⇥ Vivian Fine ⇤

Vivian Fine at 73. Photograph by Judith Cody.

⇢ Vivian Fine ⇠

A Bio-Bibliography

Judith Cody

Bio-Bibliographies in Music, Number 88
Donald L. Hixon, Series Adviser

Greenwood Press
Westport, Connecticut · London

Library of Congress Cataloging-in-Publication Data

Cody, Judith.
    Vivian Fine : a bio-bibliography / Judith Cody.
      p. cm.—(Bio-bibliographies in music, ISSN 0742–6968 ; no. 88)
    Includes bibliographical references and indexes.
    ISBN 0–313–25474–5 (alk. paper)
    1. Fine, Vivian, 1913– —Bibliography. 2. Fine, Vivian, 1913– —Discography. I. Title. II.
Series.
    ML134.F477 C63   2002
    780′.92—dc21   2001040444

British Library Cataloguing in Publication Data is available.

Library of Congress Catalog Card Number: 2001040444
ISBN: 0–313–25474–5
ISSN: 0742–6968

First published in 2002

Greenwood Press, 88 Post Road West, Westport, CT 06881
An imprint of Greenwood Publishing Group, Inc.
www.greenwood.com

Printed in the United States of America

The paper used in this book complies with the
Permanent Paper Standard issued by the National
Information Standards Organization (Z39.48–1984).

10 9 8 7 6 5 4 3 2 1

CONTENTS

PREFACE

In 1988, Vivian Fine graciously invited me to spend about eight to ten hours a day within the privacy of her rural home in upstate New York; there I was able to research amongst her personal papers and files for much of the material facts presented in this volume. She had set up a diminutive desk for me to work on that was situated in an alcove between her small kitchen and the music and family rooms. Fine allowed me almost complete access to her music and life chronicles for almost two weeks of intensive and exhilarating research.

Fortunately for music history, Fine was an excellent collector of her own memorabilia. In numerous cardboard cartons she had gathered all of her concert programs, newspaper article clippings, correspondence, photographs, school report cards, and her original music scores. The material dated back to her beginnings in the world of music in the 1920s, which was also the beginning of American modern music and including her first score from June of 1927 (see JCii).

Day by day as I explored through the stacks of Fine's early records, a clear window into the 20th century birth of American modern music began to emerge. For Fine was not a lone figure; she was an integral part, composer, confidant, and colleague to all the critical pioneers in America's new music age. She acted alongside and with Henry Brant, Charles Ives, Roger Sessions, Henry Cowell, Ruth Crawford, Aaron Copland, Martha Graham and Doris Humphrey, plus many other music and modern dance celebrities. She ranks today as the matriarch of American modern music.

Vivian and her husband, Benjamin, made me feel a bit like a houseguest in their comfortable family home. The house stood on a gentle hillock surrounded by lush lawn where Benjamin's enthralling stone sculptures sat in a natural array among the grass and plants. Often, Vivian prepared lunch for the three of us, presenting a greens salad adorned with huge vivid tomatoes that Benjamin would bring in directly from his garden, then slice just before serving for ultimate freshness.

While I was working at their home, Vivian would do most of her composing in the mornings, quietly, in an upstairs bedroom. Afternoons, the composer would sometimes spend a few hours discussing her music while we listened to tapes of her music compositions that she had carefully chosen. She clarified and elaborated upon many issues and her intentions concerning some of her later compositions, points not known before this book. Afternoons were also the time she selected for the taped and notated interviews. The majority of my taped interviews were done within the calm atmosphere of the family home, after my mornings' research through decades worth of her documents had prompted interesting new questions to ask of her.

Fine composed over 140 music compositions, and there have been hundreds of performances of her work to date. Most of her significant performances are included here in some manner. It seemed a formidable task to create a definitive listing of her works in their entirety, but with her help it came to pass. Fine was anxious to leave an authoritative compendium of her life's work for both researchers and serious students of music. Being a teacher, she often spoke to me of her great concern for historical accuracy and completeness in education. In this light, she gave me access to "early compositions" composed as a child and relatively unknown until now, so that all of her music could be part of this book.

Therefore, I have made an exhaustive attempt to make the Works and Performances chapter, which is Fine's music compendium, as complete, thorough, and accurate as possible. After my research was complete, Fine was able to personally verify almost all of my entries of the performances, dates, titles and descriptions of each of her compositions. Some of this work was done at one of our many interviews. At other times I was able to attend her music performances, some premieres, and gather firsthand information on specific compositions.

Fine would often verify a particular fact in her own penciled remark on my computer printouts that I mailed to her listing my most recent findings on her music. This double confirmation was authenticated with a JC number for each composition on my draft of her music compendium. Then she would mail it back to me. This might then lead to some time spent on a search through both of our records for the name of a missing performer for a certain concert date. If it couldn't be found I'd then need to spend time at the nearest music library to check it out. In time this became what is, I hope, a definitive listing of Fine's works. Many times an inaccuracy in a composition or in another fact has been published elsewhere. In all cases where there has been a question of fact, I have taken Fine's personal reference as correct.

Besides my trip to Fine's New York home, resulting in many taped interviews, I had other opportunities to meet with her on trips to the San Francisco Bay Area in California, where her music has a devoted following and frequent performances. These occasions gave me the delightful prospect of attending her concerts or lectures with the companionship of the composer, herself. This was a unique chance to learn from her.

Additional taped interviews were conducted in California, as were a number of notated interviews. I met with Fine a number of times when she traveled to Berkeley, San Francisco, and Petaluma, California. Often, I would telephone Fine, or she telephoned me, to discuss various music issues or for interview material. We also exchanged numerous letters over the years. She frequently sent me thick manila envelopes filled with copies of her documents (new reviews, scores, etc.), things she thought I might need in my research. Though Fine permitted few, if any, photographs in her elder years, she nevertheless kindly consented to give me a free hand to take photos of her. The frontispiece is one of the "natural light" black and white portraits that she and Benjamin especially liked.

A considerable part of this volume was put together from original source materials; thousands of original music programs, documents, newspaper clippings, reviews, interviews, letters, photographs, music scores, etc., were read, studied and annotated herein. All of these activities added up to about ten years of research and actual writing for this book.

I had met Vivian for the first time in 1981 while I was associated with the Bay Area Congress on Women in Music, in San Francisco, California (see B52). It was then that I spoke with her after a concert of her music. That night, Fine's *Missa Brevis* had been performed with eight live cellists and taped soprano. Fine was the conductor. As one of the historically great women composers, Fine was highlighted by the Congress at that event. *Missa's* beauty had profoundly impressed me, even more so since I was aware of the fact that Fine's long, distinguished career was so little known outside of a small music circle. That she was a prolific writer of music has been remarked upon by many. But, perhaps, the most remarkable thing about her creativity is that the greater amount of her creative work was accomplished in what can only be called advanced age (see Appendices 3 and 4). It seems, as this fact illustrates, that perhaps we should rethink our cultural stereotypes about old age equaling a drastic decline to an individual's creative accomplishments.

Preserving our music history by acknowledging and extending honor to our male and female composers and musicians became one of my goals ever since my first meeting with Vivian Fine. In that spirit, this book is designed to be as accessible as possible to all those who love music.

HOW TO USE THIS BOOK

Mr. Don Hixon, Series Advisor, has devised an ingenious system of cross-reference that will help to make this book (and the series) more accessible to many. He has given a letter and number value to citations in various chapters, such as "B" for the Bibliography, Chapter 2; B numbers are given to each author, e. g., B10 Anderson, Martin."D" numbers are given for each recording in the Discography, Chapter 5, e. g., D3 *Canzones y Danzas*.

Following this method; "JC" numbers are given to each composition (work) by Vivian Fine in the Works and Performance, Chapter 3.

Fine At The Piano, Chapter 4, is given a "P" number for each piano performance by Vivian Fine in her Catalog of Selected Piano Performances.

Cross-referencing to any other chapter can be easily attained using this letter-number system. To illustrate:

Chapters:

In the Discography, Chapter 5, in the above example, *Canzones y Danzas* is numbered D3, and then noted (see JC136), sending the reader to the Works and Performance Chapter for further data on that composition.

The Biography, Chapter 1, contains a study outline in the form of brief reviews and a summary. This chapter is also arranged by years. Each italicized year in the left margin is keyed to events in the Chronology, Chapter 6, marked with a corresponding italicized year. In Chapter 6 each year of Fine's life is briefly outlined, the reader can turn to the same italicized and keyed year in Chapter 1 for a detailed description of that year. In the Biography, included compositions are noted with JC numbers; B numbers refer to authors listed in Chapter 2.

The Bibliography, Chapter 2, is the largest, probably most important, part of this book. Here one can sample the critical appraisal and cultural modes of the developing modern American music while sifting through the decades presented in this chapter. It spans almost eighty years of Fine's career in the public realm, to her death in 2000. Chapter 2 is organized alphabetically by authors (each with "B" number), then cross-indexed to the other chapters using Mr. Hixon's system. Under an author's or reviewer's listing each JC number directs the reader to the specific composition in the Works and Performance, Chapter 3; "D" Numbers to the recording in the Discography Chapter, etc. The authors full name is referred to, if space permits; otherwise the B number is used. For example, B numbers are also used in the index.

In the Works and Performance, Chapter 3, Vivian Fine's compositions (works), listed by JC numbers, are shown with premieres, significant performances, performers, length of work, tempos, and instrumentation, among other information available in this chapter. Each work is cross-referenced to other chapters where needed. Reviews and literature on each composition are shown with the writer's full name (e. g., see Copland, Aaron), and can be found alphabetically listed in the Bibliography, Chapter 2.

Fine at the Piano, Chapter, 4 may be of special interest to the pianist. This piano performance chapter (listed by P numbers) lists much of Fine's repertoire as a working, "professional pianist" (as she sometimes called herself). There is an essay on Fine's career as a pianist as well as the only catalog of Selected Piano Performances encompassing her lifetime as a pianist. Also noted, are the dates, places, performers and groups for each of her music engagements. Her own piano compositions are found in Appendix 8. Chapter 4 is also cross-referenced to other chapters where needed.

The Appendices section contains 11 parts. Extensive resources for locating Fine's music are cited in Appendices 1 and 2: e-mail, fax, libraries, and phone numbers, etc. Other parts include: a statistical analysis of Fine's productivity and the creative periods of her life; details of her education; her works listed alphabetically, by genre (with her works for piano outlined), and by JC numbers; a listing showing the poets that Fine used in her music; a sample iconography for her composition, *After the Tradition*; and an alphabetical listing of all the authors cited in this book.

ACKNOWLEDGMENTS

My most heartfelt thanks must be given to my husband, David, who was an enormous help in preparing this manuscript. He did many of the tasks, that all seemed to accumulate towards the end stages. Besides being understanding and supportive, Dave was responsible for formatting the manuscript on the computer; he also compiled the "Fine's Use of Poetry in Music" guide in Appendix 9.

Vivian Fine and Benjamin Karp will live forever in my memory with the greatest gratitude for their hospitality and help. My appreciation and thanks to Peggy Karp, their daughter, for her interest and concern during the concluding months of this book. I wish to thank Dr. Birgitte Moyer, who offered pertinent comments; she also kindly volunteered to proof read Chapters 1, 2, and 3. I am grateful to Don Hixon, Greenwood series editor, who was always positive, patient and quick to offer his support and assistance.

I would also like to acknowledge the following individuals and institutions who were of great help in compiling this work: The American Music Center; Richard Jackson, The New York Performing Arts Library, New York Public Library; Marilyn Dekker, Music Specialist, Wayne Shirley, Music Librarian, Music Division and Wynn Matthias, Recorded Sound Division, Library of Congress; Riva Bacon, operations manager, music library, Braun Music Center, Stanford University.

This book is dedicated to David, husband and helpmate.

→ *Chapter 1* ←

BIOGRAPHY

NEW WORLD MUSIC: NEW STAR

1913   All that was the great age of musical Romanticism[1] was bleeding and dying under flagrant attack by those who would become the champions of the new music innovations: Igor Stravinsky's (1882-1971) *Le sacre du printemps* (*The Rite of Spring*)[2] enraged audiences at its premiere in 1913; Arnold Schoenberg (1874-1951) had not yet delivered his disdained, but in-time preponderant, twelve-tone "serial" system (1920-23), meanwhile, he utilized *Sprechstimme*[3] to polarize listeners with *Pierrot lunaire* (1912); great ballet star, Vaslav Nijinsky (1890-1950) would impale ballet aficionados with his sensate *The Afternoon of a Faun* (1912). Meanwhile, in America, Charles Ives (1874-1954)[4] was quietly creating his second piano sonata, *Concord* (1909-1915), and becoming the first original general of American composers.

Into this fresh and tumultuous onslaught of music history, middle child of three sisters, Vivian Fine was born on September 28, 1913 in Chicago, Illinois. Her mother was Rose Finder Fine. Her father, David Fine,[5] ". . . was a superintendent at Michael Reese Hospital, that's why [Fine] happened to be born there. . . ."

The young, hardworking Russian-Jewish immigrant parents took their second infant home to 1206 South Lawndale Avenue ". . . on the west side of Chicago . . . kind of lower middle class, working class . . . a short distance away was the more affluent part of the Jewish neighborhood, but it was entirely Jewish at that time."[6]

1916   Emerging child prodigy, Vivian, rapidly took her position in music circles of the era. Her musical talent was both bright and swift, recognized at the age of three when she heard a piano for the first time, then in one of her often told famous stories, threw "a tantrum" demanding a piano (lessons) of her own:

". . . Take the way she started playing the piano. . . . At a young age, making music was a means of communication for her, and playing the piano simply another form of speech . . ." (see Kino, Carol, B164)

Fine spoke highly of her mother's native talent on the piano; she realized that her mother had "almost absolute pitch and she [Fine's mother] would have become a pianist." Poverty's reality intervened though, and Rose Finder (described by Fine as "beautiful . . . [having] black hair . . . grey eyes . . . ") was forced to go to work as a secretary thereby forsaking her own piano lessons.

So it happened that the first piano young Vivian was to covet was the very same one that had been her mother's. This was to become the first instrument for Fine; in her own words:

". . . So this piano then remained at the house of the aunt, her sister [Fine's mother], and I remember going when my Mother would go over to visit her when I was three or four, probably three. I would touch the piano and I remember loving the sound of it! . . . An old upright. . . . I said I wanted to have a piano and my Mother said, 'All right, all right.' She didn't know what had come over me. I wasn't a child given to tantrums. . . . My Mother arranged — we were very poor then — to find a few dollars, and then to have the piano moved from my aunt's house to our house, and she began to teach me herself. . . . Yes, my mother was my first teacher when I was five . . . very soon she thought I ought to have a teacher. There was a neighborhood teacher, a Miss Rosen, who came to the student's house. My mother told her about me. Miss Rosen said, that she 'doesn't take children under the age of eight' . . . [but after] having heard me play, she then said she would 'take me.'"[7]

1918   The child proved herself; almost at once she was deeply absorbed in her hours practicing on the piano, though at times Miss Rosen could be quite firm, in the custom of the day, should her little Vivian miss a note. Fine called Miss Rosen her "second teacher" always remaining loyal to her Mother's advice on what direction to take in her juvenile music career. Mrs. Fine's advice was amazingly accurate for her daughter's future. Mother-piano teacher recognized that her diminutive pianist was more than ready for bigger things. This happened "even before I finished my fifth year," as Vivian Fine was to tell the author seven decades later; at that time she also discussed how her staunch and determined mother, though her family had newly arrived in America, had somehow discovered the Chicago Musical College; learned about auditions for their first scholarships; finally bringing Vivian to an audition when she was only five years old.[8]

Vivian was playing her beloved piano well beyond the level of the average child, of course. She was making her first of a great many public appearances in years to come. She was confronting her first critical audience in the tables of judges at the Chicago Musical College.[9] The scene as it appeared that day in 1918, in the audition hall as described by an interviewer in 1955 (see Kimball, Alice Mary, B162):

"Vivian, combed, scrubbed, and dressed in her prettiest, walked across a hall that seemed miles long and empty, save for a row of poker-faced judges . . . she reached the instrument [the piano], it was like coming home. She tossed off the *Skater's Waltz* with verve. . . ."

Fine won that long-ago scholarship and began an exemplary musical career. She studied under several teachers at the college, Helen Ross and a Miss Caruthers, "the piano supervisor," being two that she recalled. April 10, 1920 saw Vivian's very first concert with the other students. Julia Lois Caruthers directed the tiny students that Saturday morning when six-year-old Vivian played Crosby-Adams' *Singing and Swinging*.[10] Fine was to study and accomplish at the College through her ninth year in 1922.

JUVENESCENT GENIUS

1921   By age eight Fine was "playing the first movement of the *C-major* Mozart *Sonata* at concerts." At this time in her young career she played what was most likely her first composition on the piano. It was called *The Starving Children of Belgium*, (JCi, 1921) since this was one of the frightening topics in the media in that time period, right after the First World War armistice had been declared in 1918. Vivian performed her inspired piano work for the other children (see Kimball, B162).

Mr. Fine was working at the Jewish Theater box office in the 1920's; during that period he became acquainted with a Mr. Weinstock, father to Gertrude Weinstock. Gertrude had changed her name to Getta Gordova after the Russian equivalent of "place of wine," Getta, Fine told the author:

". . . was a rising star as a pianist in Chicago . . . Madame Herz was Getta's teacher. Mr. Weinstock and my father talked often of their daughters. My father probably discussed this with my mother and they brought me to Madame Herz. That was the fall of 1924. I was eleven."[11]

Madame Djane Lavoie-Herz (1888-1982) had been both pupil and disciple of renowned Russian mystic and composer Alexander Scriabin (1872-1915). She was pale and petite wearing her dark hair in the bobbed "roaring twenties" cap style.[12] Under Herz's tutelage "for a token payment," Vivian was indeed heavily coached in Scriabin's music; but Fine strongly states that her music studies of the time were "broad:"

"Oh, I studied the whole repertoire. . . . That is, I studied everything. Absolutely everything. From Bach, Mozart, Chopin, Haydn . . . Liszt, Schumann . . . not all the pieces in their repertoire but I studied the whole period of the pianist's repertoire . . . there was some emphasis on Scriabin, but by no means . . . was it the sole focus at all. . . . It's important to emphasize that I got a very broad pianistic education . . . I played contemporary [music of that period] . . . Debussy, Ravel, Bach, Chopin . . . with Madame Herz. . . . It was the professional repertoire of the pianist . . . [not] student pieces."

Initially, Fine was practicing piano four hours a day plus her school schedule. Very soon however, Vivian became interested in the modern music of the age: ". . . I began to concentrate, I preferred the choice of the moderns. "

Composing her own music now became the pleasant locus for the youthful pianist; Vivian could spend four or five hours of each day composing at her piano, while much less time was now spent on practicing the piano works of other composers:

"I had a few very good friends, that were musicians. . . . I went out a lot with my sister. . . . I didn't have a social life . . . and I didn't even miss it. . . . My life was centered around my work. . . ."[13]

During this period of Fine's early music training she was immersed in a world of exciting and quality music, though at the time, to this child, all seemed quite natural so that she felt completely unaware of the uniqueness of this world. Fine's "activities" revolved almost totally around her piano lessons, her music studies, practice at home, and playing in the concerts. For most of the first decade of her life, she had become profoundly engrossed in the development of her gifts in music.

As Fine would later recall: "I was making my own music. . . . The things I was most conscious of, were my teacher and my own playing. . . ."[14]

When she was about "eleven" years old the little girl, Vivian, began to regularly attend performances of the Chicago Symphony Orchestra. This was a first class orchestra of the period featuring many of "the great artists of the century." Fine, accompanied by one of her sisters or her Mother, "went every week for many years." Her parents supported her in this, as it was her nature to take great pleasure in great music. Fine would make this clear later:

"The highest excellence, the greatest pianists and violinist of the time . . . it was marvelous! I enjoyed and loved every minute of it! It was wonderful to go to all these concerts. . . ."[15]

Fine remembered, in 1986, how as a child she loved *The Firebird* (Stravinsky, 1910) and *Petrushka* (Stravinsky, 1911); but she did not recall ever hearing his *The Rite of Spring* (1913) performed as a child; she did recall hearing the works by Beethoven, Bach's *Brandenburg Concertos,* and Debussy's *Nocturnes.* Fine was also able to study the likes of Casals, Tchaikovsky, and she loved hearing Ravel and Rachmaninoff conduct. She thought Ravel was: ". . . One of the best conductors;" and of Rachmaninoff, "a wonderful conductor, but he didn't play anything more, anything very adventurous with New Music."[16]

REVIEW

Vivian Fine, born in Chicago in 1913, was a child prodigy, her large talents were recognized by both parents and teachers who gave her much support. Her mother was her first teacher. She naturally seemed to gravitate toward intense music learning with a strong desire to accomplish and develop a high level of pianist skills. At age five she won a scholarship to the Chicago Musical College, and adhered to her first mentors' (Herz's) music philosophies, then to become an outstanding child pianist. Her weekly Chicago Symphony attendance helped develop her "ear" for orchestral composing later in life. She studied with Madame Djane Lavoie-Herz, influential piano teacher, and follower of Scriabin.

CRAWFORD EDUCATES FINE: FIRST CREATIVE EXPLOSION

1924   Another amazingly talented student of Madame Djane Lavoie-Herz was Ruth Crawford (later Ruth Crawford Seeger) who began studies with her in the "fall of 1924," at Herz's studio and home on Grand Boulevard. During that year the 23-year-old Ruth was to take young Vivian to a Chicago concert where a Crawford composition was performed (her early *Violin and Piano Sonata*).[17] M. Herz saw to it that Vivian was introduced to Ruth Crawford, who had been studying music theory with Adolf Weidig at the American Conservatory in Chicago, where Ruth taught now. Herz decided that Crawford should teach Vivian music theory. Ruth took Vivian under her tutelage for no payment whatsoever, as she was so impressed with Vivian's talent. "Because we didn't have money for lessons," Fine remembered in 1988 ". . . in the fall of 1925, I would have been twelve."[18] Crawford was to become a major influence and impetus for Fine as a composer. Fine would recall that because Ruth ". . . was an avant-garde composer as my teacher . . . it made me feel that it was completely natural to be a woman and to be writing adventurous music. . . ."[19]

It would be Ruth who coached the child to begin work on her first formal composition (see JCii). Then, Fine recalled: ". . . Ruth had been playing the late Scriabin works . . . opus' 74, 75, the piano works. . . . I was playing those early on [Fine was about fourteen-years-old] . . . then I heard Ruth Crawford's music! [see McLellan, Joseph B188]. . . . Very soon I started to write in a style that was influenced greatly by Scriabin's style. . . . I found some works of [Arnold] Schoenberg, opus 19 and opus 11 . . . [also] avant-garde works of Leo Ornstein. . . . This was how I was spending my time, this is why I didn't want to go to high school. . . ."[20]

1927   The summer that Vivian was just thirteen ushered forth a torrent of her music compositions that brought some astonishment to her new mentor, Crawford:

"'. . . their profuseness, force, depth, breadth of conception . . . remarkable at thirteen. . . .'"[21]

Sometime in June of 1927 Vivian wrote down the notes to her first sixteen measure score called *Lullaby* (JCii) written in four/four time.[22] Since 1921 she had composed many incidental short pieces directly on her piano.[23] Vivian had discovered the gratification of composing music. She had also begun her first great creative cycle.

Nicholas Senn High School had seemed boring and irrelevant to fourteen-year-old Vivian. While she had good marks, earning a ninety percent in German, she did not return to Nicholas Senn after completing the second quarter in June of 1928.[24] Her parents gave their support to this arrangement. Of course, a High School diploma did not have the same priority in the 1920's that it does today. Especially for girls, as at that time Home Economics was still thought to be a suitable major. In fact, on Vivian's sixth grade report card from John Fisk Elementary School, Cooking, Sewing, and Manual Training were listed as classes that she had "missed."[25] On Christmas Eve of that year, 1928, instead of being on the school holiday break, Vivian was giving a concert at a Mrs. Eisendrath's Chicago home. The small typed program showed a

"Miss Vivien Fein [sic] . . . [performing on piano] . . . Chopin's *Polonaise B Flat Major*; Scriabin's *Four Preludes*; Scarlatti's *Sonatas in C and G Minor*; Debussy's *Gradus ad Parnassum*; Bach's *Prelude and Fugue B Flat Major*; and Liszt's *Ballade B Minor* [sic]."[26]

Besides the rigors of her self-imposed music studies, Vivian was also nurturing what would become a lifelong appreciation for poetry. One facet of her composing was to set poetry texts to her music, so that a distinct number of her works will center on poetry in the future (e.g., see JC77, JC105, JC117, JC124, and JC126) (see Appendix 9). In 1928 she began by setting a John Galsworthy text to piano and voice (JCvi).

As a child who had had constant exposure to music of the "highest excellence," while maximizing her creative gifts, Vivian had made up her mind to leave high school, with the object of dedicating herself to her music, underscoring her own composition work. So complete was her dedication and discipline that the teenager was able to accomplish this goal in a singularly rapid time-frame, with great historical consequences.

During this time Fine was naturally involved with the adventurous in her own music. Constantly exposing the musically gifted little girl to the great music of the world while she also studied and performed would produce this result; the little girl was acquiring a rich groundwork in ear training for her later orchestral compositions. As Fine later recollected her early years in Chicago:

". . . so that, I think my ease, my feeling of being comfortable with orchestration stems from this early time . . . when I heard the orchestra all the time. . . . I just got the sound of the orchestra in my ears. It felt very comfortable. It's only in this conversation that I realize that's why I feel very much at ease writing for an orchestra. Those early years going to many, many concerts with a first class orchestra, they were wonderful!"[27]

Herz and her husband, Siegfried, hosted "musical soirees" at their home where influential musical talents fraternized. Henry Cowell had performed some of his infamous methods on the piano at such an event on one of his many visits to Chicago in 1924.[28]

Champion of the musical avant-garde, Imre Weisshaus was a "Hungarian composer-pianist . . . a Cowell discovery," known by M. Herz, who would befriend and advise both Vivian and Ruth.[29] He would later have a profound effect on Vivian's music, also seeing to it that her composition, *Four Pieces for Two Flutes* (JC2, 1930), was performed at the Bauhaus, in Dessau, Germany, when Fine was seventeen.

1929 Ruth Crawford introduced Vivian to Imre who "became very interested" in Fine's autonomous atonal compositions crafted in the emancipated spirit of that age; women had fought, then won voting rights just ten years before. She admitted that his musical style had caught her attention, influencing her own developing style or idiom. She and Imre would form a bond through music that lasted a lifetime:

"It [Weisshaus's musical idiom] was angular, spare, spare, extraordinarily spare! So the material he uses for each composition is very limited . . . if there could be something called musical cubism [that would be his style] . . . but it wasn't just imitative [Fine's learning from him] . . . I did learn from that how to be more sparing. . . . I'm still quite fond of him. . . ."[30]

Dane Rudhyar (1895-1985), another avant-garde composer, also writer, was handsome, dark haired, possessing an aquiline profile that seemed to poetically peer into some mystic space.[31] He revered Scriabin, was an intellectual, these being qualities that likely endeared him to M. Herz, who had him stay at her exotically decorated apartment for a long visit in 1925.

"A four foot sculpture of a Tibetan Buddha presided over [her] piano studio. . . . Incense scented the air. A Hindu named Shandre, wearing a white turban, greeted the Herzes' numerous guests, for there were many that imbibed an atmosphere that was 'redolent of mystery.' Because Siegfried worked for Arthur Judson, the most powerful agent in the period, the Herz's 'knew everybody' — all the famous celebrity soloists and conductors and composers."[32]

In the still slightly courtly manners of the 1920's era, M. Herz plausibly would have proudly presented her star students (just such as Fine, Crawford and Gordova) to her celebrity acquaintances for their appraisal at one of her modern music parties. It was at this time that Vivian met and was "encouraged" by the young Rudhyar with at least a few known letters.[33]

Vivian said she was just "sixteen or seventeen" when M. Herz introduced her to Rudhyar who at once became "interested in my [Vivian's] music." Eager and quick to learn, Fine was to be strongly influenced by Rudhyar's "very special viewpoint about music." At that time Rudhyar, "who didn't like anything that was contrapuntal," wrote mainly piano music that was generally performed by him. Later though, Vivian would perform some of his compositions. His heavy, complex musical idiom was abruptly contrasted with Weisshaus' "spare" style. Fine spoke strongly of the inspiration Rudhyar's music had on her work in 1986:

"He [Rudhyar] was quite different . . . he liked large resonating masses, larger masses of sound. That concept has been an influence in my work . . . certain kinds of things that I write for piano. It also influenced how I played the piano, to get a yearning, a resonant, beautiful sound out of the piano. *I got this from playing his music"* (see P9). Fine would perfect the "masses" and "resonant" sounds to bring a sense of power, even majesty at times, to her piano works that would echo into her longer works far into the future.[34]

1928   When Fine was fifteen, M. Herz or Crawford ("probably Crawford") decided to bring Fine's work to the attention of established New Music composer Henry Cowell: "Henry Cowell became interested in my [Fine's] music. . . . He was in contact with both of them [Herz and Crawford] and I began corresponding with him. So . . . I was beginning to lead a semi-professional life very early on. . . . He would write asking to see compositions and he would write back comments. . . . I sent him a song and he said something about the 'tessitura' and I had never heard that word before . . . he arranged for the first performance of this first composition. . . ."[35]

1930   *Solo For Oboe* (JC1, 1929) had caught Cowell's attention so that he arranged for it to be world premiered at a concert of The Pan American Association of Composers, Inc.,[36] where he was the acting President. This was 1930, tickets were one dollar. Seventeen-year-old Fine's composition shared the program with three works by Charles Ives; *Solo For Violin* by Henry Cowell, and *Rat Riddles* by Ruth Crawford who now was both friend and mentor to Vivian (see P1).[37]

　　　　When Fine was seventeen years old, Ruth went to New York City, but before Ruth left she saw to it that Fine had a scholarship to study with Crawford's composition teacher, Adolf Weidig. Weidig had earned a "solid reputation as theorist, performer, composer," furthermore, he nurtured a direct musical "link to Brahms." Fine spent a year trying to interrelate her compositional style to Weidig's; it just didn't work. Weidig was a firm tradionalist, of course, Fine was just breaking free of these same music rules. By eighteen she had made up her mind to follow Ruth and go to New York City:

　　　　"He [Weidig] was a product of the old school and he tried very hard to understand my compositions. . . . There was no one I could associate with [teacher of composition] in Chicago. . . . I realized that I had to find someplace else to study. There was nobody with whom I could study, there was no one!"[38]

　　　　All of Vivian's associates (Ruth, Imre, Dane, and Henry) were traveling to and from New York City at that time to further their careers in the Ultra-Modern music scene. It seems natural that she would need to follow in their footsteps. Fine had made up her mind.

REVIEW

Teacher and renowned avant-garde composer, Ruth Crawford meets and inspires Fine to become a composer as well as a pianist. In the summer when she was thirteen, she begins composing in earnest, writing her first formal piece, *Lullaby*. Fine's own remarkable music draws the interests of eminent mentors: Cowell, Rudhyar, Herz, Weisshaus, Weidig. Her music was heavily influenced by

Scriabin, Schoenberg, Ornstein, later Rudhyar and Weisshaus. She left high school to pursue composing. Her music was still undergoing a formative process and was her single source of artistic exploration. These then, were the attributes in her search for her unique artistic self-hood as expressed through her music, to wit: Fine's compositions are now idiosyncratic, severely dissonant, and just as severely creative, imbued with a striking and captivating sense of newness. She deliberately excised all tonal elements from her work as though excising all that had gone before, to generate the newborn composer in the person of Fine. Her *Solo For Oboe* (JC1, 1929) world premiered at the Pan American Association of Composers; *Four Pieces for Two Flutes* (JC2, 1930), was performed at the Bauhaus, in Dessau, Germany.

During this time from child prodigy to early adulthood, young Fine was mastering the essentials of the composer's craft and exercising her perspicacious mind on this construct.

These events were the precursor to the first great creative cycle in Fine's career. Fine would compose fifty-four works in her first great creative cycle which lasted until about 1946.

CONQUERING THE NEW MUSIC CIRCLE: NEW YORK CITY

1931   By September of 1931 Vivian had gone to New York City with fifty dollars and the friendship of Ruth Crawford. Ruth was to introduce her protege, Vivian, to Walton.

Mrs. Blanche Walton was a wealthy, generous widow who had knowledgeable devotion to music, especially the new music of her era. As Fine was to say: ". . . the people who were advising Mrs. Walton, were people like Henry Cowell. . . ."[39]

Cowell had also been a "prime mover" in seeing that Ruth lived with the influential patron of music, Mrs. Walton. Walton's carefully chosen inner circle of music devotees was not an ordinary music appreciation group, however. Those who would become important, even great figures in music history held court in her New York home. Bela Bartok, when he came to the United States for the first time, ". . . made his headquarters with her [Mrs. Walton]. . . . ;" also, Adolph Weiss, Edgard Varèse and Henry Cowell. Many other individuals prominent in the artistic society of New York gathered at her home. Here, in Mrs. Walton's living room, Ruth Crawford had her first composition lesson with her future husband, the noted Charles Seeger. This was arranged by the already famous Henry Cowell, who had mentored Ruth Crawford as he was now a mentor to Vivian Fine.[40]

It was also to be in Mrs. Walton's living room that the young Vivian was presented to this music and arts aristocracy at what she called her ". . . New York debut as a composer . . . it really was that, my debut concert. . . ."[41] Winter in New York City, December thirteenth, 1931, at Mrs. Walton's elegant home; the "Programme" was headed, "Compositions of Vivian Fine"; Vivian was also the pianist of the event. Influential friends of Mrs. Walton's would be the audience for the brilliant eighteen-year-old girl composer on her debut day in the large Victorian living room, where she would perform on the brand "new Steinway piano"[42] to the select audience that Fine would describe:

". . . So that I was introduced to the New Music audience, not the musical audience, the New Music Circle! . . . around forty people. . . . The Seegers came [Ruth Crawford and her new husband, Charles Seeger]. . . ."

Fine also recalled that she indeed "was aware" at that time that it was a critical event for her music career.[43]

Aaron Hirsch with Vivian played her *Sonatina for Violin and Piano* (JC4, 1930); she soloed with her *Canon and Fugue for Piano* (JC5, 1930); *Trio for Strings* (JC3, 1930) was played, and also on that debut "Programme," Vivian had brought together the poetry of beloved poet Carl Sandburg (1878-1967) with song and piano for her *Little Suite for Voice and Piano* (JC6, 1930); his vigorous "Chicago Poems" were published in 1916.[44]

1932   The "Ultra-Modern Music," (Fine said it was so named), was given a "First Festival of Contemporary American Music" presentation at the Yaddo estate in Saratoga Springs, in upstate New York, on April thirtieth and May first in 1932 (see *New York Herald-Tribune*, February 1932, B212). The intense and dissonant new-born music of the raucous New World captured international interest; so did Vivian Fine.

Miss Fine was listed with the other "Composer-Pianists" on the Yaddo program (incompatibly printed in Old English style lettering) that day; George Antheil, Aaron Copland and Oscar Levant. She performed *Four Polyphonic Piano Pieces* (JC7, 1931) with extreme pianistic abilities well noted by the many visiting critics, who also noted the works projected a disarming atonalism, albeit intellectualism not always welcomed by some.[45] (see Saminsky, Lazare. 1932, B266, compare with Engel, A. Lehman, 1932 & '33, B91, B92, and Saminsky, 1941, B267)(see P10)

Fine was now the only woman and a key performer with the newly formed Young Composers' Group, all said to be under twenty-five years old. (see H., H. January 16, 1932, B118; *The Musical Leader*, B202; Perkins, Francis D., B231)(see P5)

Well recognized as an outstanding young pianist, Fine also had another amazing, unusual ability to sight read the Ultra-Modern Music scores. Most musicians would agree that it is very difficult to read and immediately play music written in a heretofore unknown style and, or system of notation. Fine could do this. These two twin talents, coupled with her native compositional comprehension, irrefutably made Vivian indispensable within Copland's newly formed avant-garde composers group. She became the natural choice to premiere Ultra-Modern works by such renowned figures as Ives, Copland, Brant, Cowell, Rudhyar, and others (see Fine at the Piano, Chapter 4). In 1986, Fine explained how this came about:

"... Aaron Copland ... who was not very old himself at the time. He was about thirty-two. ... He had a composers group and I became a member of this young composers group (see Copland, Aaron, B73). ... We would get together once a week and play each other's compositions. ... I was glad to function as a young composer. ... I was playing for concerts of contemporary music such as there are now. I was probably the best-known performer of contemporary piano music in New York at that time ... *there wasn't anybody else!* ... I gave a lot of first performances ... Ives, Ruth Crawford, Chavez ... then I was earning my living playing ... being an accompanist and concert pianist for modern dance."[46](see P8, P6, P15)

At the Dance Center (billed as the Intimate Theatre Studio), a first in a series, "Symposium for Moderns," subtitled on the program, "modern music, song, movements," was held on a Sunday in April of 1932. Vivian Fine played works by Dane Rudhyar and then her own *Polyphonic Piano Pieces*. Henry Brant, A. Lehman Engel and Gluck-Sandor (the choreographer) presented their music offerings.[47] Fine's *Pieces* drew a rather excellent review by Arthur Berger. Commenting on how all the works performed that night reflected the growing American sensibility in music, Berger singled out Fine's piano composition in the *New York Daily Mirror*:

"In this respect ... *Pieces* ... most successful. While the musical fabric in its contrapuntal complexity might conceivably pass for Schoenberg, the nervousness of the rhythm is American in character." [see Berger, Arthur, B27, also P9]

The depression had cost her father his job in Chicago, leading Vivian's parents to join her in New York in 1932.

CREATING MODERN DANCE IN AMERICA

Exciting surges of American wealth plummeted in the colossal stock market crash of 1929; now in the early thirties the Great Depression "was really deepening to a tremendous depth at that point. ..."

Yet, the arts still struggled and innovated onward; modern dance was being invented. Vivian found a job as a piano accompanist for dances choreographed by one of the "leading dance personalities," Gluck-Sandor. The original 1932 program from one Gluck-Sandor production (see P4), at the Dance Center, announced:

"THE FOURTH PRODUCTION IN ITS SEASON OF
BALLET REPERTOIRE"

This was Prokofieff's ballet, *The Prodigal Son*, directed, choreographed, with scenery designed by Gluck-Sandor (also sometime costume designer), who also starred as the "father" and "the impressario [*sic*]." There were ten scenes, each with a line or two of description:

"UNDERGROUND   'On his way he meets a Hoofer.'"
At the bottom of the program Vivian Fine is noted to be "At the Piano."
A New York reviewer, S.A.D., said of the ballet:
" The Center Group . . . now finds itself under the adverse conditons
of space, mechanical equipment and ventilation . . . [yet there is] realization in
high artistic purpose . . . " [referring to Fine's work] ". . . played with admirable
rhythm."[48]
An anonymous New York Tribune reviewer wrote: "Vivian Fine played
the piano, and competently." [see B217]

1934   Vivian, young, invincible with her powerful talent remembered:
"I was very busy earning a living and trying to adjust to living in New
York, alone . . . that's when I got involved with the dance world. . . . I began
to be known as a dance accompanist and a composer for dance. And this is how
I supported myself."[49]
Rent was seventeen dollars a month for Vivian's unheated "tenement"
on First Avenue and 54th Street. She had to work, and so she sought out more
jobs in the dance studios. At twenty-one she was beginning her long association
with the burgeoning modern dance movement in America, as accompanist,
concert performer, arranger and composer.
Those early, experimental years saw mostly women in the Modern
Dance companies of the era. Doris Humphrey, Charles Weidman, Jose Limon,
Hanya Holm, Rose Crystal (see Chapter 4, 1932 to 1938), and later (in the
1960's), Martha Graham were the great innovative choreographers who would
come to know and work with Vivian. These were the ground breaking
choreographers who commissioned Fine's dance compositions that were to
become fundamental to the Modern Dance as we know it today (see Ammer,
Christine, B7; Humphrey, Doris, B143, also White, Edward, B320). Yet, though
the era was rich in creativity, perhaps expressly because it was somewhat "free,"
in the dance world, as almost everywhere else during the Depression, ". . .
dancers were very, very poor. . . . All we could afford was the piano," Fine was
to say later. Creativity was still affordable.
Fine often spoke of her special abilities as a dance accompanist; she was
able to translate the movement, rhythms and timing into the music seamlessly,
almost without effort. Fine's description of this inner process:
"I would compose the music that would enhance the dance, which was
quite a trick . . . without seeing the dance, I couldn't do it. I had to get the
characteristics and the movement they had, and then I composed music to match
. . . they wouldn't give me a musical theme. . . . I had a knack for catching in
music the characteristics of the dance. . . . Not everybody can do it; to watch
movement, then compose music."[50]

1935   Fine was working hard earning wages from her piano playing by taking
a variety of jobs. She accompanied Nini Theilade, a much heralded modern ballet

dancer, in local productions such as The "Y" Pop Series on Thursday, December 28, 1933 in Newark, N. J.(see P21). Most of the music Nini required was the likes of Chopin, Debussy or perhaps Haydn. Vivian would do piano solos at the end of the night's show. At the December "Y" show she chose to play, *Serenade* by Albeniz, and some Scandinavian "Popular Melodies." In other shows during the 1935 tour, Fine played composers such as Brahms or Liszt.

Fine and Nini took their production on tour to Ottawa and Montreal, Canada, Wichita Falls and Dallas, Texas, in February and March of 1935 (see P24). Crowds were said to brave vicious "rain and storm" to see them. Nini's dancing delighted audiences and critics, with remarks such as "much superior" directed to Fine's piano solos and dance accompaniment. (see Armstrong, Israel, 1934, B14; Dallas Dispatch, 1935, B83; Powell, S. Morgan, 1935, B239; Underwood, W.L., 1935, B309; and V., M., 1935, B311)[51]

1934   Charles Seeger had taught Vivian for two lessons when she first came to New York; she was to conclude, "that didn't work out." Fine began her lengthy course of studies with Roger Sessions (1896-1985) in the fall of 1934. She was also taking classes in improvisation and eurhythmics. The Dalcroze method is a system of musical education developed by Émile Jaques-Dalcroze (1865-1950), the idea being to develop musical abilities through rhythmic movement, e.g. eurhythmics. Later, in 1948, Fine would build on this idea in her paper on rhythm in music (see Fine, Vivian. 1948, B99). Sessions was a "classically trained composer with . . . incredible knowledge of music, ency-clopedic knowledge of music," Fine recalled. Most of the time Sessions waived the usual five dollar fee for his private lessons with Vivian, who also performed his music in concert (see P29). She went there one hour a week to study harmony and counterpoint for about a year. Fine described what might take place at such a lesson:

". . . you bring in your exercises, and there were very few corrections that had to be done on mine. But he would show me, it's called voicing . . . it teaches you to manage four voices within a structure . . . when I wrote the *Four Songs* [JC8, 1933, see Upton, William Treat, B310] I was able to manage four voices. . . . Now, it's interesting what would have happened to me without the classical education which I began to receive [at that period in Fine's life]. . . ."

Having honed his student's skills in classical music education, Sessions, who Wallingford Riegger had called, "One of the great teachers of modern harmony," by then became Vivian's composition teacher until 1942. Vivian's composer friend, Israel Citkowitz had "recommended" to Sessions that he look at her compositions. Interestingly, it had never occurred to Sessions to look at Vivian's own work until that time. Within these eight years a basic shifting of focus developed in Vivian's compositions (see Ariel, B11). Her earlier works had been dissonant, stark, and now, though more in command of traditional compositional techniques, Fine's music changed both shape and direction never to return, as she would reveal:

"... at that point, my idiom had become quite tonal as compared with the previous period which was quite atonal! ... At one point I felt that I wanted to work on my own. ... I wrote the *Concertante for Piano and Orchestra* [JC42, 1944; see Composers Recording, Inc., 1960, B68] on my own. ... I felt that I didn't need a teacher anymore and I was right. Maybe I'd even studied too long with Sessions ... he was unbelievably generous in every, every way. ..."

The New Music School was founded by Roger Sessions and Paul Doepple who was the head of the Dalcroze School on 59th Street in New York. It proved necessary to use the Dalcroze premises for the New Music School, since being "very idealistic" provided them with meager income. Fine added:

"It didn't last very long ... for one thing, practically everybody was on scholarship ... I had a scholarship!"

1935 In mid-winter of 1934 Benjamin Karp and Vivian Fine were introduced through their mutual friend, Israel Citkowitz. Benjamin was a talented sculptor (see Newtown, B204; also Karp, Benjamin, B157) who had started out by graduating *summa cum laude* in physics from Syracuse University, then he won a fellowship to Vienna. Shortly after that, he decided to devote himself to his art career. The couple knew each other only four months before they married in the Spring of 1935[52] (on April 5th) at 458 W. 124th St., New York City, at "the Fine home" (see Cupid, Dan, B81). Another headline in the *New York Times* saluted the newlywed Karps with: "Marriage of the Arts."

Many hours a day were going into the dance rehearsals, accompanying, performing, music studies and of course Vivian's composing; but she would add:

"... I had an apartment to take care of, cooking to do. ... It was during the days when women were married, cooking. ... I did a lot of composing for dance ... [at the same time]."

1937 Doris Humphrey was commissioning a number of music compositions for the dance from the dazzling talents of the young pianist-composer, Vivian Fine (see Humphrey, Doris, B143; also I., K., B145)(see P22). In 1937 Vivian composed *The Race of Life* for her (JC16, 1937; see Martin, John, B186; Robin, Harry, B253); it was a modernist dance conceptualization of drawings by the noted artist James Thurber. Eventually, Fine would compose for virtually all the trailblazers in the dance world. At the same time that she was studying harmony with Sessions, Fine composed *Race of Life*, which was, as she would explain:

"... a tonal composition ... there's something good about receiving a systematic education [in classical music composition]. ... It enlarges you, it gives you a certain craft, a certain skill ... before that, I was ... *I don't know if I would have continued to compose.* ... There was something less original about the compositions that I wrote when I began to write tonal music [during this period]. The others [her earlier works] were quite original. But whether I could have continued in this way, I don't know ... it enabled me to have a mastery of writing [composing music] eventually."

When she was twenty-four, Fine began her piano studies with Abby Whiteside which would continue through 1945. Miss Whiteside, who died in 1956 at seventy-five, had authored numerous books on piano playing (see Klein, Howard, B165).

Vivian became a mother for the first time to her daughter, Peggy, on September 12, 1942. Two years before, 1940, Benjamin had a Carnegie Fellowship (see Newtown, B204). Six years later Mr. and Mrs. Karp had a second daughter, Nina, born also in September on the fourteenth, in 1948.[53] In the midst of this active music and family schedule Fine was somehow able to find time to study orchestration with the well-known conductor, George Szell (1897-1970), for one term in 1944.[54]

REVIEW

Herein is the formula that captured the attention of the music mavens of that era: Fine's musical hallmark in the beginning half (to about 1936), of the period I have named as her first *creative explosion,* 1927 to 1946, is a striking, often out-rageous, pristine originality coupled with great pianistic skills, in the person of a lovely young woman. Vivian became famous in the New Music circle of her era. Her music would mellow into a substantially tonal idiom after the mid nine-teen-thirties. Her 1931 debut as a New York composer to Mrs. Walton's New Music Circle, plus her 1932 Yaddo festival premiere established her reputation.

Fine earned her reputation and living as accompanist, arranger and composer with the trailblazers of American Modern Dance. In 1934 Fine began studying with Roger Sessions, making modern music theory the new basis for her music lexicon. Orchestration teacher, George Szell had a traditional influence on her music, but this study enabled her to enrich her music. All this resulted in her developing the beautiful, but tonal voice to her music and an abdication of her original compositional spontaneity. This quite tonal period reached a climax and would end, with her *Concertante for Piano and Orchestra,* 1944; her first long work for orchestra (fifteen minutes). Fine married Benjamin Karp in 1935 and began a family. Fine composed over fifty-four works in this first cycle, began in 1927, and which would end shortly in 1946 (see JCii through JC42).

CREATIVE AND STRUCTURAL SYNTHESIS: MID-LIFE INTERLUDE

1944   Displaying both strength and an unusual self discipline, Fine managed to schedule her life as a composer into her life as wife and mother. In 1943 Fine had begun composing her first "big work for orchestra . . ." with some valuable help from her father as baby sitter each day during her time set aside for composing:

". . . my father was very kind. He took her [the baby] for her outing, her daily airing, he took her to Washington Square Park in Greenwich Village. And during those two hours when she was out, I composed. . . ." Fine recounted.

While Fine admits that her composing was indeed "less" in these young composer-mother-wife years, nevertheless, the mid-nineteen-forties would be "breakthrough" years for her. She states that it was just then that she made one critical discovery; the conception of herself as a composer for orchestra. For the first time Vivian moved her musical consciousness away from her piano, her chamber works and into the dynamic complexities of orchestral presentation.

By this time, of course, Vivian had achieved a rather formidable music education that had transmuted her focus once again (see Appendix 5). This time it was toward the myriad and vigorous colours of that all inclusive instrument; the orchestra. She would never turn back:

"That was a big step forward for me. It was a tonal work, that's true, but it was the first time I had been able to write a long work. I hadn't been able to write a longer work. I had written longer ballets, But they weren't as involved musically as this piece was. . . . It was a big step technically for me to write a long piece, a 15 minute work . . . a piece for orchestra. After I had written that I thought I had accomplished something very important in my composing career . . . that was a big, big, big step. And I took that when Peggy was just a year old."

The work Fine spoke of was the *Concertante for Piano and Orchestra*, 1944. It was finally recorded in 1960 (JC42; see Composer's Recordings Inc., B68, D4, D5).

1947   Another crucial "breakthrough" occurred in Vivian's work when she was able to synthesize her own native musical originality with the formal musical structures she had learned so well with her eminent teachers, Sessions and Szell to create what became the cardinal pattern for her distinctive compositions thereafter. She was now expertly able to utilize tonal lines, but in a manner that suited her unique creativity, while integrating the totality of her composition with aural freedoms found in the atonal lines. This happened when she wrote *Capriccio for Oboe and String Trio* (JC43, 1944). As Fine would carefully state:

". . . I felt that that was an important breakthrough [*Capriccio*] . . . I began to return to a less tonally oriented idiom. . . . It was really the beginning of what was the basis of the rest of my musical language . . . they have tonal centers, you feel tonality, but it is not in the traditional harmony using triads. . . . I wasn't conscious of the reasons that compelled me in that direction but I evidently must have felt some need to move away from the tonal idiom that I had used in the *Concertante*. . . . There isn't a reasoned decision about it, *I just began to hear a different kind of music.*"[55]

The year 1947 brought forth a return to certain of her youthful innovations and originality in another work; *The Great Wall of China*. "*Wall*," Berger approvingly noted, had brought Fine back to her earlier "abstract" music methods, leaving the traditional harmonies far behind (see Berger, Arthur. May 1948, B29).

1948   The Karps left New York City with their new baby, Nina, and six year old Peggy for Montclair, New Jersey, where Ben was head of the Art Department at the State Teacher's College.[56]

1950   Ben and Vivian tried an "experimental venture" as a husband and wife art and musical team using classical music to highlight projected classic art works. Ben analyzed the art work while Vivian played piano. This event was at the Newtown, New York town hall where it was favorably reviewed in the local paper (see Newtown, B204 and also Kahn, Erminie, B155).

FAMILY AND MUSIC IN SUBURBAN 1950s AND 1960s

1951   Nina was three and Peggy was nine when the Karp family moved to the New Paltz suburbs at 19 Prospect Street, New Paltz in 1951. Ben had a position at the State University Teacher's College, New Paltz, as professor of art where he would teach for the next nineteen years (see *New Paltz Independent*, February 1959, B205). Private piano teaching, and after-school classes in theory and composing for children were among the outside-the-home activities that occupied Fine. She was a founder, vice-president, and also did "some performing," for the American Composer's Alliance, "at a number of colleges playing [her] own music and contemporary music."(see exs. P39, P40, P41, P42, P44 & P46). Though she was deeply "involved" in her cherished family life; Vivian managed to keep up with a meaningful amount of her diverse professional activates in music and composing.[57]

Within these busy years Fine composed, *String Quartet* (JC56, 1957); *Divertimento* (JC48, 1951); *Guide to the Life Expectancy of a Rose* (JC55, 1956); *Variations* (JC49, 1952); *Sonata for Violin and Piano* (JC50, 1952); *Sinfonia and Fugato* (JC51, 1952, D16, D17, D18); *Psalm 13* (JC52, 1953); *Variations for Harp* (JC53, 1953); *Composition for String Quartet* (JC54, 1954); and *Valedictions* (JC57, 1959). She felt that "the most important work that I wrote in those early years was the *Divertimento*." Fine made it a point never to seriously interrupt her work despite how this probably crowded her life as the mother of two young girls.[58] She held strong feelings for her role at that time:

"I have delighted in our family and can't imagine life without it. . . ." (see McKinney, Joan, April 2, 75, B187)

Yet, though Fine kept composing regularly, the overall amount of her actual compositions declined abruptly each year. In this 1947 to 1970 interlude between her two lifetime creative peaks, Fine composed thirty-three works; this being just about one half of the works composed during her two twenty-year peaks of creative productivity. (see Appendix 3 & 4)

Fine's music was still a rigid discipline pursued several hours each day, but now Fine seems to have undergone a change in her perspective. On the way from the avant-garde, brilliant "young composer around New York," to the mid-

life mother now part-time careerist, Fine appears to have become more inner
directed. She went to the City only a few times a week for her Foundation
duties. Now, far (75 miles) from New York City's vigorous New Music scene,
there was time and quiet enough to pursue these new themes, within the personal
world of home and hearth. She would tell interviewer, M. Hinderaker in 1968
(B135):
> "In our town we have a comparatively quiet village life. . . ."

This "quiet" time can be viewed as the composer's *mid-life interlude,*
insofar as the formulation and quantity of her compositions during this restrained
time.[59]

1956   Fine was working as the music director of the Rothschild Music
Foundation, giving concerts of her own works (commencing in 1956) and
researching other concert material for Bethasbee de Rothschild of the European
Rothschilds. Vivian was helping to decide the types of concerts to be given by
the Foundation. The Karps had developed a close friendship with Bethasbee de
Rothschild "in the forties in New York," where they (the Foundation) had a
"small concert hall on East 63rd Street." That was also where Vivian performed.

Because of her Foundation functions, Vivian was able to meet many
musicians and notables from the world of music, yet there were times that she
still felt somewhat "cut off from the rest of the musical world," as might any
mother.[60]

1958   Wallingford Riegger (see P43) analyzed Fine's music in his most
interesting 1958 treatise as having three "periods," an "earlier," to age 24, atonal
period; a less atonal period to age 31; and the third period, given as the time of
his treatise, being Fine's "return to atonality." Indeed, these properties existed.
But, as we shall see, by 1994, Riegger's third period, would actually fall during
the slowest creative cycle in Fine's long life. He was also deeply affected by her
A Guide to the Life Expectancy of the Rose (see Riegger, Wallingford, B251).

At least some of the themes she would select for her music reflected a
bit of the claustrophobic nature of suburban life. *A Guide to the Life Expectancy
of the Rose,* 1956 is fittingly taken from the garden section of the *Times.*
Composed in 1962, *Morning* (JC62) is for mixed chorus, piano or organ, with
a narrator quoting text taken from Thoreau's "Walden;" surely, a metaphor for
isolation and learning from the quiet life similar to Fine's life at the time. In
reality, Walden Pond was but a short drive away from Fine's home. Even
Dreamscape (JC66, 1964), a complex work conducted by Henry Brant at its
premiere, employs the universal suburban insignia as one of the instruments: the
lawn mower.

1960   Martha Graham commissioned the ballet *Alcestis* from Fine in 1960
(JC58, JC59). It was a critical success, becoming one of her far too meager
recordings (see D1, **American Record Guide**, 1962, B5; Cohn, Arthur, 1981,

B59 and 1962, B58; Sabin, Robert, B260, compare with Bramhall, Robyn, B36).

1963   Since their move, Vivian and Benjamin had become a two-career family in the suburbs of New Paltz, long before the term or concept was popular. One day stood out in Vivian's story of that 1960's decade:
       "... It was the early 60's, and yes ... because I remember the day that Kennedy was assassinated. I taught school and the children told me about this."[61]

REVIEW

The year 1947 saw Fine's landmark composition, *Capriccio for Oboe and Strings*, where she realized a creative and structural synthesis of the tonal and original elements in her music idiom. She abandoned pure tonalism, bringing back experimentation and atonalism to her music. Fine and family moved to suburban New Paltz, New York in 1951; of necessity, her career became part-time. 1947 to about 1969 was Fine's mid-life interlude. Though these years produced a sharp decline in compositions, they produce, instead, an increase in thematic and instrumental complexity expressing her seasoned development. Taking this new turn, Fine's music is again drawn from her youthful inventive prototype, but now tempered with a commanding and expert polish, adding absolute ease with her present, new found music idiom. Fine henceforth kept to this path. As the 1960's ended, Fine began the ascent to the period that I have identified as her third and final cycle; her *second* creative explosion.
       Fine's positions: "founder and chair, 1961-1965, vice president" American Composer's Alliance; director Rothschild Music Foundation 1953-1960; adjunct piano teacher 1945-48 at New York University; in 1948, adjunct teacher Juilliard School of Music, and State University Teacher's College at Potsdam, New York in 1951.[62]
       Fine wrote thirty-three works between 1947 and 1970 (see JC44 through JC76).

BENNINGTON: SECOND CREATIVE EXPLOSION

1964   New vistas would dramatically appear for Fine's visionary music in 1964. She was approached by Bennington College in Vermont; they offered her a part-time position teaching composition and piano, at much more money than she was making in New Paltz. But, it was a daunting close to one hundred miles one-way commute from New Paltz to Bennington College in Vermont. The College offered her $5000 a year for half-time teaching; this was considered a good wage in the 1960's.[63] She turned it down at first because she didn't like the long commute, but Fine was to say in 1988 that she "was finally persuaded to give it a whirl . . . it would have been a great mistake to have turned it down." She was to find a "very lively scene" at the department of music that was much to her liking.[64]

One important benefit to faculty life was the new opportunity Fine had to have her freshly created compositions performed almost without delay. Many of Fine's better known works were composed at Bennington; *Missa Brevis*, a primary example of her "layering" technique (JC79, 1972, see Kino, Carol, B164; Armer, Elinor, B12); the *Paean* (JC75, 1969); *Concerto for Piano, Strings and Percussion for One Performer* (JC80, 1972); *Meeting for Equal Right 1866* (JC84, 1976), and *Women in the Garden* (JC89, 1977).

Equal Rights and *Women* were Fine's first candid feminist themes. But, she had in fact been born a natural feminist, in that she seemed to naturally assume the obligations of self that pay homage to one's potentials. Though she had not felt it essential that love of family be the sacrifice to her art; this being the acceptable canon for women in her era.

At long last, in her fifth decade, Vivian was freed of most of a lifetime's shackles, including the necessity of earning a living *instead* of composing. She was also freed from the complex logistic difficulties routinely involved when having a work performed in concert: finding musicians, funding, venues and sponsors on a case by case or composition by composition basis. In addition she had now made powerful advancements in her mastery of the composer's craft. She was wonderfully well prepared to enter the most vitally productive two decades of her career.

In the past, no matter how worthy the piece, it might be many years, often never, until Fine could hear her work *in toto*; or be offered recording opportunities. One such case in point: Fine's *Concertante for Piano and Orchestra*, 1944 had never been premiered until 1988, forty-four years after she wrote it! The *Sonata for Violin and Piano* (JC50, 1952) wouldn't be heard by the composer for another six years, 1958. In contrast, while at Bennington, when a work was complete it was quickly heard in concert so that a cyclic motivational energy moved through performer, performance, audience and composer. Fine defined this situation precisely:

". . . Yes, I'd say that I began to compose more, because for one thing, my compositions were automatically played here [at Bennington College]. I didn't have to shop around to find a place for them to be played. . . . I had that situation where my works were going to be performed. *This was a wonderful thing to me!* . . . and performances . . . give you energy and impetus. . . ."[65]

Fine's Bennington period is characterized by great productivity, many performances, more complex compositions, and numerous commissions. She composed fifty-seven works while on the faculty (see JC66 through JC123). Her time teaching at Bennington somewhat overlaps her last, second creative cycle of music output (see analysis, Appendix 3). Fine's activities in this period would presage, as did her early creative period, substantial measures of attention from critics, prestigious music organizations, and perhaps above all, new and devoted audiences across the country.

1965   Fine composed *My Son, My Enemy*, for dance choreographer, Jose Limon in 1965 (see Hughes, Allen, August 16, 1965, B141; also Terry, Walter, B299). In the same year she wrote, *Concertino for Piano and Percussion Ensemble* (JC69, 1965). She would also perform Erik Satie's *Satiana* as part of The American Dance Festival premieres of works by Hoving and Draper, during this active year (see Cohen, B56)(see P49).

1966   Fine's *Dreamscape* (JC66, 1964) was performed at Bennington. She also gave a series of lectures and recitals of twentieth century piano music, Notre Dame University and Bard College and Bennington College (see P48, P50). She was a recipient of the Dollard Prize in 1966, among other key awards in these decades (see Morton, Brian and Pamela Collins, B198).

1969   In 1969 Vivian and her family, Ben had retired in 1967, moved near Bennington College in Vermont where they built a home in the pastoral hills of Hoosick Falls, New York, just over the Vermont border. And "then it was full time . . ." [of her faculty position]. Fine spoke of her enthusiasm for her life there with her normal modesty:
        "I had colleagues whom I liked a lot. . . . I was having my compositions performed. . . . There was a lot of energy at this place . . . forgive me, I gave it a lot of energy too. . . . I was active here as a composer, a performer, and a teacher. . . . It was a very wonderful kind of situation . . . my association with Bennington has been very fruitful. . . ."[66]

1970   As part of a Bennington "multi-media evening on the subject of war" (this was at the height of the Vietnam war), Fine organized several performances including her *The Delta* (JC76, 1969) with a poem about the horrors of wars, and Stabat Mater from *Songs of Our Time* (JC40, 1943, written at the height of the World War II), and *Adios, Bilbadito* (JC29, 1939, written at the beginning of World War II). Fine's daughter, Nina Karp, participated (see Bennington Banner 1970, B25).

1971   Fine was one of four composers recorded in 1971 in a release "Music from Bennington." (D13) where she conducted her *Paean* (JC75, 1969, see Frankenstein, Albert, B102)(see P52). Since the point in the mid sixties (when she began teaching at Bennington) events had set the stage for Fine's second creative period of accelerated composing. The second creative explosion was to begin in 1971 after a year of no finished compositions (1970). Twenty works were composed between 1971 and 1979. This trend would crescendo to a prodigious sixty-two works completed by Fine in this peak cycle between 1971 and 1994 (JC77 through JC138). This would be the most substantial creative effort of Fine's lifetime, amazingly, begun at age fifty-eight and continuing until she was past eighty years old.

1976   With her 1976, *Meeting for Equal Rights 1866* (JC84) and in 1977, *Women in the Garden* (JC89), she could explore both the intellectual and musical abstractions that feminist ideals portrayed for her. These two works garnered considerable critical acclaim. *Meeting* would premiere in the authentic Great Hall at the Cooper Union in New York City where the early Women's Right's Association debated for women's Suffrage. It was funded by the National Endowment for the Arts. Fine's *Meeting* is a vast interlacing musical work requiring three conductors; it is scored for narrator, soprano, bass-baritone, full chorus, and orchestra. Male and female voices contend within nineteenth century writings and suffrage ideals. Reviews ranged from awestruck to awful as is often the case with visionary works of art (see Belt, Byron, B23, compare with Der, A., B86 and Fuller, Sophie, B102).

1977   Fine was to further contour her music to study eminent women of history with her chamber opera, *Women in the Garden* (JC89 1977). It was written with a $8000 grant from the National Endowment for the Arts in 1974 (see Hertelendy, Paul. March 17, 1974, B127) and widely performed on both the East and West coasts. Like *Meeting* it sharply divided critics into opposing camps; most probably because of its resolutely feminist concept, yet again its intellectual center. Fine's natural intellectualism had drawn complaints in the past. Most critics admired the modernist music, saving their wrath for Fine's inherent ideas. The composer's four interacting character presentations of: Isadora Duncan, dramatic soprano; Virginia Woolf, lyric soprano; Emily Dickinson, mezzo-soprano; and Gertrude Stein, contralto or dark mezzo, were viewed either as "superbly presented" or "static" by critics Goldstein and Hertelendy, respectively (see Goldstein, Margery, B110, compare with Hertelendy, Paul. February 15 1978, B128). One tenor, Tenor, behaves in some sense as an "everyman" throughout the musical conversations (see West, William D., B319).

      Fine was indeed brave, perhaps the only one able, to bring this complicated artistic and political theme to the opera stage. She was, after all, well studied on the attributes of the women characters. Fine had a lifetime's familiarity with poetry (Dickinson, Stein), and was an expert on the Modern Dance, and had understanding of how another avant-garde spirit like Duncan might view the world. These character undercurrents could be incorporated into her own music idioms. She was called a "pioneer" because of *Garden's* artistic achievement (see Paris, Barry, B224). There is no doubt that Fine's opera was a success; *Garden*, besides being extensively critiqued, was performed many more times at important venues. More so than most contemporary operas.[67]

1979   Success of the seventies was capped when Fine was elected a member of the elite American Academy and Institute of Arts and Letters in May of 1979. This election paid homage to her lifetime of composing music in numerous genre. Another aspect of Fine's work was singled out for honor by the Academy. She was also awarded a special Citation (B5) recognizing her "substantial contribution to American Dance."[68] In 1980 she won a Guggenheim Fellowship for composition.

Almost all of Fine's many music scores were now made available through Catamount Facsimiles Editions, which was a publishing company operated by her sister, Adelaide. Several outside publishers were also publishing some of her scores[69] (see Works and Performances, Chapter 3, and also Appendix 2).

Not only the amount, but the sheer magnitude and grandeur of her compositions would flourish during this energetic cycle of creativity (see Appendix 4).

1981   But still, although Fine had many accomplishments by this time, she could still be snubbed. The Bay Area Congress on Women in Music, San Francisco, California, January 31, was one of the first conferences that brought together women in music from all sectors and areas of the United States (see Cody, Judith. 1981, B53). Men and women, learned about, and listened to contemporary and historical women's music that they, too often, had never had opportunity to study or enjoy before. Vivian Fine was one of the composers presented at that Congress; even at that late date her work was but slightly studied or not included often enough in the historical archives, considering her numerous achievements. Fine's *Missa Brevis* (JC79, 1972) was performed at an evening concert of prominent woman composers, which event received scant media attention. Visually compelling, with eight cellists, *Missa* wove a kind of cool, suppressed anticipation through its linear lines; a mood that may well have been about a decade or so before its time.

1982   *Women in the Garden* (JC89), Fine's chamber opera, was premiered by the Port Costa Players in 1978, was performed again by Carnegie Mellon University in 1979, again in 1981 by the L'ensemble Chamber Music Center (see Burrell, Margo, B41) and yet again by the San Francisco Opera Center in 1982. *Garden* would receive over fourteen performances before the decade ended. This was quite different from the situation during Fine's early years when there could be decades between performances of most of her creations (see Works and Performances, Chapter 3).

Seven decades into life, Fine was composing her way to the incredible apex of her music career. *Drama for Orchestra* (JC101, 1982) was commissioned by the San Francisco Symphony (see San Francisco Symphony, B269, B270; Pontzious, Richard. January 10, 1983, B238) and became a musical "landmark . . . first major commission in its 72-year history to a woman composer. . . ." (see Albahari, B2). The Symphony also honored Fine with the week of January 5-13, 1983 that was devoted exclusively to a retrospective of Fine's music (see P64). The premiere of her *Drama* was the centerpiece for the Vivian Fine Week (see Hertelendy, Paul. January 4, 1983, B129).

Drama is a fully realized masterpiece, employing the total spectrum of "music-drama" (see Carson, Josephine, B46). There is "tremendous colour" of orchestration, so that Fine has said of *Drama*:

"Sometimes I feel like a painter, painting with strong colours . . . creating music is sometimes like painting."[70]

Fine scored the massive aural production for a huge orchestra, "Mahler-sized," (see Shere, Charles, January 7, 1983, B284). The focus of the *Drama* was the intense psychodrama, inner directed agonies and manic joys, suggested by a group of paintings by Edvard Munch. Fine, now the master of both tonal and atonal orchestral colouration, synthesized these opposing sound elements with her "layering" techniques.[71] Emotive sound and aural visual intimations interwove in myriad musical "layers." Fine drove the huge orchestra as a powerhouse of labyrinthine rhythms, able to come to a probing focus. This sound lens then musically illuminated each of the psychological states evoked by the paintings.

Judging by the great amount of material published about *Drama for Orchestra*, it was a critical success in a very big way.[72] It was even nominated for the Pulitzer Prize in 1983; it was the runner-up. Fine was now seventy years old.

Many of Fine's older works were now to be revived, to be performed for the first time in many years, by numerous well-respected music groups. For example; *Four Pieces for Two Flutes* (JC2, 1930) was played as part of the Music of Women Composers in 1985; *Four Elizabethan Songs* (JC23, 1938) was performed at Skidmore College in 1981 after forty-three years; *Four Songs* (JC8, 1933) was played during San Francisco's Vivian Fine Week 1983; even her first public work, *Solo for Oboe* (JC1, 1929) was performed in Innsbruck, Austria. Ben showed his pride in her special week by designing and wearing a tee shirt with the Fine Week logo (see Connell, Mary, B70).

1986   On International Women's Day, March 8, a one-hour radio program (see Brookes, Tom, B38) was broadcast on Fine and her music for the International League of Women Composers (JC8, JC56, JC58, JC79, JC90, D1, D9, D11). On Fine's 73rd birthday that September 28th, the program was rebroadcast.

1987   Fine retired as a faculty member of Bennington College in 1987, where she had taught since 1964. She felt that now she could have time to write even more music. Shortly thereafter, in 1988, she and Ben would edit a book of essays about French scientist, Louis Rapkine.[73]

1988   Among her important commissions was one from the Bay Area Women's Philharmonic in Berkeley, California. This would be the BAWP's world premiere of the deeply moving *After the Tradition* (JC123, 1987). That night, the audience would respond to Fine's presence and her new work, in the most exhilarated fashion that this writer has ever witnessed (compare with Hertelendy, Paul. May 2, 1988, B).

The packed house was hushed in rapt attention during Fine's pre-concert lecture on her *Tradition*. The audience leaned forward in their seats, as if they had all become one body, reaching toward the quiet, dignified figure of Vivian Fine. Her small and compact presence provoked an aura of intense anticipation.

When describing *Tradition*, Fine said that she "had found a way to express my feelings in my own language." It is in three movements, beginning with Kaddish, a prayer for the dead, that was dedicated to Fine's friend, George Finckel. The second movement conveys "a very Jewish feeling of longing," voicing words from the 12th century Hebrew poet, Yudah Halevi, who longed for his homeland, "My heart's in the East and I am at the end of the West." "Hark! Yaweh causes the wilderness to dance," is the third, and last part of the work.

With Kaddish, the orchestra suddenly released swells of mournful, yet imposing sounds in barely sensed ancient rhythms against the kettle drums, the impression being one of clear desert winds. Secondly, the poet's yearning words are translated into strangely beautiful non linear music with the shadows of near Eastern timbres. The finale is the work of Yaweh; the most familiar tones, like coming home, are joyous forthright rhythms as the wilderness does indeed "dance" as only the dance master Fine could manage. Always, a lush spot of tonality is there as a brief touchstone, no matter how startling are the new horizons of music in *Tradition*.

The last cascade of the conductor's baton signaled swells of applause, prompting several standing ovations from the packed house. Tears were clearly evident on the cheeks of some audience members.[74]

Fine, at this zenith of her life as a composer, had at last achieved the eminence, in the world of contemporary classical music, that she richly deserved. Not by any means did this make her name a household word, but among those attuned to this particular musical domain, she was held in great esteem. There would be another major retrospective showcasing Vivian's music in addition to San Francisco's Vivian Fine Week; there was a performance retrospective at SUNY-Buffalo in 1987 (see Coon, Judith A., B71). The East Coast would have its own homage to Fine, also.

1989   Mayor Raymond L. Flynn, of Boston, declared with an official proclamation that the week of April 16-22, 1989 would be Boston's Vivian Fine Appreciation Week. Concerts and lectures on Fine's music were featured throughout the Boston area (see Boston, City of, B35). Fine was quite delighted at this prospect.

By December of 1989 she was also steadfastly continuing to work on her other commissions. Her music seemed to give her energy. Fine had just sent ten pages of a newly commissioned score, "a mono drama, a remake of a Poe Story," to Claudia Stevens (*The Heart Disclosed*, JC131, 1989). She was enthusiastically waiting "to germinate something," for an idea for a commission for Pamela Frank (*Portal*, 1989, JC132). Something else was also " in the germinating stage" that December; it was the last work and it would become the fictionalized memoir for Fine.[75]

1990   Vivian sounded quite pleased when she told me that she had had few health problems in her long life. This would change when my phone call to her revealed an "unpleasant surprise." She had a "weak and reedy voice" and sounded "sad," for she would tell me that she had pneumonia. Up to this time, Fine had been "composing some of her finest music. Comprehensive works with many years of intense experience behind them."

Saturday morning of July thirtieth, I phoned Vivian with great "trepidation concerning her state of health." But her voice seemed almost as full of health and vigor as before she had been stricken with that serious pneumonia. It was as if a weight had been lifted off of my shoulders.

"The illness came out of the blue. It started as an awful bronchitis. I never felt so sick in my life. I will have to put rest on my agenda, don't you think?" she said.

We talked of her current composing and discussed my compendium of her compositions and performances then in progress (see Works and Performances chapter 3). Fine was anxious to talk of her music; I wrote at the time:

". . . Though she does indeed sound very well, her voice still has a slight wobble. . . So strong is her will to compose music, that even with this heavy illness still weakening her, she dreaded taking time off from her loved music."[76]

Benjamin and Vivian took an apartment in San Francisco at 407 Sanchez Street during November and December in 1990. One evening while visiting the Karps there, I asked Vivian:

"Do you feel that your energy level is back to normal, Vivian?"

"Almost. I'm resting now when I feel tired, being careful, listening to the body. I feel very well. I've been doing a piece for my granddaughter, Keli. She choreographed a dance for an event here in San Francisco. You must see the program. In the notes it says, 'her grandmother composed the music.'"

This dance is probably one of three dances that Keli choreographed from Fine's *Canzones y Dances* (JC136, 1991), for guitar, flute, and cello which she was also composing, on commission, during the same time-frame.

Later that night Vivian would add:

"I've never had health problems before. Never needed to hold back my activities. So, it's difficult for me now, having to be careful about my health."[77]

Fine's 1970's and 1980's explosive peak of composing appears to decline in the early 1990's, but she still maintained a busy schedule. Her violin and piano duet for Pamela Frank, *Portal*, begun in 1989, was completed in January of 1990, premiered in April 1990 at the Philadelphia Free Library. One month later Frank performed in Alice Tully Hall in New York City.[78] Fine also composed *Songs and Arias* (JC133) in 1990, having it premiered on July 12 1990 in Portland, Oregon.[79]

Thursday evening of Oct 2, 1990 I heard *Missa Brevis*, for the second time, at the Green Room in San Francisco. This time there were but four cellos. The work immediately projected a sense of dignity, yet freshness, as the four cellists bowed in what seemed both contrasting, then conflicting melodic motifs, accompanied with a few sung words from Roman Catholic and Hebrew holy texts. The lovely taped soprano voice, multiplied by voice-overs, shadowed and then eclipsed the cellists in soft patterns of sound. These eerily interweaving music lines represented a most effective use of Fine's "layering" technique.[80] At least one critic from a major newspaper, saw Fine's work as "visionary" that evening (see Commanday, Robert, Oct 4, 1990, B65).

1991 In 1991 Fine completed a new commission for a chamber work with classical guitar, flute and cello, *Canzones y Dances* (JC136, 1991). The repertoire is limited for this combination, especially with modern music, making her work an important addition. She had begun it in 1988, though up to then she had never composed for classical guitar. *Canzones* has much that resonates with the resplendent Spanish guitar tradition, fused with what can only be 20th century, very American music harmonies. At least, this is Fine's unique contribution to this growing body of American music. In the second movement, her love affair with poets is declared with ethereal, delicately atonal music based on a Pablo Neruda poem. Of course, parts three and four, the Tango and Jiga are occasions to see modern dance composer Fine at her best, deploying her aural impressionistic images.[81] (see Cody, B54; D3,1992).

1993 The new opera! In the budding spring of 1987 Vivian came upon a story that gave her an insight for what would be her final opera, while reading obituaries in the *New York Times*.

For reasons that may forever remain clouded, Vivian was instantly attracted to the odd-ball life of another famous child piano prodigy, who went on to live a Hollywood life complete with ten wives. As Vivian read the pianist's obituary, she somehow fused the wild life of the pianist with her own rather conventional family life; but her conventional home life had run parallel to a quite eventful career in music (see Bustard, Clarke, B42). She was to see the stuff of her own life story within, what might superficially seem, the very different life imbedded in the Hungarian pianist's obituary.

This was not the first time that she had found substance in the news for her music themes. There was of course, *Guide to the Life Expectancy of a Rose* (JC55), a concept she had drawn from an article in the *New York Times*. Now, Vivian's magic music would raise her 21st century multi-media *Memoirs of Uliana Rooney* (JC138, 1994) from the still print.

On an evening meeting in December of 1989, Fine had disclosed just such an idea for an opera that she held in special regard. So thoroughly did the opera's concept appeal to Fine, that she quite plainly declared that she "would write this one *without* a commission!" [82]

Though she refused to give the name for the opera that evening, all events point toward *Memoirs of Uliana Rooney*. This was the contemporaneous production portraying the multifarious twentieth century lifetime of a ebullient composer named Uliana Rooney. Quietly, Fine would state that it was indeed, something of an autobiography (see Jones, Leslie, 1997, B152). Still composing the work in 1993, though both she and Ben had both become "a little creaky,"[83] Fine felt sure that the Dallas Opera would help her with a commission and give *Uliana* its world premiere. They had apparently expressed interest, but they would turn her down. The Dallas Opera "had studied the opera, but just couldn't do it."[84]

Uliana is the fictional, American composer in the opera's stellar role. Her electrifying life of avant-garde music, uncommon exploits, and romantic turns, coincides with twentieth century historical happenings; as does the real life composer's, Vivian (minus the romantic turns and multiple husbands!). Uliana is born of Russian-Jewish immigrants, as was Vivian. The opera begins with "an echo" of *Le sacre du printemps*, later *Pierrot lunaire* is used.[85] Professional filmmaker-librettist Sonya Friedman used film and slides to create a "newsreel" projection of history backlighting the opera's serious, and at times humorous scenes. Fine deployed much of her "earlier music . . . as motifs" throughout the opera, she added:

". . . I'm looking back into my past and seeing what happened."[86]

1994   Given enough time, grants and commissions from various sources were combined to create the expensive production that is music, theater and poetry: opera. *Uliana* was performed by the American Opera Projects, Inc., in part, in February, 1994. Fine's opera went on to its world-premiere as a fully staged production at the University of Richmond, Virginia in September of 1994; in time for her eighty-first birthday (see Bustard, Clarke, B42).

1996   Since starting her autobiographical opera, few notes of music seemed to appear on the sun-sensitive vellum sheets that Fine favored for her scores, so that she had to write in dim light, and also silently, "Sun isn't good for the vellums. . . ." She no longer used the piano to compose, it got in the way of hearing the sounds of music that she mentally created. She had once said:

"I haven't played piano to compose in twenty years. . . . The sound of the piano cramped my hearing the instrumental sounds . . . [this is] an inner hearing. . . ."[87]

In any event, it had been years since she had performed publicly. She missed her piano, it had been her companion for seventy-eight years, but hands were no long "so strong and steady."[88]

In 1996, she said, in an article, that she was at work on a special "project" for her daughter, Nina, who Fine said "is a singer." It was to be a somewhat longer work than Fine's usual piece. This would have been her last known work, as yet untitled (see Jones, Leslie. 1997, B152). Writing her music had all but come to a halt for the aged composer. August, 1996 saw another performance of *Uliana* by American Opera Projects. *Uliana* is performed again at Philadelphia, Pennsylvania's Annenberg Center in February of 1997.

2000   At the end of wintertime, on March 20, 2000, Vivian and her sister Adelaide, older by three years, were in a car accident in Bennington. Her sister lingered and then died several weeks later. Vivian was killed instantly.[89]

Vivian's husband, Benjamin, died nine months later, after a long illness.

REVIEW

Fine and family relocated near her full-time faculty position at Bennington College, Vermont. There, her opportunities in music broadened considerably for performances, recordings, and grants, thus extending her recognition, and giving her more motivation for composing, especially the complex works. Music themes now include opera and major orchestral works, dealing in involved social, sometimes feminist, more often spiritual, and psychological issues, i. e., *Drama for Orchestra, Women in the Garden, Meeting for Equal Rights 1866, After the Tradition, Poetic Fires, Missa Brevis,* and *Memoirs of Uliana Rooney.* Her opera, *Uliana,* was her last known major work. It was somewhat autobiographical. She composed more in the later half of her life than ever before.

Fine was elected to the American Academy and Institute of Arts and Letters in 1979; she received a Guggenheim Fellowship in 1980, and her *Drama for Orchestra* was nominated for the Pulitzer Prize (it was the runner-up) in 1983. Fine composed sixty-two works between 1971-94, her greatest, final, cycle of creative output (see JC77 through JC138).

Vivian Fine died in March 2000. Adelaide, Fine's sister, also died in the accident. Adelaide's firm, Catamount Facsimile Editions, ceased operations;[90] it had published most of Fine's music. Fine had willed her papers and scores to the Library of Congress (see Appendix 1).

SUMMARY

An axiomatic statistical analysis of Fine's creative output during her long lifetime revealed an astounding, bimodal distribution of her lifework (see Appendices 3 and 4) not noted elsewhere. By far the greater number of Fine's compositions were completed during two clearly distinct, approximately twenty year peak periods, or creative cycles. Only the term *creative explosion* seems apt to describe these rather dramatic peaks of Fine's music production.

The first peak cycle began with her first efforts in 1927 at age 13, until about 1946 at age thirty-three; during this time she composed fifty-four works. This figure doesn't include many early unwritten works for piano (see Chapter 3). Beginning this cycle, Fine's youthful works were arresting, dissonant and extraordinarily original; midway through this first cycle, about 1934 coinciding with her theory studies under Roger Sessions, her works became tonal, almost conservative and derivative. Her tonal idiom lasted until 1946 when she said that her "tonal period was over."

From about 1947 to 1970 was Fine's *mid-life interlude*, where the number of works she would compose in each year declined significantly to but thirty-three in the entire twenty-three year period. Exactions inherent in her role as a wife and mother were most likely responsible for Fine's decline in composing her music during this period. Careful rationing of her time allowed her to formulated the music style that continued until her death; it was "less dissonant, though not strictly tonal or strictly atonal," in aural construct. Fine's musical thematic material became more diverse, dramatic and impassioned during this cycle.

Vivian Fine's *second creative explosion* began in 1971 at age fifty-eight and lasted to about 1993 when Fine was eighty years old; during this time she composed sixty-two works. Conventional beliefs that discourage thinking of advanced age as a period of possibly, substantial productivity must be abandoned when analyzing Fine's record. Her second composing peak was even more astonishing considering her age, and the fact that the works of her second peak were also considerably longer, orchestrations and operas, than in her first peak, many containing greater instrumentation complexities than in the first creative explosion or her mid-life interlude. Here, her thematic material became quite rich and complex, often dealing with pivotal life questions (though Fine never would lose her wit or sense of musical humor).

CHAPTER ENDPAPERS

1. Historically, the Romantic period of European music spans about 1825 to the early 20th century when the innovative Ultra-Modern music champions altered the status quo music idiom to forms that endure to this third millennium. Some Romantic composers cited by the **Harvard Concise Dictionary of Music and Musicians**, 1999, are: Weber (1786-1826), Schubert (1797-1828), Berlioz (1803-69), Mendelssohn (1809-47), Chopin (1810-49), Wagner (1813-83), and Liszt (1811-86).

2. Premiered in Paris on May 29, 1913, *Le sacre du printemps* " . . . departed radically from musical tradition by using irregular, primitive rhythms and harsh dissonances. The audience . . . reacted with riotous disfavor. . . ." **New Columbia Encyclopedia**, fourth edition.

3. Schoenberg launched his new twelve-tone system, also called serial music, in his works between 1920-23:
". . . twelve pitches of the chromatic scale are ordered into a row, or series, that provides the basic pitch structure for a given composition . . . ; *Sprechstimme, Sprechgesang*: [Gr., speaking voice, speech-song) mid-way between speech and song . . . approximates reproduction of pitches . . . avoids

sustaining of any pitch . . . notated with x's . . . Schoenberg made the greatest use of it." **Harvard Concise Dictionary of Music and Musicians,** 1999.
Fine's last composition, her opera *The Memoirs of Uliana Rooney* (JC38), was interspersed with these techniques.

4. Ives, church organist-composer, was little recognized as the first truly American Ultra-Modern music composer; not until his *Concord* was performed in 1939, twenty four years after it was finished, did he receive fame. His *Third Symphony* won the Pulitzer Prize in 1947. **New Columbia Encyclopedia.**

5. Data, from Fine, she also told the author, "I was the second daughter. I had a sister [Adelaide] who was three years older than I am; and a younger sister [Eleanora] who was fifteen months younger than I am." Taped, by author, interview with Fine, at her upstate home in Hoosick Falls, New York, 9-21-1988.

6. "Michael Reese Hospital," and "affluent part of" quotes by Fine; hardworking . . . [to] . . . Lawndale Avenue: Data, *ibid.*

7. "absolute pitch," "grey eyes," and "wanted to have a piano," all quotes by Fine; . . . work as a secretary . . . : Data, taped, by author, interview with Fine, Petaluma, California, 1-20-1986.

8. "hours practicing . . . [to] . . . only five years old:" *ibid.*

9. Dates of Fine's early music education are based on her own account of her early education as taken from Fine's information sent to the author, 5-14-1990. (see Appendix 5)

10. Taken, by the author, from the original recital program at Fine's home; copy in author's collection (CAC).

11. "Mr. Fine . . . [to] . . . I was eleven:" Telephone interview, by author, with Fine, April, 1990.

12. From a 1925 photo in **Ruth Crawford Seeger, A Composer's Search for American Music,** by Judith Tick (see Tick, Judith, B301) p 128.

13. Madame Djane . . . [to] . . . "around my work:" Taped, by author, interview with Fine at her home, 9-21-88.

14. ". . . first movement of the *C-major* . . . ," & "During . . . [to] . . . my own playing:" Taped, by author, interview with Fine, Petaluma, California, 1-20-1986.

15. When she was . . . [to] . . . "all these concerts:" Taped, by author, interview with Fine, at her home, 9-21-1988.

16. Fine remembered . . . [to] . . . "adventurous with New Music:" Taped, by author, interview with Fine, Petaluma, California, 1-20-86.

17. Another . . . [to] . . . *Sonata*: Taped, by author, interview with Fine, Petaluma, California, 1-20-1986.

18. M. Herz . . . [to] . . . "lessons:" Taped, by author, interview with Fine at her home, 9-21-1988.

19. Crawford . . . [to] . . . "adventurous music:" Taped, by author, interview with Fine, Petaluma, California, 1-20-1986.

20. It would be . . . [to] . . . "high school:" *ibid.*

21. The summer . . . [to] . . . "thirteen:" Crawford's note in **Ruth Crawford Seeger**, p 60 (see Tick, Judith, B301).

22. Copy of original *Lullaby* sent to author by Fine and penciled in her hand: "First composition, June, 1927." May 10, 1990.

23. Information sent by Fine to author, 1993, headed: "Selected list of early compositions," also notes "Numerous short pieces for solo piano." These very early piano works are unaccounted for; most likely not written down. All other of Fine's childhood works (see Works and Performances, Chapter 3) are numbered Jci to Jcxiv preceding Fine's formal *opus compendium.*

24. Taken, by author, from Fine's original Nicholas Senn School semester report card, at her home. Dated June 1928, stamped, B. F. Buck, principal. Mrs. D. Fine had signed the card. CAC

25. Taken, by author, from Fine's original John Fisk School report card at her home. Dated January 1925: teacher, F. O. Wilson gave Vivian good to excellent on all grade 6B subjects, except "drawing" which drew only a fair mark. CAC

26. Taken, by author, from the original program at Fine's home; penciled in Fine's hand, "Dec. 24, 1928 . . . at Mrs. Eisendrath's — Chicago." CAC

27. As a child . . . [to] . . . "wonderful!:" Taped, by author, interview with Fine, Petaluma, California, 1-20-86.

28. **Ruth Crawford Seeger: Memoirs, Memories, Music**, by Matilda Gaume, pp 35-36 (see Gaume, Matilda, B112). Cowell may well have demonstrated his radical "tone clusters;" groups of piano keys hit with forearm or palm; perhaps his (then new) method of plucking inside the piano directly on the harp.

29. Imre . . . [to] . . . "discovery:" **Ruth Crawford Seeger**, p. 126 (see Tick, Judith, B301).

30. He . . . [to] . . . "fond of him:" Taped, by author, interview with Fine, Petaluma, California 1-20-1986.

31. From photo in: **Ruth Crawford Seeger** (see Tick, Judith, B301) p 128.

32. long visit . . . [to] . . . "composers:" **Ruth Crawford Seeger**, (see Tick, Judith, B301), "redolent" quote, interview with Fine, 1989; "everybody" quote, interview with Tristan Hearst by Nancy Reich 1985 from same, pp 45-48.

33. "encouraged" by Rudhyar, and "letters:" **The Music of Vivian Fine**, by Heidi Von Gunden (see Von Gunden, Heidi, B316), pp 34n8, 16.

34. Fine's music was always "evolving;" many reviewers discussed her style (see Riegger, Wallingford, B251; Hertelendy, Paul. 1-4-1983, B129; Saminsky, Lazare 1-1-41, B266; Shere, Charles 1-9-1983, B285; Upton Treat, William, B310; Humphrey, Doris, B143; Ariel, B11; Bramhall, Robyn, B36; Pontzious, Richard. 1-6-1983, B237; and Carson, Josephine, B46).

35. Vivian . . . [to] . . . "first composition:" Taped, by author, interview with Fine, Petaluma, California 1-20-1986.

36. *Solo For* . . . [to] . . . Inc.: Taped, by author, interview with Fine at her home 9-20-1988.

37. Taken, by the author, from the original program at Fine's home; CAC

38. When Fine . . . [to] . . . "no one:" Taped, by author, interview with Fine, Petaluma, California 1-20-86; "solid reputation . . . [to] . . . Brahms:" quote, **Ruth Crawford Seeger** (see Tick, Judith, B301) p35.

39. Taped, by author, interview with Fine at her home, 9-20-1988.

40. "prime mover;" Bartok, "made headquarters;" "mentored Ruth," Varèse, Cowell, Weiss, data: **Ruth Crawford Seeger**, (see Gaume, Matilda, B112) pp 62, 63, 64.

41. Taped, by author, interview with Fine at her home 9-20-1988.

42. "new Steinway:" From Charles Seeger's description of his first lesson with Ruth in Walton's living room on that same piano, in **Ruth Crawford Seeger** (see Gaume, Matilda, B112) p 64.

43. Taped, by author, interview with Fine at her home, 9-20-1988.

44. Taken, by author, from the original "Programme." CAC, *ibid.*

45. Taken, by author, from the original program. *ibid.*

46. Well recognized . . . [to] . . . "modern dance:" Taped, by author, interview with Fine, Petaluma, California 1-20-86.

47. Taken, by author, from the original program at Fine's home. CAC

48. S. A. D., quote taken, by the author, from an original news clipping at Fine's home; quite stained, marked by Fine: "Sun 1932;" she had underlined the quote with pencil. Probably the *New York Sun*; perhaps "Sunday." CAC

49. parents . . . [to] . . . "that point:" Taped interview, by author, at Fine's home, 9-19-1988. "leading:" Taken from original, February 10, 1932, Roerich Society program at Fine's home. Vivian found job . . . : Taken from many original programs at Fine's home. "Fourth Production:" data from original program at Fine's home. All taken by author. All CAC.

50. Rent . . . [to] . . . composer: Taped, by author, interview with Fine, Petaluma, California 1-20-1986. "dancers . . . [to] . . . was the piano:" Quotes, interview with Fine, by her daughter, Nina Karp, 1975. Fine's inner process quote, Data: Taped, by author, interview with Fine at her home, 9-21-1988. CAC

51. Fine . . . [to] . . . Liszt: data taken from original "Y" Pop Series, and Fuld Hall programs; tour data taken from numerous original programs and reviews (as shown) all at Fine's home. CAC

52. Charles Seeger taught Vivian for two lessons . . . [to] . . . "didn't work out:" Taped, by author, interview with Fine, Petaluma, California 1-20-1986. Fine began . . . [to] . . . four months: Data, taped, by author, interview with Fine at her home, 9-21-1988. Dalcroze method: **Harvard Concise Dictionary of Music** 1999. April 5, 1935, was the date on the New York wedding certificate. Benjamin Karp was born May 8, 1906 in Syracuse, New York.

53. "Marriage of the Arts:" Taped, by author, interview with Fine who read this at her home saying, "that's cute!" No copy, 9-21-1988. Many hour . . . [to] . . . born in September, 1948: data, taped, by author, interview with Fine at her home, 9-21 & 22-1988. CAC

54. George Szell, well-known conductor of The Cleveland Orchestra, Ohio; mainly Romantic period music. CD retrospective, 1997.

55. Displaying both . . . [to] . . . "kind of music:" Data, taped, by author, interview with Fine at her home, 9-22-1988. CAC

56. Karps . . . [to] . . . college: data, Taped, by author, interview with Fine, Petaluma, California, 1-20-1986.

57. family moved . . . [to] . . . activities in music: Data, taped, author, interview with Fine at her home, 9-22-1988.

58. Within these . . . [to] . . . girls: Data, *ibid.*

59. Fine's music . . . [to] . . . careerist: Data, taped, by author, interview with Fine, Petaluma, California 1-20-1986.

60. Fine working . . . [to] . . . "musical world:" Taped, by author, interview with Fine at her home 9-22-1988.

61. "It was the early sixties:" Quote, *ibid.*

62. "founder and chair" . . . State University Teacher's . . . (see Morton, Brian and Pamela Collins, B198); other positions: Data, taped, by author, interview with Fine at her home, 9-22-1988.

63. offered $5000 yearly . . . : Data, letter from Bennington College to Fine, May 19, 1964. CAC

64. In 1964 . . . [to] . . . her liking: Data, taped, by author, interview with Fine at her home 9-22-88.

65. "Yes, I'd say . . . [to] . . . impetus:" *ibid.*

66. 1969 . . . [to] . . . "very fruitful:" *ibid.*

67. See the Works and Performances, Chapter 3, for extended lists of reviews and performances on *Garden* (JC89) and *Meeting* (JC84). Fine's daughter, Peggy Karp, has the only known CD recording of *Meeting*. Phone discussion, by author,

with Peggy Karp, February, 2001.

68. Taken, by author, from the original letter: Academy to Fine, dated May 1979, at her home. CAC

69. Almost . . . [to] . . . scores: Data, Taped, by author, interview with Fine, at a friend's apartment in Berkeley, California, the afternoon of 4-29-1988.

70. "Sometimes I feel . . . " quote, Fine at her home, interview by author while studying Fine's tape of *Drama*. "tremendous colour," one of my remarks that evening. We spent many days listening to Fine's compositions as she commented on them to me, 9-15-1988.

71. "layering" one of many modernist music techniques devised by Fine; this one evolved while she studied a recording session as various tapes worked together. (see Pontzious, Richard 1-6-1983 B237; Carson, Josephine B46)

72. Selected reviews: Ariel, 1983 B11; E. Armer, 1991 B12; J. Carson, 1983 B46; R. Commanday, Jan. 7, 1983 B63; C. Crawford, 1983 B75; T. Flandreau, 1983 B101; W. Glackin, 1983 B115; P. Hertelendy, Jan. 4, Jan. 7, 1983 B129,130; C. Kino, 1983 B164; D. Landis and L. Edelman, 1982 B174; A. Levine, 1983 B176; R. Pontzious, Jan. 6, Jan. 10, 1983 B237, 238; C. Shere, Jan. 7, Jan 9, 1983 B284,285; M. Tucker, 1982 B306.

73. she and Ben . . . [to] . . . Rapkine: Data, **The Music of Vivian Fine**, (Von Gunden, Heidi B316),pp45, 138, 177; (see Karp, Vivian and Benjamin B158).

74. Among her . . . [to] . . . audience members: Data, I had attended the *Tradition* world premiere at Berkeley, California and had also interviewed Fine that afternoon and evening for nearly four hours on that date. She had been very generous with her time that day. "My own language," and "feeling of longing," are quotes by Fine from her pre-concert lecture, attended by author.

75. By December . . . [to] . . . for Fine: Data, taped, by author, interview with Fine, 12-19-1989. "remake of Poe;" "something;" and "germinating stage," Fine quotes: *ibid.*

76. This would change . . . [to] . . . "her loved music:" author's quotes, from journal entry of telephone interview with Fine; also Fine's quotes, 7-17-1990. Vivian was too weak to continue the discussion.

77. Benjamin . . . [to] . . . "my health:" Interview with Fine in San Francisco, California at their temporary apartment, November 1990.

78. Taken from original program sent to author, by Fine in June 1990; noted by Fine, "*Portal* was written in January 1990."

79. Fine's letter to author 5-14-1990.

80. I was present for both the January, 1981 and October, 1990 performances of *Missa*, with the chance to compare it with either four or eight cellists; it had a most effective sound balance with eight cellos present.

81. Fine completed . . . [to] . . . classic guitar: data, interview with Fine at her home, 9-17-1988. We discussed her latest commission (for guitar); then Fine had been kind enough to listen to my taped classical guitar compositions. She was interested in certain atonal sounds, and she had asked me to demonstrate my guitar fingerings for my various unorthodox tones on the instrument. I did so. Cody, *Nocturne,* 1979, for classical guitar, Kikimora Publishing Company.

82. "would write this one:" Fine quote, taped, by author, interview with Fine, Petaluma, California, 12-19-1989.

83. Fine's letter to author, 7-8-1993.

84. work in 1993 . . . : Data, letter from Fine, March 1993. "studied the opera . . . :" Quote, phone call to Dallas Opera, August 2000.

85. *Uliana* . . . [to] . . . used: Data, taken from original *Uliana* program, printed "a multimedia chamber opera-premiere production," 9-9-1994, University of Richmond (see Friedman, Sonya B105).

86. "newsreel;" "motifs," and "what happened," quotes by Fine, from University of Richmond opera announcement 9-6-1994 (see Patterson, Catherine B229).

87. "good for the vellums;" "sound of piano;" and "inner hearing," Fine quotes, taped, by author, interview with Fine at her home, 9-21-1988.

88. "so strong . . . :" Fine quote, phone discussion with author, June, 1996.

89. For obituaries see: B10; B15; B173; B180; B246; B278; B294; and B317.

90. Letter sent to Catamount was returned to the author, stamped by the Post Office, "box closed-no forwarding address," July, 2000. Phone discussion with Peggy Karp confirmed this and also that her mother, Vivian Fine, had willed her works to the Library of Congress (see Appendix 1).

→ *Chapter 2* ←

BIBLIOGRAPHY

Notes on this annotated Bibliography:
"See" references refer to either background information and/or relevant facts for an understanding of the specific review (e.g., see Bramhall, Robyn). "Compare with" references ask the reader to compare particular selected points of view by the various reviewers (e.g., compare with Riegger, Wallingford).

Numbers such as "JC62" refer to an individual work, and the performance data as listed in the "Works and Performances," Chapter 3. A "JC" number listed with the annotated review means that the work was mentioned in the original review, whether or not the author chose to comment on it in the annotated review.

Numbers such as "D8" refer to an individual recorded work found in the "Discography," Chapter 5.

Numbers such as "P4" refer to individual piano performances by Fine as listed in the "Fine at the Piano," Chapter 4.

B1.   A., T. "Brilliant Talent Shown by Dancer." Montreal, Canada: *The Gazette*, March 12, 1935. See: P21, P24.

    Critic T. A. lauds Vivian Fine's performance as pianist (compare with V., M. and also Powell, S. Morgan) accompanying the dancer. She was on tour with Danish dancer Nini Theilade. Fine's renditions of Debussy's and Brahms pianoforte works, *El Puerto del Vino* and *G Minor Rhapsody* were judged "much superior."

B2.   Albahari, Steven W. "Fine's San Francisco Festivity." Bennington, Vermont: *Quadrille* **15**(3):4-5, February, 1983. See: JC1, JC101, JC102, JC104.

Steven W. Albahari's lengthy article is an informative discussion concerning Fine's music presented during Vivian Fine Week (see San Francisco Symphony November 24, 1982) as celebrated by the San Francisco Symphony in cooperation with Old First and Mostly Modern Concerts, January 5-13, 1983. Albahari called Fine Week a "landmark" since it was "the San Francisco Symphony's first major commission in its 72-year history to a woman composer." *Drama for Orchestra*'s World Premiere (see Carson, Josephine) was performed and commissioned by the San Francisco Symphony. Fine's *The Women in the Garden* is mentioned, also, two compositions she was working on at the time of the article: *Canticles of Jerusalem* (see Caldwell, Mary) and *Double Variations,* just completed, (see Newlin, Dika).

High praises for Fine's musical achievements by music critics, Robert Commanday of the *San Francisco Chronicle* and William Glacken of the *Sacramento Bee* are detailed here. Mr. Albahari quotes Fine about her inspirational source for *Drama for Orchestra,* the paintings by Norwegian expressionist, Edvard Munch. Some details of her discussion (during an interview with Albahari) on Munch's "The Scream:"

> ". . . 'I was interested in some sort of dramatic sequence of movements and thought of Munch's painting "The Scream" as a dramatic movement of intensity. The starting point for the work was "The Scream." I wanted to depict this extreme emotion or state and I didn't know just how I was going to incorporate that into a musical work, I still didn't know what form the work would take, but then at one moment, looking through the paintings, I was aware I would be able to make it work. A sequential work that would be dramatic in nature. . . .'"

Article included photographs of Fine overlaid on a sheet of her music on the cover of *Quadrille*: a picture of the lobby exhibit at Davies Symphony Hall; of her and Edo de Waart at a reception in her honor; of the Davies Symphony Hall in San Francisco; of the poster-mailer sent out by the Symphony for Vivian Fine Week; of her in the company of de Waart, John Adams, Deborah Borda, artistic administrator of SFS, and SFS President Michael K. Hooker at the post-concert reception.

B3.   Albany Records. "Five Premieres. Chamber Works with Guitar." Albany, New York: Albany Records U.S., 1992. See: JC136, D3.

Vivian Fine's *Canzones y Dances* is one of the premieres on this CD with Joel Brown, guitar, Ann Alton, cello, and Jan Vinci, flute. There are five "Songs and Dances" in this work which arise (according to Fine's notes on the CD) from:

> ". . . a variety of Spanish sources . . . origins in the
> Spanish Civil War [1930's] . . . a poem by Pablo
> Neruda . . . a tango . . . the memory of my [Fine's]
> colleague. . . ."

Fine concludes with the dance, "Jiga de la Muerte (Death's Jig)," that
she believed:

> ". . . reflects the direct confrontation with the power
> of death expressed in Spanish music."[see Cody,
> Judith. February, 2001]

B4.   *Algemeen Handelsblad*, anon. [Review of R. Guralnik's 1962 concert
tour]. Amsterdam, The Netherlands: *Algemeen Handelsblad*, Fall, 1962.
See: JC33.

Referring to "new" works composed by Americans, Koutzen and
Vivian Fine, the critic from the Netherlands comments on Fine's, *Five
Preludes* (compare with Rotterdamsch, Fall 1962),

> ". . . not of too much importance."[*trans.* anon.]

B5.   American Academy and Institute of Arts and Letters. "CITATION.
VIVIAN FINE." New York City, New York: May 23, 1979.

This was a citation awarded to Vivian Fine by the American Academy
and Institute of Arts and Letters. This was on the occasion of her
election, as a member, to the Academy.

The citation was given to honor Fine's substantial contribution to
American modern dance (see Ammer, Christine and White, Edward).
Fine's concert and orchestral music were also cited; one point
mentioned was her music's "sensitivity to the foibles of contemporary
society."

B6.   *American Record Guide*. [Review of recording of Fine's *Alcestis*].
March, 1962. See: JC59, D1.

Fine composed this music for Martha Graham's dance: Alcestis (see
Sabin, Robert).

> ". . . And in Fine's case the structures and lines are
> magnificently clean and very exciting."

B7.   Ammer, Christine. **Unsung — A History of Women in American
Music**. Westport, Connecticut: Greenwood Press, 1980. See: JC2, JC8,
JC16, JC17, JC24, JC30, JC31, JC55, JC58, JC59, JC70, JC75, JC77,
JC79, JC80, JC84, JC89, D1, D9, D13, P22.

Incorporates numerous details of "enormously prolific" Fine's music history and the particulars of many of her compositions. Also, mentioned are *Concerto for Piano Strings and Percussion* (1972), *Missa Brevis* and *Two Neruda Poems* (see Shere, Charles October 27, 1981), all having been part of a special program featuring Vivian Fine's music. Ammer included a quote from a *New York Times* review (see Henahan, Donal 1973) on this program. Fine is also quoted on her early student-teacher relationship with composer Ruth Crawford (see Gaume, Matilda and also Tick, Judith).

Ms. Ammer outlines Fine's early career as composer for the modern dance (see White, Edward) in collaboration with the great choreographers of this century:

> "In 1937 Fine wrote her first ballet score, *The Race of Life*, for Doris Humphrey. . . . There followed *Opus 51* (1938), for Charles Weidman. . . . Then two ballets for Hanya Holm, *Tragic Exodus* (1939) . . . [and] *They Too Are Exiles* (1939). . . . Humphrey wrote about Fine: 'She has an uncanny sense of what to choose as sound and that *sine qua non* for dance composers, a complete understanding of body rhythm and dramatic timing. . . . *Alcestis* (1960), commissioned for Martha Graham. . . . *My Son, My Enemy* (1965) . . . for Jose Limon. . . . Fine had written at least one work for each of the leading dance companies in America over a period of two decades" [see American Academy and Institute of Arts and Letters].

B8.   Anderson, E. Ruth. Fine, Vivian. **Contemporary American Composers. A Biographical Dictionary**. Boston, Massachusetts: G.K. Hall & Co., 1976, p. 136-137 and 1982. See: JC8, JC24, JC25, JC32, JC42, JC45, JC51, JC53, JC55, JC57, JC58, JC65, JC68, JC73, JC75, JC77, JC79, JC80.

Anderson's dictionary entry for Fine contains approximately 250 words sketching many of this composer's achievements in the world of music. Latest performance noted is *Fantasy* on May 22, 1979 in New York. It is herein noted that Fine has "other works in all genres."

B9.   Anderson, Jack. **The American Dance Festival.** Durham, North Carolina: Duke University Press, 1987, 324pg.

B10.   Anderson, Martin. "Obituary: Vivian Fine." London, England: *The Independent*, Newspaper Publishing PLC, Obituaries, April 4, 2000, pg.6.

In the opening paragraph of Anderson's thoughtful obituary for Fine, he writes:

> ". . . In spite of the widespread respect she enjoyed, as composer and as performer, her music is poorly represented in the catalogues even on her own side of the Atlantic and deserves better. . . ." [see Works and Performances, also compare with Morton, Brian].

Anderson chronicles Fine's early rise and her teenage musical triumphs that caught the eye of Aaron Copland (see Copland, Aaron, also Randel, Don Michael) and Henry Cowell among other distinguished names.

Later Anderson writes of Fine's music:

> ". . . fine balance between dry dispassion and a sense of lurking power . . . her sound world slightly forbidding . . . an understated sense of humour. . . ." [compare with Gann, Kyle, also Greene, David Mason]

Photograph captioned, "Fine: lurking power."

B11. Ariel. "On Music: Vivian Fine." San Francisco, California: *THE VOICE* 5(3), January 28, 1983. <u>See</u>: Jcii, JC8, JC50, JC83, JC97, JC101.

THE VOICE profiles Vivian Fine's sensibilities as a contemporary composer; noting her first scored work, *Lullaby*, which was written with the encouragement and inspiration given to the teenage Fine, by her teacher, Ruth Crawford. The almost fourteen-hundred word article offers material on the composer's early music education. Ariel directed commentary especially through the compositions performed during the full week devoted to celebrating Fine's music. This was Vivian Fine Week (see San Francisco Symphony November 29, 1982), and a unique tribute from the San Francisco Symphony. Ariel discusses the development of *Drama for Orchestra* (see Carson, Josephine). According to Ariel, Fine's early studies with Roger Sessions explain his compositional impact on her creative style as a composer (compare Riegger, Wallingford):

> "One of the great teachers of modern harmony, Sessions filled out Fine's theoretical background."

On the structures within *Teisho* Ariel explained:

> "*Teisho* from 1977 is like the *Drama* in carrying with it extra musical ideas. In this Violin-Piano piece, Fine imagined the music as the sermons of a Zen Master. Like the orchestral piece, this literary scheme has technically little to do with music, except that the psychological state imagined in *Teisho* has a lean,

epigrammatic mysticism to it. What was musically exciting in these sermons was the way harmonic structures that are smaller than the full 12 tones, but much larger than anything Mozart would have recognized emerged from open-ended dialogue. Here was post-modernism at its finest."

B12. Armer, Elinor. "A Conversation with Vivian Fine: Two Composers Talk Shop." *Strings*, Volume V, Number 5, March/April, 1991, pg.73. <u>See</u>: JC101.

This five page interview by Ms. Armer generally queries Ms. Fine on her professional use of "strings" in her compositions over the years. As for *Missa Brevis,* Fine states here that it "work[s] very well" with eight cellos, ". . . even sixteen . . ." Armer questions Fine:
"Your Missa Brevis [1972, JC79] is another example of strings with voice."
  Fine responds:
". . . an interesting combination — four cellos and taped voice. . . . I loved the sound of four cellos, and the idea occurred to me of writing this Mass. . . .
Four different vocal tracks were made initially, then freely combined; I compose *with* the tracks, so to speak. That worked very well, one voice singing four tracks with the complementary cello parts."

B13. Armitage, Holly. "Bennington Workshops: Something for Everyone." Bennington, Vermont: *Bennington Banner*, July 8, 1978.

Outline of the Bennington College four-week summer workshops in arts, poetry, music and drama. Fine was a teacher at Bennington College.
Article includes a photograph of Vivian Fine instructing students around a piano, marking a pupil's score on the piano.

B14. Armstrong, Israel C. "Nini Theilade Arouses Genuine Enthusiasm of Big Ottawa Audience." Ottawa, Canada: *The Citizen*, February 20, 1934. <u>See</u>: P24.

"Clever young accompanist" to Danish dancer, Nini Theilade, Vivian Fine at age twenty-four, also was the piano soloist at a sold out concert in Glebe Collegiate Auditorium. It was noted that Fine performed "very acceptably".

B15.   *Associated Press, The.* "Vivian Fine, 86; Musical Composer, Teacher."
Bergen County, New Jersey: *The Record*, Bergen Record Corp. Source:
Wire services, Saturday, March 25, 2000; All Editions, News, pg. A15.
See: JC18, JC31, JC58, JC70, JC84, JC89.

> Two hundred and seventy words describe Fine, her long career in
> musical arts, and her death on a Monday in Bennington, Vermont. Her
> works are said to have
>> ". . . expressive dissonance . . . rhythmic edges. . . ."

B16.   B., A.E. "Cortes, Vivian Fine Music Heard at Donnell Center." New
York City, New York: *New York Herald-Tribune*, February 8, 1959.
See: JC55, JC56.

> Critic's comments on *A String Quartet* were that it was
>> ". . . technically proficient . . . strong and warm."
>
> Observing *A Guide to the Life Expectancy of a Rose* the critic was less
> enthusiastic (compare with Riegger, Wallingford), saying that it was
>> ". . . marred by overstraining in search of humor; a
>> single amusing idea was made to support . . . [the]
>> entire work . . . thus stretched beyond the breaking
>> point."

B17.   B., A.V. [Berger, Arthur V.] "Music." New York City, New York: *New
York Daily Mirror*, January 28, 1932. See: P6

> Summarized review describing one of the very early activities that
> began what we know today as contemporary music. The reviewer wrote
> that Henry Cowell was the leader of a symposium to discuss the newly
> developing "American polyphonic music" at the New School of Social
> Research (see Engel, A. Lehman 1933) in New York City. Others who
> would help in the program included important composer figures of that
> era: Ruth Crawford (Seeger) (see Gaume, Matilda, also Tick, Judith),
> Carl Ruggles and Wallingford Riegger (see Riegger, Wallingford 1958).
> Henry Brant (see Bramhall, Robyn April 29, 1988) and Vivian Fine
> performed and were noted as being as "composers in the making."
> The reviewer was impressed with the gathering together of such
> eminent music leaders and he believed that the audience should have
> been larger. Berger called these audience members:
>> ". . . partisans of the ultra-modern faith. . . ."

B18.   B., A.V. [Berger, Arthur V.] "Pan-American Association." New York
City, New York: *New York Daily Mirror*, February 17, 1932. See: P15.

Vivian Fine performed along with Adolph Weiss, John J. Becker, the New World String Quartet, Georgia Kober, Radiana Pazmor, and the Pan-American Association of Composers' chamber orchestra. The event was at the New School. Henry Cowell was the director of the Pan-American Association at that time and he
> ". . . presented a concert of Mexican, Argentine, and native works. . . ."

B19.   B., A.V. [Berger, Arthur V.] "Saminsky on Jewish Music and Musicians." Boston, Massachusetts: *Boston Evening Transcript*, mid-1930's.

Critique of *Music of the Ghetto and the Bible* written by Lazare Saminsky and published by Bloch Publishing. Vivian Fine along with other outstanding young composers of the era are referred to by the author:
> "Again, while it is gratifying to observe the names of such younger talents as Vivian Fine, Henry Brant and Jerome Moross mentioned in the present volume, the assertion that they group themselves about Henry Cowell is without basis."

B20.   Bachelder, Marilyn. **Women in Music Composition: Ruth Crawford-Seeger, Peggy Glanville-Hicks, and Vivian Fine**. Ypsilanti, Michigan: Master's Thesis, Eastern Michigan University, EMU Library, 1973.

B21.   Barnes, Clive. "Dance: Graham Triple Bill in Brooklyn." New York City, New York: *The New York Times*, November 3, 1968. See: JC58, D1.

Clive Barnes offered harsh criticism for Martha Graham's dance *Alcestis*, the music was composed by Vivian Fine, (compare with *American Record Guide*, 1962; also see Sabin, Robert) labeling it a
> ". . . minor work . . . lacking . . . definition and conflict . . . fatally flawed by dull music. . . ."

B22.   Baxter, Robert. "In Review, From Around the World: Philadelphia." *Opera News* 61(17):58, 1997. See: JC138.

Baxter reviews Fine's *The Memoirs of Uliana Rooney*, making a strong statement for Fine's "sixty-five-minute chamber opera . . . [following] Uliana from her childhood . . . to age eighty-five. . . ." One must notice that this age sequence parallels Fine's own age and occupation throughout the 20th century; Uliana is also a "composer" in Fine's own description of her opera (see and compare Jones, Leslie 1997). Baxter judges the opera, *Uliana Rooney*, as a combination that is:

> ". . . satirical and touching, [unfolding] in a series of fragmented scenes . . . film sequences . . . [a] feminist message with a naive charm that disarms criticism . . . jaunty score . . . boldly drawn sketch. . . ."

This Philadelphia premiere production (see Webster, Daniel 1997) is pronounced as "well-prepared:" Baxter adds positive comment on the lead singers. This final opera of Vivian Fine's life was performed at Annenberg Center on February 28, 1997 as part of the Relache Ensemble's "salute" commemorating the National Women's Month. American Opera Projects "collaborated" with Relache for this premiere night in Philadelphia.

B23. Belt, Byron. "Oratorio's Bicentennial Salute Witty and Noble." Long Island, New York: *Long Island Press*, May 21, 1976. <u>See</u>: JC84.

Meeting for Equal Rights 1866 premiered at an Alice Tully Hall concert by the Oratorio Society of New York. Byron Belt, wrote both affirmatively and eloquently on this work by Fine; he found Fine's *Meeting* both "impressive" and "moving" (see and compare with A. Der and also Fuller, Sophie). Furthermore, Mr. Belt added that *Meeting* was

> ". . . a stirring . . . timely piece devoted to the unhappily still struggling cause of Equal Rights. Taking a feminist viewpoint . . . full of righteous rage — which is understandable — and compassion — which is more important. . . . [Vivian Fine's *Meeting*] provides the first current significant artistic statement for women's rights other than literature."

B24. *Bennington Banner* (anon.). "String Quartet Concert Thursday." Bennington, Vermont: *Bennington Banner*, Wednesday, May 17, 1967.

Announcement for a concert at the Carriage Barn at Bennington College.

> "Miss Vivian Fine, pianist, will assist the Bennington String Quartet. . . . [She is] also a well-known composer. . . ."

This article includes a photograph of Vivian Fine.

B25. *Bennington Banner* (anon.). "The Mayfest 'Requiem'." Bennington, Vermont: *Bennington Banner*, May 25, 1970. <u>See</u>: JC29, JC40, JC76.

Reviewed as a "multi-media evening on the subject of war." Fine organized several performances, *The Delta*, with a poem, about the horrors of war, by Poet Michael Dennis Brown. She also arranged two other presentations with music:

> ". . .'*Stabat Mater*,' [from *Songs of Our Time*] song
> of a mother's sorrow sung by Catherine Sterlee and
> Nina Karp [Fine's daughter], with Sarah Tenney on
> percussion . . . cellist George Finckel and Nina Karp,
> playing a bell, presented *Adios, Bilbadito*."

B26.   *Bennington Banner* (anon.). "'Women in the Arts' Program at Bennington College, Saturday." Bennington, Vermont: *Bennington Banner*, November 16, 1973. See: P52.

This brief piece mentions that Vivian Fine was the piano accompanist to mezzo-soprano Betty Allen in a concert featuring songs of Schubert, Wolf, Ravel and Mendelssohn. Fine also moderated a discussion profiling Ms. Allen's

> "work, her music and her life as a Black woman in
> the world of music. . . ."

B27.   Berger, Arthur. [No Title]. New York City, New York: *New York Mirror*, April, 1932. See: JC7. See: P9.

Dance Center performance with compositions by Vivian Fine. Other performers were, A. Lehman Engel, Henry Brant, Gluck-Sandor, dancer, and sopranos Radiana Pazmor and Ruby Mercer.

> ". . . Miss Fine's *Polyphonic Pieces* [see Engel, A.
> Lehman   October   1932]   were   perhaps   most
> successful."

B28.   Berger, Arthur. "Yaddo Music Festival." New York City, New York: *New York Daily News*, May 2, 1932. See: JC7.

Arthur Berger calls Fine's *Polyphonic Pieces* "unique discoveries. . . ." (see and compare with Engel, A. Lehman October 1932).

B29.   Berger, Arthur V. "Ditson Concert: Chamber Group is Heard at McMillin Theater." New York City, New York: *The New York Times*, May, 1948. See: JC45.

Berger critiqued a Ditson Chamber Concert where Vivian Fine's *Great Wall of China* (her musical viewpoint on a section from the Kafka story) was performed along with some Satie, George Perle and Stephen

Wolpe. Berger said that Fine's new work
> ". . . marks a return, after an interlude of conservative
> Romanticism, to her earlier, more abstract style, but
> with less profile than she had as a kind of child
> prodigy among composers. . . ."

B30.   Berlin [newspaper unknown]. "Hermann Trio Review." August 12,
1953. See: JC3.

> "The youngest and most arbitrary [original?] work —
> great freedom of harmony and rhythm, the
> instruments were very harshly put one against the
> other." [*trans.* anon.]

B31.   Berliner, Milton. "Melodic Percussion." Washington, DC: *The
Washington Daily News*, January 9, 1964. See: JC48.

> "More impressive was Vivian Fine's brief but bright
> *Divertimento for Cello and Percussion. . . ."* [see
> Borg, Alan].

B32.   Block, Adrienne Fried and Carol Neuls-Bates. **Women in American
Music, A Bibliography of Music and Literature**. Westport,
Connecticut: Greenwood Press, Inc., 1979, 302 pages. See: JC16, JC24,
JC58, D1.

Block and Neuls-Bates have compiled an important source book and
research guide to women's music. Not only are composers and their
works listed, there are also comprehensive guides to: "Reference Materials, Collected Works, Historical Studies, Literature about Women as
Patrons and Educators in Art Music . . . Performers of Art Music" and
more. Vivian Fine is referenced under a number of headings such as:
> "Literature about women as composers of art music [p. 152]
> Vivian Fine and Lucia Dlugoszewski [co-author and
> choreographer] discuss [*Dance Perspectives* **16**:8-11,
> 21-25, 1963] the relationship of their music to dance
> in this symposium of composers and choreographers.
> The following works by Fine are considered: *"The
> race of life"* [sic] (WIAM 4412), which was written
> for Doris Humphrey; *"Opus 51,"* written for Charles
> Weidman; and *"Alcestis,"* written for Martha Graham.
> Biographical sketches of the 2 composers and
> chronological lists of their dance scores are included."

There is a discography listing Fine. Also, the book is illustrated with
seven pages of excellent and hard to locate black and white photographs
of early women in music.

B33.   Boenke, Heidi M. (Compiler). **Flute Music by Women Composers:
        An Annotated Catalog**. Westport, Connecticut: Greenwood Press,
        1988, p. 38-39. See: JC2, JC45, JC60, JC61, JC65, JC66, JC82, JC99.

        In this extensive catalog, Ms. Boenke observes that Fine is "prolific"
        and records ten of her works where the flute is utilized. Boenke finds
        Duo for Flute and Viola (1961) "Difficult" and to have "rhythmic
        interest, shifting pulse."
            Noted on Fine's composition, *The Great Wall of China* (1948), is that
        she used "standard notation and technique" in this four movement work
        for flute, mezzo-soprano, cello and piano; Boenke adds that it ranges
        from "easy to moderate" for the flutist.

B34.   Borg, Alan. "Modern Chamber Music Concert Reviewed." New Paltz,
        New York: *The Oracle*, State University Teachers College, November
        21, 1958. See: JC48, P44.

        The Humanities Division, in cooperation with the American
        Composers Alliance presented a concert.
                "In the selection *Variations for Four Drums and
                Viola* [*Divertimento* (1951) written originally for cello
                and percussion] we noted that the drums were tuned
                differently for each variation."

B35.   Boston, City of. "Proclamation." Boston, Massachusetts: April 16-22,
        1989.

        The following official "proclamation" was presented to Vivian Fine
        to announce Boston's Vivian Fine Appreciation Week (see Caldwell,
        Mary).
                "PROCLAMATION
                WHEREAS: Vivian Fine has contributed in an
                outstanding manner to creative thought and music in
                this century as a composer, pianist and teacher and is
                considered by many to be the Dean of Female
                Composers in America today; and
                WHEREAS: Vivian Fine has distinguished herself as
                the recipient of a Guggenheim Fellowship and having
                awards from the National Endowment for the Arts
                and the Ford Foundation as well as teaching music for

over twenty years at Bennington College in Vermont;
and
WHEREAS: Vivian Fine will lecture and have music
played during Boston's Share A Composer Program
which will feature music by Boston Musica Viva,
Boston University, Tufts, Harvard, Northeastern,
University of Massachusetts, the Boston Conservatory
and the Longy School; NOW
THEREFORE, I, RAYMOND L. FLYNN, Mayor of
the City of Boston, do hereby join with the entire
Boston community in proclaiming April 16-22, 1989
as
VIVIAN FINE APPRECIATION WEEK
in the City of Boston and I urge all my fellow
Bostonians to join me in recognizing this truly
outstanding individual and her contribution in adding
to the quality of life in our city.
[Signed by the mayor]."

B36.   Bramhall, Robyn. *"After the Tradition* (1987). Vivian Fine (b. 1913)."
Berkeley, California: Program Notes of Bay Area Women's
Philharmonic, April 29, 1988. <u>See</u>: JC123.

"Chicago and New York of the 1920's and '30's
reigned as the major American centers for 'serious'
music, and Vivian Fine spent several important years
of her musical training in each city. The American
Conservatory, in her native Chicago, was her musical
home from age twelve, and offered valuable
inspiration and instruction from the likes of Ruth
Crawford, who was gaining a reputation as a daring
and talented new composer. Fine may never have
thought to compose without that first assignment from
Crawford, and most of Fine's early compositions
showed Crawford's influence in their prevailing
dissonance.
In 1931, Fine journeyed to New York, where her
piano studies were continued in conjunction with
composition lessons with Roger Sessions. As she married and reared two daughters, Fine continued to perform and compose, adding university teaching to her
schedule in 1945 (New York University, the Juilliard
School and Bennington College). Commissions from
America's major dance companies allowed Fine to

create much successful ballet music, most of which leans more toward the tonal. Other commissions, from the San Francisco Symphony and others, along with a Guggenheim fellowship and grants from the National Endowment for the Arts, the Ford Foundation and the Martha Baird Rockefeller Foundation resulted in a vast variety of intriguing works.

Many of Fine's compositions are based on her personal experiences, convictions and associations, which may account for the noted uniqueness of each of her works. As composer Henry Brant wrote, 'No two Fine pieces are alike either in subject matter or instrumentation; each new work appears to generate its own style appropriate to the subjects, and there are no mannerisms which persist from work to work.' Thus, without quoting a single Jewish melody or consciously utilizing the traditional Middle-Eastern modalities, Fine communicates her connection with her Jewish roots in tonight's world premiere, *After the Tradition*.

The work takes its name from the title of a book by Robert Alter, with each of its three movements drawing inspiration from Hebrew writings. 'Kaddish' is the traditional prayer for the dead, and this musical version is a memorial to Fine's friend, the late George Finckel, cellist and teacher. 'My heart's in the East and I at the end of the West' is from a poem by the Hebrew poet Judah Halevi, who lived in Spain in the 12th century. The music here is in the vocal style, its wandering melodies evoking a definite sense of poetry. 'Hark! Jaweh causes the wilderness to dance' is a line from the 29th Psalm, and the increased activity and expanding instrumentation help to express the joyfulness of the 'tradition.' Fine explores this tradition musically for the first time with this piece, which was commissioned by BAWP for tonight's concert."

B37.   Brandt, Maarten. "Huntingdon Trio: Perfect Ensemble." Arnhem, The Netherlands: Arnhem's newspaper, September 5, 1983. <u>See</u>: JC99.

The critic from the Netherlands comments (in Dutch) on the works of American composers, David Loeb, *Four Nocturnes*, and Vivian Fine, *Music for Flute, Oboe and Cello*. Much praise for the Huntingdon Trio, however, Brandt is harshly negative about the American compositions:
"... the two pieces do not represent much, there being a questionable mishmash with most stylistic components but no articulated idiom, yet there is nothing comparable that can be discerned."[*trans.* JC]

B38.   Brookes, Tim. "The Maverick Impulse and the Gifted Child." Windsor, Vermont: *Vermont Public Radio Program Guide* VIII, March, 1986. <u>See</u>: JC8.

Long, informative article that questions the beginnings of intellectual and musical genius in the case of the young Vivian Fine. Her parents' complete acceptance of the child, "Vivian's abstract curiosity" as a form of talented passion rather than disobedience is cited as one cause for her positive development. Brookes comments:
"Within the last five years Fine, who teaches at Bennington College and lives a hundred feet across the border into New York state, has become generally recognized as one of America's leading composers. Described by Gunther Schuller as 'in this grand old American maverick tradition of . . . Ives, Harry Partch and John Cage,' she has won awards from the Guggenheim and Rockefeller foundations, has received commissions from the San Francisco Symphony and the Library of Congress, and has been elected to the American Academy and Institute of Arts and Letters."

B39.   Brookes, Tim. "Conversations with Vivian Fine. A Maverick Tradition." Bennington, Vermont: *Quadrille* 18(3), Spring, 1986. <u>See</u>: JC8, JC56, JC58, JC79, JC90, D1, D9, D11.

Tim Brookes' interview material reveals Fine's thoughts about the women who supported and influenced her career in the world of music. She said that her mother, an aunt and teacher-mentor, Ruth Crawford Seeger (see Gaume, Matilda) were these encouraging and motivational women. Her aunt owned the first piano that the three-year-old baby Vivian had ever even heard. She was enchanted by this piano. Throughout her early years, Vivian's mother was "supporting" her musical endeavors. A photo of Fine at her piano in her New England home is with the article.

"International Music [Women's] Day was celebrated
March 8th with the premiere broadcast of a special
one-hour program about VIVIAN FINE. Produced as
a pilot for the International League of Women
Composers, it included . . . some of Fine's most distinguished works — the ballet *Alcestis, Missa Brevis,
Momenti* for piano, and two never-before broadcast
works, her 1932 *Four Songs* and 1957 *String Quartet.*
Public radio stations nationwide will have the
program available for rebroadcast on September 28th,
Vivian Fine's 73rd birthday."

B40.   *Burlington Free Press* (anon.). "Bennington Composer to Premier Work
at Trinity Library." Burlington, Vermont: *The Burlington Free Press,*
October 24, 1985. <u>See</u>: JC89, JC101, JC108.

An announcement of the dedication of the $1.2 million library at
Trinity College. Vivian Fine's choral and instrumental composition, *A
Song for St. Cecilia's Day* was commissioned for the function.
According to the article, The Vermont Symphony Orchestra string and
trumpet ensemble was conducted by Fine, while singers from the
Bennington Chorus, the University of Vermont Concert Choir, Trinity
Choir and over one hundred musicians participated in the performance.
Fine's *The Women in the Garden* and her *Drama for Orchestra* were
mentioned. A reception followed the concert.

". . . Based on a poem by Dryden which celebrates
learning, *A Song for St. Cecilia's Day* was
commissioned in conjunction with the 60th
anniversary of the founding of Trinity by the Sisters
of Mercy. It has been supported in part by a grant
from the Vermont Council on the Arts. . . ."

B41.   Burrell, Margo. Cambridge, New York: *Program Notes* for *The Women
in the Garden* performance by L'Ensemble Chamber Music Center,
August 29-30, 1981. <u>See</u>: JC89.

Margo Burrell's review is a perceptive discussion of the four women
listed in the cast of Fine's opera *The Women in the Garden* (see Fine,
Vivian and Judith Jamieson and compare with S., C. also Commanday,
Robert, March 1982 and April 1982), Emily Dickinson, Gertrude Stein,
Virginia Woolf and Isadora Duncan. Fine received a Grant from the
National Endowment for the Arts to compose this opera.

"Throughout *The Women in the Garden* her [Fine's]
own voice joins the four listed in the cast. Did a

common denominator shape these four uncommon
women? We found her in search of an answer. All, it
is true, were born in a century when, to quote Anne
Bell, 'a lady was, in a refined way, a domestic
animal.' All were nonconformists, rebels, innovators,
each struggling in her own — often lonely — way to
make the world safe for eccentricity."

B42. Bustard, Clarke. "'Memoirs' of Music on the Plains. Chamber Opera
at UR was Inspired by Obituary." Richmond, Virginia: *Richmond
Times-Dispatch*, Sunday, September 4, 1994. <u>See</u>: JC138.

Bustard's piece clarifies the interesting conception of Fine's final
chamber opera, *Memoirs of Uliana Rooney*. Fine discovered the major
character's, Uliana's, beginnings in an obituary in the *New York Times*.
The deceased, "who had been one of the weirder personalities of gilded-
age Hollywood . . ." also married ten times, gave the composer a notion
for her next opera.
The character was gender reassigned, and in a partnership with
librettist, Sonya Friedman (see Friedman, Sonya), became an entirely
fictional opera heroine, Uliana. Fine described it as "'a humorous,
satirical piece. . . .'"
Fine is quoted as stating that the opera is "'a semi-autobiographical
memoir of my composing from the earliest times to the present.'"
Bustard further sets *Memoirs* world premiere at the University of
Richmond, where Dr. Fred Cohen directed "Currents" in the Camp
Theatre on September 9, 1994. This was the "first [performance] . . .
fully staged with full instrumentation."

B43. Caldwell, Mary (Ed.). "Learning from Performers. Vivian Fine Week
Honors Eclectic Composer." Cambridge, Massachusetts: *The Arts
Spectrum* **25**(16):1, Office for the Arts at Harvard and Radcliffe,
Harvard University, April 14, 1989. <u>See</u>: JC2, JC89, JC104, JC111,
JC113, JC116, JC118, JC128.

In this profile of Vivian Fine, Mary Caldwell reported on the special
"tribute," Vivian Fine Appreciation Week in the Boston area (see
Boston, City of), that had been sponsored by Northeastern University,
Tufts University, Boston University, University of Massachusetts
(Boston), Boston Conservatory of Music and Harvard University. The
Boston area Fine Week was held April 16-22, 1989. Of interest, is that
in 1982 there had been a similar, but unrelated, tribute to Fine in San
Francisco (see San Francisco Symphony November 29, 1982).

Caldwell wrote that Radcliffe and Harvard presented a discussion program where Fine discussed what she had "learned" through the "performers" she had worked with over her extensive composing career. This was on April 20 as part of Fine Week.

Ms. Caldwell commented on two Harvard concerts featuring new works by Vivian Fine. On April 16 there was a "contemporary and traditional" Jewish music concert, "*After the Tradition* (see Bramhall, Robyn)," sponsored by *Mosaic* magazine featured the world premiere of Fine's *Canticles for Jerusalem*. Fine's inspiration for *Canticles* was drawn from Psalm 137 with words from Hebrew poets Yehuda Amichai (living), and Judah Halevi (medieval). The reporter also mentioned that the Harvard Wind Ensemble featured new works by Fine on April 22 (see *Four Pieces for Two Flutes* and *The Triple-Goddess*).

Fine's long and illustrious career as composer for the modern dance (see Ammer, Christine and also White, Edward) is remarked upon by Caldwell. Also commented on are the then recent works by Fine; *Inscriptions* (1986), *Sonata for Violoncello and Piano* (1986), *Ma's in Orbit* (1987) and *The Human Mind* (1987). Caldwell explained that Ms. Fine, as a creator of music, was always

> ". . . open to different styles and experimentation in musical composition . . . always focused on her own musical conceptions. Her music tends to be atonal. . . . [Fine's] concern has been to find ways to express extreme emotion in her music with her own idiom and style."

B44.   Capparela, Richard. "10 Women Composers Focus for Concert." Albany, New York: *KITE*, March 9, 1977. See: JC23, JC85

A concert in the well-known "Composer's Forum" series; this concert highlighted the compositions of ten women in a "Program of Music by Women." Fine's offerings, *Elizabethan Love and Bird Songs* and *Nightingale* (compare with Pontzious, Richard January 10, 1983) were created with a commission from the "Composer's Forum."

> "Tour de Force
> *Nightingale* is an avian tour de force. . . . Woodblock, triangle, suspended cymbal and voice created a nostalgic, almost mystical mood which left me wishing that the work were longer."

B45.   Carnegie-Mellon University. "Program Notes for *Women in the Garden* performances." Pittsburgh, Pennsylvania: Carnegie-Mellon University, College of Fine Arts, February 22, 1979. See: JC89

These are program notes on Fine's *The Women in the Garden* (see Fine, Vivian and Judith Jamieson) performed at the University.

B46.   Carson, Josephine. "Vivian Fine: *Drama for Orchestra* (After Paintings of Edvard Munch)." San Francisco, California: *Program notes of San Francisco Symphony*, January 5-8, 1983. See: JC1, JC2, JC7, JC16, JC24, JC42, JC58, JC59, JC75, JC79, JC84, JC89, JC90, JC91, JC101, JC102, JC104, D1, D4, D9, D11, D13, D14.

Dr. and Mrs. Ralph I. Dorfman commissioned Vivian Fine's *Drama for Orchestra* to be premiered by the San Francisco Symphony. This was to be the masterwork in the SFS's homage to composer Fine, in their event called "Vivian Fine Week" (see San Francisco Symphony November 29, 1982).

Josephine Carson's comprehensive program notes (close to three thousand words) are an outline and description of interest to readers and scholars concerned with the construction of *Drama for Orchestra*. Carson clarifies that the composer was less concerned with visual imagery of the paintings than with Munch's "impetus" prior to painting. For composer Fine, this impetus became a "series of powerful psychological states" to be realized in the creation of *Drama for Orchestra*. Her method of composition is here explained as "'layering.'"

Carson paraphrases Fine and explained that "'layering'" is how Fine employs "linear ideas that are written separately" are eventually combined to "realize her expressive purposes." Fine began this style of composing during her work with tape manipulation in the electronic music studio, according to Carson (see and compare Pontzious, Richard January 6, 1983, also Armer, Elinor). This seemed a more unfettered approach to Fine's art.

Fine's interesting narrative (see Albahari, Steven W.) on *Drama for Orchestra* is included and it delineates five elements beginning with Midsummer Night; the central figure being "A woman in the fullness of life." With The Embrace, the "lovers rush" together; there are "surging movements of ardent love." Jealousy is musically stated through a "violent agony of obsession." Perhaps, the most recognized visual element is Munch's The Scream; here seen as "when the world is experienced as fragmented horror." The work concludes with Two Figures by the Shore culminating in the composer's "assertion of the power and joy of Life." Some details of Fine's insights:
[Midsummer Night:]

> "'. . . A woman in the fullness of life . . . exper-
> iencing the magic of the summer's night. Over the
> strings . . . appears a melody for oboe . . . english
> horn repeats the oboe theme; sudden, sharp, muted.

. . . Brass instruments are a third element; harp . . .
lower strings enter . . . bird-like trills in the wind instruments. . . .

[The Embrace:]

. . . warm, lyrical impulse flowing through . . . wide-
ranging melodic line . . . by strings reinforced by
winds. . . . Over the bass and cello . . . a motif in
third added by wind instrument . . . the movement
ending quietly with a solo violin accompanied by
vibraphone, harp, pizzicato cellos . . . double basses.

[Jealousy:]

. . . orchestra . . . seems to be undergoing . . . violent
agony of obsession. The basic motif is a twisting five-
note figure . . . piano and xylophone double the
speed. . . . Throughout . . . increases and decreases
in sound contribute to . . . agonized pulsation. . . .

[The Scream:]

. . . expression of the ultimate existential agony . . .
drawn-out sounds of the scream are interspersed by
dissociated memories . . . a wail (trumpets). . . . A
section for percussion and piano in which the fabric
of . . . sound disintegrates. . . . convulsive chords.

[Two Figures by the Shore:]

. . . oceanic rocking rhythm . . . motifs from previous
movements. The effect . . . as if a kaleidoscope were
used to combine the same elements in new
ways. . . .'"

Carson also includes long quotes by both composers Henry Brant and
Henry Cowell, Fine's early mentor.

Brant describes Vivian Fine's work as he views it. One image he uses
is "highly compressed music-drama, or . . . abstracted ritual in concentrated musical terms."

Cowell wrote of his early meeting with her when she was just fifteen-
years-old. He had great respect for her amazing natural gifts. He was
also quite aware of Vivian's inner motivational strengths and indicated
that she would only be satisfied with doing her "very best" [see and
compare with Cowell, Henry].

B47.   Chamber Music, 6(3):52, 1989. See: JC130.

Vivian Fine's *Madrigali Spirituali* for string quartet and trumpet was
premiered on August 29 at the Music From Angel Fire Festival in New
Mexico, USA.

B48.   Chapin, Louis. [Review]. New York City, New York: *The Christian Science Monitor*, January 2, 1963. See: JC33

Mr. Chapin comments on Fine's *Five Preludes* as being "comparably pleasing" and says that they "lean" to "pianistic brilliance." He elaborates on Mr. Guralnik's ability as a pianist most positively.

B49.   Chon, Richard. "Hallwalls Presents Some Fine Music, Indeed." Buffalo, New York: *The Buffalo News*, April 27, 1987. See: JC7, JC17, JC23, JC112, JC116

Mr. Chon reviewed a retrospective of the works of Vivian Fine as part of the North American New Music Festival at Hallwalls Vault. His viewpoint on Fine as a person and composer is both parts intelligent probing and positive reaction. He commented on the beginnings of her amazingly vital and long career in the 1930's; began at a time when few composers chose the Ultra-Modern idiom and there was little, if any, financial aid to students of such arcane music. Nevertheless, Vivian Fine "survived" all this and more, managing to succeed. Chon makes some unusual, exceptionally interesting observations on Fine's music.
Fine's compositions performed at the retrospective, with comments by Mr. Chon were, *Four Polyphonic Piano Pieces* (see and compare with Engel, A. Lehman October 1932, and also Berger, Arthur April 1932): ". . . stern, declamatory statements . . . recalls Bach's dense voice-leading . . . ;" *Four Elizabethan Songs*: ". . . alternately somber . . . frolicking moods . . . spare, economical . . . ;" *Toccatas and Arias* (1986)(see Coon, Judith A.), for harpsichord: ". . . recall[s] the player piano music of Conlon Nancarrow with rich, plangent major chords. . . . ;" and lastly, *Ma's In Orbit*, which is "episodes" of *The Race of Life* (see and compare with Robin, Harry; also Humphrey, Doris). The reviewer said that *Ma's:* ". . . fast-paced series of programmatic episodes . . . blithe, syncopated sarcasms . . . capture that 1930's spirit found in those recordings Count Basie made. . . ."

B50.   Church, Francis. "Young Pianist Tackles a Taxing Program." Richmond, Virginia: *The Richmond News Leader*, November 27, 1984. See: JC33

Review of performance by pianist Kit Young which included the *Five Preludes* by Vivian Fine. Church mentions they are "easily accessible" and that the last movement, "featuring runs in the upper register, is a virtuoso piece."
As a point of interest, Ruth Crawford Seeger's *Kaleidoscopic Changes on an Original Theme, Ending with A Fugue* was also chosen for this program.

B51.   Claghorn, George. **Women Composers and Songwriters. A Concise Biographical Dictionary**. Lanham, Maryland: The Scarecrow Press, Inc., 1996, p.68. See: JC16, JC24, JC45, JC55.

Six of Fine's compositions are cataloged in Claghorn's dictionary. Drama for Orchestra, 1982 is noted.

B52.   Cody, Judith (Editor). **Resource Guide on Women in Music**. San Francisco, California: Bay Area Congress on Women in Music, San Francisco State University, or Kikimora Publishing Co., Los Altos, CA, 1981, 48 pp. See: JC58, JC42, JC75, JC51, D1, D4, D13,D16.

This **Resource Guide** was issued during the Bay Area Congress on Women in Music, in January, 1981. It has lists of various music groups, libraries, films, musicians, composers, and related women in music, mostly in the San Francisco Bay Area at that period in time.

B53.   Cody, Judith. Review of the recording: "Image and Impressionism for Classical Guitar, Flute, and Cello:" Fine's *Canzones Y Dances*. Los Altos, California: February, 2001. See: JC136, D3.

The flavor of Spain moves throughout Fine's *Canzones Y Dances* (1991), along with Fine's (very American) unexpected, interesting harmonies.

1 *Adios, Bilbadito:* recalls Bilbadito's vanquishment during the Spanish Civil War. It is introduced simply with bright, brittle atonal chords plucked high on the fingerboard of the guitar. Then a chordal almost romantic section with the flute and cello carrying brief, tonal melodies as three instruments work in effective, imaginative contrast.

2 *Oda a las Ranas:* from a Pablo Neruda poem. Beginning brusquely (perhaps the frog's "serenade?"), at times evocative of Albeniz, the ethereal atonal flute (the "twisting vine" of the poem) "raises" to a gorgeous impressionistic interplay among the three instruments. The guitar work here is refined, delicate.

3 *Tango: The Frog Prince & The Señorita:* This third part is frankly tango, and also frankly tonal, permitting Fine's mastery of the dance to glow through. Her dance rhythms are marked with opulent guitar strums that profile the intense flute melodies in dense inner passage work as all three instruments join in a passionate crescendo.

4 *Soliloquy:* a dedication to Fine 's colleague, Louis Calabro is a mournful guitar dirge on the "dance of death" with a musical contrast to the last (fifth), somewhat intellectual section, *Jiga de la Muerte*, where the guitar assumes its most difficult almost scherzo passage work against the lento flute in a instrumental meshing with Fine's trademark:

beautiful, dynamic rhythmic patterns.

Some of these dances were derived from earlier Fine works (see JC29, JC95, JC115) but in their present reconstruction demonstrate her emotional amalgamation with enormous intellectual maturity to voice her commanding musical erudition.

Though these works may not be a great virtuoso challenge for classical guitar, they are difficult enough; indeed, the height of musicianship in expression is required. Guitarist Joel Brown succeeds at this demanding task, as does all the chamber ensemble. The recording provides a rare opportunity to study contemporary composers and players for this genre. The other interesting composers on this CD are Loris O. Chobanian; Anthony G. Holland; Carver Blanchard; and Andrew York. (see also Albany Records)

B54.   Cody, Judith. Review of Fine's 1948 article: "Rhythm as the Basic Tool in the Learning of Musical Skills." Los Altos, California: January, 2001. See: B99.

This is a most intriguing article (originally a "talk," for unknown groups) dealing as it does, with Vivian Fine's inner processes as a piano prodigy. Her article is, sadly, unpublished yet it gives a glance into Vivian Fine's deeper ideas on music training for the child. It is almost four thousand words long, and is titled "Rhythm as the Basic Tool in the Learning of Musical Skills;" there is a subtitle also, "A Guide for Primary School Music Teachers 1948." Fine had sent a photocopy to this writer in 1993, she wanted to be sure that her paper was included in this bibliography (see Fine, Vivian. 1948).

Fine discusses her frustrations with her piano practice "from the age of five-years on," even though she was richly gifted with "natural endowments," somehow the young girl Fine was unable to achieve the sort of musical satisfaction that she thought she was entitled to. Indeed, she was a ferocious learner on her piano. Abby Whiteside, her piano teacher, is credited here with "ideas" that Fine shared and that helped her with her piano development.

In Fine's viewpoint, there are "two fundamental elements" that should be an important part of a young child's study of music. These are the "aural image" and "rhythm." According to her, there is little of "the exhilaration of rhythm," where the children "use their whole bodies," to music in the teaching of music. She believed that teaching of exactitude, notes, keys, etc., removes the young music student from the music's rightful, often forgotten, provence, e.g.; "playing is a pleasure."

Indeed, what Fine recommended was a course of piano "experimenting" that was not unlike her own improvising as a youth, when her parents allowed her to experiment freely at her piano, no matter how unconventional it might prove. She suggests about "two years" for this stage of "creative experience . . . though the resultant sounds many be hard on the parents."

It seems here as if Fine is saying that music, including conducting, is a total experience for the performer, if done correctly. That the entire body or "torso" must be involved in the "perception" of rhythm for the music to have authenticity. She cites the art of jazz, which she held in high regard, as the perfect example of this concept, as opposed to the rote rigors of classical training. Fine believed that the study of notes should not begin "for a long time." This could cause a conflict with many contemporary teachers, and must have been somewhat shocking in her talk of 1948. (Fine still believed this in the 1990's, speaking quite firmly of her music training ideas, at that time, to this writer).

Certain of Fine's music theories deserve rethinking today, as they are the considerations of not only an important modern composer, but also a dedicated music teacher; Fine was both of these.

B55.   Cohen, Aaron I. (Editor). **International Encyclopedia of Women Composers, Second Edition** [2 volumes]. New York City, New York: Books & Music (USA) Inc., 1987, p. 236. <u>See</u>: JC1, JC2, JC3, JC7, JC8, JC9, JC10, JC16, JC17, JC18, JC21, JC23, JC24, JC25, JC26, JC27, JC30, JC31, JC32, JC33, JC36, JC37, JC39, JC40, JC41, JC42, JC43, JC44, JC45, JC46, JC47, JC48, JC49, JC50, JC51, JC52, JC53, JC54, JC55, JC56, JC57, JC58, JC60, JC61, JC62, JC63, JC65, JC66, JC67, JC68, JC69, JC70, JC71, JC72, JC73, JC74, JC75, JC77, JC78, JC79, JC80, JC82, JC83, JC84, JC85, JC86, JC88, JC89, JC90, JC91, JC92, JC94, JC97, JC99, JC101, JC107.

Cohen includes a considerable number of Fine's compositions in all genre; also other pertinent data of interest on this composer.

Statistics (not readily available elsewhere) on women composers in countries of the world ["Composers by Country and Century"] help place Vivian Fine [also other composers] in an incontrovertible context.

B56.   Cohen, Selma Jeanne. "Draper, Hoving Share Honors in Premieres." New London, Connecticut: *The Day*, August 9, 1965. <u>See</u>: P49.

The American Dance Festival's premieres works by choreographers, Paul Draper and Lucas Hoving. In passing, Fine's production of *Satiana* is mentioned with a positive note. This is the music and witty text of Erik Satie, which, according to the reviewer, had never been "staged before."

B57. Cohn, Arthur. "Review: *Concertante for Piano and Orchestra.*" *American Record Guide* **11**, 1960:218. <u>See</u>: JC42, D4.

An altogether negative statement on the record release of Fine's *Concertante (for Piano and Orchestra)*. Cohn believes the work "cling[s] to the yoke of academicism" and accuses the composer of "worship" in these regards. *Concertante* "is dated and out-of-date" Cohn said (compare with Cohn, Arthur 1981 and also Jones, Ralph E.).

B58. Cohn, Arthur. "Review of Recorded Music." *The Music Magazine*, February, 1962. <u>See</u>: JC59, D1.

A review of an "all-female disc" pronounced as "worthy" by the writer, Arthur Cohn. He is pleased with the works of Julia Perry, Louise Talma and Vivian Fine whose work is recorded here. Miss Fine's *Alcestis* (see Sabin, Robert and compare with *American Record Guide* 1962, Cohn, Arthur 1981 & 1960 and also Barnes, Clive) is heard as:
> ". . . highly intense . . . especially cogent in its dark orchestration. . . ."

B59. Cohn, Arthur. "Reviews of *Alcestis, Concertante for Piano and Orchestra, Paean.*" New York City, New York: **Recorded Classical Music**, Schirmer Books, Macmillan Publishing Co., 1981, pages 626-627. <u>See</u>: JC42, JC59, JC75, D1, D4, D13.

Cohn had excellent comments on Fine's *Alcestis* (see Sabin, Robert, and compare with *American Record Guide* 1962; Cohn, Arthur 1962; and also Barnes, Clive) as performed for this recording by the Imperial Philharmonic of Tokyo, CRI-SD-145. He wrote that the "structures" were "very exciting."

Vivian Fine's *Concertante for Piano and Orchestra* by the Japan Philharmonic Orchestra, CRI-S-135E, was billed, by Cohn, as "healthily academic but not dull" (compare with Jones, Ralph E.; Cohn, Arthur 1960; and French, Richard F. and also *HiFi Stereo Review*). Quality of recorded sound was considered less than the best.

Fine's *Paean*, Eastman Brass Ensemble, CRI-S-260, presents words from "Ode to Apollo" by Keats (see and compare with *Richmond Times-Dispatch*). Mr. Cohn observed interesting and unusual vocal effects such as;
> ". . . fractured sounds . . . and cheerleaderlike repetitions. . . . These are differentiated against brass pungency (trumpets and trombones). . . ." [compare with Frankenstein, Albert].

B60.   Commanday, Robert. "Let the Music Do the Talking." San Francisco, California: *San Francisco Chronicle*, March 31, 1982. <u>See</u>: JC89.

In this short article, Mr. Commanday discusses the meaning of the "text" (or lyrics) to the two new operas to open at the Herbst Theater. Vivian Fine wrote one of the operas, *The Women in the Garden* (see Fine, Vivian and Judith Jamieson), the other was by John Harbison. They were produced by the San Francisco Opera Center.

The writer seems to say that attempting to understand the "elusive words" too literally (of Fine's opera), would be almost impossible. Then just what is the importance of the opera's words? Commanday quotes Fine a lot to help assuage this dilemma. [It is not clear if Fine's quotes are from an interview or perhaps, notes]. Some details from Fine's commentary about *The Women in the Garden* as in Commanday's article:

> "'It's the process of [the women in the garden] getting to know each other as artists and as women . . . being drawn together at an emotional, not an intellectual, level . . . text should be glanced at only so you'll recognize . . . words . . . musical considerations were paramount. . . .'" [compare Kaplan, Arthur; Ratliff, William; Goldstein, Margery November 1981].

B61.   Commanday, Robert. "Women, Myth — A Stunning Double Bill." San Francisco, California: *San Francisco Chronicle*, April 3, 1982. <u>See</u>: JC89

Robert Commanday reviewed Fine's opera, *The Women in the Garden* (see Fine, Vivian and Judith Jamieson), and thought it most praiseworthy. He called Fine's score, "beautifully proportioned," among other laudable statements. A few of Mr. Commanday's comments on the interrelations of the four famous women cast members:

> ". . . The reality of individuals being what they truly are, separated from what they say on the conversational surface . . . four artists of highest sensibility discover each other in this way. . . ."

B62.   Commanday, Robert. "Stop Looking, Listen." San Francisco, California: *San Francisco Chronicle*, October 24, 1982. <u>See</u>: JC79, JC90, JC91, D9, D11, D14.

Mr. Commanday reviewed a record release from Composers Recording, Inc., featuring works by Vivian Fine.

While Commanday. refers to Fine's *Momenti* for piano, as "jewels waiting for recitalists." However, he found faults with Fine's *Quartet for Brass*; at least within the central sections. Of Fine's ten-movement *Missa Brevis* (a short Mass), commissioned for the San Francisco Symphony in 1972, Commanday had only affirmative statements pronouncing that it was

". . . a most original work using both Latin and Hebrew words and phrases. . . . There is singing by Jan DeGaetani, in solo and in quadruplicate [electronic tape recordings]. . . . Four cellos accompany her elsewhere and play four movements alone. It's a moving statement. . . ." [see Kino, Carol; also compare Shepter, Dale D. and Commanday, Robert October 4, 1990].

B63. Commanday, Robert. "Remarkable Individualism at the Symphony." San Francisco, California: *San Francisco Chronicle*, January 7, 1983. See: JC89, JC101.

In this review of Vivian Fine's *Drama for Orchestra* (see and compare with Carson, Josephine), Robert Commanday wrote movingly and eloquently of her "distinctive" creativity in symphonic music. Writing about the qualities of *Drama*'s five movements; Midsummer Night, The Embrace, Jealousy, The Scream and Two Figures by the Shore, Commanday used phrases such as, "compelling," "flow and sweep are beautiful," "rhythmic thrust," "climactic outcry" and in the last scene, "joyful." Some convictions Commanday expressed on the merits of Fine's *Drama:*

". . . The harmonic strength in Fine's music originates in part with chordal structures formed from her melodies . . . [also] the potent rhythmic impulse that courses through and generates Fine's music. . . ." [compare with Pontzious, Richard, January 7, 1983].

B64. Commanday, Robert. "'Mostly Modern' Brings Together Some Pioneers." San Francisco, California: *San Francisco Chronicle*, January 15, 1983. See: JC8, P64.

This is a short review on the "Mostly Modern" concert that was part of Vivian Fine Week (see San Francisco Symphony November 29, 1982). Mr. Commanday said the program was "provocative" and represented "innovative composers" who had been part of Henry Cowell's (circa 1925) New Music Society and *Quarterly* (see Shere, Charles January 15, 1983). Of course, Vivian Fine was one of these illustrious composers and performed on the piano (a duet with violin) Ruth Crawford Seeger's *Violin and Piano Sonata* (1926) (see McLellan, Joseph, 1982).

Commanday further noted that the performance of Fine's *Four Songs* (1933) (see and compare with Gilbert, Steven E. and also Upton Treat, William) was "rich in tone and overtones of meaning."

B65.   Commanday, Robert. "A Few Pearls Among New-Music Offerings." San Francisco, California: *San Francisco Chronicle*, October 4, 1990. See: JC79, D3.

Robert Commanday reviewed a Composers Inc. concert held in the Veterans Building Green Room in San Francisco, California. Works by four composers were featured, George Perle, Fred Lerdahl, David Sheinfeld and Vivian Fine. Commanday found Vivian Fine's concert offering that evening to be the least "distinctively" projected of the four composers present.

Fine's *Missa Brevis* for soprano on tape, and four cellists was the most "visionary work" yet the "least satisfying" stated the reviewer, Commanday (see and compare with Commanday, Robert. October 24, 1982 and also Shepfer, Dale D.). Mr. Commanday also believed that Fine's work

> ". . . did not hold together . . . left touching moments
> and a sense of sketchiness and incompletion. . . ."

B66.   Composer's Forum Program Notes. "Contemporary Music for Viola and Piano." Albany, New York: The Arts Center, November 20, 1974. See: JC80, P54.

Brief quote by Vivian Fine describing her *Concerto for Piano Strings and Percussion for One Performer*, 1972. Fine asserts that the pianistic impetus the performer experiences while on the keyboard, should not be

> ". . . involved with herself in the serious business of
> being a pianist."

B67.   Composers, Inc. Program Notes. [Untitled]. San Francisco, California: Composers, Inc., Green Room, Veteran's Building, March 11, 1986. See: JC91, D14, D15.

Brief program note comments from Vivian Fine on the construction of her *Quartet for Brass*. The movements are called, Variations, Fanfare, Eclogue, and lastly, Variations. While the third movement is said to have a "sense of dialogue," Fine's Variations contain

". . . free transformations of original material." [see
Shepfer, Dale D.; Severinghaus, Wendy 1987].

B68.   Composers Recordings, Inc.. *"Concertante for Piano and Orchestra,
Vivian Fine."* [Liner notes]. New York City, New York: Composers
Recordings, Inc., 1960. See: JC42, D4.

Reiko Honsho was the pianist while Akeo Watanabe conducted the
Japan Philharmonic on this record of Vivian Fine's *Concertante.*
Jacob Glick, a noted violist and "colleague" of Fine's at Bennington,
is quoted on the record liner about his interpretation of the *Concertante
for Piano and Orchestra.* Some of Glick's astute observances on the
first movement are:
". . . impressive argument for a two-movement format
. . . rigorous economy of material [Andante] . . . lyric,
romantic [compare with Gann, Kyle, 1997] . . . volup-
tuous dialogue between soloist and orchestra. . . ."
But a few of violist Glick's comments on the second movement:
". . . baroque drive. . . . The two-part cadenza is extremely effective . . . conclusive with a conciseness
that charms and disarms."

B69.   Composers Recordings, Inc. "American Masters Vivian Fine." New
York City, New York: CRI, CD, 1992. See: JC42, JC51, JC58, JC79,
JC90, JC91, D2, D5, D10, D11, D15, D18.

Six of Fine's better known and more often performed works are on
this CD: *Concertante for Piano and Orchestra, Missa Brevis, Alcestis,
Quartet for Brass, Momenti,* and *Sinfonia and Fugato.*
Heidi Von Gunden declares in the CD's liner notes, that *Concertante*
was composed:
". . . at the end of Fine's study with Sessions [Roger]
. . . [seeing] sketches of the *Concertante,* both teacher
and student sensed that lessons were no longer needed, Sessions saying 'Now we are Colleagues'. . . ."
[compare with Composers Recordings, Inc., 1960 and
also French, Richard F.].

B70.   Connell, Mary. "Some of Life's Great Lessons? Learning to Dance."
Petaluma, California: *Argus-Courier,* January 10, 1986. See: JC58,
JC101, JC115, D1.

Ms. Connell writes of the three-generation family gathering of Vivian
Fine and husband Ben Karp with their daughter, Peggy Noton and

husband David with their daughter Keli and her business partner James Campbell, who all happen to be learning to ballroom dance together at Petaluma Dance Theater which is co-owned by Keli Noton. Keli is "adept" at ballet, jazz dance and choreography. The writer mentions that "Peggy is no artistic slouch, either." Vivian Fine's daughter "still teaches piano."

In passing, Fine's short composition, *Tango With the Frog Prince* is discussed and its performance by the Dance Theater Workshop in New York City as part of a Tango Marathon there. Also mentioned, is that husband, Ben Karp is "a well known sculptor."

This is a rare and pleasant glimpse of Fine's family life.

> "When Keli, her parents and grandparents were polled
> as to why they wanted to master ballroom dance,
> there arose a chorus of 'It's romantic!' . . . As for
> grandmother Vivian Fine, she's delighted with it all.
> . . . 'And I'm very happy to be a part, in a small way,
> of the Petaluma Dance Theater, and to know that my
> granddaughter is one of its directors. . . .' Lifting up
> his plaid work shirt, Ben Karp revealed a self-
> designed T-shirt declaring Vivian Fine Week [see San
> Francisco Symphony November 29, 1982] at the San
> Francisco Symphony."

B71.   Coon, Judith A. *"Program Notes."* Buffalo, New York: Department of Music, State University of New York at Buffalo, Baird Recital Hall, February 9, 1987. See: JC89, JC112, D9.

Background information and short discussion on Fine's five *Toccatas and Arias*; these, having been composed for Barbara Harbach:
> "consist of five movements which unite in a sort of
> arch form. The first *Toccata* is based on baroque style
> toccatas" [see Chon, Richard].

B72.   Cooper, Michael. "Nearwitness Account of the First Three Meet the Woman Composer Concerts at the New School." New York City, New York: Publisher unknown, October 8, 1976. See: JC63, JC80, D7, P61.

Michael Cooper reviewed a concert of music by women where Vivian Fine's *Fantasy for Cello and Piano* (1962) and her *Concerto for Piano Strings and Percussion* were performed. Some of his thoughts on *Fantasy* are;
> "It leaps and plummets — hangs by a toe and drops,
> burrows underground . . . creates a system of its own
> tensions and releases."

Mr. Cooper said of Fine's *Piano Strings* that
"In its uniqueness we hear shrieks and thumps we
have not heard before. . . ."

B73.   Copland, Aaron. "The Composer in America, 1923-1933." *Modern Music*, 1933.

Excellent background study on the birth of what still is now called and was then, in 1933, called Modern Music, also known here as "radical music." Copland sees this momentous musical event as being "born" at the end of the "World War." This is, of course, World War One; the other great war is as yet unknown. He delineates a picture of modern music as beginning in "various countries of Europe" painting traces from the Schoenberg Group leading, eventually, to the shores of the New World in the nineteen twenties. New York was the center of this "radical" new sound until it slowly "seeped" its shocking coloration into all of the country.

Audiences responded at times with "snickers and sarcasm;" oddly, some seventy years into the future there is often the same unenlightened response at contemporary compositions performed in this era. In 1933 Copland had concluded that the advent and accommodation of audiences to this new sound of music had become "inevitable."

Copland makes mention of composers forming an older and younger generation of the "American school"; these elder "men" included: Bloch, Ives, Jacobi, Ornstein, Ruggles, Saminsky, and Varèse. These great legends, in turn, were instrumental in the formation of the younger group of legends-to-be and include, Antheil, Chavez, Copland, Cowell, Hanson, Harris, McPhee, Rudhyar, Sessions, Virgil Thomson and Randall Thompson. The later being those in vogue at the time of Copland's article. As for those composers who would become the future of American Modern Music (compare with Saminsky, Lazare February 1, 1941); Aaron Copland specifies

". . . the coming generation of composers in America.
The first phalanx is already in sight: Henry Brant,
Paul Bowles, Israel Citkowitz, A. Lehman Engel,
Vivian Fine, Irwin Heilner, Bernard Herrman, Jerome
Moross, Elie Siegmeister. . . ."

B74.   Cowell, Henry. [Title unknown]. *Musicalia*. Date unknown, probably early 1930's.

Henry Cowell wrote on various composers of modern music and he commented on the young Vivian Fine [this was most probably written in the early 1930's]:

"Among the composers in the central part of the
United States the most interesting figure is Vivian
Fine. . . . Her work possesses a good sense of form,
and reveals a restless and agile talent." [see Copland,
Aaron].

B75.   Crawford, Caroline. "Effective, Exciting New Music." Palo Alto,
California: *The Peninsula Times Tribune*, January 6, 1983. <u>See</u>: JC101.

Ms. Crawford reviews Fine's *Drama for Orchestra* (see   Carson,
Josephine) stating that;
"the repertory of modern American music gains a
dramatic, lively and intriguing work . . . but there is
also lyricism and melodic, soft coloration." [compare
Commanday, Robert January 7, 1983; Shere, Charles
January 7, 1983; Hertelendy, Paul January 7, 1983;
Glackin, William; and Moor, Paul].

B76.   Crouch, Tim. "Reflections of a Classical Programmer." *Radio
Magazine*, Lawrence, Kansas. Date unknown, but likely early 1970's.

Tim Crouch wrote a long and lively article chronicling "New Trends"
in music. Vivian Fine is cited along with her early mentor, Henry
Cowell, "who absorbed and reinterpreted the music of many cultures."
Crouch commented on the music of Luciano Berio (see Hertelendy,
Paul March 10, 1974), "whose ear is a veritable time tunnel." He
reflected on Fine's (born 1913) contemporary, John Cage (born 1912),
who said about ordinary noise, "'When we listen to it, we find it
fascinating.'"
Mr. Crouch quotes Vivian Fine from an interview with KANU
producer Ev Grimes:
". . . 'sound is a manipulable material, just like any
other medium, like paint . . . architecture, anything
else. People don't think of it that way, though, and
often their ears aren't sensitive enough to isolate that.'
Take her words as a challenge!"

B77.   Crutchfield, Will. "Juilliard Presents 3rd In Contemporary Series." New
York City, New York: *The New York Times*, January 24, 1985. <u>See</u>:
JC45.

Crutchfield reviewed a Juilliard concert that was the third in its
"Focus!" series. The writer was not impressed with the overall quality
of the concert that Tuesday evening in New York City. He called Stefan

Wolpe's work, "ranting" and also "bad music." Vivian Fine's composition, *Great Wall Of China*, is deemed "better" but Crutchfield sees the work as one that:
> "perambulates along under the text . . . undermining
> . . . effectiveness. . . ."

B78.   Crutchfield, Will. "Jayn Rosenfeld Offers a Flute Recital." New York City, New York: *The New York Times*, date unknown but several days after the concert of February 28, 1988. <u>See</u>: JC117, D6.

Jayn Rosenfeld's performance as flutist is reviewed with a comment on Vivian Fine's seven flute movements, *Emily's Images*. This was a premiere of Fine's composition.
> ". . . Vivian Fine's *Emily's Images,* a set of seven
> short movements inspired by first lines of Emily
> Dickinson poems, each delightfully pictorial. . . ."

B79.   Cummings, David. **Random House Encyclopedia Dictionary of Classical Music**. New York City, New York: Random House, 1997. <u>See</u>: JC55, JC58, JC75, JC89, JC101, JC107, JC123.

Brief citation, but also remarks that Fine was a "performer of contemporary piano works from 1931. . . ."

B80.   Cummings, David M. (Editor). **International Who's Who in Music and Musician's Directory (in the Classical and Light Classical Fields)**, 16th Edition. Cambridge, England: International Biographical Centre, 1998-1999, p. 169-170. <u>See</u>: JC3, JC18, JC42, JC50, JC56, JC66, JC71, JC73, JC86, JC89, JC91, JC97, JC101, JC106, JC107, JC113, JC119, JC123.

Fine is cited as having "many grants and commissions"; a fair number of her works cited as well.

B81.   Cupid, Dan. "Cupid's Arrows Hit Handful of Spring Victims." New York City, New York: *New York Daily Mirror*, Monday, April 1, 1935. <u>See</u>: P26.

Amusing, socially slanted article describing the marriage of Ben Karp and Vivian Fine. A photograph of the "lovely" twenty-one-year-old Fine appeared with this piece, plus a second photograph of Ben Karp at his work of sculpturing. Details from the captions read:

"[first photo] We won't Karp; we, too, think it's Fine.
[second photo] Noted sculptor weds noted
pianist. . . ."

According to this account, their marriage occurred at 453 W. 124th
St., in New York City. This was on March 30, 1935, which was a
Saturday, in the afternoon.

Mr. Karp's background is given as a sculptor who has won a
fellowship to Europe recently. Fine is but twenty-one-years at the time
of the marriage and was said to be

". . . one of the most distinguished pianist-composers
in America. . . ."

B82.   *Curari Internazionale del Teatro* (anon.). Italy: September 15, 1970.

Brief review, in Italian, of musicians Pietro Elvin and Anna Gabrieli's
tour in America where "they went to the Bennington Composers'
Conference in Vermont." Vivian Fine is mentioned as having
participated at the Conference:

". . . Pietro Elvin . . . instead he performed music by
contemporary American masters, including Reginald
Boardman and Vivian Fine. The well-known Vivian
Fine has composed a suite of chamber songs (arias)
dedicated to him ." [*trans.* JC]

B83.   *Dallas Dispatch* (anon.). "Young Dancer Charms Large Crowd With
'Toe-Work.'" Dallas, Texas: *Dallas Dispatch*, [May] 6, 1935 [*sic* 34].
See: P24.

This is a quite short review of a dance program featuring dancer, Nini
Theilade, who is described as Danish. It was at McFarlin Auditorium.
This would have been part of a tour with Theilade and Fine:

"Vivian Fine, [piano] accompanist, played three selections
admirably."

B84.   *Darmstadter Echo*. "Amerika-Haus Kassel. Hermann-Streichtrio."
Darmstadt, Germany: November 26, 1953. See: JC3.

Original review was written in German, of which only a portion was
available. The Hermann-Streichtrio performed Vivian Fine's composition, *Trio* [*Trio for Strings*]. Fine was just seventeen-years-old when she
composed the first of the *Trio*. Of this selection by "Amerikanissche
Komponistin," [American Composer] Vivian Fine, the writer states
(compare with *Darmstadter Tageblatt*. November 25, 1953):

> "This is a student level composition in the renowned
> neo-classic style . . . admittedly, the lyrical middle
> passage contains moments of tense excitement,
> betraying very noteworthy talents ." [*trans.* JC]

B85. *Darmstadter Tageblatt.* "Kammermusik mit Streich-Trio." *Darmstadter Tageblatt*, November 25, 1953. <u>See</u>: JC3.

Original written in German. A review of a string trio concert where Fine's *Trio for Strings* was performed and received some positive commentary. Vivian Fine is singled out as one of the world's few female composers.
One movement is criticized as being without profile, while the other is said to have no personal contouring, "personliche Konturierung." The middle movement receives a different sort of comment:

> "The middle movement had sections of such powerful
> expressiveness that one listens most attentively
> (compare with *Darmstadter Echo.* November 26,
> 1953), and one could envision inestimable compos-
> itions from a future period [of Ms. Fine's] — were
> the materials condensed somewhat ." [*trans.* JC]

B86. Der, A. "Oratorio Society: Fine Premiere." *High Fidelity/Musical America*, August, 1976:MA26-27. <u>See</u>: JC84.

A. Der offers, in this review, favorable comment on Fine's music for her cantata, *Meeting for Equal Rights 1866*, yet unfavorable comment on the text for this work (this was the premiere). *Meeting* is constructed of sections from talks by such as Frederick Douglass, Horace Greeley and others that were controversial arguments for and against women's suffrage made after the Civil War. A. Der wrote that Fine

> ". . . botches her case for sexual and racial equality
> in her haphazardly constructed text. . . . Their works
> make little forensic impact . . . out of context. . . . A
> gratuitous section on Biblical persecution of the Jews
> confuses matters further" [see and compare with Belt,
> Byron and also Fuller, Sophie].

Der finds the musical contrasts between male and female choral parts, accompanied at significant points, by calming strings or discordant brass during the debates over women's suffrage to be "often quite vivid." Der was most impressed with Fine's employment of "Ivesian clashes."

Article includes a photograph of Vivian Fine.

B87. Ditsky, John. "Fine: *Quartet for Brass, Momenti and Missa Brevis.*"
Fanfare 7-8, 1982:120. <u>See</u>: JC79, JC90, JC91, D9, D11, D14.

> Ms. Fine's compositions, *Quartet for Brass*, *Momenti*, for solo piano
> and *Missa Brevis*, for taped mezzo-soprano and four cellos are reviewed
> here. Mr. Ditsky makes note of the fact that Vivian Fine has recently
> been awarded a sponsoring award by the American Academy and In-
> stitute of Arts and Letters; also that *Momenti* is dedicated to Roger Ses-
> sions. Of her *Quartet for Brass* he says "technically fascinating . . .
> pleasurable." He proclaims *Missa Brevis* as
>> ". . . lovely. . . . The collage of voice tracks . . . and
>> cello accompaniment creates a haunting piece that
>> leaves a lasting impression" [compare with Shepfer,
>> Dale D.].

B88. Donner, Jay M. Review: "*Missa Brevis, Momenti and Quartet for
Brass.*" *The New Records*, May, 1982: 7. <u>See</u>: JC79, JC90, JC91, D9,
D11, D14.

> Mr. Donner "recommend[s]" Miss Fine's new recording (CRI-SD-468
> by Composers Recording, Inc.) here. There are positive comments for
> *Quartet for Brass*, "skillful and energetic," yet no enthusiasm for
> *Momenti*. He views   Jan DeGaetani's performance of Fine's *Missa
> Brevis* as a "spectacular execution" (compare with Ditsky, John) whilst
> viewing the whole as
>> "a trifle overextended . . . still worthy for its unique
>> concept."

B89. Donoghue, John D. "Trinity Dedication Music Was Fine." Burlington,
Vermont: *The Burlington (Vt.) Free Press*, October 26, 1985. <u>See</u>:
JC108.

> Donoghue reviews the dedication concert for the new library at Trinity
> College, The Thomas A. Farrell Family Library. This was also the
> occasion of the sixtieth anniversary of Trinity and Bennington Colleges
> since 1925 when they were founded to educate women. *A Song for St.
> Cecilia's Day* was Vivian Fine's offering for this particularly close-to-
> home occasion (She taught at Bennington College during this period).
> Fine conducted the Vermont Symphony String and Trumpet Ensemble
> performing her composition. Susannah Waters was soprano with
> Michael Downs the baritone. Choral singers were drawn from the ranks
> of the Bennington College Chorus, the Trinity College Choir and the
> University of Vermont Concert Choir. The reviewer found *Song*, an
> eight-part cantata, to be a "piece of enduring merit" (compare with

Saminsky, Lazare, February 1, 1941). He predicts that the music may last as long as have the lyrics from John Dryden's words (at the time of this review, 1985, this amounts to 298 years):

> "Fine writes thoughtfully for voices yet with an appreciation of the origin of the words. . . . The writing for instruments was supportive and the trumpet fanfare glorious."

B90. Dyer, Richard. "Music Review: The Boston Musica Viva, Richard Pittman, Music Director, in a Concert in the Longy School Last Night. Musical Expressions of Substance." Boston, Massachusetts: *The Boston Globe*, Globe Newspaper Company, Section: Arts & Film; April 22, 1989, pg.10. See: JC 127.

Highlights a concert of the Boston Musica Viva (see Miller, Margo) featuring two "striking new works"; one work by Olly Wilson who is an "eminent black composer," and one by Fine who is an "eminent woman composer." Mr. Dyer begins his thoughtful review by offering the cogent argument that:

> "Music has neither color nor sex. But it can express these things. . . Fine's [work] was very much a woman's statement. . . ."[compare with Fruchter, Rena]

Vivian Fine's work that night was *Asphodel* (1988); that is a William Carlos Williams poem set to a musical score and employing coloratura soprano. *Asphodel* concerns "long marriage . . . weathering of storms. . . ." Dyer reports that *Asphodel* is a "lovely piece" and that soprano Maria Tegzes:

> ". . . vocalizes flowering melismas of reconciliation over music that lifts the voice and wafts it like a gentle breeze. . . ."

Mentioned here is the celebration of Fine's 75th birthday during a week devoted to presentation of her music. This was the "Fine Week" proclaimed by Boston (see Boston, City of).

B91. Engel, A. Lehman. "Music Notes." *The Symposium: A Critical Review*, October, 1932. See: JC7, P10.

A review of the music festival programs at Yaddo at Saratoga Springs, New York. Numerous celebrated modern music composers of the time were present and performed, among them were; Copland, Henry Brant, Carlos Chavez, Harris, Israel Citkowitz, Sessions, Walter Piston, Ives, Wallingford Riegger and the lone woman composer present, Vivian Fine. A. Lehman Engel writes that Fine's is "technically equipped" for most musical intricacies (compare with Saminsky, Lazare, September-

October 1932). He states her *Four Polyphonic Piano Pieces* as "music in its purest form" (compare with Berger, Arthur, April 1932 and also Chon, Richard) and further says that he was

". . . moved by the sheer truth-beauty which emanates
from them."

B92.   Engel, A. Lehman. "Vivian Fine — Henry Brant." New York City, New York: *Young Israel*, 1933. S̲e̲e̲: JC2, JC7

Mr. Engel puts forth the theory in this treatise, that the "real" artists will discover the "new mode" for their art, and that these great men and women of history had childhoods very different than what we commonly think of as "'childhood'"(see Brookes, Tim). This, because most often their younger years were spent devoted to complex studies and accumulation of skills. For instance, he explained that these artists "studied diligently" during their childhood and teenage years: Michelangelo, (art and "anatomy"); Mozart, (composing and skills at piano); Beethoven ("radical ideas" and music skills) and Wagner (composed the opera *"The Fairy,"* at twenty).

As for the "new mode," or "radical" concept, that these prodigies discover; it is often met with discomfort, distrust and "calumny." Engel clarifies this by his statement:

"We are fast forgetting the men who wrote the
comfortable, successful music of his time. After a few
more years, we will not know them at all."

Later Engel adds two composers that he believes of "special interest," being unusually talented and very young. Vivian Fine and Henry Brant, both nineteen, one year ago at the time of his article (1932), have had their work selected for performance at Yaddo (see *New York Herald-Tribune,* February 1932) where there was a Festival of Contemporary American Music. Aaron Copland had thought up this "idea."

Engel was much impressed with the young Vivian, who he wrote, "composed much and has had several noteworthy performances." Mentioned are Fine's early performances, *Oboe Sonatina* (Pan-American concert in New York), *Four Pieces for Two Flutes* (International Society for Contemporary Music in Hamburg), and *Four Polyphonic Piano Pieces*, performed at Yaddo (see Engel, A. Lehman, October, 1932):

". . . [Fine] is the only woman in a group of young
modern composers which has been assembled together
in New York"[compare with Copland, Aaron].

[A photograph of Fine at the age of nineteen or twenty is with the article and, also, a photograph of Henry Brant]

B93. Ericson, Raymond. "Flute and Viola Concert." New York City, New York: *The New York Times*, February 23, 1962. See: JC60.

Fine's flute and viola work, *Iconomachy*, [*Duo for Flute and Viola*] is given luke-warm comment in this short review. Though the reviewer indicated certain passages between flute and viola as being "deftly arranged" he questions
". . . images Miss Fine was warring against . . .
could not be fathomed."

B94. Ericson, Raymond. "'Cookbook' with Musical Beat is Served Up by Bennington." New York City, New York: *The New York Times*, May 17, 1972. See: JC48.

Raymond Ericson reviewed a program titled, "Music From Bennington" (College) held at Carnegie Recital Hall in New York City. The program of musicians and composers included both the college faculty and students. As faculty, Vivian Fine presented her *Divertimento* for cello and percussion here billed as
" . . . a lively duet for an unlikely combination. . . ."

B95. Everett, Thomas. "Five Questions, Forty-one Answers." *The Composer* **5**(1):22-27.[n.d.].

From the journal *The Composer*, Thomas Everett, a member of the editorial staff concocted several questions that were to be asked of several composers. Vivian Fine was included along with Roger Harris, Joshua Missal, Carl Della Peruti, Klaus George Roy, Ulysses Kay, Sergio Cervetti and Galen Wilson. Sample questions and answers:

" [interviewer]: Have you ever judged a composition contest? [Fine answers]: 'No.'
[interviewer]: Do art forms in one medium affect another? [Fine answers]: 'Perhaps.' . . ."

B96. Ewen, David. **American Composers. A Biographical Dictionary**. New York City, New York: G.P. Putnam's Sons, p. 220-222. See: JC1, JC2, JC3, JC7, JC8, JC16, JC17, JC18, JC23, JC24, JC30, JC31, JC55, JC58, JC65, JC69, JC70, JC80, JC84, JC89.

Ewen gives background and biographical information on Fine and most of her works up to 1980. Of Fine's creative activity in the year 1975 he writes:

> ". . . she secluded herself in Cuernavaca, Mexico to
> write *The Women in the Garden* to her own libretto,
> and on February 12, 1978, the Port Costa Players
> produced it in San Francisco. . . ." [see Fine, Vivian
> and Judith Jamieson].

B97.   Fine, Vivian and Lucia Dlugoszewski. "Composer/choreographer.
Choreographer/composer." *Dance Perspectives* **16**:8-11, 21-25, 1963.
<u>See</u>: JC16, JC24, JC58, D1.

See Block, Adrienne Fried and Carol Neuls-Bates.

B98.   Fine, Vivian and Judith Jamieson. Cambridge, New York: Program
Notes: *The Women in the Garden* performance by L'Ensemble Chamber
Music Center, August 29-30, 1981. <u>See</u>: JC89.

Fine's opera, *The Women In The Garden*, is outlined in these
extensive program notes with Vivian Fine's description of the
reflections and articulated interactions of four celebrated women and the
single male character. American poet Emily Dickinson, dancer Isadora
Duncan, novelist Virginia Woolf and writer Gertrude Stein meet in
music and lyrical processes that are "surreal, dream-like," and enhanced
through a "plotless, freely-associated libretto."
Fine adopted selections from texts and letters written by the women,
in life, to become their words, lyrics and personal stories. As a point of
actual fact, they did not meet in real life. The character, The Tenor, is
cast in multiple roles signifying primal male relationships in the
women's lives. Fine cast him as father to Dickinson, lover (fantasized)
to Dickinson and lover (Gordon Craig) to Isadora. Gertrude and The
Tenor sing duets in scene five and at the opera's conclusion, when they
leave the stage with their arms linked in friendship.
The opera begins when

> ". . . Gertrude sings of man, human nature . . . time.
> Emily of 'that sacred closet entitled memory,' Isadora
> of her affinity for the sea, and Virginia of novel
> writing and the effect of sex upon the novelist. . . .
> Scene 4 opens with a long lament sung by Isadora on
> the loss of her three children. . . . Scene 6 . . .
> [Virginia's] story of the difference an inheritance can
> make to a woman. . . . Scene 7 . . . Emily and The
> Tenor sing of her decision to remain with her father.
> . . . Scene 8, the four women continue to draw on
> each others' words as well as their own. . . ."

B99.   Fine, Vivian. "Rhythm as the Basic Tool in the Learning of Musical
            Skills." 1948, Hoosick Falls, New York and Library of Congress (see
            Appendix 1).

            Manuscript "Rhythm as the Basic Tool in the Learning of
            Musical Skills;" subtitled "A Guide for Primary School Music
            Teachers." was an unpublished paper written by Vivian Fine
            in 1948 (See Cody, Judith January 2001).

B100.   Flanagan, William. "Review of Records." *HiFi Stereo Review* **6**,
            1962:76. <u>See</u>: JC58, JC59, D1.

            This is a terse review of "lady composers" whose work is rated as
            "so-so" by Mr. William Flanagan. Louise Talma, Mary Howe, Mabel
            Daniel, Julia Perry and Vivian Fine's compositions are recorded on this
            Composers Recording Inc. release. Vivian Fine's work, *Alcestis*, (see
            Sabin, Robert and compare with American Record Guide, 1962) takes
            brief mention as
                       ". . . competent and appropriately murky."

B101.   Flandreau, Tara. "Review: San Francisco Symphony." San Francisco,
            California: *Bay City News Service*, January 6, 1983. <u>See</u>: JC101.

            Both a "capsule" review and main review cover the prestigious Vivian
            Fine Week (see San Francisco Symphony, November 29, 1982)
            celebrated in San Francisco that began with the world premiere of her
            symphony composition *Drama for Orchestra* (see Carson, Josephine)
            which was written in 1981-82. Edo de Waart conducted *Drama* with the
            San Francisco Symphony's "salute" to Fine. Brahms' *Violin Concerto
            in D* and Mozart's *"Linz" Symphony* were also on the evening program.
            Flandreau determines Fine to be a "master orchestrator with a very
            personal style" while listening to Fine's musical work studying the
            intense emotions underlying the revelations of yet another great artist,
            Norwegian painter Edvard Munch. The piece is in five movements,
            "Midsummer Night," "The Embrace," "Jealousy," "The Scream" and
            "Two Figures by the Shore." It is the last movement, "Two Figures by
            the Shore," where the reviewer finds fault; concluding that too much
            material is squeezed into the brief section. Flandreau expresses the wish
            that this movement was "longer" in order to "adequately balance" the
            intensity of the fourth part, "The Scream." As for the first movement,
            "Midsummer Night," and the others, the writer contends:
                       ". . . a wealth of ideas and colors, in gestures of
                       sometimes abruptly different character, emerge and
                       develop. The movement, like most of the others in the

piece, has an overall arch form — growing to an
intense climax . . . slowly . . . peacefully dies away."
[compare Shere, Charles January 7, 1983; Moor, Paul;
Hertelendy, Paul January 7, 1983].

B102. Frankenstein, Albert. "Review: *Paean.*" *High Fidelity Magazine,*
October, 1971:110-112. <u>See</u>: JC75, D13.

Three composers from Bennington College faculty are represented on
this disc titled "Music from Bennington." Vivian Fine presents her
work, *Paean* (see *Richmond Times-Dispatch*). Frank Baker narrates
while the Eastman Brass and the Bennington Choral Ensemble render
Paean with Vivian Fine conducting. *Paean* is not the first choice of Mr
Albert Frankenstein; first choices were works by Brant and Calabro.
However, his conclusions on Fine's work remain positive:
". . . singers shout and scream and wail . . . like a
cheering section. . . . Vivid, entertaining, sometimes
moving" [compare with Cohn, Arthur 1981].

B103. French, Edward. "Concert Merges Tapes, 'Live' Sound." Albany, New
York: *Knickerbocker News*, November 21, 1974. <u>See</u>: JC80, P54, P55,
P58.

Mr. French reviews contemporary music for piano and viola. The
Composers' Forum in Albany, New York presented the concert at the
Arts Center. Vivian Fine was both the composer and the pianist for her
Concerto for Piano Strings and Percussion. Fine was also pianist
performer for Jean Eichelberger Ivey's *Music for Viola and Piano.* This
work was composed for Fine and violist Jacob Glick who accompanied
Fine that evening. Works by Roger Hannay, Henry Cowell and Thea
Musgrave were also on that evening program.
French adjudges Fine's and Glick's performance as "exemplary"
noting that Fine's own composition, *Concerto*, was "highly effective."
He stated that:
". . . Fine extracted every possible kind of sound from
the piano, using the keyboard and sundry other
means. . . . As an experiment in sonics this piece was
highly effective . . . while quite free in form, still
held together."

B104. French, Richard F. "Review of Records." *The Musical Quarterly* **46**(4),
1960: 548-551. <u>See</u>: JC42, D2.

Somewhat technical review that covers the work of a number of composers including Vivian Fine's *Concertante for Piano and Orchestra*, Copland's *Dance Symphony*, Cowell's *Music 1957*, Franco's *The Cosmos* and Ruggles' *Organum* among others. Mr. French believes that the above works of Fine and Franco "betray weaknesses" that are not visible in the numerous other works included in this review.

These flaws in Fine's *Concertante* appear to be the reviewer's opinion that this composition must have been written in three movements at one time and furthermore, that it was the *first* [my italics] movement that was "discarded" by the composer. Or, perhaps, never recorded at all. According to Mr. French, it is also highly possible (based on the final movement's "tonality") that the vanished movement was composed in "A major."

Technical flaws additionally observed by Mr. French are that Miss Fine's *Concertante*

"... displays no highly articulated harmonic usage
... harmonic and contrapuntal usage ... unrelated to
... [a] formal plan. ..." [compare with Composers
Recordings, Inc., 1960 and 1992].

B105.   Friedman, Sonya. "NOTES on Memoirs of Uliana Rooney." Program Notes. Richmond, Virginia: The University of Richmond, Current Resident Ensemble, Sept. 9, 10, 1994. See: JC138.

Friedman, who is an award-winning documentary film writer, producer, director and Academy Award nominee, calls Fine's opera heroine, Uliana:

"... a fictitious, feisty, feminist American composer
... a thoroughly American prodigy ... dared to turn
composer in days when women were not even
allowed to play in orchestras. ..."

Ms. Friedman wove the opera's compelling contemporary elements so that "... words, music and film/slide projections ..." tell Vivian Fine's somewhat true life history through the eyes of a fictional composer highlighted with twentieth century spectacle (see Patterson, Catherine and also Bustard, Clarke).

B106.   Fruchter, Rena. "Music; American Women Focus of Concert." New York City, New York: *The New York Times*, The New York Times Company, Sunday, February 26, 1989, Late City Final Edition, Section 12NJ; pg.8. See: JC58.

Details of the then forthcoming concert at the Shea Center at William Paterson College are reported. The Wayne Chamber Orchestra

performed compositions by Vivian Fine and Mary Howe to
commemorate Women's History Month. Murray Colosimo conducted.
Fruchter goes on to cite:

> ". . . dangers of classifying artists as male or fe-
> male. . . ."

as discussed among Fine, Mr. Colosimo, harpist Kathleen Bride and
cellist Gretchen Lochner (compare with Dyer, Richard, 1989).

B107.   Fulkerson, Christopher. "Program Notes: Teisho." San Francisco,
California: Ariel, A Contemporary Vocal Ensemble. See: JC83.

B108.   Fuller, Sophie. **The Pandora Guide to Women Composers, Britain
and the United States 1629-Present**. San Francisco, California:
Pandora, an Imprint of Harper Collins Publishers, 1994. See: JC1, JC2,
JC8, JC16, JC24, JC30, JC31, JC42, JC55, JC58, JC75, JC79, JC84,
JC101, JC107, JC123, JC138.

Sophie Fuller delivers a well thought out, comparative history on the
evolution of women composers in the United States and Britain. Her
book manages to be entertaining as well as educational while sketching
many intriguing lives of these early women in music. Two of the most
fascinating musical lives herein are Ruth Crawford Seeger's [see Judith
Tick and Gaume, Matilda] and Vivian Fine's. Crawford (later, Seeger
was her married name) was to become the educator and inspiration for
Fine. Fuller elaborates on Fine's 1976 work, *Meeting for Equal Rights
1866*, as:

> ". . . putting the text together from various 19th-
> century writings and speeches about women's
> suffrage. It is a complex work needing three
> conductors but displaying Fine's sense of humour in
> many of its touches, such as the musical suggestion of
> Johannes Brahms' famous lullaby when the text is
> presenting the argument that woman's place is in the
> home" [compare with Belt, Byron and also Der, A.].

B109.   Galardi, Susan. "Premieres: The Composer Speaks — Vivian Fine on
Poetic Fires." *High Fidelity/Musical America* 35:18, February, 1985.
See: JC59, JC107, D1, P63, P67.

This is an engaging profile piece on Vivian Fine highlighting her
forthcoming concert, on February 21, 1985. This was to be her *Poetic
Fires,* for piano and orchestra with the American Composers Orchestra
conducted by Gunther Schuller, with Fine performing at the piano.
Poetic Fires was commissioned by the Koussevitsky Foundation. Fine,

being accomplished in the fine art of orchestral colorations has always been responsible for the creation of her own orchestration; she also "composes in full score" according to Galardi.

Susan Galardi writes that it was after Fine premiered a Ruth Crawford Seeger violin sonata in 1982 (Fine had not performed on stage at the piano for many years until then) that Fine decided to play piano on stage, again. What convinced her to return was the fact that "her piano playing elicited enthusiastic reviews" (compare McLellan, Joseph, November 11, 1982, also Holland, Bernard, March 1 1983). A short while later she began to write the piano-orchestral work *Poetic Fires*.

As has been often noted, poetry is a reoccurring theme in Fine's work. In the case of her *Poetic Fires,* this composition contains segments of Greek poetry; specifically, bits of poetic structures from the poets, Aeschylus and Homer. The article further says that, the work was written after the eminent composer's sojourn to Greece leaving her with memories of the Greek writings. Though, interestingly enough, only when the musical work was complete did Fine assign the lines of poetry that would "describe the music." Galardi writes that Vivian Fine has stressed that the orchestra does not accompany the "solo" pianist and that, indeed, *Poetic Fires* was not written as a concerto. Rather, Fine explained that:

> "'. . . there is much more of an interweaving of the
> sounds of the piano and orchestra. . . . Orchestration
> [is] transparent . . . lyric and articulated piano pas-
> sages come through.'"

Article includes a photograph of Vivian Fine at the piano.

B110.   Gann, Kyle. **American Music in the Twentieth Century**. New York City, New York: Schirmer Books, Simon & Schuster, Macmillan, p. 106, 1997.

Examining the evolution of what is sometimes called "modern classical music" in America, Kyle Gann investigates complex interactions among the robust mix of composers and their unique new music creations in the American society of the nineteen-hundreds. Within Gann's chapter titled "Atonality and European Influence," Gann brings together Fine, Piston, and Persichetti in a comparative triad:

> ". . . In fact, as a descriptive category, neoclassicism
> is forced to cover a wide range. If one generalizes it
> to extend to the filling of classical forms with new
> materials, then Walter Piston, Vivian Fine, and Vin-
> cent Persichetti must be included, even though their
> works are lyrically romantic and emotively expansive,

devoid of Stravinsky's ironic emphasis on rhythmic
surprise. . . ."
Gann states this view of Ms. Fine's music:
". . . Her compositions are classical as to form and
romantic as to feeling. . . ." [compare with Greene,
David Mason and Anderson, Martin]

B111.   Gann, Kyle. "Symphonist Stakes Her Claim." New York City, New
York: *The New York Times*, Sunday, April 25, 1999, late Edition-
Final, Section 2; Arts and Leisure Desk, pg. 34.

This is a thirteen-hundred-plus word article on Ms. Coates, "female
symphonist," within which the writer includes the name of Vivian Fine
among a list of fourteen other women composers whom Gann insists
don't have:
". . . a symphony among them. . . ."[see Appendix 8]

B112.   Gaume, Matilda. **Ruth Crawford Seeger: Memoirs, Memories, Music.**
Metuchen, New Jersey: The Scarecrow Press, Inc., 1986, 268 pages.

Gaume's 268 page study on the life of Ruth Crawford contains much
interesting background data with facts also impinging on the life of the
young Vivian Fine. The book also contains a wealth of large and most
charming family photographs. Ruth kept detailed journals, letters and
notes, all written in an exuberant, idealistic style. Gaume quotes a good
deal from this rich depository, left by Ruth, and we are lucky, indeed
to have insight into a rare and gifted female composer from our own
era. Gaume notes that the greatly talented Ruth was Fine's teacher and
her inspiration to compose:
"During the years Ruth and her mother spent
together in Chicago, Ruth was quite busy studying,
composing, and teaching. Besides teaching at the
conservatory and at Elmhurst College, Ruth taught
theory and composition, probably privately. She was
understandably impressed with the talent of one of her
students, a thirteen-year-old girl named Vivian Fine.
Fine first became acquainted with Ruth when they
were both piano students of Djane Lavoie-Herz. Herz
thought that Fine, an unusually talented young girl,
needed more in-depth music study than piano alone
could provide so she suggested that Ruth teach her
theory, which served in those days as a prelude to the
study of composition. Fine remembers Ruth vividly
and feels that her work in theory and composition

with Ruth was decisive in pointing her on the road to her very successful composing career. Ruth's approach to teaching Fine paralleled rather closely the training Ruth received from Weidig at the conservatory, i.e., liberal doses of strict, conventional harmonic training tempered with the opportunity for original work at every turn and a very informal and free approach to the teaching of composition, allowing and encouraging Fine to experiment as Weidig had done to her. When Ruth went to New York in the fall of 1929, Weidig gave Fine the scholarship that Ruth had had, so she knew and understood his teaching techniques first hand, as she did Ruth's."

B113. George, Earl. "Fine Enters New Composing Field with *Women in the Garden.*" Syracuse, New York: *Syracuse Herald America*, March 25, 1984. <u>See</u>: JC89, JC101, JC104.

Women in the Garden (see Fine, Vivian and Judith Jamieson), Fine's chamber opera, was to be performed at the Civic Center's Currier Theater by the Society for New Music in Syracuse, New York. Therefore followed this profile article, by Earl George, drawn from a telephone interview with Vivian Fine. Mr. Earl George began by discussing Fine's studies with the famed Ruth Crawford at about age twelve (see Gaume, Matilda) and her early teacher for one semester, noted musician George Szell, from Mannes School in New York City. Fine credits Crawford with giving her the "'encouragement'" that motivated her to lead the life of a composer of music.

Many of the distinguished composer's accolades are remarked upon and include: a Guggenheim Fellowship, a grant from the National Endowment for the Arts and an award from the American Academy and Institute of Arts and Letters. Fine mentioned that her recent opus, *Drama for Orchestra* (see Carson, Josephine) was "nominated for the Pulitzer Prize." *Drama* was still "widely heard on PBS" reported Earl George.

George noted eminent names from the world of modern dance who had commissioned Fine to create dance music (see White, Edward). There was also some discussion on the fact that three of the cast of *Women in the Garden* (see Fine, Vivian and Judith Jamieson) are renowned women of letters. Fine's reason for this, she stated, was that she "'compiled'" the opera's libretto from actual words the women had written.

In a brief aside the article mentions Fine's new commissions of the time: *Canticles for Jerusalem,* also, a trio for oboe and strings commissioned by Sigma Alpha Iota (the national music fraternity for women) and a commission for a voice and string quartet. The later two works were currently in progress at the writing of the article.

B114. Gilbert, Steven E. "'The Ultra Modern Idiom': A Survey of New Music." Dallas, Texas: *Perspectives in New Music* 12, Fall, 1973, pp. 310-314. See: JC8.

Engrossing, yet readable, technical music analysis (see and compare with Upton, William Treat) of Fine's *Four Songs* for voice and string quartet. Just the third song, "She Weeps Over Rahoon", employs all instruments of the quartet. Gilbert said that Vivian Fine chose text for each of the four songs from diverse literary sources. Beginning with an anonymous English poem "O Western Wind," written in the sixteenth-century, inspiring the text of the first song; a poem by Herrick becomes text for the next song. Lastly, from our twentieth century, James Joyce's "Pomes Penyeach" contributes passages for the third and fourth songs.
Steven E. Gilbert expresses his "admiration unequivocally" for Fine's *Four Songs* and in this regard he states:
> ". . . Vivian Fine's work shows how techniques
> related to serial composition can be applied in a very
> personal way, yet with consistency and logic. . . ."

B115. Glackin, William. "Former Child Prodigies Create Striking Concert." Sacramento, California: *Sacramento Bee*, January 7, 1983. See: JC101.

A commendatory review of the world premiere of Vivian Fine's *Drama for Orchestra* (see Carson, Josephine) during the event-filled Vivian Fine Week (see San Francisco Symphony November 29, 1982). It was performed by the San Francisco Symphony in Davies Hall. Also on the program was twenty-one-year-old violinist Dylana Jensen performing the Brahms *Violin Concerto*. Glackin compares both as once starting out as child prodigies. Fine was sixty-nine in 1983. The writer was deeply impressed with their talents while noting the apparent happiness both expressed to "prolonged applause" at their separate works. Fine "looked pretty young herself," he remarks.
Background concepts for *Drama for Orchestra* are discussed as being inspired by the paintings of Norwegian artist, Edvard Munch, as the five movements (each about twenty-two minutes, according to Glacken) arise from the psychological states preceding his five paintings; "Midsummer Night," "The Embrace," "Jealousy," "The Scream" and "Two Figures by the Shore." Glacken concludes that Fine's *Drama* has succeeded

"brilliantly" in terms of its artistic objective and realization; noting that it deserves a "long career." The reviewer states that *Drama* is a "powerhouse of dramatic musical communication." (Compare with Flandreau, Tara; Hertelendy, Paul, January 4, 1983 and also Moor, Paul):

> "If the name Vivian Fine isn't ringing any bells in your memory, you needn't be embarrassed. The striking thing about her career is that while her talent has been recognized by the upper levels of music (and dance) from a very early age, she has never won the fame of an Aaron Copland or a Virgil Thomson."

B116. Goldstein, Margery. "How Does Our Garden Grow?" Boston, Massachusetts: *Sojourner*, November, 1981. See: JC89.

Margery Goldstein reviews Vivian Fine's *The Women in the Garden.* This chamber opera was performed by the Boston Musica Viva on October 4 and October 2 at Yale University's Sprague Hall in New Haven and also at Harvard University's Sanders Theater in Cambridge where it was taped by station WBUR for radio. Goldstein is enthusiastic; commenting on the opera as "a wonderfully engrossing hour" and on the talent of Fine as "abundant." She regards Fine's opera "as a discussion of Woman as Artist" and subsequently adds that the music is "accessible" yet remains "rewarding" to audiences acquainted with contemporary classic music. Concerning the cast and framework (see Fine, Vivian and Judith Jamieson) the reviewer adds that:

> "Action is always subordinate to musical structure . . . but characterization is very important. The personalities of the four women (superbly presented, far more than a mere impersonation of famous figures) create drama in the absence of plot."

B117. Greene, David Mason. **Greene's Biographical Encyclopedia of Composers**. Garden City, New York: Doubleday & Company, Inc., 1985, p 1250, See: JC16, JC42, JC51, JC58, JC75, JC79, JC83, JC89, JC90, JC91.

In this hefty tome surveying the contributions to musical history of innumerable composers, Greene presents a studied, albeit brief, history of Ms. Fine's long career. Greene pronounces Fine:

> "An avoider of circumscribed systems, Ms. Fine at first leaned toward atonality, then toward the diatonic, and finally compromised between the extremes. Her

choice of subjects in her stage and vocal music shows
imagination and wit. . . ."

B118. H., H. "Young Composers Presented." New York City, New York: *The
New York Times*, January 16, 1932. See: JC2, P5.

H.H. attended the start-up concert of "excessively contemporary
music" by the Young Composers' Group (see and compare with *The
Musical Leader*), "planned" by Aaron Copland, then "organized" by
Elie Siegmeister and Irwin Heilner. According to H.H., the purpose of
this ultra-modern music group was to "further the work of composers
under 25 years old." To that end, H.H. reviewed their concert at the
New School (see and compare with B., A. V.) later writing that the
young composers concertizing that night were Jerome Moross, Israel
Citkowitz, A. Lehman Engel, Irwin Heilner, Vivian Fine, Elie
Siegmeister, Henry Brant and Bernard Hermann. "Assisting artists"
included Vivian Fine on piano and Henry Brant. Fine's *Four Pieces for
Two Flutes* was performed at this very "first" program of the Young
Composers' Group causing the critic, H.H., to interject on "the delicacy
of Miss Fine's second flute piece" (see and compare with Perkins,
Francis).
   H.H. also declared the concert's new music to be
         ". . . an art whose idiom is changing as rapidly as the
         harmonic language . . . whether that material outrages
         or pleases the unaccustomed ear. . . ."

B119. *Haagsche Courant*. [Review of R. Guralnik's 1962 concert tour]. The
Hague, The Netherlands: Fall, 1962. See: JC33.

Short review (in Dutch) of Robert Guralnik's performance in The
Hague as part of his European concert tour. Brief mention of Vivian
Fine's *Five Preludes*, as performed by Guralnik on his tour, they were:
         ". . . full of charm and virtuosity. . . ." [*trans.* anon.]

B120. Hall, Charles. **A Twentieth-Century Musical Chronicle. Events 1900-
1988**. Westport, Connecticut: Greenwood Press, 1989. See: JC57, JC68,
JC89, JC101.

The brief entry in Hall's **Musical Chronicle** highlights five of Fine's
compositions including 1983 *Drama for Orchestra*.

B121. Hall, Charles J. **A Chronicle of American Music 1700-1995**. New
York City, New York: Schirmer Books, Prentice Hall International,
1996. See: JC7, JC16, JC17, JC18, JC33, JC35, JC41, JC42, JC49,

JC50, JC54, JC56, JC58, JC59, JC70, JC72, JC73, JC74, JC78, JC87, JC89, JC90, JC101, JC102, JC107.

Mr. Hall has a distinctive presentation for the study of musical history. Each year is divided into informative categories such as: "Historical Highlights, World Cultural Highlights and Music — The Cultivated/Art Music Scene." Both the political and artistic significant events of that year are cited within each category. The music publications of the specific year are further subdivided into: "Choral, Opera, Piano, Symphonies, etc," where the composers are noted. For example, one can learn at a glance that in 1982 some of the new music published included works by contemporaries Philip Glass, *The Photographer*; Richard Adler, *Wilderness Suite;* Vivian Fine, *Drama for Orchestra* and her *Double Variations for Piano*.

B122.   Hasden, Nikki C. [Review]. Chattanooga, Tennessee: *The Chattanooga Times*, October 16, 1982. <u>See</u>: JC79, JC90, JC91, D9, D11, D14.

Short review of Vivian Fine's record release (CRI SD 434) of *Quartet for Brass* called "a charming work . . . superbly executed"; *Momenti* called "delightful" by Nikki Hasden who also affirms that *Missa Brevis* is

> "fascinating and unusual . . . other worldly sounds
> . . . concluding this excellent contemporary recording"
> [compare with Shepter, Dale D. and also Henahan, Donal].

B123.   Haskins, John. "Guralnik's Program Loaded with Interest." Washington, DC: *The Evening Star*, June 11, 1962. <u>See</u>: JC33.

Review of Robert Guralnik's concert piano performance during a Phillips recital on the evening of June 11, 1962. Fine's work, the *Five Preludes*, were said to have
> "had much to commend them. . . ."

B124.   Henahan, Donal. "Concert: Music by Vivian Fine Performed at Finch." New York City, New York: *The New York Times*, April 17, 1973. <u>See</u>: JC65, JC77, JC79, JC80, D9.

Review of a program of Vivian Fine music at Finch College Concert Hall where a first performance of *Missa Brevis* was conducted by Fine. The work gave reviewer Donal Henahan an

". . . impression of distant times and cool cathedrals"
(compare Shepter, Dale D. with Commanday, Robert
October 4, 1990).

Of *Concerto for Piano Strings and Percussion*, with Fine the pianist,
the writer says,

". . . absorbing in its aural sensitivity . . . in its ton-
gue-in-cheek manner (a parody, perhaps, but of
whom?)" (compare with Hertelendy, Paul, March 10,
1974).

Henahan comments that Fine writes "elegant and inventive
works. . . ." Jan DeGaetani sang Fine's songs, *The Confession* and *Two
Neruda Poems* (compare with Shere, Charles, October 27, 1981). The
latter

". . . crawling along in hushed beauty. . . ."

B125. Henahan, Donal. Concert review [unknown headline]. New York City,
New York: *The New York Times*, The New York Times Company;
Information Bank Abstracts, Saturday, May 22, 1976, pg. 21. <u>See</u>: JC84.

B126. Hertelendy, Paul. "Vivian Fine's Gift Glows at Festival." Oakland,
California: *Oakland Tribune*, March 10, 1974. <u>See</u>: JC79, JC80, D9.

Quite favorable review of Vivian Fine's performance in her triple role
as conductor, composer and pianist at the Mills College festival of
women's music. Fine presented her *Missa Brevis* for four live cellos
with soprano Jan DeGaetani as the taped voice (see and compare with
Commanday, Robert, October 24, 1982 & October 4, 1990; also
Shepfer, Dale D.). This work evoked the comment, "great lyric gift,"
from the reviewer. He felt her newer compositions had influences of
Luciano Berio (see Crouch, Tim), Henry Cowell, John Cage's "prepared
piano" and something of "Stockhausen's 'one-man band' effect."

Of Fine's conducting of the all-woman ensemble the reviewer says it
"achieves a rare tranquility."

Concerto for Piano Strings and Percussion is recalled as a "violent
clump of clangers" as Mr. Hertelendy defines the influences of Cage,
Cowell and Stockhausen in this context (compare with Henahan, Donal,
1973).

Fine's *Missa Brevis* was seen by Hertelendy as exactly the opposite,
being music that was

". . . comforting as a saintly touch . . . just as beautiful."

B127. Hertelendy, Paul. "Women are Battling for the Baton." Oakland,
California: *Oakland Tribune*, March 17, 1974. <u>See</u>: JC79, D9.

This long article is a concise overview of the woman composer in history *a propos* a four-day music festival held at Mills College that commemorated International Women's Day, March 8. Vivian Fine appeared at this festival (see Hertelendy, Paul, March 10, 1974). It would make an excellent introduction to a course on our composers of both genders.

Paul Hertelendy goes on to cite some of the severe repressions against the female composer, also many rarely known, fascinating stories about these women's musical careers. One was the infamous story of composer Carlos Salzedo who believed composing was the province of the male sex only and that the female is "'born to compose babies.'"

Hertelendy mentioned other tales about a number of women composers who, though unknown to the general public, have earned the respect of music scholars. They include the accomplished Fanny Mendelssohn, sister to Felix. Fanny's songs were published with her famous brother's name as the composer. France produced the likes of Germaine Tailleferre and Lili Boulanger, sister to Nadia. Hertelendy proclaims Lili Boulanger (Winner of the Grand Prix de Rome for composition and the first woman so honored) as "the finest feminine talent since Nannerl Mozart."

Then there was Clara Schumann married to Robert, Elena Giuranna, Betsy Jelas, Miriam Bauer, Peggy Glanville-Hicks, Ruth Crawford Seeger, Thea Musgrave, though a prolific composer, had a single record catalogued (in 1974) and Grazyna Bacewicz, prolific writer of symphonies and chamber works, who Hertelendy states "most neglected" and what a "pity" her work is so unknown and not performed.(compare Hollender, Barbara D.)

As for the contemporary women composer, Mr. Hertelendy refers to Julia Perry, Julia Smith, Louise Talma, Miriam Gideon and one he called "vanguard of the avant-garde," Pauline Olivares.

Hertelendy reported that $25,000 of grant monies was awarded to eight women composers. One of the awardees was Vivian Fine who received $8,000 from the National Endowment for the Arts to write an opera. He considers Fine as:

> "One of the most prominent Americans is Chicago-born Vivian Fine (1913). . . . Her works have been recorded from the Japan Philharmonic to the Eastman Brass Ensemble. Her piano pieces are best-known, but she writes skillfully for voice, as evinced particularly by the evocative *"Missa Brevis"* (1972). . . . Her work is moving and almost hypnotic, like the best vocal pieces of Crumb and Berio."

Article included a photograph of Fine at the piano.

B128.   Hertelendy, Paul. *"'Women in the Garden'* — Almost Opera." Oakland, California: *Oakland Tribune*, February 15, 1978. <u>See</u>: JC89.

This is one of the most unfavorable reviews of Vivian Fine's opera *The Women in the Garden* (see Fine, Vivian and Judith Jamieson). It was premiered at the San Francisco Conservatory of Music with a nine musician orchestra conducted by Alan Balter.

The four celebrated women in the cast, Isadora Duncan, Emily Dickinson, Virginia Woolf and Gertrude Stein, are said by Hertelendy, to act like a group of "withdrawn psychiatric patients" dwelling on negativity. Some of the "colossal" problems in Fine's opera, as told by Hertelendy were; lack of "conflict" and "action" (compare with Goldstein, Margery; Shere, Charles, March 1982 and also Von Bachau, Stephanie) and too many "ambiguities." Also, there was no theatricality, except one instance, wrote the critic, when the conductor lost his baton yet continued with pointed finger instead. Mr. Hertelendy declared his opinion of Fine's *Women* saying that it was

> ". . . an embroidered sampler more than . . . a world premiere opera. . . . Fine's garden yields static cameo portraits of outstanding American women writers. . . . [Fine's opera] cannot sprout . . . drama or characterization needed to restore them as living, blooming entities."

B129.   Hertelendy, Paul. "Vivian Fine Orchestrates a Symphonic Coup. Composer's New *'Drama'* Unveiled." San Jose, California: *San Jose Mercury*, January 4, 1983. <u>See</u>: JC77, JC89, JC101, D9, P64.

> "Composer Vivian Fine flew in from Vermont for Vivian Fine Week [see San Francisco Symphony, November 29, 1982]. After more than 50 years of composing, this nationally prominent figure is finally in the San Francisco Symphony limelight.
>
> Nobody had organized a 'women in music month,' but Fine's week is only one of several important women's concerts and events coming up in the Bay Area during the first weeks of 1983. Women are playing a new and stronger role in classical music, well reflected in the concert calendar. For instance:
>
> o . . . Starting with songs she wrote before her 20th birthday, Fine Week — with events starting Wednesday — will present 50 years of Fine's American music.

o For the first time in its 72-year history, the San Francisco Symphony commissioned a symphonic piece by a woman for a regular subscription concert. Fine's opus, *"Drama for Orchestra,"* will be unveiled Wednesday night at Davies Symphony Hall and repeated Saturday at Cupertino's Flint Center. The solo violinist in that program is Dylana Jensen . . .

o The indefatigable maestro (and UC Berkeley alumna) Antonia Brico, 80, a prominent Berlin conductor in the early 1930s who was later shut out of American opportunities for decades, is returning to the Bay Area to conduct the Mozart Festival of Alameda opening on Jan. 30.

o The Oakland Symphony's subscription concerts Jan. 11-15 are being led by a Frenchwoman, Catherine Comet, in a program of Beethoven, Hindemith and Howard.

o Mostly Modern, a contemporary ensemble under Laurie Steele, is performing in San Francisco Jan. 13, with composer Fine at the piano.

o The South Bay's Joyce Johnson Hamilton continues as music director of her two far-flung orchestras in Walnut Creek and Napa. Her Napa Symphony will play the *Festival Overture* by Californian Emma Lou Diemer Feb. 2.

The Bay Area is several leagues ahead of the rest of the country in women's involvement for classical music, whether as professional orchestral musicians, soloists, conductors or composers. In addition, the nearby Cabrillo Festival has featured women composers in the past.

The major focus falls now on Fine, an articulate and active professor from Bennington College who turns 70 Sept. 28 — and goes like 60 all the time, to the constant amazement of her students. Her brain moves faster yet, providing interview answers that are neatly organized into sequential paragraphs and chapters.

Her commissioned symphony work being unveiled Wednesday, *'Drama for Orchestra'* [see Carson, Josephine], incorporates her novel concept: music inspired not by a painting itself — as in this case Edvard Munch's 'The Scream' — but by what lies behind it.

'I was looking for a dramatic sequence,' she explains. 'I wanted to depict the prior psychological and emotional state of the painter and what was going through his mind.'

She calls it a very dramatic piece, inspired partly by a set of Munch paintings called 'Love.'

'Some of it is rather brutal. Munch's intensity is overpowering. I hope that my work is lyrical and fervent.'

She characterizes her current style as post-romantic lyricism.

This is a far cry from the changes of her music as a precocious teen-aged composer, which prompted composer Henry Cowell to remark on her 'unlady-like dissonances.' She was in tune with the avant-garde of the 1920s and 1930s, in the time of Varese, Antheil and other experimentalist.

Despite the widespread prejudice in America against women in music — the bigger orchestras had no women players at all except for harpists — Fine escaped, partly because she studied with one of the most successful women composers, Ruth Crawford Seeger [see Gaume, Matilda].

'I have nothing to complain about," she notes. "But I think prejudice is blatant in society.'

She recalls an exchange with a 'well-known (male) composer' when a piece of hers was played in 1958. 'Did you do it yourself?' was his ingenuous but well-meant query. 'Do you do it yourself?' she replied.

By the time she was 16, performances of Fine's work were being arranged by Cowell, whose *New Music Quarterly* on Jones Street in San Francisco brought out the work of this fast-rising Chicagoan.

Her *Two Neruda Poems,'* [see Shere, Charles October 27, 1981] to be played Sunday at San Francisco's Old First Church, features her as pianist, striking strings inside the piano with techniques derived in part from Cowell.

The young Fine was influenced early on by many composers and styles, not the least among them Dane Rudhyar, the composer-astrologer-philosopher from Palo Alto [California]. She eventually developed her own 'voice' and well-disciplined (if cautious) idiom.

Fine has a variety of accumulated work, much of it traditional in feeling. She wrote a bicentennial opera, *'Women in the Garden,'* and composed several dance scores for Doris Humphrey, Martha Graham and Charles Weidman. A number of her instrumental ideas, such as in *'Missa Brevis'* (1977), derive from collage techniques learned in electronic music. Without breaking windows or turning up the dissonance of the avant-garde's megawatt amplifiers, she shows herself an inventive spirit, open to ideas and ready to synthesize in varied ways through conventional instruments."

B130.   Hertelendy, Paul. "Violinist Ignites Brahms Concerto." San Jose, California: *San Jose Mercury*, January 7, 1983. See: JC101.

San Francisco Symphony performance at Davies Symphony Hall of Vivian Fine's *Drama for Orchestra* (see Carson, Josephine). Hertelendy stressed that had there been projections of "relatively unknown" Edvard Munch's paintings during the performance it would have improved the concert since these works had inspired the music. This was a somewhat lukewarm review of *Drama* (compare with Glackin, William; Moor, Paul, and also Commanday, Robert, January 7, 1983).
". . . often with big gaps of register and texture between her [Fine's] musical line and her accompaniment. It is a lucid, well-crafted work. . . ."
(compare with Pontzious, Richard, January 6, 1983).

B131.   Hertelendy, Paul. "Musical Survivor Finds Composer's Lives Easier Now." San Jose, California: *San Jose Mercury*, April 29, 1988. See: JC79, JC83, JC89, JC117, JC123, D9.

Hertelendy interviewed Vivian Fine and employed a question and answer verbatim format for most of this profile piece. This was occasioned by the world premiere of Fine's symphonic composition, *After the Tradition*, (see Bramhall, Robyn) which was to be performed by the Bay Area Women's Philharmonic on April 29th in Berkeley, California. Her early studies with Ruth Crawford Seeger (see Gaume, Matilda) and Roger Sessions are mentioned by Hertelendy, along with her celebrated early career in modern dance (see Ammer, Christine).

Vivian Fine told of the forthcoming biography, on her composing career, by writer, Judith Cody (publisher: Greenwood Press).

The writer described Vivian as a "low-key soft-spoken woman" who happened to be "a pioneer in her field" during a historical period "when female composers in America were virtually unknown and unrecognized." Touched upon are her "numerous major prizes," "more than 100 works" and "prejudice and poverty in the arts."

Paul Hertelendy queried the eminent composer on several points relating to the business and difficulties of the composer lifestyle. Some examples are:

"Q Aren't there immense pressures associated with full-time composing?

A 'No, I found it very rewarding. In the last 20 years I got many grants and awards. . . .'

Q Did you have any inkling around then how the whole music world would grow?

A 'No, not at all. The situation is so different. In the very early 1930s, when I started out, there were only 12 avant-garde composers in the country. Now there are thousands. . . .'"

B132.   Hertelendy, Paul. "Women's Orchestra Stakes Out its Turf." San Jose, California: *San Jose Mercury*, May 2, 1988. See: JC123.

"I was astonished to find something of Charles Ives' innovation lurking within Vivian Fine. Ives was essentially combative in his music, while on the verge of her 75th birthday Fine remains a gentle, benign commentator.

Yet Fine's piece for chamber orchestra, *'After the Tradition,'* given its world premiere Friday by the Bay Area Women's Philharmonic [see Bramhall, Robyn], lets loose softly colliding blocks of sound: a harmonious entity from the strings, a conflicting one from the winds. It's good old polytonality, of course, but toned down from adversity to dissonance: Ives revisited.

Like much of Fine's music, *'After the Tradition'* does not 'go' anywhere so much as it creates a mood, then moves on; or in this case, three moods, one for each movement.

These reflections on the Jewish tradition begin with the stasis of 'Kaddish,' marked by long pedalpoints and the wan thud of kettle drums. An oboe solo dominates 'My heart's in the East and I at the end of the West,' a segment which Fine admits is a song at heart. The closing segment, in which God makes the wilderness dance, is as lively as you might expect, with the added surprise that God has the wilderness not 4/4, not 3/4, but an elusive five beats to the measure. The finale is boisterous and rousing. The performance ran 15 minutes, several minutes longer that the composer had predicted.

Rousing audience

The performance at the First Congregational Church in Berkeley got a standing ovation; the Bay Area Women's Philharmonic drew one of the most animated symphony audiences I have encountered in America. Of course the philharmonic represents not just a musical enterprise, but a social cause. You can probably count the female conductors in the professional symphonic world on your fingers, and the all-women orchestra (like the women's philharmonic) on your thumbs.

Much to the philharmonic's credit, it stakes out its own turf. It features mostly women composers, commissioning new works regularly in addition to playing works by Cecile Chaminade, Germaine Tailleferre and, next season, Clara Schumann. . . ."
[Remainder of article covers the rest of the program.]

B133.   *Het Vrije Volk* (anon.). [Review of R. Guralnik's 1962 concert tour]. Amsterdam, The Netherlands: Fall, 1962. See: JC33.

Brief, favorable review (in Dutch) of pianist Guralnik during his European tour stop in Amsterdam. On the introduction of Vivian Fine's work for piano, *Five Preludes*, the reviewer said that:
". . . The new pieces were pianistically clever and original. . . ." [*trans.* anon.]

B134.   *HiFi Stereo Review* (anon.). "Review: *Concertante for Piano and Orchestra*." *HiFi Stereo Review* **6**, 1960: 60. See: JC42, D4.

Brief mention of Vivian Fine's recording of *Concertante for Piano and Orchestra* (compare with Jones, Ralph and French, Richard) as being   "lyrical . . . expressive . . . lacking striking individuality."

B135. Hinderaker, Miriam. "Brilliant Composer-Concert Pianist Adding Enrichment to Arts Panorama." Oshkosh, Wisconsin: *Daily Northwestern*, February 27, 1968. See: JC51, D16.

Wisconsin State University-Oshkosh's Panorama of Arts made Vivian Fine the focal point during her one week visit. Miriam Hinderaker interviewed Fine for this excellent profile piece highlighting "composer-concert pianist" Fine's long background in music and describing her functions at the Panorama of Arts. Fine's husband, noted sculpture and teacher at State University of New York, traveled with her. Ms. Hinderaker reported that as a focus of the Panorama of Arts, Fine would begin with a lecture-recital; investigate music theory and appreciation with lectures and seminars; and visit piano, modern dance and voice classes.

Fine's evening lecture-recital covered a "who's who of modern composers." Fine ended the concert performing two of her works, including *Sinfonia and Fugato*, 1952.

Part of Hinderaker's interview brought to light Vivian Fine's thoughts on "serious" versus "rock" music:

". . . Commenting on the seemingly endless abilities of youngsters to listen to loud 'pop' music, Miss Fine was unworried. 'These are just stages,' she said.

Distinguishing the difference between serious contemporary music and pop or rock, this composer explained that serious contemporary is, of course, the more complex — a continuation of a long trend which began in the 16th Century with Palestrina.

Pop or rock is influenced by sonorities or adventures in sound, she continued, a structure which relates to folk music with rhythm the strong pulse."

[Article included a photograph of Fine holding a music score.]

B136. Hixon, Don L. and Don A. Hennessee. **Women in Music. An Encyclopedic Biobibliography, Second edition**. Metuchen, New Jersey: The Scarecrow Press, Inc., pp. 350-351, 1993, 2 volumes.

Key reference work in the compilation of women's musical history. Accessible format presented with clarity, and containing a wealth of both critical and interesting data on a great number of women composers & musicians seldom found elsewhere (e. g. Fine as an "electronic music composer," also a "writer on music"). Indicating the reason for this much larger, now two volumes, edition of their book (since the 1975 edition), the authors write in the preface:

> ". . . the tremendous upsurge of interest in women's
> music that has occurred in the intervening years.
> . . ."[that would reasonably include Vivian Fine's
> music]

Thirty-eight other source titles are listed under Vivian Fine's entry.

B137.   Hodgson, Moira. **Quintet: Five American Dance Companies**. New York City, New York: Morrow, 1976, 161 pgs.

B138.   Holender, Barbara D. "Women's Music Slighted." Buffalo, New York: *Buffalo News*, July 14-18, 1984. <u>See</u>: JC89.

> "I spent the weekend of July 11-13 at the Women
> In Music Symposium on the State University of
> Buffalo Amherst Campus, and I would like to know
> where everyone else was. Where were the students,
> teachers, musicians and professed music lovers who
> should have been supporting these composers and
> performers, not because they were women but
> because they were worthy?
>
> Why, when the New Music Festival received
> extensive daily coverage in The News, was there no
> mention of this symposium, which offered such a
> variety of new music? After the initial article
> announcing the schedule of events there was not a
> word. Why did Sunday's paper ignore Joan Tower's
> powerful, exciting chamber concert of Friday night,
> and Vivian Fine's witty, challenging opera [*Women in
> the Garden*, see Fine, Vivian, and Judith Jamieson]
> performed on Saturday night? These are well-known
> composers of acknowledged ability and impressive
> credentials; it is insulting to pass them by.
>
> Barbara Harbach deserves acclaim for organizing
> the symposium and bringing together so many
> accomplished women — composers, conductors,
> instrumentalists, vocalist — in seminars and recitals.
> She was ill-served by the press and public, but the
> real losers were those who missed a rare opportunity
> to hear the music of women from the 17th century to
> the present [see Hertelendy, Paul, March 17, 1974]."

B139.   Holland, Bernard. "Music. Noted in Brief. Rosalind Rees, Soprano, Kimball Wheeler, Mezzo." New York City, New York: *The New York Times*, June 11, 1981. See: JC100.

Short review of a traditional classical music program which also incorporated the premieres of three works by American composers. Bernard Holland mentioned that Vivian Fine's work *Gertrude and Virginia* (see and compare with McKinney, Joan) was one of these premieres held at Carnegie Recital Hall. The program selections were sung by Kimball Wheeler, the mezzo-soprano and Rosalind Rees, who was the soprano. Holland stated that Fine's musical contribution
> "was a whimsical dialogue between the two writers, Gertrude Stein and Virginia Woolf. Miss Fine's touch was unfailingly light."

B140.   Holland, Bernard. "Concert: Tashi Plays the Beethoven Septet." New York City, New York: *The New York Times*, March 1, 1983. See: P63.

In this succinct review, Holland comments on a program by Tashi held in New York City at the 92nd Street Y [YMCA, Young Men's Christian Association]. Proclaimed as one of the "rare delicacies from our time" (*Violin and Piano Sonata* by Ruth Crawford Seeger), Bernard Holland further commented on the pianist, Vivian Fine as displaying
> "a wonderful crystal clarity at no sacrifice of power"
[compare McLellan, Joseph November 11, 1982].

B141.   Hughes, Allen. "Dance: End of a Festival. Limon's *'My Son, My Enemy'* Is Given." New York City, New York: *The New York Times*, August 16, 1965, page 23. See: JC70, D9.

Mr. Hughes reviewed the American Dance Festival at Connecticut College, which offered the premiere of choreographer Jose Limon's *My Son, My Enemy* (see and compare with Terry, Walter) with music composed by Vivian Fine (see Ammer, Christine). There were three other dance works on the program that night. Mr. Hughes was least pleased with Fine's and Limon's dance, "*My Son*," finding the dance one of "unrelieved hyperactivity" and "brutality" that totally disregarded the "subtleties of interaction between father and son" (the Czar, Peter, and Alexis). Hughes was not at all impressed with Fine's music for Limon's furious familial modern dance:
> "Miss Fine's music does not illuminate the progression of the dance. It is a series of starts and stops provided by piano, strings and percussion and does not say very much at all."

B142. Hughes, Allen. "Eight Composers Offer New Works." New York City, New York: *The New York Times*, September 20, 1968. See: JC68.

What Allen Hughes, rather harshly, hailed as eight of "the unlikely combinations of composers" (Blake, Thomas, Reif, Greene, Weigl, Seletsky, Hannay and, of course, Fine) gathered in a concert held at Town Hall in New York City. "This listener had to leave," quote the critic, after two hours. However, Hughes did remark on Vivian Fine's *The Song of Persephone* (for unaccompanied viola):
        ". . . And how did Miss Fine's academic study for
        the viola get in there?"

B143. Humphrey, Doris. "Music For An American Dance." *American Composers Alliance Bulletin*, Vol. VIII(1): 4-6, 1958. See: JC16, JC24, P22.

Imminent American choreographer of the modern ballet, Doris Humphrey, wrote a fascinating but somewhat short article of her impressions on composer for the modern dance, Vivian Fine. This was a companion article to Riegger's "The Music of Vivian Fine" (see Riegger, Wallingford). At the end of the article there is listed many of Fine's works and performances, even the performance times, from 1930-1956.

Fine had composed a large number of modern dance scores for most of the great modern dance choreographers in America (see Ammer, Christine). As a young woman, she had also been piano accompanist to the modern dance. Miss Humphrey called Fine the "true collaborator" and selected a work by Fine, that had been composed for Charles Weidman (*Opus 51*), as one that "stands out" for her. Doris Humphrey then discussed her idea for a dance that had, in time, become a collaboration with Fine. This dance was called *"The Race of Life."* It was based on a "series" of popular drawings by James Thurber (see Robin, Harry and also Martin, John):
        ". . . Vivian and I both loved his dry and improbable
        humor . . . the episodes met all the requirements for
        dance: plenty of action, contrast, independence from
        words. The scenes were all quite short, six of them,
        and had subject matter with a challenging image; *The
        Beautiful Stranger, Night Creatures, Indians, Spring
        Song,* culminating in the achievement of the goal
        . . . gold, pearls and money.
        . . . Fine met all these moods with imagination . . .
        full awareness of their Thurberian gaucherie and
        humor . . . she added to the all-piano score a Flexo-
        tone [see White, Edward] whose sliding eeriness

exactly met the requirements of [a] weird scene. In its
entirety it was a notable score — bright, humorous,
expert.
. . . in the dance field she has an uncanny sense of
what to choose as sound and that *sine qua non* for
dance composers, a complete understanding of body
rhythms and dramatic timing."

B144.   Husarik, Stephen, Ph.D. (editor). **American Keyboard Artists, Second
Edition**. Chicago, Illinois: Chicago Biographical Center, 1992-1993; p.
124. <u>See</u>: JC42, JC58, JC79, JC91, D1, D4, D9.

B145.   I.,K. "Humphrey and Weidman In Solo Dances." New York City, New
York: *The New York Times*, January 7, 1935. <u>See</u>: JC11, P22, P25.

K.I. tells, in his/her brief review of solo dances in recital, that Doris
Humphrey and Charles Weidman performed their own choreography to
the musical compositions of Vivian Fine. The event was held at the
Guild Theater in New York City. The pianist accompanying the dancers
in the early part of the program was the young Vivian Fine whom the
critic, K. I., judged as "excellent."

Of her compositions, there were somewhat different conclusions. Miss
Humphrey's dance, *"Credo"*, was judged, by K. I., "a fitting salute" for
this recital. "Curiously," determined the reviewer, Mr. Weidman's
choreography and dance, and his
". . . intent to convey the varying intensities with
which affirmations can be rendered . . . was an exhaustive gamut of possibilities. . . . Purely as dance
and composition, one felt a lack of connective tissue
or motive, though there were considerable vitality and
ingenuity in the statement of the work."

B146.   *ITA Journal*. Premieres [Discourse of Goatherds]. *ITA Journal* **18**:32
no.3, 1990. <u>See</u>: JC129.

B147.   Jacobson, Marion. "The Forum's Musical Metaphors." Washington
D.C.: *The Washington Post*, Wednesday, March 28, 1990, Final Edition,
Style, p. D14. <u>See</u>: JC45.

Fine was one of three contemporary composers highlighted in a
special concert by the Contemporary Music Forum. It was aptly called
"Visions Poetic and Dramatic." *The Great Wall of China*, was chosen
by Fine for her statement that Monday evening. Marion Jacobson
interpreted the *Great Wall* as manifesting

> ". . . Moments of high drama — spoken declamation
> . . . erratic interjections, . . ." [compare with Ross,
> Alex and Kosman, Joshua]

Jacobson goes on to observe that this very drama coexists alongside
". . . subtle poetic development. . . ."

B148. Jamieson, Judith and Vivian Fine. "Synopsis of *The Women In The Garden.*" Syracuse, New York: *Society for New Music, Program Notes*, March 27, 1984. <u>See</u>: JC89.

See Fine, Vivian and Judith Jamieson. Cambridge, New York for similar program notes.

B149. Johnson, Rose-Marie (compiler). **Violin Music by Women Composers, A Bio-Bibliographical Guide**. Westport, Connecticut: Greenwoood Press, 1989, p. 45, 99, 110-111, 128, 139, 162, 181-182. <u>See</u>: JC3, JC8, JC18, JC36, JC43, JC48, JC50, JC54, JC55, JC56, JC76, JC83, JC88, JC89, JC103, JC107.

Ms. Johnson notes that Ms. Fine was a Pulitzer Prize nominee. A number of Fine's works for violin (solo and chamber pieces) are included in this "Guide" with commentary. Of Fine's 1933 song, "Comfort to a youth that had lost his love [part of *Four Songs*]," (voice, violin, viola) it is observed that:

> ". . . The phrase . . . is a perfect Schoenbergian row.
> The declamation has been considered extraordinary
> . . ." [compare with Gann, Kyle].

B150. Jones, Barrie (General Editor). **The Hutchinson Concise Dictionary of Music**. Chicago, Illinois: Fitzroy Dearborn Publishers, 1999, p. 217. <u>See</u>: JC55, JC58, JC75, JC89, JC101, JC107, JC123.

"U.S. composer" Vivian Fine is logged in the "Concise Dictionary."

B151. Jones, Leslie. *The Solo Piano Works of Vivian Fine*. Ann Arbor, Michigan: Dissertation Abstracts International Section A, 55:2629A, March, 1995. The Humanities and Social Sciences, University Microfilms International, 300 North Zeeb Road, Michigan 48106-1346.

B152. Jones, Leslie. "Seventy Years of Composing: An Interview with Vivian Fine." Amsterdam, The Netherlands: *Contemporary Music Review* **16**, Parts 1-2, 1997, pp 21-26. <u>See</u>: JC2, JC7, JC16, JC23, JC24, JC30, JC35, JC44, JC55, JC63, JC69, JC71, JC77, JC79, JC83, JC84, JC89, JC101, JC121,, JC136, JC138.

Jones interviews Fine on her musical development, "reminiscences," compositional techniques among other things, in this quite informative article. Fine told the interviewer about her latest work (the interview was in 1996), which she called a "solo dramatic" composition that she likened to "*Erwartung*." Fine's daughter, Nina Karp, apparently wrote a "text" that Fine was "setting" to a rather long piece of music of "twenty to twenty-five minutes." (This "Nina's" composition, if completed, would have been the last known work by Fine). She spoke of her other daughter, Peggy Karp, as "very musical," and also a pianist.

Jones queries: "Many of your solo instrumental works . . . have a Baroque derivation. . . ." [see and compare Composers Recording, Inc., 1960]

Fine answers: "Yes; it's because I am a pianist."

Later on Fine is asked about her latest opera, *Memoirs of Uliana Rooney* (1994).

Fine answers:

> ". . . It's the high-speed biography of a woman com-
> poser [Uliana Rooney] . . . a stylistic newsreel. . . .
> She zips through life — from a send-up of *Pierrot
> Lunaire* to the turbulence of the 1960's. It isn't
> strictly autobiographical . . . because I have had one
> husband for almost sixty years and Uliana has a ten-
> dency to change husbands when her musical style
> changes . . . there are a lot of quotes from my music.
> . . ." [see Bustard, Clarke and also Friedman, Sonya].

B153.   Jones, Ralph E. "Review: *Concertante for Piano and Orchestra.*" *The New Records*, June, 1960: 3-4. See: JC42, D4.

Mr. Jones emphasizes the educational significance of listening to contemporary music. Jones states that he listens to a considerable amount of new music on records; because of this he has a brief, but of interest, comment (see and compare with Cohn, Arthur 1981 and French, Richard F. and also *HiFi Stereo Review*) on Vivian Fine's *Concertante for Piano and Orchestra*. He states that this work

> ". . . is cast in the classical mold. The "cadenza" of
> the second movement is especially interesting. Vivian
> Fine is one of the few successful women in the field
> of composition today."

B154.   Jones, Ralph E. "Review: *Alcestis.*" *The New Records*, December, 1961:5. See: JC58, JC59, D1.

Reviewing a Composers Recordings Inc. release of a collection of compositions by women composers, ("the ladies,") Mr. Jones mentions Vivian Fine's segment, *Alcestis* (see Sabin, Robert and compare with *American Record Guide*, 1962) as created for Martha Graham and company but offers no comment whatsoever. The critic insisted that only a single piece "does very much to advance the cause;" Louise Talma's *Toccata for Orchestra*. The National Council of Women in the United States partly sponsored this record leading Mr. Jones to explain that "the cause" is

> "The intention, of course, is to contradict the prevailing belief that the world of composition is a man's world."

B155.   Kahn, Erminie. "Vivian Fine, American Composer and Concert Pianist in Lecture-Recitals and Concerts." New York City, New York: Brochure by Erminie Kahn, Artist Representative, 5601 Riverdale Avenue, New York, New York. Date not noted but probably mid-1980's. See: JC42, JC59, JC70, D1, D4, P48, P53, P56, P57, P63.

This artist's brochure, produced for Vivian Fine, highlights her status as a concert pianist, renowned American composer and teacher of composition and music composition for the modern dance.

Mentioned is her recent commission, by the Rockefeller Foundation, *My Son, My Enemy*, which was a dance piece composed for the Jose Limon company, also Fine's works, *Concertante for Piano and Orchestra*, recorded by the Japan Philharmonic Symphony Orchestra and *Alcestis*, a recording by the Imperial Philharmonic of Tokyo.

> ". . . [Vivian Fine] is available countrywide for lecture-recitals, concerts . . . college-university visits of events formal and informal . . . workshops in composition or in composition for the modern dance . . . meetings with dance groups . . . activities of the music department."

B156.   Kaplan, Arthur. "San Francisco Opera Center. Rare Operas Excellent Young Talent are Forcefully Combined." *High Fidelity/Musical America* **32**:28-29, September 1981. See: JC89.

Kaplan wrote on how, recently founded, the San Francisco Opera Center began its first season with a presentation of three operas ranging from Scarlatti's *The Triumph of Honor*, written in 1718, to Harbison's *Full Moon In March* and Fine's *The Women in the Garden* (see Fine, Vivian and Judith Jamieson), the later two circa 1977. The performance was at Herbst Theater and was pronounced an "auspicious start" in

Arthur Kaplan's short review. Kaplan added (compare with Hertelendy, Paul, February 15, 1978 and Von Bachau, Stephanie and also Putman, Thomas, June 20, 1986):

> ". . . interrelationships among the texts . . . build to a stunning climax. . . . Fine writes so expressively for the voice . . . the best sections . . . were overwhelming in their effect. . . ."

B157.   Karp, Benjamin. **Ornamental Carpentry on 19th-Century American Houses.** New York City, New York: Dover Publishers, 130 pages, 1981.

Also called *Fantasies in Wood*, this is a beautifully photographed book of 19th-century houses'lavish wood details, with architectural close-ups of these Victorian beauties. In a 1988 interview at his home, Mr. Karp pointed out that he took many of the photos in the pre-Civil War established city of Troy, in upstate New York. Troy, perched on the banks of the Hudson River, is rich in splendid examples of historic edifices, and but a fifteen-minute drive from Hoosick Falls, New York, the home of Mr. and Mrs. Karp (Benjamin Karp and Vivian Fine). Most of these black and white photo studies were in the upstate New York and Vermont areas.

B158.   Karp, Vivian and Benjamin, editors. **Louis Rapkine 1904-1948.** North Bennington, Vermont: The Orpheus Press, 1988.

Essays about French scientist, Louis Rapkine, edited by the Karps (see Chapter 1, n72).

B159.   Kasander. [Review of R. Guralnik's 1962 concert tour]. The Hague, The Netherlands: *Vrije Volk*, Fall, 1962.

Brief mention (in Dutch) covering "clever playing" by pianist Guralnik during concert in The Hague. Also mentioned is how he "showed his virtuosity" in his performance of Vivian Fine's composition, *Five Preludes* . [*trans.* JC]

B160.   *Kassel.* "Hermann-Streichtrio im Amerikahaus." Kassel, Germany: March 26, 1953. See: JC3.

> ". . . Trio of Vivian Fine goes against the grain in its reckless line and is somewhat lacking in continuity. . . ." [in German, *trans.* anon.]

B161.   Kay, Richard and Markham, Kika. "Flute And Viola In Harmony."
London, England: *London Times*, January 31, 1964. <u>See</u>: JC60.

Generally favorable review of a musically varied concert directed to
the flute, viola or the combination. Vivian Fine's work, *Iconomachy*
[also called: *Duo for Flute and Viola*, 1961], brought a different
reaction from the critic:
> ". . . here the battle was evident enough but the
> characters of the disputing statues remained obscure
> and the struggle eventually became a bore."

B162.   Kimball, Alice Mary. "Vivian Fine's Career Began At Age Three."
Barre, Vermont: *Barre Daily Times*, July 29, 1955. <u>See</u>: JCi, JC23.

Charming profile piece depicting Vivian Fine's early childhood as a
musical prodigy with many new details and fresh insights added. Miss
Kimball tells the famous tale of the gentle mannered three-year-old Fine
who longed to play piano so much that she amazed her parents when
she threw a big "tantrum" and demanded piano lessons. She got them
and so began her lifetime of music devotion.
At eight-years of age, Fine wrote her first piece, *The Starving
Children of Belgium* as told here:
> "Vivian worked hard at piano lessons. Then after
> World War I and German jackboots over Belgium, a
> lot of concern over the pitiful Belgian children. . . .
> [She] was inspired to dream up her first piece . . .
> composed of dark purple chords, one more lugu-
> brious than the one before. It made her little
> playmates weep and toss [coins] into tin cans for the
> Belgian kids. . . ."

B163.   *Kingston Daily Freeman.* [Review, anon.]. Kingston, New York: August
25, 1955.

Clipping from Vivian Fine's files remarking on three of her piano
compositions, "dialogisms," as
> ". . . strong . . . dynamic . . . full of vita-
> lity."

B164.   Kino, Carol. "Vivian Fine. American Composer." San Francisco,
California: *City Arts Monthly*, January, 1983. <u>See</u>: JC1, JC2, JC79,
JC101, D9.

On the occasion of Vivian Fine Week (see San Francisco Symphony, November 29, 1982), celebrated with the San Francisco Symphony and Mostly Modern presenting a concert of her works, Carol Kino published this lengthy, and very informative profile on Fine. She includes early childhood background information (see Kimball, Alice Mary) and enlarges upon Fine's voyage through young adulthood as an experimental composer and piano accompanist to the modern dance (see White, Edward and also Ammer, Christine) after her move to New York City. There, Fine attended workshops led by Henry Cowell at the Young Composers League where she was the only member of her sex.

Kino refers to Fine's *Drama for Orchestra* (see Carson, Josephine) describing this prominent composer's strategy for creating her symphony.

Missa Brevis, for taped vocals and four live cellos, is brought up as an opportunity to expound on Fine's 'layering or collage' method combining "linear ideas" in order to find the desired amalgamation (see and compare with Carson, Josephine and also Commanday, Robert, October 24, 1982).

Furthermore, Carol Kino stated her observations on this

> "exemplary modern composer whose work has enough range in character, style and texture to support three different programs in one week, you couldn't go far wrong with Vivian Fine. Active as a composer and pianist for nearly 65 years, she's written extensively for nearly every sort of instrument and ensemble imaginable. She writes more symphonic works now than ever before. . . ."

B165. Klein, Howard. "Foundation Money Made It Happen." New York City, New York: *The New York Times*, August 28, 1966. See: JC51, D17.

Somewhat favorable review of Vivian Fine's work for piano, *Sinfonia and Fugato*. This was part of a two-disk set of 24 American composers' piano works, "beautifully performed," recorded by New Victor (2-disks LM 7042; stereo LSC 7042). The Abby Whiteside Foundation, Inc. funded this "guide to selecting modern repertory by pianists."
> " Varying Value
> Of varying intensity, ambition and value are the remaining works: . . . Vivian Fine's *Sinfonia and Fugato* . . . [etc,]"

B166. Kosman, Joshua. "Celebrating Women's Music. Vivian Fine's Birthday." San Francisco, California: *San Francisco Chronicle*, May 2, 1988. See: JC123.

The Bay Area Women's Philharmonic performed a work it had commissioned by Vivian Fine, *After the Tradition*, in Berkeley's First Congregational Church. This was also in celebration of Fine's seventy-fifth birthday. Background for the composition is remarked on (see Bramhall, Robyn). JoAnn Falletta was the music director and the horn soloist was Janet Popesco. Joshua Kosman judged *After the Tradition* (compare with Hertelendy, Paul May 2, 1988) to have been

> ". . . a wonderful 16-minute work in three movements. . . . The writing is clear and forthright. . . . The piece makes its points with a remarkable eloquence. . . . Fine displays a rare melodic gift. . . ."

B167. Kosman, Joshua. "Varèse Stands Out Among 'Mavericks'." San Francisco, California: *San Francisco Chronicle*, Monday, June 19, 2000, pg. B3.

The Chronicle's music critic, Joshua Kosman, lauds Edgard Varèse's "thunderous orchestral essay '*Ameriques*.'" He continues thusly:

> ". . . Its potent, hard-edged marriage of '*The Rite of Spring*' with the urban sounds and rhythms of . . . New York . . . creates a magnificently boisterous wall of sound. . . ." [compare with Ross, Alex]

Michael Tilson Thomas conducted the San Francisco Symphony.

B168. Kox, Wil. "Admirable Scheepenzaal Concert." Arnhem, The Netherlands: *De Nieuwe Krant*, September 6, 1983. <u>See</u>: JC99.

Reviewing (in Dutch) the "all American" Huntingdon Trio, the writer sees them as "excellent" performers who, among numerous selections, also performed Fine's *Music for Flute, Oboe and Cello*. Mr. Kox (see and compare with Brandt, Maarten, 1983) directed these few words to:

> ". . . the generally moderate tonal idiom of Loeb or Fine . . . ." [*trans.* JC]

B169. Kozinn, Allan. "4 Scarlatti Piano Sonatas." New York City, New York: *The New York Times*, May 26, 1988. <u>See</u>: JC90, D4.

Pianist Christine Dewyk's Sunday afternoon recital is critiqued here with a mention of her interpretation of Vivian Fine's *Momenti* as "endowed with character and charm." Mr. Kozinn's interpretation of Fine's work was as

> ". . . six vignettes that alternated between hazily soft edged and rhythmically sharp. . . ."

B170. Kozinn, Allan. "Chamber Group Offers 5 Premieres." New York City, New York: *The New York Times*, June 9, 1988. See: JC119.

Quite favorable review of five works performed by the Catskill Chamber Players; two were by Henry Cowell and Lou Harrison with one work by Vivian Fine. Fine's wind quintet, *Dancing Winds*, was seen by the critic, Mr. Kozinn, as being able
". . . to break the sugary spell. Slightly acerbic . . . touches of humor and a lively sense of dialogue . . . wit and concision."

B171. Kozinn, Allan. "Concentration and Finger Power." New York City, New York: *The New York Times*, February 1, 1989. See: JC112.

Kozinn writes of pianist Veda Zuponcic's "uncompromisingly difficult" works for piano for her concert at Weill Recital Hall. The concert started with Fine's 1987, *Toccatas and Arias*, which is noted here as a "first performance." It was indeed the world premiere of this work. Kozinn was apparently most impressed with the *Toccatas*
". . . thunderous explorations of the keyboard's full range. . . ."
and also impressed with pianist Zuponcic's interpretation of the demanding piece.

B172. Kozinn, Allan. "Pamela Frank, a Violinist, in New York Recital Debut." New York City, New York: *The New York Times*, Sunday, April 22, 1990, Section B: The Arts/Cultural Desk, pg. 9. See: JC132.

Mr. Kozinn relates that violinist Ms. Frank had had a work commissioned especially for this debut which was one of the Great Performers Series at Lincoln Center. This premiered work was *Portal*, by Vivian Fine. Kozinn describes *Portal* as:
". . . a robust opening . . . slow, haunting middle section . . . intense, extroverted finale . . . in a Spartan language. . . ." [compare with Anderson, Martin]

B173. Kozinn, Allan. "Vivian Fine, 86, a Composer for Voice, Orchestra and Ballet." New York City, New York: *The New York Times*, Friday, March 24, 2000, Late Edition-Final, Section B, Pg.9. See: JC16, JC18, JC24, JC30, JC31, JC58, JC70, JC84, JC89, JC138.

B174. Landis, David and Linda Edelman. "San Francisco Symphony presents Vivian Fine Week Jan. 5-13: World Premiere of SFS-Commissioned Work Featured." San Francisco, California: San Francisco Symphony,

Public Relations, November 29, 1982. <u>See</u>: JC8, JC50, JC82, JC83, JC85, JC89, JC97, JC101.

Landis and Edelman summarized the extraordinary event, Vivian Fine Week (see San Francisco Symphony November 29, 1982) conferred upon this famous composer by the San Francisco Symphony in cooperation with Old First Concerts and Mostly Modern. Landis and Edelman remarked that Fine's *Drama for Orchestra*, commissioned by the San Francisco Symphony, was one of the "highlights." The writers wrote a schedule of the music, lecture, concert and exhibit events that went on in the Bay Area during Fine Week. They also noted Fine's career in modern dance (see Ammer, Christine and White, Edward), her numerous awards and her chamber opera, *The Women in the Garden*. Fine's opera was produced by the San Francisco Opera in 1981.

> ". . . Vivian Fine has been on the teaching staff of New York University, the Juilliard School of Music and the New York State University at Potsdam. She was one of the founders of the American Composers Alliance, serving as its vice-president from 1961 to 1965 and since 1964 she has taught at Bennington College in Vermont. . . ."

B175. Lebrecht, Norman. **The Companion to 20th-Century Music**. New York City, New York: Simon & Schuster, 1992, p. 120. <u>See</u>: JC55, JC89.

Perfunctory reference to Fine's lifework; but two works are listed.

B176. Levine, Amy Miller. "Honors Go to Fine." Walnut Creek, California: *Independent Journal*, January 21, 1983. <u>See</u>: JC59, JC89, JC101, D1.

Amy Miller Levine interviewed Vivian Fine on the occasion of her recently premiered symphony, *Drama for Orchestra*, which was commissioned by Dr. and Mrs. Ralph I. Dorfman for the San Francisco Symphony as the centerpiece for a salute to her, Vivian Fine Week (see Carson, Josephine and San Francisco Symphony, November 29, 1982).

Levine wrote that Fine was organizing materials in readiness for the events during "Fine Week" as she met with the interviewer in a San Francisco, North Beach studio. She spoke of her background in music, early education (see Riegger, Wallingford) and of her mother's positive influence on her "'commitment to music.'" In passing, Fine's *The Women in the Garden*, aided with an NEA Grant (see Hertelendy, Paul, March 17, 1974), and also a commission from Martha Graham for *Alcestis* were reported.

The interviewer said of Vivian Fine Week that
> ". . . the event made history because it is the first time that a woman has been given this chance. . . . A prolific composer at home in many mediums, she seems to thrive on her work, truly enjoying her success. Although she has no specific style per se, there is a strong sense of line and lyricism in many of her compositions."

B177. Library of Congress. "Program Notes for the Concert 'New Music' Between the World Wars at The Coolidge Auditorium." Washington, DC: November 12, 1982. See: JC8, JC45, P63.

Comments on Cowell's publication "*New Music*" which originally published most of the works heard at this concert where Vivian Fine performed on piano. Reference was made to the publication in "*New Music*" of Fine's *Four Songs* and *The Great Wall of China*. Fine performed the first public performance of Ruth Crawford's *Sonata for Violin and Piano* (1926) on this program (see McLellan, Joseph 1982; Holland, Bernard March 1, 1983).

B178. Library of Congress. "Premiere of Vivian Fine Work to Mark Founder's Day." Washington, DC: *Information Bulletin* v.44, no.43, October 28, 1985. See: JC8, JC105.

The Elizabeth Sprague Coolidge Foundation commissioned a string quartet and soprano work to celebrate her birthday (Sprague's). Vivian Fine wrote *Ode to Henry Purcell* for Founder's Day, an annual event each October 30.
The concert was taped for radio WETA-FM (on December 12) and heard elsewhere through American Public Radio. In this announcement Fine was mentioned as
> ". . . one of the founders of the American Composers Alliance, serving as its vice-president from 1961 to 1965, and was music director of the Rothschild Foundation from 1953 to 1960."

B179. Library of Congress. "Program Notes for the Founder's Day Concert, The Elizabeth Sprague Coolidge Foundation." Washington, DC: The Coolidge Auditorium, October 30, 1985. See: JC105.

This was the premiere of Fine's *Ode to Henry Purcell*, 1985 (see Library of Congress, October 28, 1985), for soprano and string quartet, at the Coolidge Auditorium in the Library of Congress. Remarks included Fine's faculty appointments at the Juilliard School, the State University of New York at Potsdam, Bennington College, and New York University.

B180. *Los Angeles Times.* "Obituaries; Vivian Fine; Composer Of Ballet Scores, Operas." Los Angeles, California: Times Mirror Company, Saturday, March 25, 2000, Home Edition, Part A; pg.22. See: JC16, JC24, JC30, JC58, JC70, JC89, JC138.

B181. Lowens, Irving. "Timpani Features Fine Phillips Recital." Washington, DC: *The Washington Evening Star*, June 9, 1964. See: JC48.

The critic, Irving Lowens, called this "unusual recital," which featured the timpani, "a substantial musical success." Jesse Kergal was the soloist at the Phillips Collection. Lowens wrote a positive comment, relating that Vivian Fine's *Divertimento for cello and percussion* (cello, percussion and timpani)
> ". . . involved the soloist in some astounding gym-
> nastics; it was indeed quite diverting — both to the
> eye and the ear. . . ."

B182. Luse, Betty R. "Pianist Plays with Authority." Newport News, Virginia: *Daily Press*, November 4, 1983. See: JC102.

Favorable review of *Double Variations for Piano Solo* by Vivian Fine performed at Phi Beta Kappa Memorial Hall at the College of William and Mary. The pianist was Claudia Stevens and the program was repeated in December at Carnegie Hall, New York. Ms. Luse reported that *Double Variations for Piano Solo* was one of the "outstanding" pieces, adding:
> ". . . Though lacking in tonality, the textures and
> colors of sound and the complex rhythmic variations
> created an exciting and listenable work."

B183. Lynerd, B.A. "Discovery: the Sky's the Limit: A Celebration of 20th Century American Music for Flute." *Women of Note* 5(1):110, 1997. See: JC82, JC117, D6, D8.

A note of the recording of *Emily's Images* and *The Flicker* on Crystal CD's.

B184. Malitz, Nancy. "San Francisco Gives Ovation to Vivian Fine." *USA Today*, January 6, 1983. See: JC101.

A short piece commenting on Vivian Fine Week in San Francisco (see San Francisco Symphony, November 29, 1982) and the premiere of her *Drama for Orchestra* performed there in Davies Hall. Nancy Malitz regarded Fine Week as a "precedent-setting" occasion and wrote that the seventy-year-old Fine was the

> ". . . doyenne of American female composers, [Fine] was astounded by the celebration surrounding the premiere. . . ."

B185.   MacAuslan, Janna and Kristan Aspen (compilers). **Guitar Music by Women Composers: An Annotated Catalog**. Westport, Connecticut: Greenwood Press, 1997, p. 52. See: JC136, D3.

Canciones y danzas [*Canzones y Dances*], a chamber work with guitar, flute and cello composed by Vivian Fine, is recorded in this catalog. This was Fine's only known work for classical guitar (see Cody, Judith, 2001).

B186.   Martin, John. "Dance: Lorca's New York. Juilliard Performs Doris Humphrey's Choreography of Poet's Work." New York City, New York: *The New York Times*, April 28, 1956, 10:6. See: JC16.

Mr. Martin mentions that *Race of Life*, (1934) written for dancer-choreographer Doris Humphrey by Vivian Fine is a "revival;" the ballet having been inspired by the art work of James Thurber (see Humphrey, Doris). Mr. Martin wrote no review of the dance as he candidly admitted "the hour was late" and Julliard was very far from his home.

B187.   McKinney, Joan. "Vivian Fine: A Woman of Note." Oakland, California: *Oakland Tribune*, April 2, 1975. See: JC2, JC65, JC79, D9.

A brief overview of Vivian Fine's career as a composer touching on her early childhood as a musician and on her studies with Ruth Crawford Seeger (see Gaume, Matilda) and remarking on the composer's works for the modern dance with greats, Doris Humphrey, Martha Graham, Jose Limon, Charles Weidman and Hanya Holm (see Ammer, Christine and also White, Edward). Her manuscripts for the modern dance had been placed on exhibit at the Lincoln Center Library of the Performing Arts in 1974.

As this article was written, Miss Fine was on sabbatical since she had just received a National Endowment for the Arts grant for $8000 to write a chamber opera, "entitled 'Famous Women,'" (which was to become *Women in the Garden*) and a composition for string quartet and chorus.

Fine was also giving a series of concert-lectures at the California State University at Hayward and at the University of California in Berkeley. A photograph of Fine at the piano is included with the article. Fine's *Four Pieces for Two Flutes*, *The Confession* and *Missa Brevis* were performed. Joan McKinney comments on Fine's chamber opera in progress, "Famous Women" that it

> ". . . will include Gertrude Stein, Virginia Woolf and Isadora Duncan. It will be, she [Fine] hopes, 'a witty work.' It may also embrace some of the feelings that Ms. Fine had developed as a result of the women's movement.
>
> . . . Ms. Fine hopes that any form of musical 'segregation' will eventually disappear, and that music by women will be included, no longer as a 'token,' but as good programming in concerts."

B188. McLellan, Joseph. "Brave 'New Music' at the Library of Congress." Washington, DC: *The Washington Post*, November 11, 1982. See: P63.

[Not mentioned in this review is that this Library of Congress program was organized by Vivian Fine.]

Mr. McLellan discusses the November 1982 premiere of Ruth Porter Crawford's (sic) *Sonata for Violin and Piano* written in 1926. Crawford, who died in 1953, had taught composition to the young Fine. Vivian Fine was the "magnificent partner," on piano, to violinist Ida Kavafian for the sonata which was praised as "a masterpiece" by the critic. Mr. McLellan believed that such concerts as this, should "become one of its [the Library of Congress] most distinguished traditions."

Included in this "remarkable" concert were the works of Henry Cowell, Carlos Chavez, Wallingford Riegger, Adolph Weiss, Dane Rudhyar, Aaron Copland and Colin McPhee much of whose music had appeared in *New Music* magazine (1927).

In her role as pianist, Fine performed *The Corpse*, by Leon Ornstein and a Carlos Chavez sonatina for violin and piano:

> "Kavafian . . . had a magnificent partner in Vivian Fine. . . . (She) donated the manuscript of the sonata to the library. Fine, better known as a composer but also a superb pianist, played in two other striking works. . . ." [compare Holland, Bernard March 1, 1983].[see B177]

B189. McLellan, Joseph. "Eloquent Sessions; Atlantic Quartet Excels at 'Founder's Day.'" Washington, DC: *The Washington Post*, Thursday, October 31, 1985, Final Edition, Section: Style; pg. B2. See: JC105.

Ode to Henry Purcell, for voice and string quartet, by Vivian Fine made a "world premiere" at a special concert held in the Library of Congress commemorating 'Founder's Day' [see Library of Congress, October 28, 1985 and October 30, 1985]. Fine's work had been commissioned by the "eponymous foundation sponsors." McLellan contends that Fine's composition is:

> ". . . a significant addition to the limited repertoire for
> voice and string quartet. . . . Her [Bryn Julson] deeply
> involved, musically precise performance contributed
> greatly to the music's impact. . . ."

B190. Mengelberg, Karel. [Review of R. Guralnik's 1962 concert tour]. Rotterdam, The Netherlands: *New Rotterdamse Courant*, Fall, 1962. See: JC33.

Quite short commentary on pianist Robert Guralnik's tour stop in Rotterdam. His playing is seen as "almost perfect" while Vivian "Fine's well written *Five Preludes*" [*trans.* JC] are given a favorable word (compare with *Rotterdamsch Parool*, 1962).

B191. Mersel, Constance V. "3 Artists Perform In Vassar Concert." Poughkeepsie, New York: *Poughkeepsie Journal*, November 1, 1962. See: JC48, JC64.

Favorable review of concert at Vassar College where Fine's *Divertimento for Cello and Percussion*, (1951) was performed "excitingly" by Sterling Hunkins, cellist with percussionist James Coover. Fine's *October Pieces* were dedicated to Hunkins and she played them on piano. Of *Divertimento* Ms. Mersel states:

> ". . . cello plays fluid, lyric lines, the percussion
> section emits tense, terse, rhythmically complex
> statements . . . different instruments lent variety to
> both texture and pitch . . . audience was enthusiastic."

B192. Mertz, Margaret. "Meet MFAF Festival Composer Vivian Fine." Sangre de Cristo, New Mexico: *Sangre de Cristo Chronicle*, August 24, 1989. See: JC130.

Ms. Mertz compares Vivian Fine to Georgia O'Keefe in this long profile article on the occasion of her composer-in-residence for the 1989 Music from Angel Fire. Fine had composed a new work for Angel Fire, that would be *Madrigali Spirituali* (see Noble, David), written for trumpet and string quartet. This work premiered on August 27 at a concert honoring women composers. On September 1, Fine's *Teisho* (see Ariel, January 1983) was performed in Taos.

Margaret Mertz wrote of hearing the world premiere performance of Fine's *Triple Goddess* on April 22, during Boston's Vivian Fine Week (see Caldwell, Mary). Mertz wrote that *Goddess* was

> ". . . based on the story of the triple goddess — Night, Order and Justice — who rules the universe, while her courtship with the Wind results in the birth of Eros, who in turn creates the earth, sky, sun and moon of our world. . . . The music . . . is dense, deep and very slow. The sounds enfold the listener . . . instruments of the wind ensemble emerge singly from the chorus of low brass . . . builds slowly to a loud climax . . . ends in strength — truly a mirror image of a creation myth."

The reporter covered some of the important details of Fine's long career in music (see Gaume, Matilda and Ammer, Christine and also White, Edward). When Mertz asked Fine "why" she might have created such and such a composition; Vivian Fine's reply was characteristically concise and clear:

> ". . . 'I just had an idea, and I did It.' No complicated psychological explanations or intellectual analysis supports her work . . . if she feels creative, she writes music."

B193. Miller, Margo. "Marquee; A New Music Harvest Will Be Reaped in October." Boston, Massachusetts: *The Boston Globe*, Sunday, April 16, 1989, City Edition, Section: Arts & Film; pg. B42. See: JC51, JC128.

Miller reports on the start of a new music festival, New Music Harvest/Boston 1989, also there is mention of a Boston area-wide program "Share a Composer," (see Boston, City of; April 16-22, 1989); Fine was chosen for this "Share a Composer" program and was therefore involved in numerous public discussions on her methodology of music composition. Her talks and concerts took place in a wide variety of institutions according to Miller, who states that Vivian Fine:

> ". . . this 'Dean of American Women Composers,' as she is often called, rates a flow chart to keep track of her activities."

Miller further noted some of the places Fine's works, and/or talks, were performed: Plymouth State College, Plymouth, N.H., the Boston Musica Viva, Longy School of Music in Cambridge, the Boston Musica Viva (see Dyer, Richard, April 22, 1989), Boston University, Tufts University, Harvard University, Northeastern University and the Boston Conservatory. At Sanders Theater, The Harvard Wind Band Ensemble

performed *Triple Goddess*, a first performance (see Mertz, Margaret).
"Fine's visit" ended with the American Women Composers' fourth
annual marathon which was at the First Parish Church, Watertown, here,
Fine's *Sinfonia and Fugato*, was performed.

B194.   Mitgang, Herbert. [headline unknown]. New York City, New York: *The
New York Times*,; Information Bank Abstracts, Thursday, May 22, 1980,
Section 3, pg. 18.

Announces "awards ceremony" for Fine's induction, with ten others,
into the American Academy and Institute of Arts and Letters.

B195.   *Montclair Times*. [Review anon.]. Montclair, New York: March 8, 1951.
See: JC33, P39.

Brief but positive remarks for Vivian Fine's piano performance of her
own *Five Preludes*. Place unknown.
    ". . . compelling confidence . . . musical insight. "

B196.   Moor, Paul. "San Francisco Symphony: Fine *'Drama for Orchestra'*
[premiere]." *High Fidelity/Musical America*, 33:24, April, 1983. See:
JC89, JC101.

A lively and favorable review of Vivian Fine's *Drama for Orchestra*
(after paintings of Edvard Munch), performed during Vivian Fine Week
(see Carson, Josephine and also San Francisco Symphony, November
29, 1982) by the San Francisco Symphony. Dr. and Mrs. Ralph I.
Dorfman had commissioned *Drama* for the SFS and this was its world
premiere. Moor wrote that the audience reaction was one "bordering on
ovation" to the performance of *Drama* under the baton of Edo de
Waart. Moor termed the audience's powerful statement "a rarity" for
most contemporary classic music today.
    Paul Moor comments that it is the "The Scream," the name of the
fourth movement, where he judged that Fine "most brilliantly" realizes
her art (compare with Flandreau, Tara and also Glackin, William). The
writer believed that the program should have included at least black-
and-white photographs of the five Munch paintings that inspired Fine's
symphony (compare with Hertelendy, Paul, January 7, 1983)
    Also remarked upon, is Fine's *The Women in the Garden* performed
by the San Francisco Opera in 1982.
        "The San Francisco audience absolutely *loves* Vivian
        Fine and her music. . . . Obviously an unusually
        warm reception awaits her here any time she cares to
        return."

B197. Moore, Kevin. "Musicians Outshine Compositions." Syracuse, New York: *Syracuse Herald-Journal*, March 28, 1984. See: JC89.

Review of a program of "untested" modern music which included Vivian Fine's *The Women in the Garden* (see Fine, Vivian and Judith Jamieson). Fine's 1977 *Garden* had been performed, "tested," about eight times before this review. Mr. Moore found the hypothesis forming the opera "fascinating;" celebrated women meet in a "surreal situation." Fine chose Virginia Woolf, Gertrude Stein, Isadora Duncan and Emily Dickinson for the rendezvous in her "surreal situation" sung to a small yet "seemingly loyal" audience at Carrier Theater and presented by the Society for New Music. Mr. Moore wrote, with good reason, that the performance of the opera "was strong" though he remarked that as long as one could read the opera's text, Fine's work was "vivid," adding that it was

> ". . . possible that the libretto is too philosophically complex for totally effective musical treatment. The opera is deserving, however, of much closer attention than can be given in a single, first hearing" [compare with Goldstein, Margery; Hertelendy, Paul, February 15, 1978; Shere, Charles, March 1982; also Morton, Brian and Pamela Collins].

B198. Morton, Brian and Pamela Collins (eds.). **Contemporary Composers**. Chicago, Illinois: St. James Press, 1992. See: JC1, JC2, JC3, JC7, JC9, JC10, JC16, JC17, JC18, JC21, JC23, JC24, JC26, JC27, JC30, JC31, JC32, JC33, JC35, JC36, JC37, JC39, JC40, JC41, JC42, JC43, JC44, JC45, JC46, JC48, JC49, JC50, JC51, JC52, JC53, JC54, JC55, JC56, JC57, JC58, JC59, JC60, JC61, JC62, JC63, JC65, JC66, JC67, JC68, JC69, JC70, JC71, JC72, JC73, JC74, JC75, JC77, JC78, JC79, JC80, JC82, JC83, JC84, JC86, JC87, JC88, JC89, JC90, JC91, JC92, JC93, JC94, JC97, JC98, JC99, JC101, JC102, JC104, JC105, JC106, JC107. Article includes references to JC1, JC24, JC26, JC42, JC45, JC55, JC58, JC89, JC101, JC102.

There is listed a sizable amount of Fine's compositions by category, more than can easily be found elsewhere. Her Dollard Prize, 1966; other awards are noted. The latest work listed is Fine's *Ode to Purcell* (1984). Bea Weir has divergent and interesting commentary on Fine as a composer. Among the authors keen observations; Fine's ". . . considerable dramatic force [of Fine's orchestral works], . . ." and in the vocal composition, *Guide to the Life Expectancy of a Rose* Weir notes, "her instinctive feminism. . . ." Fine's extraordinarily received chamber

opera, *The Women in the Garden*, 1977, ". . . merits a revival . . ." according to Weir, whose essay on Vivian Fine concludes:
> "An important presence on the American scene, Fine is still too little known elsewhere. She is [a] highly significant composer, original, unfailingly individual and wry, quite unlike anyone else."

B199. *Music Educators Journal.* "Premieres: *A Bust for Eric Satie.*" *Music Educators Journal* **66**:106, March, 1980. <u>See</u>: JC92.

Announcement of the premiere in Bennington, Vermont of *A Bust for Eric Satie*, May 11, 1979.

B200. **Music in Print. Master Composer Index 1999.** Philadelphia, Pennsylvania: MUSICDATA. Inc., Music-in-Print Series, Vol. XC, Vol. XCa (A-L), 1999. <u>See</u>: JC8, JC45, JC86, JC94.

The Music-in-Print series contains many volumes such as; String Music-in-Print, Classical Vocal Music in Print, Orchestral Music in Print, etcetera. Only five of Fine's works are listed in the **Master Composer Index.**

B201. *Music, The.* "Meet the Composer: Press Release for the Aviva Players Concert Series." New York City, New York: The Mannes College of Music, March 12, 1979. <u>See</u>: JC83.

Announcement for a "Meet the Composer" event presented by the Mannes College of Music with the Aviva Players and Vivian Fine as the guest. This was the world premiere of Fine's *Teisho* (1977) (see Ariel, January 1983) which was commissioned by the Aviva Players. The work is for mezzo-soprano, violin and piano. Fine is hailed as
> ". . . one of America's best known women composers. . . ."

B202. *Musical Leader, The.* "New Forms of Composition." *The Musical Leader*, January, 1932. <u>See</u>: JC2, P5.

An arresting account describing the first concert where the Young Composers' Group (eight) displayed their various compositions in the modern music idiom of that era (1932).
Some of the composers offering their works were: Bernard Hermann, Jerome Moross (who used texts from *Jabberwock* and *Those Gambler's Blues* in his two songs), Israel Citkowitz (whose *Sonatina for piano* subtitled *Invention*, *Chorale* and *Rondino* were "excellently played" by

Fine), Irwin Heilner, Henry Brant (he and Fine played Engel's work *Phobias*) Elie Siegmeister and the lone female, Vivian Fine (*Four Pieces for Two Flutes*).

Vivian Fine on "fascinatingly rhythmical" piano and Henry Brant on percussion terminated the concert with an anonymous *Music for Five and Ten Cent Store* (Henry Brant). The work incorporated a goodly selection of kitchen "instruments." The audience had a splendid time "vigorously" supplying applause.

> "Young Composers Group Together — Milk Bottles and Kitchen Equipment Employed"
> "Time must prove whether their neo-classic tendencies, atonal harmonizations, and definite attempt to eschew any display of personal emotion will form a school. . . . [Fine's work] studies in dissonant counterpoint which showed balance and especially in the second number a certain degree of poetry."

B203. Newlin, Dika. "Piano Concert Aimed at Connoisseurs." Richmond, Virginia: *Richmond Times Dispatch*, November 7, 1983. See: JC102.

Dika Newlin's short commentary on a contemporary music lecture-recital given to honor Elliott Carter's seventy-fifth anniversary in the North Court Recital Hall at the University of Richmond. Among the five new works commissioned for the event was Vivian Fine's *Double Variations* which was a composite of her own motif together with one of Carter's. Newlin wrote that there was

> ". . . no discrepancy in the materials of this multi-textured work filled with dramatic contrasts and intellectually controlled dissonances."

B204. Newtown [Announcement.] "Romanticism and Impressionism in Painting and Music." Newtown, New York: June, 1950.

Announcement of an "experimental venture" where husband and wife team, Benjamin Karp and Vivian Fine, presented an "informal lecture and concert" (see Kahn, Erminie) evening. This was an exploration of classical music (performed on piano by Miss Fine) and visual arts (analysis by Mr. Karp) from "Romantic expression into the Impressionistic." A profile of sculptor and teacher Mr. Karp, this piece cited his Carnegie Fellowship; his sculptures in the Metropolitan Museum and the Museum of Modern Art; also, that he was the head of the Art Department at the State Teacher's College, Montclair, N. J.

Mention is made of Fine's notable background credits. She was to play works by Debussy, Chopin and Liszt. The event took place on June

24th at 8:30 in the Edmond Town Hall in Newtown in the Alexandria
Room.
> ". . . since these two artists are not only gifted . . .
> thoroughly trained professionals, it should prove to be
> an entertaining . . . exciting evening. . . ."

B205. *New Paltz Independent.* "Vivian Fine Heard on Composer's Forum."
New Paltz, New York: about February 8, 1959. <u>See</u>: JC55, JC56.

Short comment on Vivian Fine's chamber-opera, *A Guide to the Life
Expectancy of a Rose* (staged by Martha Graham) and her *String
Quartet*, both in concert at the Composer's Forum at the Donnell
Library Center, New York City. This piece quoted quite positive
appraisals, from the *New York Times* and the *Herald-Tribune*, on Fine's
music. At the time of the article, Fine's husband taught at the State
University Teacher's College, New Paltz;
> ". . . In private life Miss Fine is wife of Benjamin
> Karp, professor of art. . . ."

B206. *New Paltz Independent.* "Celebrated Dancer to Present Work by Vivian
Fine." New Paltz, New York: April 13, 1960. <u>See</u>: JC58, D1.

Announcement for a new Graham Dance Company modern dance with
music created by Vivian Fine and named *Alcestis* (see Sabin, Robert).
It was a work for chamber orchestra to be performed at the 54th Street
Theater in New York City on April 29th, 30th and May 5th and 8th,
1960. Fine had dedicated *Alcestis* to the renowned Martha Graham who
> ". . . will dance the principal role, with . . . three
> male soloists. . . ."

B207. *New Paltz Independent* (anon.). "Vivian Fine To Play In Riegger's
Quintet." New Paltz, New York: April 20, 1960. <u>See</u>: P45.

B208. *New Paltz Independent and Times* (anon.). "Vivian Fine's Work To Be
Played At Carnegie Hall." New Paltz, New York: February 14, 1962.
<u>See</u>: JC42, JC58, JC60, D1, D4.

A new Vivian Fine composition (*Duo for Flute and Viola*) is
announced entitled "*Iconomacky* [sic] (war against images)." The work
was to be premiered at Carnegie Recital Hall and was reported to have
been written for flutist Claude Monteux (conductor of the Hudson
Valley Philharmonic Symphony). Walter Trampler played viola.
   Mention was made that Fine's *Alcestis* was being performed for the
third year in a row by the Martha Graham company at the Broadway

Theater in New York City in the coming March. In passing, the *Times* relates that Miss Fine was also the newly elected vice-president of the American Composers Alliance.
> "In private life Miss Fine is Mrs. Benjamin Karp of
> 19 Prospect St., New Paltz."

B209. *New Paltz News.* [Review, anon., of ICSM concert at New Paltz State Teachers College, April 16, 1953]. New Paltz, New York: April 23, 1953. See: JC36, P40.

Brief remarks on Vivian Fine's *Three Pieces for Violin and Piano* saying that they were
> ". . . most interesting selections . . . unusual composi-
> tions. . . ."

B210. *New Paltz News* (anon.). "Chamber Music Concert Is Scheduled for the College." New Paltz, New York: November 12, 1958. Also, *The Oracle*, November 14, 1958 (the college newspaper). See: JC48, P44.

Announcing a free concert of American composers and their musical works for percussion instruments. The concert was held in the College Union Lounge at the State University Teachers College, New Paltz on the Tuesday afternoon of November 18, 1958. Vivian Fine's *Divertimento for Cello and Percussion* was performed and she also acted as a pianist;
> "Miss Fine, who resides in New Paltz, will also be
> represented as a composer. . . . Fine has composed
> dance works for Doris Humphrey, Charles Weidman
> and Hanya Holm. . . ."

B211. *New York Herald* (anon.). "Tribute Paid to Russia in Concert at Town Hall." New York City, New York: May 1, 1944. See: JC43, P36.

The *New York Herald* reported the following facts on a concert (directed by Lazare Saminsky) sponsored by Congregation Emanu-El and in honor of Russia; young Russian composers' piano works were performed as well as Russian folk songs, religious music and modern Russian piano music; also on the program was
> ". . . Vivian Fine's well made *Capriccio on a Russian
> Theme* [*Rhapsody on a Russian Theme*], written for
> the piano and played by Miss Fine. . . ."

B212.   *New York Herald-Tribune* (anon.). "American Composers Will Meet at Yaddo to Give and Discuss New Works." New York City, New York: February 27, 1932. See: JC7, P10, P11.

As related in this announcement, seventeen American composers had their compositions selected to be premiered at a Yaddo festival of music and conference with composers and critics. Among those so distinguished were Vivian Fine, with her *Four Polyphonic Piano Pieces*, (see Engel, A. Lehman, October 1932) and George Antheil.

In 1932 Yaddo, at Saratoga Springs, was still the private estate of Mr. and Mrs. Spencer Trask where fifteen of the composers would be guests. The event spanned April 29th to May 4th 1932.

"Several hundred invitations have been issued for the three concerts, which will be given on Saturday morning, Saturday evening and Sunday afternoon."

B213.   *New York Sun*. [No title, anon.]. New York City, New York: April 25, 1932. See: P9.

A capsule announcement for integrating "interests" of "modern music, song and movement [dance]" at a new series of symposiums. This first event was said to be for "moderns" and held at the Dance Center. Vivian Fine, A. Lehman Engel, Ruby Mercer and Henry Brant were some of the composers and artists assisting that Thursday evening.

B214.   *New York Times* (anon.). New York City, New York: review broadcast over WQXR because newspaper not being printed, December 22, 1958. See: JC50.

Capsulized radio review of the Composer's Showcase at the Nonagon Gallery. Vivian Fine's *Sonata for Violin and Piano* was performed. The anonymous writer wrote that according to Eric Salzman, Fine's work contained

". . . substance . . . free chromatic idiom with great skill. . . ." [compare with Von Gunden, Heidi]

B215.   *New York Times* (anon.). "Reprise." New York City, New York: *The New York Sunday Times*, February 15, 1959. See: JC55.

A brief round-up of area music performances. From the Modern Music list, "outstanding performances" included Fine's *A Guide to the Life Expectancy of a Rose*, a chamber opera, which was reported to be

". . . the most 'entertaining' work at the Composer's Forum."

B216.   *New York Times.* [no title, anon.]. New York City, New York: The New
York Times Company, Information Bank Abstracts, Section 3, pg. 23,
Friday, April 4, 1980.

Announces the election of eleven new members to the American
Academy and Institute of Arts and Letters including Vivian Fine.

B217.   *New York Tribune* (anon.). "Prokofieff Ballet Is 4th Offering Of Dance
Center." New York City, New York: Date Unknown, 1932. <u>See</u>: P4.

Vivian Fine was the young pianist accompanying the American
premier of Prokofieff's *L'Enfant Prodigue* at the Dance Center's newly
inaugurated programs for the ballet.
"Vivian Fine played the piano and competently."

B218.   Nilsson, B.A. "'Women in Music' is Refreshing." Albany, New York:
Albany Times-Union, March, 1987. <u>See</u>: JC97.

This concert featuring "Women in Music" hailed such composers as
Clara Schumann, Cecile Chaminade and Vivian Fine (*Trio for Violin,
Cello and Piano*).
B. A. Nilsson summarized Fine's work as "characteristically lean and
dissonant." Fine was present. Expounding on the "justification" for this
category of concert that spotlighted music by women, Nilsson said that
". . . some justification . . . could be found in the fact
that composer Vivian Fine . . . was learning music
before women were allowed to vote."

B219.   Noble, David. "Fine's *'Madrigali Spirituali'* Featured Depth, Power."
Albuquerque, New Mexico: *Albuquerque Journal*, August 29, 1989.
<u>See</u>: JC130.

In this commendatory critique Vivian Fine's new work, *Madrigali
Spirituali*, was seen by David Noble, to be
". . . Everything you could ask for from a 12-minute
quintet . . . simplicity, approachability, depth, power
. . . beauty . . . diffused, slightly austere harmonic
language . . . was virtually atonal. . . . [*Madrigali
Spirituali*] breathed fresh melodic air . . . combined
. . . transparency . . . spiritual uplift of Renaissance
polyphony . . . [and] plain sentiment of Anglo-Amer-
ican fold melody . . . the complex psychological probing of musical modernism."

Madrigali is a quintet for trumpet and strings in six movements. It was especially composed for the Music from Angel Fire festival where Fine was composer-in-residence (see Mertz, Margaret) for 1989. Noble related that it was performed at Angel Fire resort's Village Haus as part of a concert of women in music. He added that a composition by Fine's early teacher and mentor, Ruth Crawford was also performed. The audience was as impressed with Fine's work as was the critic, Mr. Noble.

B220.   Page, Tim. "Music: Schuller Leads U.S. Composers Group." New York City, New York: *The New York Times*, February 23, 1985. See: JC107, P67.

Various works are recapped here, by Mr. Page, as performed by the American Composers Orchestra at Alice Tully Hall in New York City. The night's "dreary" program was conducted by Gunther Schuller. Vivian Fine was piano soloist for her piano concerto *Poetic Fires* (from the Greeks) (see and compare with Galardi, Susan). Page asserted that
        ". . . Sounds came and went — evanescent, some-
        times lovely . . . little apparent sense of thrust to their
        argument . . . there might be more drama in the solo
        part than Miss Fine allowed. . . ."

B221.   Page, Tim. "De Waart On Mozart: 'A Purity.'" New York City, New York: *The New York Times*, January 25, 1986. See: JC101.

Edo de Waart is interviewed by Tim Page on his musical interests, past and present. As past director of the San Francisco Symphony he developed his "reputation as a new-music specialist" and desired to continue this in his Minneapolis career.
    De Waart also discussed the composers whose works he premiered with the San Francisco Symphony. Some of those composers were, he said, Elliott Carter, Ellen Taaffe Zwilich, Roger Sessions and Vivian Fine [*Drama for Orchestra*]. De Waart added:
        ". . . The composers we played in San Francisco
        didn't have much in common with one another, but
        all were eloquent musicians. . . ."

B222.   Page, Tim. "Music: Song Cycles of 20's and 30's." New York City, New York: *The New York Times*, September 30, 1986. See: JC8.

The Alliance for American Song presented a musical program entitled "American Song Cycles of the 1920's and 1930's." As told by Tim Page, the event was held at the Gustavus Adolphus Lutheran Church on a Sunday afternoon. Some of the composers whose works were represented were Vivian Fine, Virgil Thomson and Henry Cowell. Page said that mainly, the program was "an engrossing one" and added these "engrossing" thoughts about the *Four Songs* (see and compare with Gilbert, Steven E. and also Shere, Charles, January 15, 1983) by Vivian Fine:

> ". . . an early work and scored for soprano and string quartet, called to mind a particularly pristine, angst-free distillation of Alban Berg — spare, contrapuntal music that is angular but always singable."

B223.   *Pan Pipes of Sigma Alpha Iota.* "Judges Named for SAI Competition." Winter, 1983.

Report on a solo piano composition competition for Sigma Alpha Iota Inter-American Music Award for the triennial 1981 to 1984. Composer-judges were the "distinguished American composers," Vivian Fine and Miriam Gideon.

Fine's early background (see Gaume, Matilda) and "varied compositions" were noted.

B224.   Paris, Barry. "'Women in the Garden': Something New in Opera." Pittsburgh, Pennsylvania: *Pittsburgh Post-Gazette*, February 23, 1979. See: JC89

A somewhat different viewpoint is put forth by Barry Paris in his critique of Vivian Fine's chamber opera *Women in the Garden* (see Fine, Vivian and Judith Jamieson August 1981) performed at Carnegie-Mellon University. "Actual historical figures" coming together in an imaginary meeting, as do the opera's Gertrude Stein, Virginia Woolf, Isadora Duncan and Emily Dickinson, is extremely unusual in the "rarified atmosphere of opera." Therefore, the critic views Fine as a "pioneer" shaping the "brilliant" female characters into "viable theatrical property" (compare with Goldstein, Margery also Putnam, Thomas, June 20, 1986 and also Hertelendy, Paul, February 15, 1978 and Moore, Kevin).

Overall, a positive, constructive commentary though Mr.Paris believes there is need of certain script refurbishment. On Fine's score Mr. Paris sees no such disharmonies and he declared it to be

> ". . . full of dissonance, sudden changes in rhythm and key, dispensing almost completely with melody and harmony, eerie and melancholy . . . almost always very intriguing. . . . It's the enchantingly stark precision of the pure music itself which rescues these "Women" from their dubious libretto and gives the work its potentially powerful impact. . . ."

B225. Parmenter, Ross. "Music: A New Concert-Giving Group. B. de Rothschild Unit Inaugurates Series." New York City, New York: *The New York Times*, May 16, 1956, 39:1. See: JC55.

The B. de Rothschild Foundation for the Arts and Sciences inaugurated its first concert in what was Martha Graham's major dance studio (her dance school was located in the basement of the building) at the former Lenox Hill Children's House.

Ross Parmenter went on to describe the concert in Graham's studio. Five front rows were folding chairs. The Rothschild Foundation had commissioned Fine's *Guide to the Life Expectancy of a Rose* for this premiere performance. *Il ritorno d'Ulisse in patria*, by Monteverdi, dominated most of the program's time while other music selections seemed "wisps by contemporary composers." This rendition of Vivian Fine's *Rose* had Earl Rogers, tenor, and Miss Beardsley as the singers with violin, harp, clarinet, flute and cello. Mr. Parmenter observed (compare with Riegger, Wallingford) that Fine's *Rose*

"... was a sung version of an article about hybrid tea
roses. . . . After fourteen-minutes the humor implicit
in setting so unlikely a text was frayed. . . ."

B226. Parmenter, Ross. "Filling a Gap: A Summary of Reviews of Unpublished Days." New York City, New York: *The New York Times*, January 4, 1959. See: JC50.

News item recapping some of the area's smaller music performances. They had received no reviews during the past seventeen days when no newspapers had been published in New York City. Mr. Parmenter writes about Vivian Fine's composition performed at the Composer's Showcase :

. . . *Sonata for Violin and Piano* had "substance,
strength and consistency." [see and compare Von
Gunden, Heidi]

B227. Parris, Robert. [Review]. Washington, DC: *The Washington Post*, June 12, 1962. See: JC33.

Succinct remarks on Vivian Fine's "little preludes" [*Five Preludes*]. Place or event unknown. The fifth prelude is deemed by Robert Parris as "quite stunning." The critic's opinion of the other four preludes is that they were "depressingly nondescript."

B228. Parsons. **The Mellon Opera Reference Index**, 1986, v.2. See: JC55.

Operetta, one act: *The Guide to the Life Expectancy of the Rose*, February 7, 1959, Donell Library Center, New York City, New York.

B229.   Patterson, Catherine. "A Fine Romance. Currents World-Premieres *'Memoirs of Uliana Rooney*,' a Multimedia Chamber Opera." Richmond, Virginia: *Richmond Times-Dispatch*, Style Weekly, September 6, 1994. <u>See</u>: JC138.

Patterson interviewed Vivian Fine on her then new opera *Memoirs of Uliana Rooney*, in 1994, when Fine was eighty-years-old. She says that the opera is "autobiographical," but Fine makes sure to mention for the record that Uliana's marriage score, she is wed eight times in the opera, is not to be confused with the composer's real life. Fine was "married to the same man for 50 years."

The opera has a "whimsical, hopeful" conclusion: Uliana remarries her second husband. (see Bustard, Clarke)

Sonya Friedman is the filmmaker and librettist. The article announces *Uliana's* world-premiere at the University of Richmond's Camp Theater; performed by the new music ensemble, Currents.

B230.   Pennell, Knowlton E. "Chamber Percussion Numbers Mark Storm King concert." Middleton, Vermont: *The Middleton Times Herald*, August 21, 1962. <u>See</u>: JC48.

Concerning the final chamber music event of the summer at the Storm King Chamber Music Concert series, reviewer Pennell was impressed with the unusual program including two modern works for percussion ensemble, or "musical explosives." James Coover was the percussionist and the musical director was Sterling Hunkins. Apparently, Galliard's *Para Alejo* was the original program selection. But, at the last minute Vivian Fine's *Divertimento for Cello and Percussion* was selected as a replacement for the Galliard work. There is no reason stated. Pennell expresses ample enthusiasm for the percussion "numbers" with these words for the Fine composition:

> "This is a weird avant-garde piece which makes the ear strain for compatibility. The strange barrage of soft dissonances responding between 'string' and 'skin' made originality almost lose its meaning. One would hesitate to say that a rapport had been established, but the eagerly-alerted atmosphere indicated that a general 'sizing up' was rippling through the audience."

B231.   Perkins, Francis D. "Junior Group of Composers Offer Concert." New

York City, New York: *New York Herald Tribune*, January 16, 1932.
See: JC2, P5.

Francis D. Perkins reported that in the first concert of the Young
Composers' Group (see *The Musical Leader*) the young Vivian Fine
performed as both pianist and composer. She played Israel Citkowitz's
sonatina for piano and joined Henry Brant to perform a ballet scene
from *Brum Phobias*, by composer A. Lehman Engel. In the later half
of the youthful concert, Fine's *Four Pieces for Two Flutes* was intoned
by Robert Bolles and Carl Moore.
Mr. Perkins stated unequivocal interest, throughout his critique, for the
work of the eight fledgling musical geniuses. He wrote of them and,
lastly, Miss Fine's work for two flutes:
> "20 Works by 8 American Musicians, All Under 25,
> Make Up Program. Members' Age Limit 28. Diatonic
> Paths Eschewed for Dissonant Harmonies. . . . [Fine's
> work] made able use of the contrast between the
> upper and lower register of the instrument."

B232.   *Perspectives of New Music.* "For Aaron. An Offering." *Perspectives of
New Music*, 1981:19.

B233.   *Perspectives of New Music.* "In Memorium Roger Sessions. 1896-1985."
Spring-Summer, 1985, p. 144-146. See: JC90, D4.

Vivian Fine contributed a copy of her score for *Momenti*, a piano solo,
to this issue of *Perspectives* where it was reprinted. Her score was
signed and notated in her own writing:
> "In honor of the 150th anniversary of Schubert's
> death and dedicated to Roger Sessions."

B234.   *Philadelphia Evening Bulletin.* [Review, anon.]. Philadelphia,
Pennsylvania: November 22, 1946. See: JC35, P37.

In a piano recital in Mitten Hall, at Temple University, Vivian Fine
performed her "main number," Schumann's *G minor Sonata*, then
presented her own piano work, *Suite in E-flat major* for this
> ". . . interesting program and [Fine] earned enthus-
> iastic applause. . . ."

B235.   *Playbill.* "Martha Graham and Her Dance Company." New York City,
New York: *Playbill* (a weekly magazine for theatergoers), April, 1960.
See: JC42, JC55, JC58, D1, D4.

Over the years, Martha Graham had collaborated with numerous composers who form the profiles in this article. As indicated in *Playbill*, Vivian Fine, as newcomer to the Martha Graham Company, was also profiled here including a mention of her *Concertante for Piano and Orchestra*. Fine's earlier collaboration with Graham , *A Guide to the Life Expectancy of a Rose* (see Riegger, Wallingford), "with staging by Miss Graham" and, also, Fine's "new" composition *Alcestis* (see Sabin, Robert) is included here.

B236. Pontzious, Richard. "Symphony's Plans: Big Names, Missing Names." San Francisco, California: *San Francisco Examiner*, April 21, 1982. See: JC101.

Comment on the recently released events and concerts planned for the 26-week 1982-83 San Francisco Symphony subscription season. Plans for the new season of music
". . . include[s] a mini-festival honoring American composer Vivian Fine. . . ." [see San Francisco Symphony, November 29, 1982]

B237. Pontzious, Richard. "Fine Music Not Played Well." San Francisco, California: *San Francisco Examiner*, January 6, 1983. See: JC8, JC101.

"One of the most important activities on the San Francisco Symphony's busy calendar is the yearly mini-festival of living composers, a week-long event inaugurated last year with programs featuring music by Sir Michael Tippett, and continued this week with music by Vivian Fine.
This week, Edo de Waart and the orchestra are playing Fine's new *'Drama for Orchestra.'* On Sunday, the 69-year-old composer will participate in an all-Fine Chamber concert at the Old First Church. Next Wednesday she'll be at the San Francisco Conservatory for a free public symposium. A week from today, the Mostly Modern Orchestra will play her *'Four Songs'* at the Vorpal Gallery.
Rarely does a community have the opportunity to hear so much variety from a single artist in such a concentrated time. Imagine, having been able to participate in a question-and-answer session with Beethoven; having been close enough to Wagner to query him about a passage in 'Tristan.' That's the kind of experience the Symphony is providing, with

these modern-day meet-the-composer concerts.

Of the music we hear, who can accurately gauge its worth? Some of it will be highly successful. Some will be forgotten in a month. It's not important. The benefit is in the experience and the close proximity to composers whose music may be played for generations.

Last night, the Symphony's subscription audience heard the world premiere of Fine's *Drama,'* a work for large orchestra conceived after paintings by Scandinavian artist Edvard Munch.

It's an intriguing work, not so much a grabber as a piece that nibbles at the ear. While a tonal center may be hard to pin down, several traditional flowing melodic lines and rich *tutti* chords provide a distinctively Romantic flavor. Melodies are built on intervals that recall music by Bela Bartok. Many are harmonized and orchestrated in a manner not atypical of Shostakovich.

Built by layering fragmented pieces one atop the next, its fragments deserve closer scrutiny, the placement of those fragments, hours of study.

Each of the score's five separate movements represents a state of feeling evoked by five of Munch's paintings. "The Scream" is just what the title suggests. "The Midsummer Night" unfolds following a lovely oboe melody played over hushed, sustained strings. "The Embrace" might have been created to capture the impulsiveness of young lovers, while "Jealousy" finds the lovers — and the orchestra — in turmoil, only to be calmed again in "Two Figures by the Shore."

The imagery is never clouded, yet one longs for music with greater depth. The emotions have a superficiality, an obviousness. Perhaps it's the method of composition, the layering of ideas, but this reviewer continually longed for the introduction of contrapuntal invention.

A second hearing is definitely in order, as is another week of orchestral rehearsals and another month of study by de Waart. Even with score in hand, it is difficult to fully enjoy the music's richness. The maestro had his head buried in the manuscript, and the orchestra was on safari looking for lost notes.

It was not a good night for the hometown band or its leader. De Waart appeared to be suffering jet lag following his return from conducting engagements in Europe. The *"Linz" Symphony* of Mozart, with which he opened the concert, had all the freshness of day-old beer. As Michael Steinberg reminds us in his unusually brief program notes, the symphony's first movement is supposed to be festive, not funereal.

One might also remind de Waart that the first movement's development section requires a tightly pieced-together performance. The puzzle pieces can't be strewn all over the stage, as they were last night. With so blatant neglect of the obvious, its useless to complain about such things as phrasing and articulation.

The basic elements of performance didn't get better with the last work of the program, Brahm's *Violin Concerto*. In for the solo, and her Symphony debut, was Dylana Jenson, 21-year-old protegee of Nathan Milstein. How she plays on any given night, I cannot say. Last night, she started strongly and went down hill. Her tone was raw, her approach to the score markedly unsophisticated. Undoubtedly she has a substantial amount of technique at her disposal, but it wasn't on hand for this performance. She looked nervous, and she sounded that way.

It's unfortunate that the Symphony extends itself to feature a major composer, then plays her work with so little care, but it's a crime that they do it, then surround it with muck. Absolutely 27th-rate." [compare with Shere, Charles, January 7, 1983; Hertelendy, Paul, January 7, 1983 and January 4, 1983; also Commanday, Richard, January 7, 1983]

B238. Pontzious, Richard. "Seven Works Seek a Theme." San Francisco, California: *San Francisco Examiner*, January 10, 1983. See: JC77, JC82, JC83, JC85, JC89, JC97, JC101.

"Composer Vivian Fine is currently the object of the San Francisco Symphony's affections. Her *'Drama for Orchestra'* was premiered Wednesday, while several of her chamber pieces were played by Symphony members yesterday at the Old First Church.

After hearing seven of her works, I'm baffled. Her stylistic choices are so varied [see and compare with quote of Henry Brant in Bramhall, Robin, 1988], it's difficult to tell whether recent pieces represent artistic growth or new directions. No one score relates to the last. If there's a single unifying factor, it is in the construction of the pieces. While Fine may not be the most artistically inspired or inspiring of composers, she is without question a skilled, sensitive craftswoman.

Her works tend to open threateningly, with material that's at once tonally ambiguous and atonally ambitious. Seldom, however, do they end up that way. Final movements in large works and closing moments in smaller scores are remarkably conciliatory.

The opening of her *Trio for Violin, Cello and Piano* (impressively rendered by Daniel and Machiko Kobialka and Peter Shelton), is a cacophony of sound, with each of the instrumental voices pulling in opposite directions. The texture is harsh, violent, confused. Musical activity is lost under volcanic explosions of sound. In the elegiac finale, however, the mood is placid. Calm has been restored, melodies have become part of a harmonically austere tapestry.

Although the 30-year-old violin sonata ends with a spirited finale, the sense of resolution is the same. Beautifully executed by the Kobialkas, the sonata is a richly expressive, intense, emotional work.

'Teisho,' a collection of pieces for violin and piano, is less effective. Created, one presumes from the title, as representations of Zen sermons, I found the harmonic figures in the violin and the abstract wanderings in the piano forced. It may have been the performance, but I found the piece lacking in compositional clarity and potency [see and compare with Ariel, January 1983].

In her libretto for *'Women in the Garden,'* a chamber opera produced by the San Francisco Opera Showcase a year ago, Fine used texts from several sources. For *'Nightingale,'* a song for mezzo-soprano and light percussion, she borrowed from Keats, T.S.

Eliot, John Lyly, Richard Barnefield, and the **Ency-clopedia Britannica.** As in the opera, the verse is transposed, with one line of Keats butting up against another of the Lyly. The result is disconcerting verbal nonsense [compare with Capparela, Richard].

Musically, however, she's on to something. Though the technique is oversimplified in this score, the idea is solid. If only she would allow her audience to enjoy the verse without the transpositions, as she does in two *Neruda Poems, 'The Turtle'* and *'Ode to the Piano'* [see and compare with Shere, Charles, October 27, 1981].

In these settings as well as in *'The Flicker,'* for solo flute, Fine's sense of the drama and humor are obvious. Certainly nothing was lost on flutist Leone Buyse or mezzo Stephanie Friedman, whose vocal portrayal of the songs was done with the composer sitting at the keyboard and hovering over the piano strings, plucking out an accompaniment."

B239. Powell, S. Morgan. "Nini Theilade Dances Her Way Into Hearts Of Montreal Audience." Montreal, Canada: *The Montreal Daily Star,* March 12, 1935. See: P24.

In this positive review of the "beautiful" twenty-year-old dancer Nini Theilade in her debut, Vivian Fine is also given an enthusiastic critique. Powell notes that Fine was the "masterly . . . ideal accompanist" to the dancer and offered her own solo rendition of Debussy's *La Puerta del Vino* on the pianoforte.

". . . an ideal accompanist, exhibiting perfect under-standing of . . . mood . . . rhythm. . . ."

B240. Press, Jacques Cattell. **Who's Who in American Music, Classical First and Second Editions.** New York City, New York: R.R. Bowker Company, 1983 and p. 180, 1985. See: JC75, JC77, JC84, JC86, JC89, JC101.

This volume's one hundred and six word biographical entry on the works and awards of Vivian Fine notes:

". . . her composition study with Ruth Crawford-Seeger and Roger Sessions, piano study with Djane

Lavoie-Herz & Abby Whiteside."

B241. Putnam, Thomas. "'Women In Music' — A Promising Star." Buffalo, New York: *The Buffalo News*, July 20, 1986. <u>See</u>: JC89

Mr. Putnam covered part of a three-day symposium at the State University of Buffalo Amherst campus. He wrote that *Women In Music* was organized by Barbara Harbach. Vivian Fine's chamber opera, *The Women in the Garden* (see Fine, Vivian and Judith Jamieson), was the music symposium's "big event," though there were some 28 events and two other operas. The concert was sparsely attended.

Four paragraphs, by Putnam, suggest one dilemma of the 1980's; considering, what does one call a female who composes or a female who happens to be a musician?

Putnam indicates that he had spent considerable thought and made efforts at fairness in his address of women in music; mentioning that he found terms such as "women composer wordy," and "woman flutist exclusive." He had once used "concertmistress" then discovered his "mistake." Parenthetically, he states that Vivian Fine voiced no opposition to the title "Women in Music." Putnam's analysis of *Garden* is genuinely positive; he also remarks on its "feminist spirit" (Compare with Ratliff, William and also Burrell, Margo).

> "The text is somewhat irrational. The music for the four female voices is remarkable, a richly textured quartet. The Tenor relates to the women [see and compare with West, William D.]. . . . The opera has feminist spirit, but is amusing, not bitter. . . . The opera is amusing and lively. Its density is not too thick. The orchestra provides some lightness in its jazzy, ragtime music, and the scoring is sensitive, often spare and carefully colored." [see Fine, Vivian. 1948]

B242. Putnam, Thomas. "Harpsichordist Barbara Harbach Amplifies Instrument, Composers." Buffalo, New York: *The Buffalo News*, February 10, 1987. <u>See</u>: JC112, D19.

A review on the occasion of Barbara Harbach's recital for harpsichord. According to Putnam, two harpsichords were employed for her recital; one of which was amplified. One of the contemporary works she performed on the amplified harpsichord was Vivian Fine's *Toccatas and Arias*; this work having been especially composed for Ms. Harbach. The recital took place at the State University of Buffalo Amherst Campus in Baird Recital Hall. Mr. Putnam directed a number of favorable

remarks to Fine's *Toccatas and Arias*; some of them follow:
"... It is bracing ... brisk, playful ... clear. ...
[Her] music emphasizes the play of the mind; line
seems uppermost in her music. ... It is not trading
on some well-used emotion. ... [Her music] is neo-
classical. ..."

B243. Rabben, Linda A. "First the Notes, Then the Music." Grinnell, Iowa:
The Grinnell Magazine, Fall, 1981. <u>See</u>: JC97.

Ms. Rabben's almost fourteen-hundred word article stands out as a
unique, educational exploration of Vivian Fine's music. Through the
living interaction of composer, musicians and music one can gain
deepest insight into the meaning of the living composition.

The Mirecourt Trio had commissioned a work by Fine, *Trio for
Violin, Cello and Piano,* and would premiere *Trio* at the Unity Temple
in Oak Park, Illinois. In order to study the complex process that the
Mirecourt Trio, in collaboration with the composer, would have to
undertake to bring *Trio*'s "threateningly complex" score sketched from
an idea in the mind of Fine to finished music before the audience;
Rabben chose to follow this process, step by step. The reporter traveled
with violinist Kenneth Goldsmith, cellist Terry King, and pianist John
Jensen, throughout the rehearsals until the process was complete at the
premiere night.

Rabben reported that there had to be numerous collaborative moments
with the composer, Fine, both over the phone and later in person.
Matters of tempo, phrase and interpretation had to be defined, shaped
and mastered during countless hours of rehearsals.

Ms. Rabben explained how each member of the trio began by
practicing their part alone, at home, until the three finally were
comfortable performing all parts together. The chamber ensemble would
continue to rehearse Fine's work during the 12-day tour. After hearing
Trio ten times the reporter wrote, "it's a genuinely moving experience."

"The first half of the second movement moves
devilishly fast, considering its complexity. ... By the
third rehearsal, they could play the first movement in
tempo. ...
... at the fourth rehearsal, when they played the first
movement through at tempo. ... It seemed less
gothic, more romantic. ... Jensen said at the fifth
rehearsal's end that Fine had asked them to make the
piece 'rhapsodic' and they'd added rubati, accents and
other interpretative elements to fulfill her intentions.
... Intellectual angularity smoothed by interpretive

devices, the second movement really began to make
sense at the eighth rehearsal. . . ."

B244. Randel, Don Michael. **The Harvard Biographical Dictionary of
Music.** Cambridge, Massachusetts: The Belknap Press of Harvard University Press, 1996, p.268. See: JC58, JC59, JC75, JC89, JC90, JC101

". . . Copland was an important supporter after her [Fine's] arrival in
New York. . . ." [at the age of only eighteen-years][see Copland,
Aaron], Randel mentions.

B245. Ratliff, William. "The Opera Showcase Was an Interesting, but
Inconclusive, Experience." Palo Alto, California: *The Peninsula Times
Tribune*, April 2, 1982. See: JC89

In his review of Vivian Fine's chamber-opera, *The Women in the
Garden* (see Fine, Vivian and Judith Jamieson), Mr. Ratliff believed that
it started with a "fascinating idea" but somehow "didn't quite work"
(Compare with Putnam, Thomas, July 20, 1986 and Shere, Charles,
April 3, 1982). *The Women in the Garden* was performed under the auspices of the American Opera Project at Herbst Theater in San Francisco.
    Audience members were provided with librettos, wrote Ratliff. Though
some parts of Fine's opera came across, according to the critic the
"fascinating idea" of four women of genius meeting, Gertrude Stein,
Emily Dickinson, Virginia Woolf and Isadora Duncan, left him with
these thoughts:
> "It sounds good on paper, but for me it didn't quite
> work. First, many of the words did not project. . . .
> No one could read it [the libretto] since the lights
> were too low . . . sung philosophy tends to be pre-
> tentious and/or trivialized philosophy. Take Stein's
> opening and closing lines: 'Man is man was man will
> be gregarious and solitary. . . .' Oh, ho hum."

B246. Raymond, Jennifer. "Vivian Fine." London, England: *The Guardian*,
Guardian Newspapers Limited, April 10, 2000, pg.20. See: JC7, JC18,
JC42, JC55, JC84, JC89, JC101, JC138.

Background details along with praise form the body of this obituary
for Vivian Fine. Ms. Raymond writes of Fine as a: ". . . prolific composer . . ." and creator of a ". . . tremendous repertoire. . . ."

B247. Reinthaler, Joan. "Huntingdon Trio." Washington, DC: *The Washington
Post*, Monday, May 4, 1981, Final Edition, Performing Arts, p. B9. See:

JC99.

> Vivian Fine's *Music for Flute, Oboe and 'Cello* has sparse but positive mention in this summary of the year's fifth concert by the Huntingdon Trio performed at the National Gallery as part of the American Music Festival. Fine's work had been written under a commission from the Huntingdon Trio. Ms. Reinthaler responded to *Music for Flute, Oboe and 'Cello* by writing that Fine's composition
>> ". . . maintained a compelling intensity and energy
>> level while exploring intriguing ideas."

B248. Reis, Claire Raphael. **Composers in America; Biographical Sketches of Contemporary Composers with a Record of their Works**. New York City, New York: Macmillan, 1947.

B249. *Richmond Times-Dispatch*. [Review, anon.]. Richmond, Virginia: November 25, 1973. <u>See</u>: JC75, D13.

> Review of a concert at Virginia Commonwealth University and, in addition, favorable comment for a new recording by four faculty composers from Bennington College in Vermont. This was a Composers Recordings, Inc., SD 260 entitled "Music From Bennington" (see and compare with Frankenstein, Albert). Vivian Fine's *Paean* along with the works of Henry Brant, Louis Calabro and Lionel Nowak were included on the record.
> Fine's composition was inspired by three excerpts from "Ode to Apollo," by the poet Keats, and is performed by women's chorus, brass ensemble and tenor-narrator. Ms. Fine conducts on this release.
>> "The chorus makes use of a large gamut of groans,
>> hisses, shrieks and cheers. Ms. Fine enjoys playing
>> with a line like: 'From a virgin flower flows/ A hymn
>> of spotless chastity. . . .'"

B250. Richter, Marion Morrey. "A Salute to American Women Composers. 1970 NFMC 'Parade' Concert in New York." *Music Clubs Magazine*, Spring, 1970:13-15. <u>See</u>: JC63, D7.

> Ms. Richter reported the events of a radio broadcast program highlighting women composers in America and "originated" at Carnegie Recital Hall. Quite favorably mentioned is the world premiere of Vivian Fine's *Fantasy for Cello and Piano* which was broadcast by WNYC in New York City, according to the reporter.
> The article included a photograph of Fine with four other women composers present at the concert.

Richter had this to say about composer, Fine:
> ". . . long known for her distinguished contribution to
> American Music. . . . Her works have been widely
> performed in this country and Europe. . . . *Fantasy* is
> a strongly structured work. . . . A work of power and
> originality. . . ."

B251. Riegger, Wallingford. "The Music of Vivian Fine." *American Composer's Alliance Bulletin*, **VIII**(1):2-6, 1958. See: JC2, JC8, JC16, JC17, JC42, JC55, D4.

In this approximately seventeen-hundred word treatise, Wallingford Riegger analyzes Vivian Fine's music throughout various periods in her life. He outlines her childhood studies on a music scholarship to the Chicago Musical College (at the age of five), piano with Djane Lavoie-Herz, harmony and composition with Ruth Crawford Seeger (see Gaume, Matilda and also Tick, Judith), counterpoint with Adolf Weidig, then more of the same with the addition of orchestration with Roger Sessions (see Copland, Aaron). Fine was to carry on her piano education under the tutelage of Abby Whiteside.

Fine's "earlier period" ends in 1937 and is "atonal" and illustrates no "twelvetone writing," according to Mr. Riegger (see and compare with Ariel). The "charming" *Four Pieces for Two Flutes* is his example from this period and demonstrated Fine's "mastery of dissonant counterpoint."

1937 to 1944 was the "second period" in Fine's music life with *The Race for Life* (see and compare with Robin, Harry), composed for Doris Humphrey (see and compare with Humphrey, Doris), an example of this "more diatonic style" as the outstanding trait in this period. Riegger further added, that *Race for Life*, had been "brilliantly scored for small orchestra."

At the time of the article, 1958, Mr. Riegger identified a third and last period in Fine's career, this "marked by a return to atonality, tempered occasionally by key impressions" (compare with S., C. June, 1978). He selected *A Guide to the Life Expectancy of a Rose* as the hallmark of this "third and last period." An article by S.R. Tilley in the *New York Times* was Fine's inspiration for *Rose*. Riegger comments:
> ". . . By the use of exaggerated stresses and clever
> prosody she has transformed the pedestrian serious-
> ness of the words into something hilariously funny."

Henry Cowell (see. Carson, Josephine January 1983) is quoted from a review in *Musicalia* as he wrote that he believed Vivian Fine was one of the "the most interesting" of the composers in the United States.

Riegger quotes from an in-depth musicology analysis, by William

Treat Upton (see Upton, William Treat), of the early songs of Vivian Fine. Here, her two songs are seen as exemplary representatives of the art of song, "well nigh perfect," according to Treat in 1938.

Also quoted is Lazare Saminsky (see Saminsky, Lazare, February 1, 1941), as seen in the *Musical Courier*, as he describes Fine's contribution to music in overwhelmingly positive terms touching upon her songs (compare with Shere, Charles, January 15, 1983) and also *Concertante for Piano and Orchestra*.

Riegger closed his essay with the thought that (in 1958) "recognition" for Fine's outstanding work in music was "long overdue." Certain details from his commentary on *A Guide to the Life Expectancy of a Rose*:

> ". . . Throughout . . . there is plenty to intrigue the academic mind . . . the haunting beauty of these words: 'The flowered climber cannot be relied on in all cases' [Example 5: depicts three-part canon]. . . . This is first stated instrumentally, then repeated *in toto* with the voice *au dux*. There are recurring themes, or rather fragments, but seldom a direct repetition as such, thus heightening the disarming casualness of the music. At the close, lest one take it all too seriously, the 'man' intones again and again the provocative thought, 'And it is, and it is . . .' while the 'woman' . . . has the complete sentence: 'And it is impossible to quote any real statistics as to the longevity of a rosebud. . . .'"

B252.   Riemann, Hugo. **Erganzungsbande, Hrsg. C. Dahlhaus**. Mainz, Germany: B. Schotts Sohne, vol.1 (A-K), 1972.

B253.   Robin, Harry. "Miss Morini Triumphs At Philharmonic Concert." New York City, New York: *The New York Times*, April 16, 1961. <u>See</u>: JC17.

This is a short review of a program by the Hudson Valley Philharmonic that included Vivian Fine's *The Race of Life*, originally written as a modern dance for Doris Humphrey in 1937 (see Humphrey, Doris). Mr. Harry Robin refers to *Race* as "THE NEW WORK" (his caps) and wrote with enthusiasm about its new presentation along with images of Thurber's drawings (James Thurber's drawings were instrumental in forming the concept of *Race*; a witty perspective on an "American middle-class family"). The effect caused the audience to laugh during most of the orchestra's performance adding to the evening's "fun."

Robin's exuberant remarks include:

> "[Fine's] music is extremely witty and well adapted

to the drawing . . . or was it vice-versa? . . . Unusual
musical effects . . . a 'flexitone'[*sic*] [see White, Ed-
ward] and a police siren.
  Altogether a delightful concert!'"

B254. Rockwell, John. "Music By Women Given In Festival." New York City,
New York: *The New York Times*, March 10, 1975. See: JC45

Mr. Rockwell reviewed a long afternoon concert featuring music by
women as part of an International Women's Arts Festival and declared
it a "rewarding affair." Women from many cultures contributed music
along with Vivian Fine's *The Great Wall of China*.
  Writing that most of the compositions weren't "overtly feminist,"
Rockwell later remarked on three compositions that he called
  ". . . Western classical avant-garde music . . . a bit
  short on vitality next to the other music, although a
  compulsive Kafka setting by Vivian Fine did stand
  out [*The Great Wall of China*]."

B255. Rockwell, John. "Song: Miss Schonbrun." New York City, New York:
The New York Times, March 1, 1978. See: JC77.

John Rockwell reported on an event called the First Festival of
Women's Music at the City University of New York Graduate Center.
Historical women composers (see Hertelendy, Paul March 17, 1974)
were featured and also contemporary music. The reviewer said the
highlight was a troubadour song written in the twelfth century by the
Countess de Dia. Certain other selections were by Fanny Mendelssohn-
Hensel, Clara Schumann, Lili Boulanger, Ursula Mamlok and Vivian
Fine who offered her *Two Neruda Poems* (see and compare with Henahan, Donal, 1973 and also Shere, Charles, October 27,1981). Among
many selections, Fine's work brought forth Rockwell's comment:
  ". . . and two fascinating Pablo Neruda settings by
  Vivian Fine [*Two Neruda Poems*]. No sweeping
  generalizations about the place of women composers
  in history were possible on the basis of this music
  alone [the entire concert]. But the music itself was
  often very fine."

B256. Ross, Alex. "Record Brief [CRI CD 658]." New York City, New York:
The New York Times, Sunday late edition, Sec. 2, August 28, 1994; pg.
24; See: D21, P64.

Review of Ruth Crawford compositions including, *Three Songs to*

Poems by Carl Sandburg and *Piano Study in Mixed Accents*. This "all-Crawford CD" is described as having:

> ". . . ecstatic charge . . . vision of ordered chaos
> comparable to Varèse's greatest works." [compare
> with Kosman, Joshua June 19, 2000]

Vivian Fine honors her early mentor and teacher (see Gaume, Matilda, also Tick, Judith), by performing Crawford's' piano works along with pianist Joseph Bloch on this CD (compare Holland, Bernard, March 1, 1983 also Mclellan, Joseph, November 11, 1982). Other performers were: Patricia Berlin, mezzo-soprano, Ida Kavafian, violinist and the Lark Quintet.

B257. *Rotterdamsch Nieuwsblad*. [Review of R. Guralnik's 1962 concert tour, anon.]. Rotterdam, The Netherlands: Fall, 1962. <u>See</u>: JC33.

Brief, quite positive comments (in Dutch) on Vivian Fine's *Five Preludes* played as part of pianist Robert Guralnik's 1962 well-received concert tour. The critic said that:

> ". . . [*Five Preludes*] are full of diversity, with bril-
> liant fast movements and an exceptionally beautiful
> slow movement. . . ." [*trans.* JC](see and compare
> with *Rotterdamsch Parool*, 1962)

B258. *Rotterdamsch Parool*. [Review of R. Guralnik's 1962 concert tour, anon.]. Rotterdam, The Netherlands: Fall, 1962. <u>See</u>: JC33.

Brief, quite negative comment on Vivian Fine's *Five Preludes* performed as part of pianist Robert Guralnik's 1962 concert tour: (Compare with *Rotterdamsch Nieuwsblad*, Fall, 1962)

> ". . . Fine's short pieces [*Five Preludes*] were not too
> important. . . ." [*trans.* JC]

B259. S., C. "Port Costa Players: Fine premiere." *High Fidelity/Musical America*, June, 1978:MA-20-21. <u>See</u>: JC89.

Concerning the premiere performances of Fine's chamber opera, *The Women in the Garden*, (see Fine, Vivian. and Judith Jamieson), C. S. wrote an analytical, positive critique. The review indicated three performances in both San Francisco and Oakland, California in February, 1978. *Garden* played to "capacity" audiences; there were standing ovations for Vivian Fine. C. S. stated that the Port Costa Players' production had been excellent.

Four famous women, Emily Dickinson, Gertrude Stein, Isadora Duncan, Virginia Woolf and one man, the Tenor, become the cast in an imaginary meeting. C.S. mentioned the often quoted description given by Fine of her opera as 'plotless.' Disputing Fine's 'plotless' summation, C.S. outlined what she designated as a dramatic plot: "the individual woman's response to the experience which shapes her sensibility" (compare Hertelendy, Paul. February 15, 1978 and also von Bachau, Stephanie).

"Evocation," rather than "dramatic gesture" shapes Fine's opera where the use of "extended recitative" heralds opera in the "tradition of Wagner and Debussy." Also, according to C.S., Erik Satie's (see Schmidt, Frank G. and Cohen, Selma Jeane and compare with Shere, Charles, April 3-8,1982) *Socrates* is analogous to Fine's opera "poem:" both move in parallel delineation without traditional dramatic action but with suggestive interaction, "simply" persuading with "logical . . . graceful musical statement."

Referring to two un-named San Francisco newspaper critics, C.S. stated that after their premature and loud exit the two then uncompromisingly disdained Fine's opera in their reviews. Apparently, this was after the two had viewed the performance just briefly (see Tircuit, Heuwell, 1978).

Details of C.S.'s analysis of *The Women in the Garden*:

> "The music is contrapuntal . . . orchestra stating lyrical melodies with tonal implications in free juxtaposition. [Fine's] opera alternates . . . counterpoint and simpler melodic statements with chordal accompaniment. . . . Patterns proceed simply, now falling on a common beat, now going their own ways, following ideas in Messiaen and Ives to express the mutual support of diverse voices."

B260.   Sabin, Robert. "Martha Graham. Greek Cycle Extended." *Musical America*, May 1960:31. <u>See</u>: JC58, D1.

Short review of a cycle of "dance dramas" that Martha Graham choreographed on various Greek themes. Vivian Fine's *Alcestis* was one of the themes from the era of Greek gods. Admentus was to die (Death is Thanatos) but his wife, Alcestis, traded places with him and subsequently is saved by the god, Hercules. This is a world premiere for Fine's work on April 29. Mr. Sabin stated it was a "novelty" and also "ravishingly beautiful." While Sabin found the production visually "intoxicating" he had less enthusiasm for Fine's music (Compare *American Record Guide*, 1962 and also Cohn, Arthur. 1981 and 1962):

> ". . . something of a disappointment . . . dignified and unobtrusive . . . but retains a wintry pallor throughout."

B261. Sable, Barbara Kinsey. "Vivian Fine: *Missa Brevis* [Record Review]."
NATS Bulletin, Nov/Dec/ 1982:51. <u>See</u>: JC79, D9.

Capsule record review of Vivian Fine's *Missa Brevis* (Compare with
Shepfer, Dale D. and also Commanday, Robert, October 4, 1990). Ms.
Sable declares *Missa Brevis* to be an "excellent" composition and a very
"usable" selection in the modern music repertory. She believes it would
also be appropriate for women's chorus and added that the
"... tonal concepts are tightly woven ... beautifully
accomplished. ... I commend this work. ..."

B262. Sadie, Stanley. **The Grove Concise Dictionary of Music.** London,
England: MacMillan Press, p. 257, 1988. <u>See</u>: JC55, JC58, JC75, JC79.

Sadie says of Fine that her: "... early works [were] ... stern,
dissonant contrapuntal. ... [Later] relaxed ... wider expressive range,
touched by humour." *A Guide to the Life Expectancy of a Rose* is used
as an example of Vivian Fine's musical use of "humour." Indeed, she
was able to accomplish a wry wit in the midst of moderate dissonant
tones, at times, at least.

B263. Salzman, Eric. "Vivian Fine Heard On 'Composers' Showcase.'" New
Paltz, New York: *New Paltz Independent*, January 7, 1959. <u>See</u>: JC43,
JC46, JC50.

Evidently, parts of Mr. Salzman's review of Vivian Fine's program
(originally in the *New York Times*) were copied in the *New Paltz
Independent*. Fine was a New Paltz resident so area media commonly
mentioned that she was the wife of Benjamin Karp. Karp was Professor
of Art at the State University Teachers College. The concert was at
Nonagon Gallery in New York City and was a "Composers' Showcase"
program on December 21, 1958 (see *New York Times*, December 22,
1958).
Fine's *Sonata for Violin and Piano, Capriccio for Oboe Quartet* and
Second Solo for Oboe brought comments: Salzman reported that *Sonata*
had "substance, strength;" while he decided that *Capriccio* and *Second
Solo* though having adeptness, seemed "less convincing." One
determinant in Fine's *Sonata*, yet noted in *Capriccio* and *Second Solo*
is, according to Salzman, Fine's
"... technique of building up a structure out of long,
beautifully wrought phrases. ..." [see and compare
Von Gunden, Heidi; Parmenter, Ross. 1959]

B264. Salzman, Eric. "Vivian Fine Wins Music Acclaim." New Paltz, New

York: *New Paltz News*, January 10, 1959. <u>See</u>: JC43, JC46, JC50.

The *New Paltz News* had reprinted Salzman's review on Vivian Fine's December 21, 1958 concert for "Composers' Showcase" at Nonagon Gallery in New York City (see Salzman, Eric, January 7, 1959). The *New Paltz News* thought the review to have been "of special interest here" since, they wrote, Fine lived in New Paltz and was married to Benjamin Karp.

B265. Samford, C. Clement. "Pianist Presents Concert of Contemporary Music." Newport News, Virginia: *Daily Press*, May 14, 1968. <u>See</u>: JC51, D16, P50.

This review pertains to a lecture-recital of contemporary music (see and compare with Schmidt, Frank G.) developed and performed by "noted composer-pianist" Vivian Fine for the Collegium Musicum series at the College of William and Mary. According to Samford, Fine's program was "perhaps the most significant" concert since the series inception.

At this last program in the series, Fine performed at the piano and also lectured on the works of many significant 20th century composers. She played numerous short compositions by composers Alexander Scriabin, Arnold Schoenberg, Anton von Webern, Eric Satie, Olivier Messiaen, Charles Ives and Henry Cowell engendering enthusiasm and positive remarks from C. Clement Samford. Fine's *Sinfonia and Fugato* was her "well conceived" choice for the concert's finale.

> "Miss Fine has been on these programs here before and it was a welcome return. Her program was broad in scope and a good cross section of the various musical forces which have been at work since the early days of the century."

B266. Saminsky, Lazare. "New Faces Among Our Composers." *Musical Courier*, February 1, 1941. <u>See</u>: probably JC18, JC23, JC37, P48.

Saminsky's treatise elaborates, at length, on his idea that the New York City, of the 30's and 40's, was a kind of massive marketplace for the "musical world;" a "stock exchange" where new music credos were "brazenly" promoted at the cost of ethics or even the need for much talent. In this music commodity motivated "world" only the most driven, "agile" contenders garner the fickle attention of the "public." Whilst in the midst of this ferocious struggle those milder mannered, although "true leaders" of the modern music movement, were "brushed aside" leading Mr. Saminsky to assert:

". . . how often drive passes for talent and loud
claims for rights."

Saminsky regarded Roy Harris, Roger Sessions, and William Schuman
as the "premier" composers within the musical culture of 1941; he re-
gretted that they were not "warrior(s)." this induced him to write of the
"new . . . gifted" composers being "brushed aside" by the packs of ag-
gressive, lessor lights of music. The "irresponsible public" seemed to be
only "vaguely" aware of those with great talents but with quiet
"claims."

Saminsky listed several of these "gifted" composers: Elliott Carter,
Normand Lockwood, Miriam Gideon, Edward Cone, Alvin Ettler and
Vivian Fine, among others (see and compare with Aaron Copland,
1923-33).

He wrote of Fine's serenity and "outstanding mastery" of her craft; he
was deeply impressed with her songs (see and compare with Upton
Treat, William); her "admirable music." Saminsky realized that even
though Fine was "well and favorably known" to the inner circle of the
music culture, what we, today, call *mainstream America* knew little
about young Vivian Fine or her "extraordinary" abilities (see and
compare with Riegger, Wallingford).

These are some of Saminsky's observations on what he headlined as
Fine's "Story":

". . . A brilliant musician. . . . Agile pianist,
admirable coach, extraordinary reader at sight of most
difficult scores. . . .

Some years ago I first saw the works of Vivian
Fine. She was then a child of fifteen. I was amazed
by the power and precocity of her superb musical
brains capable of tackling the most intricate harmonic
concepts.

Her former radicalism *a outrance* and cerebralism
have now disappeared, leaving no trace. In her
Allegro Concertante [may be *Prelude for String
Quartet*, 1937] for strings it is a delight to follow the
novel diatonic flow of the charmingly gay piece with
its firm polyphonic-thematic backbone.

Even more impressive are her splendid songs — the
attractive *Epigram*, of a limpid vocal line and imaginative instrumentation [probably *Epigram and Epitaph*]; *Bloom*, for voice and string quartet, enchanting
in its human substance and parallel weaving; lumi-
nous, lovely expressive vocal line and counter-voices
of the strings. Then there is *Dirge* (after Shakespeare)
[probably *Four Elizabethan Songs*] for voice, viola

and cello, a piece beautiful in its emotional depth and
a calm, clear-eyed mastery mirroring an amazingly
potent, fine intellect.
    Think of the stoicism of this extraordinary girl who
has lived here for years without ever hearing her
admirable music played or seeing it published!"

B267.   Saminsky, Lazare. *"Chroniques et Notes." Le Revue Musicale*,
          September-October, 1932. <u>See</u>: JC4.

In this condensed review (in French), Mr. Saminsky listed the
participants at the recent Yaddo Festival (See *New York Herald-Tribune*,
February, 1932) highlighting new music. Roger Sessions, Charles Ives
and Vivian Fine were among those present. As for Fine's *Four
Polyphonic Piano Pieces* the critic remarked (compare with Engel, A.
Lehman, October, 1932 and also Saminsky, Lazare, 1941):
    ". . . an extremely capable young girl, but that very
    precociousness is somewhat unpleasant. . . ." [*trans.*
    JC]

B268.   *San Francisco Chronicle.* "Bay Area Women's Philharmonic Commis-
          sions Fine Work." San Francisco, California: June 12, 1987. <u>See</u>:
          JC123.

Announcement of the commission for a classical orchestral work to be
composed by Vivian Fine (this would become *After the Tradition*), for
the Bay Area Women's Philharmonic (see Bramhall, Robyn). The
commission was said to be "in observance of the 75th birthday" of Miss
Fine. Works by other composers were also commissioned for this 1987-
88 concert season and included Germaine Tailleferre and Marianne
Martines.

B269.   San Francisco Symphony. "News Release for 'Vivian Fine Week' (Jan-
          uary 5-13), Davies Symphony Hall." San Francisco, California: Novem-
          ber 29, 1982. <u>See</u>: JC8, JC50, JC82, JC83, JC85, JC89, JC101, P64.

    "SAN FRANCISCO SYMPHONY PRESENTS
    VIVIAN FINE WEEK JAN. 5-13: World Premiere of
    SFS-Commissioned Work Featured."
This news release announced the San Francisco Symphony's "week-
long salute" to Vivian Fine, composer, and listed the numerous events
scheduled to celebrate this occasion. (An unrelated Vivian Fine
Appreciation Week would be "proclaimed" in Boston in 1989; see
Caldwell, Mary and Boston, City of). The news release stated that

Vivian Fine Week had been presented by the SFS in cooperation with Mostly Modern and Old First Concerts. As the centerpiece of the special week, the SFS had commissioned Fine to write a symphony for full-scale orchestra. This would become Fine's *Drama for Orchestra* (see Carson, Josephine), which was conducted by SFS Music Director Edo de Waart. Fine's *The Women in the Garden*, which had been performed by the San Francisco Opera, was alluded to.

The events and activities of Vivian Fine Week were:

Throughout the entire week, there was a "special exhibit" with Fine's "original manuscripts" (music scores written by the composer, herself) on display in Davies Symphony Hall.

On January fifth, the Week began with SFS Composer-in-residence John Adams' morning lecture about Fine's works and her creative methodology. Afterward, there was an Open Rehearsal of Fine's *Drama* with the SFS and Mr. de Waart. Both events were free and open to the public. On evenings of January fifth and seventh, *Drama for Orchestra* was performed at Davies Symphony Hall; there was an afternoon concert on January sixth. On January eighth there was an evening performance of *Drama* at Flint Center in Cupertino (fifty-miles south of San Francisco, just north of San Jose, California).

Sunday, January ninth, saw a chamber music program highlighting some of Fine's chamber works covering almost three decades (see Pontzious, Richard, January 10, 1983). Old First Concerts co-sponsored the program with the San Francisco Symphony. Fine's works performed, in Old First Church, were *Sonata for Violin and Piano* (1952); *The Flicker* (1973); *The Nightingale* (1976); *Teisho* (1977) and *Trio for Violin, Cello and Piano* (1980).

For January twelfth, Vivian Fine hosted "a free symposium for students of the San Francisco Conservatory and the general public, affording an opportunity to talk informally with the composer about her work."

On January thirteenth, Mostly Modern held a concert as a "tribute" to the New Music Society of Henry Cowell (see Kino, Carol, January 1983) and featuring Fine's *Four Songs* written in 1933 (see Upton Treat, William, 1930-38). Another special feature was the West Coast premiere of *Sonata for Violin and Piano*, (see McLellan, Joseph, November 1982) by Ruth Crawford Seeger who was Fine's childhood teacher and mentor. Fine accompanied on the piano.

B270.   San Francisco Symphony. "Program Announcement for Vivian Fine Week (January 5-13)." San Francisco, California: January 5, 1983. See: JC8, JC50, JC82, JC83, JC85, JC89, JC101.

Short announcement for the "Vivian Fine Week" (see San Francisco

Symphony, November 29, 1982). *The Women in the Garden*, Fine's chamber opera performed in 1982 by the San Francisco Opera, is alluded to. Fine's accolades, commissions and recordings are mentioned.
". . . exciting opportunity . . . hear one of America's
eminent composers. . . ."

B271. Sandved, Kjell Bloch. **The World of Music; An Illustrated Encyclopedia**. New York City, New York: Abradale Press, 4 volumes, 1963.

B272. Sartori, Claudio (Direttore; Riccardo Allorto, Vice-direttore). **Enciclopedia della musica**. Milano, Italy: Ricordi, 4 volumes, 1963-1964.

B273. *Schenectady Gazette*. "Season's End [Photo]." Schenectady, New York: May 2, 1979. See: JC91, D14.

Caption to a photo concerning a recent American Composer's Forum. This last program spotlighted women composers. The photo depicts the President (of Union College) and Mrs. Norman P. Auburn and also composers Sarah Mennely Kyder, Vivian Fine and Alison Nowak, "discussing the evening's concert." Fine's *Quartet for Brass* was premiered at the forum.

B274. Schiavo, Paul. "Notes on the Program: Portal." New York City, New York: Alice Tully Hall, Great Performers at Lincoln Center, April 19, 1990. See: JC132.

Short quote from Fine on her work for violin and piano, *Portal*, written in 1990, which was commissioned by violinist Pamela Frank and dedicated to Frank:
"'Changes of character of a Baroque Sonata . . .
opens . . . *un poco maestoso* . . . [next parts] playful,
serene, ardent . . . latter section based on a quotation
from Carl Ruggles' *Portals*.'"

B275. Schmidt, Frank G. "Vivian Fine Creates Strange Recital Sounds." South Bend, Indiana: *South Bend Tribune*, April 29, 1966. See: JC72, P48, P55.

Schmidt's review of a lecture-recital program of modern piano music of significant contemporary composers at the University of Notre Dame campus. The program was created by Vivian Fine; she was also the pianist.

As told by Schmidt, Fine emphasized works by such as Arnold Schoenberg, von Webern, Erik Satie, Henry Cowell, Charles Ives and Oliver Messiaen. He wrote that Messiaen's was the most memorable piece, while saying that certain Satie works had "unusual charm." Fine was quoted as stating that she was "'probably the only pianist now playing his work.'"

Four Piano Pieces were Fine's choice for the finale; Schmidt commented:

> ". . . sometimes the sounds were like the feeling when a bee is buzzing around and you don't know how or when it will strike."

Schmidt commented on Fine's lecture:

> ". . . [She] did make sense of the music in a charming, informal manner. . . ." [see and compare with Hinderaker, Miriam]

B276. Schubart, Mark A. "Young Composers Offer New Works Here; Present-Day Writers Show to Advantage." New York City, New York: *The New York Times*, April 17, 1946. <u>See</u>: JC36.

Mr. Schubart expressed positive sentiments over the musical efforts of the youthful associates of the Forum Group of the International Society for Contemporary Music at Times Hall. Among the young composers were Ben Weber, Jeanette Siegel and Vivian Fine. Fine's *Three Pieces for Violin and Piano* impressed the reviewer who said that her music was

> ". . . accessible . . . to audience. . . . Her violin pieces are striking . . . with the exception of a somewhat overlong Andante, well put together. They are likable, pleasing, and, at times, affecting music."

B277. Schupp, Enos E. Jr. "Review: *Paean*." *The New Records*, August, 1971: 6. <u>See</u>: JC75, D13.

Short review of Fine's record release, "Music from Bennington." The reviewer judged that Fine's *Paean* (see and compare with *Richmond Times Dispatch* and also Frankenstein, Albert), which was inspired by Keats' "Ode to Apollo," was

> ". . . an exercise . . . using modern choral techniques, mostly excluding singing. . . ."

B278. *Seattle Times, The*. "Passages." Seattle, Washington: Sunday Night Final Edition, April 2, 2000, pg. A19.

B279. Severinghaus, Wendy. "New Fine Work Uses Whitman Poems." Bennington, Vermont: *The Bennington Banner*, January 6, 1987. Also: Brattleboro, Vermont: *Brattleboro Reformer*, January 15, 1987. <u>See</u>: JC111, JC113.

Profile piece on Vivian Fine on the occasion of a new commission written for Lise Messier and Nan Nall; a work for two sopranos to be accompanied by piano. (Fine was a local resident, living but a few miles from Bennington). Severinghaus said that the pianist for the world premiere in Brattleboro was Glenn Parker. According to Severinghaus, Fine used concepts from five poems written by Walt Whitman as texts and inspiration for her *Inscriptions* which had been composed on a Living Composers Grant from the National Endowment for the Arts.

A work of Fine's, in progress at the time, a percussionist's piece for Jan Williams, is remarked on, along with *Sonata for 'Cello and Piano* a recently completed chamber work.

> "Fine . . . said . . . that 'the poems were 'One's Self I Sing,' 'Look Down Fair Moon,' 'A Child Said What Is The Grass,' part of 'When Lilacs Last In the Dooryard Bloom'd' and 'Inscriptions.'
> 'I like to write using text,' she said."

B280. Severinghaus, Wendy. "Sounds Encouraging." Bennington, Vermont: *The Bennington Banner*, April 20, 1987. <u>See</u>: JC91, D14, D15.

Ms. Severinghaus reported on a portion of an "outstanding" concert by the Purchase Brass that she heard one "cold" day. She was instantly captivated by the music; a concert of works by Bennington composers (see and compare with *Richmond Times-Dispatch*).

Vivian Fine taught at Bennington College and her musical offering was *Quartet for Brass* (1978) included with works by Lionel Nowak, Allen Shawn, Louis Calabro and Peter Golub. The concert was at the Mount Anthony Union High School.

As much as Severinghaus had enjoyed the music, it was *Quartet for Brass* that had caught her "imagination" (compare with Woolmington, Rob and also Shepfer, Dale D.). She commented that Fine's music had been

> ". . . beautiful, and very moving — and, like the other signs of spring . . . very encouraging."

B281. Shepfer, Dale D. "Guide to Records: FINE: *Quartet for Brass (1978); Momenti (1978); Missa Brevis (1972)*." *American Record Guide*, October, 1982:14. <u>See:</u> JC79, JC90, JC91, D9, D11, D14.

Dale D. Shepfer's commendatory critique describes Vivian Fine as a "yet unlauded composer" (see and compare with Glackin, William and also Riegger, Wallingford) while expressing positive insights into her recording of *Quartet for Brass*, *Momenti* and *Missa Brevis* (see and compare with Commanday, Robert, October 24, 1982 and October 4, 1990, also compare with Henahan, Donal, 1973 and Hertelendy, Paul, January 4, 1983). He said that it was a "model example," noting that *Quartet* "should" become a permanent part of the programs of brass groups:

> ". . . innovative material . . . unusual crescendo-glissando combinations . . . an occasionally quasi-pointillist usage of the brasses come as delicious surprises."

The critic noted that Fine's *Momenti* utilized "the full range of the keyboard" and, though "atonal," it contained some melody.

According to Shepfer, Fine's work with the "greatest artistic significance" was her "oddly haunting Mass," also termed "a stunning musical achievement." Here, he wrote one of the more detailed, engrossing analyses of *Missa*; some of his thoughts while studying *Missa Brevis*:

> ". . . brilliant . . . demanding use of cellos . . . throughout the piece, covering an enormous tessitura . . . employing harmonics . . . amazing resemblance to the standard string quartet . . . two *Omni* sections . . . a vocal strand . . . persistently serene and ethereal. . . . the intensely tragic *Lacrymosa* . . . voice floating like a song lost in deep space. . . . beautifully proportioned performances. . . ."

B282.   Shere, Charles. "Friedman, Brandwynne Perform Splendidly Despite Chamber's Program, Other Musicians." Oakland, California: *Oakland Tribune*, October 27, 1981. See: JC77.

In this review of a song-recital with mezzo-soprano Stephanie Friedman, Mr. Charles Shere, apparently, was most impressed with *"Two Neruda Poems"* (compare with Henahan, Donal, 1973) written by Vivian Fine. The recital was presented by the San Francisco Chamber Music Society. The poem "Oda a la piano" (Ode to a Piano; Neruda's piano is a surreal mouth with whale-like jaws) was said by Shere to have been "witty . . . dramatic . . . a surreal piano concert." While the lazily paced "La Tortuga" (The Turtle) musically describes Pablo Neruda's poem as:

> ". . . philosophical implications of a poem describing a tortoise finally transcending his long life and joining

'the other boulders.'"

B283.   Shere, Charles. "Opera Double Bill that Features Women Scores in Every Respect." Oakland, California: *Oakland Tribune*, April 3, 1982. See: JC89.

In two performances, the San Francisco Opera's Opera Showcase presented a "double bill" featuring operas, *The Women in the Garden* (see Fine, Vivian and Judith Jamieson) by Vivian Fine and *Full Moon in March* by John Harbison. Critic, Charles Shere, wrote that there wasn't a "more provocative double bill" than this pair of operas. He wrote a kind of side-by-side comparison (compare with von Bachau, Stephanie) of the two works that strongly favored Fine's *Women*.

Shere stated that Fine's work seemed to have a French derivation; "Debussy and Satie come to mind" (compare with S., C.). He also wrote that *Women* was "anti-symbolism" while in contrast *Full Moon* was somewhat "conventional" and Straussian. Additionally, he said of Fine's opera that it was

> ". . . conversational . . . differing values of those four remarkable women interact, not in . . . dramatic conflict, but in response to their own experiences with men (Dickinson . . . her editor, Woolf . . . her father, Stein . . . Hemingway, Duncan . . . her stage designer) — and . . . to one another.
> . . . more promising for the theater. . . .'The Women' suggests . . . really communicative theater . . . [where] plot narrative gives way to . . . narrative of mood and idea."

B284.   Shere, Charles. "Edo de Waart Leads Symphony in Fine 'Linz'." Oakland, California: *The Oakland Tribune*, January 7, 1983. See: JC101.

This is a generally positive review of the premiere of Vivian Fine's *Drama for Orchestra* (see Carson, Josephine) as performed by the San Francisco Symphony. *Drama* had been commissioned by the SFS.

Shere wrote that *Drama* was written for a large orchestra, one that was "Mahler-sized" reporting on the unhappy reality that new works are given but "three rehearsals," even if complex. However, he stated that *Drama* was "rewarding to listen to . . . clear and refreshing . . . ," though he had said that at the Wednesday concert the work had "seemed subdued and uneasy." Fine composed her orchestral work in five movements inspired by Norwegian artist Edvard Munch's paintings. Shere commented on Fine's design incorporating these five-movements, saying that they

> "... suggest a program akin to ... Arnold Schoen-
> berg's *"Transfigured Night,"* based on ... dramatic
> tension between a pair of lovers. ... the idea of a
> five-movement orchestral cycle of moods recalls
> Schoenberg's *Five Pieces, Op. 16."*

B285. Shere, Charles. "A Fine Week Honors a Human Composer." Oakland, California: *The Oakland Tribune,* January 9, 1983. <u>See</u>: JC79, JC89, JC101, D9.

Charles Shere outlines some of the music and lecture events during the extraordinary Vivian Fine Week (see San Francisco Symphony November 29, 1982) devoted to a retrospective of the Fine's works. Mr. Shere interviewed Fine just before this occasion. She was 70 years old at the time and still teaching at Bennington College in Vermont. Fine disclosed to Shere that her very first "'publication'" (1933, Fine was 19) was in Cowell's *"New Music,"* a journal founded by him. Fine makes the affirmation that she "'wouldn't have been a composer'" without a directive from Ruth Crawford, her teacher, that the 13-year-old Vivian write her first music composition (see Gaume, Matilda). She remarked that she wants to be thought of as a "'composer'" rather than a "'woman composer'" explaining that a composer is "*'human* first.'"

Shere also discussed the 1978 premiere of Fine's *Women in the Garden,* when he was concerned with the early departure of two San Francisco critics (see S., C.) who then wrote bad reviews of Fine's opera. (*Women* was not performed as part of Fine Week). Shere wrote that this conjecture was "male" whereas Fine was "female."

His own remarks on the *Women* (see Shere, Charles, April 3, 1982) were, in general, favorable. During this period Fine was composing her new commission from the San Francisco Symphony which would become *Drama for Orchestra* (see Carson, Josephine) and the "centerpiece" of Vivian Fine Week, said Shere.

Fine made these statements to Shere about her chosen art:

> "'Composition demands rare single-mindedness: your
> medium doesn't guarantee completion.' (You see the
> painting or the poem immediately, but a composition
> has to be performed.) 'Not many women have been
> able to achieve such single-mindedness in a male-
> dominated society.'"

B286. Shere, Charles. "Mostly Modern Concert was Tribute to Milestone Works." Oakland, California: *The Oakland Tribune,* January 15, 1983. <u>See</u>: JC8, P64.

Charles Shere reviewed one of the concerts of the San Francisco Symphony's Vivian Fine Week (see San Francisco Symphony, November 29, 1982), which was a program of "eccentric American music" from the 1920's to the 30's, often called "modern" music today (see Copland, Aaron and also Saminsky, Lazare, February 1, 1941).

According to Shere, the music was representative of the era of the New Music Society, founded in 1925 by Henry Cowell, Vivian Fine's mentor (she would have been twelve and studying piano). The concert was by Mostly Modern at San Francisco's Vorpal Gallery and included Fine's *Four Songs* for mezzo-soprano and string quartet (see Shere, Charles, January 9, 1983).

Shere cited both Fine's *Four Songs* plus her piano accompaniment, with violinist Daniel Kobialka, of Ruth Crawford Seeger's, *Violin and Piano Sonata* (1926) (see McLellan, Joseph, November 1982) as the "centerpiece of the concert." Ruth Crawford had been both teacher and mentor to the thirteen-year-old Vivian.

The reviewer, Mr. Shere, was greatly impressed (compare with Saminsky, Lazare, February 1, 1941 and Upton Treat, William, 1938) with Fine's *Songs*, written when she was twenty years old, inspired by poems titled "O Western Wind, When Wilt Thou Blow," "Comfort to a Youth That Had Lost His Love," "She Weeps Over Rahoon" and "Tilly" (see Gilbert, Steven E., Fall 1973):

> ". . . They are astonishing: fully mature, intelligent, inspired pieces . . . using melodic and contrapuntal procedures very like those . . . [in] her present manner. . . . The text-setting is marvelous. Only Virgil Thomson's setting of the English language rivals it among 20th century composers: . . . natural, perfectly speech-like, yet measured and expressive."

B287. Slonimsky, Nicolas. **Music Since 1900**. New York City, New York: Schirmer Books, 1994, p. 876, 889. See: JC84, JC89.

B288. Slonimsky, Nicolas (Laura Kuhn, Editor). **Baker's Biographical Dictionary of Twentieth-Century Classical Musicians**. New York City, New York: Schirmer Books, 1997, p 402. See: JC3, JC16, JC18, JC24, JC30, JC31, JC42, JC43, JC45, JC52, JC57, JC58, JC66, JC70, JC71, JC73, JC74, JC78, JC84, JC86, JC87, JC89, JC91, JC97, JC101, JC105, JC106, JC107, JC113, JC119, JC123.

Contains over thirty of Fine's compositions in various genre, with the latest work being *After the Tradition* for Chamber Orchestra (1988). Slonimsky has written that Vivian Fine is:

> ". . . particularly adept at writing vocal and instru-

mental works in a dissonant but acceptable style."
[Compare with Gann, Kyle, 1997]

B289. Soler, Josef (Editor). **Diccionario De Musica**. Barcelona-Buenos Aires-Mexico, D. F.: Ediciones Grijalbo, S. A. 1985.

Vivian Fine is listed in this *referencia* as a:
"Comp. y pianista norteamer."

B290. *Spartan, The.* "Chamber Artists To Salute Women At CSC." Castleton, Vermont: *The Spartan*, Castleton State College newspaper, March 4, 1987. <u>See</u>: JC97.

Announcement for a performance by the Capitol Chamber Artists to feature music composed by women and about them at Castleton's Fine Arts Center. Vivian Fine's *Trio for Violin, Oboe and Piano* was performed. The composer was present. Ms. Fine is called
". . . one of the most important women composers of
the century."

B291. Spengler, David. "Walden Defies Music's Gravity." Bergen County, New Jersey: *The Record*, November 3, 1975. <u>See</u>: JC63, D7.

Short review of the Walden Trio's performance in Ridgewood, New Jersey. Among the five contemporary composers they played was Vivian Fine offering her *Fantasy for Cello and Piano*. Spengler said of Fine's composition that it
". . . explores the emotion as well as the arithmetic
that can be mined in 12-tone writing. . . . A pleasure
to think about . . . joy to listen to . . . contemporary
music that you don't have to kid yourself into liking."

B292. Stodelle, Ernestine. "Two Veterans Move From Drama to Comedy." New London, Connecticut: *London Day*, August 8, 1966.

Spare review of a dance recital at Palmer Auditorium, Connecticut College, for part of the 19th American Dance Festival. Dancers were Ruth Currier and Lucas Hoving in a production set to texts by Erik Satie, *Satiana*, and played on piano by accompanist, Vivian Fine, who took part in the production. As noted by Stodelle:
". . . she and her piano are part of the action."

B293. Stodelle, Ernestine. "She's Still Number One." New Haven, Connecticut: *The New Haven Register*, May 18, 1975. <u>See</u>: JC58.

Ms. Stodelle commented on a Martha Graham Benefit, asking $50. to $10,000. per ticket, that was at New York's Uris Theatre in June, 1975.

Graham began her dance career in April, 1926 (Vivian Fine was 13) she employed the music of such as Ravel or Rachmaninoff, wrote Stodelle. Fine wrote *Alcestis* (see Sabin, Robert) for her.

Graham's dance style had drastically changed since then, and according to the writer she now (in 1975) had fewer dance numbers but Graham used modern music (see White, Edward) and choreographed for

> ". . . even one production with music especially commissioned from less romantic composers, such as Robert Sharer, Vivian Fine [*Alcestis*], Charles Surinach, etc."

B294.   *Stuart News, The/Port St. Lucie News.* "Obituaries. Vivian Fine." Stuart, Florida: Stuart News Company, Saturday, March 25, 2000, Local, p. B6. <u>See</u>: JC18, JC84.

Fine's musical composition "style" is said to have:
> ". . . evolved gracefully over the years. . . ."

B295.   Swain, Jean. "Chamber Artists Salute Women In Music." Rutland, Vermont: *Rutland Daily Herald*, March 10, 1987. <u>See</u>: JC97.

Jean Swain reviewed a concert featuring the works of women: one contemporary work was composed by Vivian Fine, *Trio for Violin, Cello, and Piano* (1980). The Capitol Chamber Artists performed the works at the Castleton State College Fine Arts Center.

Remarking on the "sparse" amount of "published" compositions and "record(s)" of their performances, Ms. Swain attributes one reason for this to the fact that it was thought "unseemly" (not nice!) for a lady to be active in the world of music. Ms. Swain said of Fine's performance:
> ". . . Designed in modern idiom. . . . [Fine's] two-movement piece started out with searching . . . reflective themes in the strings, conveyed in dissonant harmonies . . . interrupted rhythms, to arrive at a final quiet resolution" [see Rabben, Linda A.].

B296.   Swift, Pat. "'Women in Music' Program At UB Will Spotlight Opera." Buffalo, New York: *Buffalo News*, July 10, 1984. <u>See</u>: JC89, JC101, JC105, JC107.

Announcement for a symposium on women's music at the State University of Buffalo Amherst Campus presented by the New Music Society of Syracuse. Vivian Fine's *Drama for Orchestra, Ode to*

Purcell and *Poetic Fires* are alluded to by Ms. Swift who began her piece:

> ". . . Vivian Fine's opera *The Women In The Garden* [see Fine, Vivian and Judith Jamieson] will be one of the highlights of a symposium on "Women in Music. . . .""

B297. *Symphony.* Washington, DC: *Symphony* **41**:32, no.5, Sept.-Oct., 1990. See: JC130.

Announcement of the performance of *Madrigali Spirituali,* 11/2/90, JoAnn Falletta, conductor, Karen Baccaro, Trumpet. Commissioned by BAWP as part of the program by the Bay Area Women's Philharmonic, Berkeley, California.

B298. Teeter, Paul. "College Hears Terkel's View." Rutland, Vermont: *Rutland Herald*, May 16, 1983.

Mr. Teeter commented on a ceremony to honor the inauguration of Michael Hooker as president of Bennington College. A processional music work *Auguries*, for soprano, piano, trumpet, clarinet and percussion, was written by Vivian Fine, Jeffrey Levine and Lionel Nowak. They all were musicians or composers teaching at the College. Studs Terkel and Governor Snelling were present.

> "The sometimes discordant, sometimes classically beautiful piece was so unique it was mentioned by both Terkel and Snelling. . . ."

B299. Terry, Walter. "Out of the Pages of History — A Dance Plot." New York City, New York: *New York Herald Tribune*, August 16, 1965. See: JC70

Walter Terry offered a somewhat negative critique (compare with Hughes, Allen, August 16, 1965) of the modern ballet, *My Son, My Enemy*, choreographed by Jose Limon with the score by Vivian Fine (see Ammer, Christine). The event was at Connecticut College who also commissioned the work with money from the Rockefeller Foundation.

Four segments of the dance are called "Visions," "Fantasies," "Judgement" and "Vengeance." These titles were inspired by a violent love-hate letter sent to Alexis by his father, Peter the Great, Czar of Russia, wrote Terry. Mr. Limon danced the Czar. Terry is generally positive about the "spectacular" choreography, though he insisted that it was much too long. Terry maintained that Fine's score also had

> ". . . its relentless side, especially . . . that section

where one hears . . . a muffled voice ranting endlessly
on the brink of madness. Elsewhere . . . we hear the
clank of chains, the flogger's explosive strike and
other pertinent sounds interwoven with her musical
fabric. . . ."

B300. Thompson, Oscar, Editor in Chief. **International Cyclopedia of Music
and Musicians,** Ninth Edition. New York City, New York: Dodd,
Mead & Company, 1964.

B301. Tick, Judith. **Ruth Crawford Seeger, A Composer's Search for
American Music.** Oxford, England: Oxford University Press, 457
pages, 1997. See: Pn4.

Tick's thick tome, 457 pages, is extensively researched and once
started it is difficult to put down. The exciting early days of American
Modern Music, with portraits of the early composers, are meticulously
delineated, giving this reader a sense of "what it might have been like
back then." Tick's book is mainly about Ruth Crawford, of course, but
the background knowledge is relevant to Fine's history as well:
Crawford was Fine's model and inspiration as well as her teacher. This
is also the milieu that begot Fine's Ultra-Modern Music, indeed much
of what is modern music today; so it is most worthy of study by the
interested student of music. Special problems confronting the female
composer, together with many statistics, are also documented here:
"Between 1880 and 1910, while the population of the
United States almost doubled, the number of musician
and music teachers increased almost five times . . .
classical music established itself as a cultural industry.
. . . Middle- and upper-class women emerged as the
'chief promoters of culture,' the majority of conservatory students, and — within the workplace — the
rank and file of new music teachers . . . in the 1920
census [Vivian was seven-years-old then], music and
music teaching, at 56 percent female, still ranked third
. . . among . . . 'feminized' . . . occupations. . . . Female musicians clustered around the lower-status
lower-paying rungs to the professional ladder. . . .
The great majority of musicians out in the world, on
stage as performers, in print as composers, were
men."
Ruth Crawford, born in 1901, was only twelve years older than her
student, Vivian Fine; both youthful composers shared a somewhat
parallel path in the new dissonant music of their era.

Fine is quoted, mentioned, or contributes, by way of her correspondence with Crawford, to the historical details of Crawford's life and times (see also Gaume, Matilda) in Ms. Tick's detailed historical study; see pages: 59-63, 72, 76, 86, 89, 95, 106, 113, 118-124, 127, 131, 133, 150, 159, 175, 181-183, 198, 224, 226-227.

B302.   Tircuit, Heuwell. "Pianist Premieres Her Work." San Francisco, California: *San Francisco Chronicle*, March 7, 1974. See: JC80, P53.

Mr. Tircuit reviewed Vivian Fine's 20th Century music lecture-recital quite negatively (see and compare with Schmdt, Frank G. and also Hinderaker, Miriam).

Fine performed on piano the works of Messiaen, Scriabin, Satie, Webern, Ives and Cowell. Mr. Tircuit had few positive comments for the works of these composers, arguing that Messiaen was the only true "'modern'" composer on Fine's program. He remarked on Fine's *Concerto for Piano Strings and Percussion* (1972):

> ". . . a three-legged work, one each on the graves of
> Scriabin, Cowell and Cage. Even if you did not like
> the piece, the choreography was great fun."

B303.   Tircuit, Heuwell. "Five Characters in Search of an Opera — or Something." San Francisco, California: *San Francisco Chronicle*, February 14, 1978. See: JC89.

Mr. Tircuit wrote an unfavorable review of the San Francisco debut of Vivian Fine's chamber opera, *The Women in the Garden* (see Fine, Vivian and Judith Jamieson).

As he apparently saw it, a particular "philosophy" (not identified here) of Fine's, endeavored to become an opera, this then "defeated" the opera. This method cannot usually succeed, Tircuit stated (compare with Putnam, Thomas, June 20, 1986 and also Shere, Charles, March 1982 and von Bachau, Stephanie). Nevertheless, the critic had a positive remark as well as the negatives; some details from Tircuit's commentary:

> "Nothing really happens in this *'Garden'* . . . [the
> four women] seem to have nothing to say to each
> other . . . no situation of conflict outside the inner
> minds of [the four women]. . . . On purely musical
> grounds, Fine achieved craftsmanly, artistic effects.
> . . . As an opera, it was beyond sitting out, despite a
> good performance [see S.,C. 1978]."

B304.   Tircuit, Heuwell. "A Survey of Vivian Fine's Chamber Music Career."

San Francisco, California; *San Francisco Chronicle*, January 11, 1983.
See: JC50, JC77, JC82, JC83, JC85, JC97, P64.

Mr. Tircuit reviewed a special concert presenting six of Vivian Fine's
compositions for small chamber works. This concert represented her
work from 1952 and was part of the San Francisco Symphony's tribute
of a week devoted to Fine's music (see San Francisco Symphony,
November 29, 1982). Basically, this was a favorable review but there
were exceptions.
   Heuwell Tircuit stated that Fine's "sensational pianism . . . inspired"
mezzo-soprano Stephanie Friedman in the "masterful settings" of the
Two Neruda Poems (1971) (see and compare with Shere, Charles,
October 27, 1981). Pablo Neruda wrote the poems, "Ode to the Piano"
(Oda a la piano) and "The Turtle" (La Tortuga). Of "Turtle," Tircuit
said that it was
             ". . . gravely contemplative . . . rich in magical
             stillness — and . . . curiously tragic."
remarking on "Ode to the Piano:"
             ". . . a wild burlesque-illustration of the poem's inside
             jokes . . . the piano soars and glides along. . . ."
Tircuit wrote that Fine's *The Nightingale* was "eloquently moving."
However, he stated that the "instrumental" works "fell down," all being
on the "dour side, rarely attempting bravura effects." He added that they
"seemed emotionally detached." Fine's *Trio for Violin, Cello and Piano*,
The Flicker, and *Teisho* received slight, yet negative notice. But *Trio*
was said to have been "moving" in the "slow movement."

B305.   Trimble, Lester. "Record Reviews: Classical Collections. Recording of
            Special Merit." *Stereo Review*, September, 1972: 106. See: JC51, D16.

Short summary and review of a new record release and "lost treasure"
titled, "New Music for the Piano." As told by Lester Trimble the
"reissue" of a 1966 Victor album included numerous contemporary
music compositions for the piano (see and compare with Klein, Howard,
August 28, 1966). CRI-SD-288, two records.
   Vivian Fine's *Sinfonia and Fugato* was included along with other
contemporary composers such as, Weber, Babbitt, Kraft and Glanville-
Hicks. Robert Helps was the "superb" pianist. Trimble's positive
remarks were general in nature:
             ". . . Performance: Excellent.
             Recording: Excellent.
             . . . growing progressively more amazed and elated by
             the feast of first-rate American music contained
             thereon . . . the prevailing atmosphere of the music is

American and unmistakenly so."

B306. Tucker, Marilyn. "Fine Celebration for a Busy Composer." San Francisco, California; *San Francisco Chronicle*, December 29, 1982. See: JC1, JC8, JC89, JC101, JC102, JC104.

Marilyn Tucker wrote this article profiling composer Vivian Fine for the upcoming event, Vivian Fine Week (see San Francisco Symphony, November 29, 1982) as inaugurated by the San Francisco Symphony in 1982. The Symphony commissioned and premiered Fine's *Drama for Orchestra* (see Carson, Josephine) as the highlight of the week. Tucker remarked that Fine's *The Women in the Garden* had been "a hit" of the San Francisco Opera Center's 1982 "spring season."

Fine's teenage composition, *Solo for Oboe*, was her first public performance through Henry Cowell, Tucker wrote. She also mentioned that *Four Songs* (1933) (see Gilbert, Steven E., Fall 73 and Upton Treat, William), by Miss Fine, would be performed by Mostly Modern as part of Fine Week events; adding that *Songs*, as a historical point
"... had their premiere in San Francisco 50 years ago under the sponsorship of Henry Cowell's New Music Society [Fine's first score was published in *New Music*]."

The 1927 composition, *Sonata for Violin and Piano*, written by Fine's childhood teacher and mentor, Ruth Crawford Seeger (see Gaume, Matilda), is remarked on here, by Tucker, as a keepsake that Fine had "had in her possession since she was a teenager in 1927." The work was performed during Vivian Fine Week with Fine at the piano. It was the West Coast premiere (see McLellan, Joseph, November 1982).

At the time of this article, Fine had "just completed" *Double Variations* (see Newlin, Dika) and was "working on a song cycle," titled *Canticles of Jerusalem* (see Caldwell, Mary), reported Ms. Tucker.

B307. Tyler, Sean. **International Who's Who in Music and Musicians' Directory.** Cambridge, England: International Biographical Centre, 1998-1999, p. 169-170. See: JC3, JC18, JC42, JC56, JC66, JC71, JC73, JC86, JC89, JC97, JC101, JC106, JC107, JC113, JC119, JC123.

This directory inventories many of Fine's "honours" and compositions, with her *Dancing Winds* [woodwind quintet] from 1987 being the latest date.

B308. Ulrich, Allan. "Two 1977 One-Acts at S.F. Opera." Los Angeles, California: *Los Angeles Times*, April 7, 1982. See: JC89

Critic Allan Ulrich gave Vivian Fine's *The Women in the Garden* (see Fine, Vivian and Judith Jamieson) numerous minus points during its San Francisco Opera Center production. He states that there was no "dramatic conflict," only "static, radiantly expressed attitudes" (compare with S., C. and Shere, Charles, March 1982), that the composer just handed each of the four brilliant women their quotes and scripts and then Fine

> ". . . steps back from the situation and hopes that
> feminists sympathies will prevail. . . ."

However, Mr. Ulrich wrote that there was certainly a lot within Fine's work that "demands admiration" such as Fine's proficiency in integrating eclectic texts.

> ". . . with extraordinary clarity, a masterful sense of
> contrasts and a capacity for sheer beauty in the vocal
> composition . . . orchestral interjections are always
> pointed and discreet."

B309. Underwood, W.L. "Danish Dancer Wins Wichita." Wichita Falls, Texas: *Wichita Falls Record*, [May] 8, 1935[34 sic]. See: P24.

Underwood's brief commentary told of five-hundred-plus members of the North Texas Civic Music Association eager and awe-struck who merrily "sloshed" onward in a fierce winter storm to see the young dancer, Nini Theilade, perform (see Powell, S. Morgan and V., M.). Her piano accompanist that rainy night was the young Vivian Fine. Underwood wrote that the dancing had been "excellently" aided by young Fine who also played a solo of Chopin preludes and Liszt's *Waldesrauschen*. These last solos "commanded prolonged applause."

B310. Upton, William Treat. *A Supplement to Art-Song in America, 1930-1938*. Oliver Ditson Co., 1938. See: JC8.

Mr. Upton analyzed Vivian Fine's *Four Songs* which were published, in 1933, pronouncing them very excellent indeed (see Riegger, Wallingford. and compare with Gilbert, Steven E., also Shere, Charles, January 15, 1983). The songs were titled, "The lover in winter plaineth for the spring," from the 16th century, for voice and viola; "Comfort to a youth that had lost his love," poetry by Robert Herrick, for voice, violin and Viola; "She weeps over Rahoon," for voice and string quartet, and "Tilly," for voice, two violins and cello, text by James Joyce. Here, Upton scrutinizes Fine's song inspired by the words of Robert Herrick:

> ". . . we behold the ancient mold shattered to frag-
> ments, and song emerging as a purely instrumental
> form. . . . The voice part here, considered as an atonal

melody, is well conceived. Indeed its first phrase, from the viewpoint to Schoenbergian atonality, is well nigh perfect, for in its fourteen tones it makes but one repetition and omits no single tone of the duo-decuple scale. . . . Could anything be more natural in its rhythmical nuances than the setting of the first phrase, 'What needs complaints, when she a place has with the race of saints?' The rhythmic alertness and spontaneity (almost that of the spoken words) is one of the outstanding excellences of the composition . . . and such a nice balance between the vocal and the two instrumental lines that, taken together, the three form a homogeneous whole. . . . As a miniature chamber work, and as a composition representing atonality in one of its peculiarly individual phases, this composition is eminently successful."

B311.   V., M. "Debuts de Nini Theilade, jeune et jolie danseuse." Montreal, Canada: *La Presse*, Mardi 12, 1935. See: P24.

The original was in French: this is a capsule review on the "lovely young dancer," Nini Theilade's performance at the Imperial Theatre of Montreal. Vivian Fine accompanied her on the piano on many occasions (see Underwood, W.L. and Powell, S. Morgan):
". . . Miss Vivian Fine accompanied on the piano. She played the dance, *Impressions of Tahiti*, extremely well and because of that solo, there was much applause, and quite precisely so, for the music had such intelligent qualities." [*trans.* JC]

B312.   Veil of Isis, The. "Program Notes for Open Wings, A Conference on Women in Classical Music." San Francisco, California: Community Music Center, March 16, 1980. See: JC26.

Brief notes on Vivian Fine's career background since a choral work she composed was being performed by the Veil of Isis (this is a women's choral group). Fine's work is *The Passionate Shepherd To His Love and Her Reply*, according to these notes Fine composed it in 1938 and it was premiered thirty-seven years later by "Anna Crusis Women's Choir . . . in 1975 in Madison, Wisconsin."

B313.   *Vermont Woman*. "Her Own Way of Seeing." March, 1986.

This is a short excerpt from the program "Vivian Fine" produced by

Ev Grimes for National Public Radio. It included photos of Fine at the piano and of Fine conducting.

In this article Fine remarked on her early beginnings in music (see Gaume, Matilda and also Ariel). She wrote her first piece of music at 13 at the request of her teacher and mentor Ruth Crawford Seeger. Fine spoke of her women teachers and her mother, women who had profound influences on her love of music. There were men in her life when she was older who were also "'supportive'" (Henry Cowell was an early mentor to Fine). Fine spoke with great commitment of her lifelong devotion to her chosen work:

> "'I love to compose music. My mind concentrates effortlessly, as in nothing else I do. It is a form of meditation. . . .'"

B314.   Vinton, John. **Dictionary of Contemporary Music**. New York City, New York: E.P Dutton, 1974.

B315.   von Bachau, Stephanie. "REPORT: U.S. San Francisco/Bay Area." *Opera News* 47 (1):34. See: JC89.

Stephanie von Bachau reported on Fine's chamber opera, *The Women in the Garden*, (see Fine, Vivian and Judith Jamieson) and its San Francisco Opera Center performance on a double bill with John Harbison's *Full Moon in March*. She wrote of Fine's opera's "total clarity" as opposed to the difficulty in understanding Harbison's lyrics. (compare with Ratliff, William, April 2, 1982)

Commenting that *Women* was a "feminist" work that neither preaches nor is angry, the writer explained that Fine has masterfully crafted the "actual words" of these four celebrated women so that the effect is "ongoing discussion about the concerns of women in a hostile world." Dramatic action takes the form of "human interaction" and a "metaphysical" controversy rather than a conventional plot (Compare with Shere, Charles, March 1982 and also Goldstein, Margery).

Von Bachau affirms that Fine's chamber opera happens to be

> ". . . a remarkable contemporary work, with a tintinabulating orchestral score of delicate beauty, thoroughly idiomatic (if difficult) vocal lines, emotional penetration and . . . civilized, wholesome warmth."

B316.   Von Gunden, Heidi. **The Music of Vivian Fine**. Lanham, Maryland: Scarecrow Press, 1999, 187 pages. See: JC50

Von Gunden recounts her technical analysis of various compositions by Fine. A case in point is her outline of Fine's 1952 *Sonata for Violin and Piano* (a 16 minute work also called *Violin Sonata*). The writer says of this composition's first movement, that it:

> ". . . is an ABAB shape created by the beginning 'Energico, confuoco (ca eighth-note=144)' constituting the A section, which changes in measure 27 to a contrasting 'delicato, cantabile' two-voice canon. . . ."

On the second movement:

> ". . . Both instruments present contrasting material, the piano's implied minor ninth chord with its pedal root and the violin's long lyrical melody. . . There is a midpoint recapitulation, but the movement resembles a series of variations due to the prominent repetition of the piano motif and violin melody. . . ."

And the third:

> ". . . Due to the frequent repetitions of the beginning material, this movement assumes a rondo shape of ABACA of uneven proportion with A being measures 1-34, B measures 35-43 with a tempo change to 'Meno Mosso,' A measures 44-52 with a return to the original tempo, C measures 53-81 as a freer and more developmental section, and another return to A in measures 82-90. . . ." [compare with Parmenter, Ross. 1959; Salzman, Eric. January 7 and 10, 1959]

Studying issues of interest to the musicologist, Von Gunden offers similar analyses of other Fine works. The book contains numerous short examples (copies) of Fine's music. Among other things, the book has biographical material, good photographs, and a five page bibliography.

B317.   *Washington Post, The.* "Deaths Elsewhere." Washington, D.C.: Sunday, March 26, 2000, Final Edition, Metro; pg.C06. <u>See</u>: JC58, JC70.

B318.   Webster, Daniel. "Light-spirited Opera Sounds Feminist Note." Philadelphia, Pennsylvania: *Philadelphia Inquirer*, Thursday, February 27, 1997, Section C, p. 1. <u>See</u>: JC138.

Pre-opening article (with photos) on Vivian Fine's opera *Memoirs of Uliana Rooney* (1993). (see Baxter, Robert, also Jones, Leslie, 1997)

B319.   West, William D. "Syracuse [review of *The Women in the Garden*]." *Opera News*, April 1984, p. 46. <u>See</u>: JC89.

Mr. West expressed enthusiasm for Fine's *The Women in the Garden* (see Fine, Vivian and Judith Jamieson) performed by the Society for

New Music at the Carrier Theater. West related, in his short review, that
the Tenor, Maurice Black, acted the role without "extremes" inherent
in "male arrogance" while he was also "gently expressive." West
viewed The Tenor (a male actor cast in multiple roles) as the
"representative" from the "male-dominated world."

Overall it was an "intense, passionate presentation," extremely
"impressive" to West, who pointed out the "sensitive tone-painting"
achieved by Fine and the great contrasts of Stein's "cooler
conversational aphorisms" with Dickinson's "intensity."

B320.   White, Edward. "Manuscripts of Leading American Woman Composer
         Presented by the New York Public Library at Lincoln Center." The New
         York Public Library, Public Relations Office, New York City, New
         York. April 1, 1974. See: JC16, JC17, JC24, JC30, JC31, JC55, JC58,
         JC59, JC70, JC80, D1.

         In this announcement, from the New York Public Library, Edward
         White described an exhibition that was called "Vivian Fine and Five
         Dancers." It was on view from April through May 1974. Memorabilia
         of Fine's three decades of collaboration with the most famous dancers
         and choreographers of the twentieth century were arranged for display
         (see Ammer, Christine and Humphrey, Doris).
         The writer, Edward White mentioned that five of the dancers in the
         exhibition, followed by a dance composition Fine composed for them,
         were, Hanya Holm, *Tragic Exodus* (1939), exodus of Europeans during
         World War II, and *They Too Are Exiles* (1940), tyrannized citizens
         become "exiles" within "their own homes;" Doris Humphrey, *Race of
         Life* (1938), (see Robin, Harry); Charles Weidman, *Opus 51* (1938), a
         "humorous" work; Jose Limon, *My Son, My Enemy* (1965), (see Terry,
         Walter) and, perhaps the most well-known dance, *Alcestis* (1960), (see
         Sabin, Robert) created for Martha Graham.
         Some of Vivian Fine's historical items that were in the display
         included, compositions of the above dances and others that were not
         published or recorded, numerous photographs, copies of reviews,
         programs and dance related letters and the full orchestral scores from
         Alcestis and *My Son, My Enemy*. Fine's works, *A Guide to the Life
         Expectancy of the Rose* (see Riegger, Wallingford), also *Concerto for
         Piano Strings and Percussion* are remarked upon. Mentioned, was her
         new work in progress, at that time, *Finnegan's Wake*.
                   ". . . One of the leading woman composers in the
                   United States has furnished original manuscript scores
                   for a new exhibition in the Music Division of the
                   New York Public Library at Lincoln Center. . . . Me-
                   morabilia of Vivian Fine's achievements in com-

> position for dance, including her own flexatone (an instrument resembling a tiny musical saw used to produce a unique percussion effect) open the exhibition. . . ."

B321. WNYC. "Radio Station Program Guide." New York City, New York: September 28, 1986. <u>See</u>: JCii, JC8, JC33, JC56, JC79, JC90, JC101.

B322. Wooley, Al. "From 1:1 to Infinity . . . with One Lens." *U.S. Camera*, November, 1961, 24(11):70-71.

U.S. Camera magazine had used an entire page for a portrait photograph of Vivian Fine. The caption indicates that the photo was shot as a kind of "demonstration" for specialized camera equipment.

B323. Woolmington, Rob. [No Title]. Bennington, Vermont: *The Bennington Banner*, November 11, 1976. <u>See</u>: JC86

The Vermont Symphony Orchestra performed a work, *Romantic Ode*, written by a local composer and teacher at Bennington College, Vivian Fine. She lives but a few miles outside of Bennington, Vermont. Here, the Symphony performed at Mt. Anthony Union High School on an autumn's Saturday night. Aaron Copland's *Hoe Down* was also on the bill.

In this capsule review, Woolmington reveals negative feelings for Fine's work (compare with Severinghaus, Wendy, April 20, 1987). As the orchestra played Fine's *Romantic Ode*, Mr. Woolmington thought that it

> ". . . seemed to lack an inner elasticity in performance. . . . The instruments moved correctly. . . but somehow, lacked the quality of dance that sets music to life."

→ *Chapter 3* ←

WORKS AND PERFORMANCES

1921-1931

Early compositions:

JCi   **The Starving Children of Belgium**; about 1921, piano (See: Kimball, 1955)

JCii   **Lullaby**; June, 1927, piano (See: Ariel, 1983; WNYC, 1986; noted by Fine as her first composition, see Chapter 1, 1927)

JCiii   **Piece for Two Flutes**; February, 1928.

JCiv   **Poem for Voice and Piano**; text by John Galsworthy, June, 1928.

JCv   **Song for Voice and Piano**; text by Richard Dehmel; September 12, 1928.

JCvi   **Two Movements for Wind Instruments**; August 22-September 6, 1929.

JCvii   **Piece for Soprano, Clarinet and Cello**; August 24, 1929.

JCviii **Prologue and Allegro**; tenor, mezzo-soprano, coloratura, 2 bassoons and English horn; October 23-27, 1929.

JCix   **Two Pieces for Solo Clarinet**; 1929.

JCx   **Three Stanzas from the Japanese**; texts by Ono No Yoshiki (902 A.D.) and two anonymous poems; voice, piano and oboe; January 22-February 8, 1930.

JCxi   **Lizard**; voice, flute, and clarinet; text by D.H. Lawrence; March, 1930.

JCxii   **Suite for Piano**; in three movements; May, 1930.

JCxiii **A Drinking Song**; text by Henry Carey; voice and piano; undated but probably 1930-1931.

1929

SOLO FOR OBOE   **JC1**
>   Allegretto; Lento; Con spirito.
>   Catamount Facsimile Editions[1]; 4 min. 45 sec.
>   Also called: **Oboe Sonatina** (See: L. Engel, 1933)
>   See: S. Albahari, 1983; J. Carson, 1983; A. Cohen, 1987; L.
>   Engel, 1933; D. Ewen, 1982; S. Fuller, 1994; C. Kino, 1983;
>   Morton and Collins, 1992.
>
>   Premiere:
>   1930 (April 21): New York City, New York; Carnegie
>   Chamber Hall; The Pan American Association of Composers,
>   D. Desarno, oboe. Performance arranged by Henry Cowell.
>
>   Selected performances:
>   1980 (October 30): Innsbruck, Austria; Hall at the Center for
>   New Music, tour of James Ostryniec, oboe.
>
>   Broadcasts:
>   1980 (November): Austrian radio re-broadcast of James
>   Ostryniec's concert.

1930

FOUR PIECES FOR TWO FLUTES   **JC2**
>   Grazioso, un poco giocoso; Lento tristo; Stridente; Poco
>   Allegro
>   MarGun Music, Inc.; 5 min. 30 sec.
>   Also called: **Four Pieces for Violin and Oboe**
>   See: C. Ammer, 1980; J. Carson, 1983; A. Cohen, 1987; L.
>   Engel, 1933; D. Ewen, 1982; S. Fuller, 1994; H.H., 1932; L.
>   Jones, 1997; C. Kino, 1983; **Musical Leader**, 1932; W.
>   Riegger, 1958.
>
>   Premiere:
>   1931 (December 1): Dessau, Germany; Bauhaus; Program
>   arranged by Imre Weisshaus (based on the works presented as

---

[1] *Catamount is no longer in business; Fine's scores, that they had published,
are now available from the Library of Congress, see Appendix 1.

part of Pan American Association of Composers); Nicolo Draber, flute, Hanna Smid, violin.

Selected performances:
1931 (December 8): Hamburg, Germany; Logenhaus Welckerstraße; Internationale Gesellschaft für Neue Musik (Sektion Deutschland) (International Society for Contemporary Music), III. Konzert, Frauen als Komponisten; Eva Hauptmann, violin and Albert Reinhardt, oboe.

1932 (January 15): New York City, New York; The New School Auditorium; The First Concert of The Young Composers' Group; Robert Bolles and Carl Moore, flutes.

1975 (April 4): Berkeley, California; 1750 Arch Street, University of California at Berkeley, Department of Music, Morrison Hall, lecture-recital; Karla Warnke and Barbara Chaffe, flutes, San Francisco Conservatory of Music Players.

1975 (April 6): Hayward, California; California State University at Hayward, Music Building; Karla Warnke and Barbara Chaffe, flutes, San Francisco Conservatory of Music Players.

1976 (June 26): Green Mountain, Vermont; Green Mountain Arts Collaborative; parts 1 and 2, performers not identified.

1985 (January 31): Fort Wayne, Indiana; Indiana University, Recital hall, Music of Women Composers, Jan Hudson and Angela McKinney, flutes.

1989 (April 20): Boston, Massachusetts; Northeastern University, Department of Music, Music at Noon, Ell Center Ballroom; Jordana Bernstein, Eric Byunn, flutes, played the first and last pieces. A performance as part of Vivian Fine Appreciation Week in Boston.

1989 (April 22): Cambridge, Massachusetts; Harvard University, Sanders Theater, Harvard Wind Ensemble (Jordana Bernstein and Eric Byunn, flutes), played the first and last pieces. The conclusion, "A Salute to Vivian Fine," of Vivian Fine Appreciation Week in Boston.

1989 (October 30): Richmond, Virginia; University of Richmond, North Court Recital Hall, The Contemporary Music

Ensemble, Patricia Werrell and Susan West, flutes. Guest composer: Vivian Fine

TRIO FOR STRINGS   JC3
Allegro con spirito; Intermezzo; Rondo
Violin, viola, cello
Catamount*; 9 min. 30 sec.
See: A. Cohen, 1987; D. Cummings, 1998; D. Ewen, 1982; R-M. Johnson, 1989; N. Slonimsky, 1997; S. Tyler, 1998.

Premiere:
1953 (November 23): Darmstadt, Germany; Amerikahaus; Hermann Trio, Karl-Albrecht Hermann, violin, Elizabeth Kramer-Buche, viola, and Alexander Molzahn, cello.

Selected performances:
1931 (December 13): New York City, New York; Home of Mrs. Blanche Walton; A Program of Compositions by Vivian Fine; Aaron Hirsch, violin, David Mankovitz, viola and Olga Zundel, cello.

1953 (December 8): Berlin, Germany; United States Information Center, Berlin Amerika Haus; Hermann Trio.

1958 (August 31): Woodstock, New York; Polari Gallery, Concert of Contemporary Music; Alice Smiley, Louis Tavelli, Cynthia Britt.

SONATINA FOR VIOLIN AND PIANO   JC4
Comodo [Con brio]; Lento; Ritmico
Publisher unknown (see App. 1); duration unknown

Premiere:
1931 (June 27): Chicago, Illinois; American Conservatory of Music, Kimball Hall; A Program of New Compositions, written by members of Mr. Adolf Weidig's class; Mary Jones, violin and Vivian Fine, piano.

Selected performances:
1931 (December 13): New York City, New York; Home of Mrs. Blanche Walton; Program of Compositions by Vivian Fine; Aaron Hirsch, violin and Vivian Fine, piano.

CANON AND FUGUE FOR PIANO   JC5

Publisher unknown (see App. 1); duration unknown

Premiere:
1931 (December 13): New York City, New York; Home of
Mrs. Blanche Walton; A Program of Compositions by Vivian
Fine; Vivian Fine, piano.

LITTLE SUITE FOR VOICE AND PIANO   JC6

Sea Chest; Sleep Impression; Two Stranger's Breakfast
Publisher unknown (see App. 1); duration unknown
Text: Poetry of Carl Sandburg

Premiere:
1931 (December 13): New York City, New York; Home of
Mrs. Blanche Walton; A Program of Compositions by Vivian
Fine; Radiana Pazmor, voice and Vivian Fine, piano.

1931-1932

FOUR POLYPHONIC PIANO PIECES   JC7

Catamount*; 7 min.
See: A. Berger, April, 1932, May, 1932; J. Carson, 1983; R.
Chon, 1987; A. Cohen, 1987; L. Engel, 1932, 1933; D. Ewen,
1982; C. Hall, 1996; L. Jones, 1997; J.Raymond, 2000.

Premiere:
1932 (April 30): Saratoga Springs, New York; First Yaddo
Festival of Contemporary American Music; Vivian Fine, piano.

Selected performances:
1932 (April 21): New York City, New York; The Dance
Theater, Symposium for Moderns; Vivian Fine, piano.

1933 (April 1): New York City, New York; Home of Ira
Hirschman; Program of American Music of Today; Vivian
Fine, piano.

1933 (April 23): New York City, New York; Tudor City,
Windsor Tower; Soirees de New York; Piano Group performed
by Vivian Fine: *Two Dances, Lied* by Hindemith, *Piano Piece
(Scherzando)* by Fine, and *"36"* by Carlos Chavez.

1975 (August 7): Hanover, NH; Rollins Chapel, Dartmouth College; Vivian Fine, piano.

1987 (April 26): Buffalo, New York; Vivian Fine, A Retrospective; State University of New York at Buffalo, Hallwalls, North American New Music Festival, Stephen Manes, piano.

1933

FOUR SONGS   **JC8**

Mezzo-soprano, 2 violins, viola, cello
New Music Press [also: Editions], San Francisco, July 1933; 7 min.
Text: 1. The lover in winter plaineth for the Spring (16th Century anon.), voice and viola; 2. Comfort to a youth that had lost his love (Robert Herrick), voice, violin, viola; 3. She weeps over Rahoon (James Joyce), voice, 2 violins, viola, cello; 4. Tilly (James Joyce), voice, 2 violins, cello.
See: C. Ammer, 1980; E.R. Anderson, 1976; Ariel, 1983; E. Armer, 1991; T. Brookes, March, 1986, spring, 1986; A. Cohen, 1987; R. Commanday, Jan. 15, 1983; D. Ewen, 1982; S. Fuller, 1994; S. Gilbert, 1973; R-M. Johnson, 1989; D. Landis and L. Edelman, 1982; Library of Congress, 1982; **Music in Print**, 1999; T. Page, Sept. 30, 1986; R. Pontzious, 1983; W. Riegger, 1958; San Francisco Symphony, 1982; C. Shere, 1983; M. Tucker, 1982; WNYC, 1986; W. Upton, 1938.

Premiere:
1933 (February 5): New York City, New York; The League of Composers, performers not identified.

Selected performances:
1966 (October 4): New York City, New York; Judson Hall; Text 1 only, Judith Alban-Wilk, voice and Stanley Hoffman, viola.

1968 (May 15): Bennington, Vermont; A Faculty Concert, Carriage Barn, Bennington College; mezzo-soprano, not identified, Eric Rosenblith, violin, Olga Gussow, violin, Orrea Pernel, viola, Gael Alcock, cello.

1976 (January 31): New York City, New York; Town Hall, Janis-Rozena Peri, soprano and unidentified string performers.

1983 (January 13): San Francisco, California; Vorpal Gallery; Mostly Modern Series as part of "Vivian Fine Week" (January 5-13) sponsored by San Francisco Symphony; Stephanie Friedman, mezzo-soprano and Mostly Modern Quartet, performers not identified.

1986 (September 28): New York City, New York; "American Song Cycles of the 1920's and 1930's," Gustavus Adolphus Lutheran Church, Alliance for American Song, performers from the following: Cheryl Bensman, Christine Schadeberg, Michael Brown, Robert Kuehn, Walter Hilse, William Trigg, William Komalko, Catherine Aks and an ensemble under the direction of Roger Zahab.

Broadcasts:
1986 (April 19): Boston, Massachusetts; WGBH 89.7 FM, Vivian Fine: A Celebration of Her Music.

1986 (March 8, September 28): National Public Radio, first in a series by the International League of Women Composers, WNYC program "Live from Merkin Concert Hall"; a tribute on Fine's 73rd birthday by Ev Grimes and Karen Pearlman.

DIVERTIMENTO   JC9
Chamber ensemble
Oboe, clarinet, bassoon, piano, percussion
Catamount*; 5 min.
See: A. Cohen, 1987.

Reading:
1952 (September): Saratoga Springs, New York; 25th Anniversary Yaddo Music Festival of American Works, performers not identified.

FOUR LYRIC SONGS   JC10
Chamber music
Mezzo-soprano, piano
Catamount*; 10 min. 45 sec.
Text: 1. The Riddle (Emily Dickinson), 1933, 2 min. 30 sec.; 2. A Flower Given to My Daughter (James Joyce), 1935, 2 min. 15 sec.; 3. Adios, Bilbadito (anon.), 1939, 1 min.; 4. Sonnet, To one who has been long in city pent (John Keats),

1939, 2 min.; 5. Lines from Whitman, 1941, 3 min.
See: A. Cohen, 1987.

Never performed except for no.3 which was part of Hanya
Holm ballet *They Too Are Exiles*, (1939 see JC31).

1934

AFFIRMATIONS   **JC11**

Dance for Charles Weidman, choreography
Piano
Publisher unknown (see App. 1); duration unknown.
Commission: Charles Weidman
See: E. Armer, 1991; I.K., 1935.

Premiere:
1934 (November 17): New York City, New York; Washington
Irving High School Municipal Auditorium, Charles Weidman
and Dance Co., Students' Dance Recitals, accompanied by
Vivian Fine.

Selected performances:
1934 (November 18): Baltimore, Maryland; The Dance
Theater, 100 E. Monument Street; Charles Weidman and
Dance Co., accompanied by Vivian Fine, piano.

1935 (January 6): New York City, New York; Guild Theater;
Charles Weidman and Dance Co., accompanied by Vivian
Fine, piano.

1935 (March 14 & 15): Boston, Massachusetts; Repertory
Theater; Doris Humphrey and Charles Weidman and Dance
Group, accompanied by Vivian Fine, piano.

1935 (October 12): New York City, New York; Washington
Irving High School Municipal Auditorium, Doris Humphrey
and Charles Weidman and Dance Co., Student's Dance
Recitals, accompanied by Vivian Fine, piano.

1935 (October 30): Newark, New Jersey; Fuld Hall; "Y"
Concert Series Committee, Young Men's and Young Women's
Hebrew Association; Charles Weidman and Dance Co.,
accompanied by Vivian Fine, piano.

THIS BELIEVING WORLD   **JC12**
Movements: Hebrew; Spanish; Mexican; American
Piano
Publisher unknown (see App. 1); duration unknown
Commission: Elizabeth Waters

Premiere:
1934 (December 27 and 28): New York City, New York; The
Chamber Dance Series, Hans Weiner Studio Hall; Elizabeth
Waters, dancer; accompanied by Vivian Fine, piano.

QUEST (CONVERGENCE AND AFFIRMATIONS)   **JC13**
Dance for Charles Weidman
Piano
Publisher unknown (see App. 1); duration unknown
See: E. Armer, 1991.

Premiere:
1937 (April 15): Norton, Massachusetts; Wheaton College;
Doris Humphrey and Charles Weidman and Dance Co.,
accompanied by Vivian Fine, piano.

1935

CONVICTION   **JC14**
Dance for Rose Crystal
Piano
Publisher unknown (see App. 1); duration unknown
Commission: Rose Crystal

Premiere:
1935 (September 13): New Canaan, Connecticut; Henry W.
Saxe Junior High School; Dance Recital of Rose Crystal;
accompanied by Vivian Fine, piano.

INVICTUS   **JC15**
Dance for Rose Crystal
Piano
Publisher unknown (see App. ??); duration unknown
Commission: Rose Crystal

Premiere:
1935 (September 13): New Canaan, Connecticut; Henry W.
Saxe Junior High School; New Canaan Community Orchestra
Association, accompanied by Vivian Fine, piano.

1937

THE RACE OF LIFE   **JC16**
Ballet for Doris Humphrey based on drawings of James
Thurber (adapted from a fantasy about an American family)
Piano, percussion (dance version)
Catamount*; 22 min.
See: C. Ammer, 1980; E. Armer, 1991; A. Block and C.
Neuls-Bates, 1963; J. Carson, 1983; G. Claghorn, 1996; A.
Cohen, 1987; D. Ewen, 1982; V. Fine and L. Dlugoszewski,
1963; S. Fuller, 1994; D. Greene, 1985; C. Hall, 1996; D.
Humphrey, 1958; L. Jones, 1997; A. Kozinn, 2000; *Los
Angeles Times*, 2000; J. Martin, 1956; J. Raymond, 2000; N.
Slonimsky, 1997; E. White, 1974.

THE RACE OF LIFE   **JC17**
Orchestra (1956 version):
          2-0-2-1, 2-2-2-1, timpani, percussion, piano, strings
Catamount*; 19 min.
See: C. Ammer, 1980; R. Chon, 1987; A. Cohen, 1987; D.
Ewen, 1982; C. Hall, 1996; H. Robin, 1961.

Premieres: Dance
1938 (January 23): New York City, New York; Guild Theater;
Doris Humphrey, Charles Weidman, Jose Limon and Dance
Company, accompanist not identified.

          Orchestral
1961 (April 16): Poughkeepsie, New York; Hudson Valley
Philharmonic; Claude Monteux, conductor. This performance
used slides of the Thurber drawings.

          Dance and orchestra
1956 (April 27, 28, 29): New York City, New York; Juilliard
Dance Theater; Doris Humphrey and Dance Company; using
the orchestral score for the first time, orchestra not identified,
Frederick Prausnitz, conductor.

Selected performances: Dance
1939 (March 25): Des Moines, Iowa; Roosevelt High School;
Dance Club of Drake University and the Des Moines Physical
Education Association; Charles Weidman, Doris Humphrey,
Jose Limon and Group; accompanied by Lionel Nowak, piano.

PRELUDE FOR STRING QUARTET   **JC18**
Two violins, viola, cello
Montevideo: Instituto Interamericano Musicologia, Vol. V,
October, 1941; 6 min. 30 sec.
Also called: **Prelude and Elegiac Song for String Quartet**;
also **Elegiac Song**
See: *Associated Press*, 2000; A. Cohen, 1987; D. Cummings,
1998; D. Ewen, 1982; C. Hall, 1996; R-M. Johnson, 1989; A.
Kozinn, 2000; J. Raymond, 2000; N. Slonimsky, 1997; *Stuart
News*, 2000; S. Tyler, 1998.

Premiere:
1939 (March 26): New York City, New York; Town Hall
Club; The League of Composers; Frederick Dvonch, Dorothy
Kesner, Edward Neikrug, George Neikrug.

Broadcasts:
1986 (April 19): Boston, Massachusetts; WGBH 89.7 FM,
Vivian Fine: A Celebration of Her Music.

PIECE FOR MUTED STRINGS   **JC19**
(for the children of Spain)
String orchestra
Catamount*; 4 min.
Also called: **Prelude and Elegiac Song.**
PIECE FOR FLUTE AND MUTED STRINGS   **JC20**
(version of the above)
Quartet; Flute, violin, viola, cello

Premiere:
1971 (August 8): Lenox, Massachusetts; Merrywood Music
School; Merrywood String Orchestra, Jacob Glick, conductor.

Selected performances:
1976 (December 1): Bennington, Vermont; Bennington
College, Carriage Barn; A Bicentennial Offering of American

Chamber Music for Strings; Frank Baker, Jacquelyn Bertles, Chris Finckel, Michael Finckel, George Finckel, Jacob Glick and Gretchen Paxson.

1978 (December 6): Bennington, Vermont; Bennington College, Greenwall Music Workshop; The Bennington College String Orchestra.

LYRIC PIECE FOR VIOLONCELLO AND PIANO   **JC21**
LYRIC PIECE FOR VIOLONCELLO AND STRING
QUARTET   **JC22**
Catamount*; 4 min. 45 sec.
See: A. Cohen, 1987.

Premiere:
1972 (May 10): Bennington, Vermont; Bennington College; Martha Siegel, cello, Lilo Glick and Leonard Rowe, violins, Jacob Glick, viola, Barbara Mallow, cello.

1938

FOUR ELIZABETHAN SONGS   **JC23**
No. 1, Daybreak (John Donne), no.2, Spring's Welcome (John Lyly), no.3, Dirge (William Shakespeare), no.4, The Bargain (Sir Philip Sidney).
Voice and piano.
Soprano, piano
Catamount*; 1 min. 15 sec.; 1 min. 30 sec.; 1 min. 30 sec.; 1 min. 30 sec.
Note: Composed in the time period between the years 1937 and 1941
See: , R. Capparela, 1977; R. Chon, 1987; A. Cohen, 1987; D. Ewen, 1982; L. Jones, 1997.

Premiere:
1940 (May 1): New York City, New York; Composer's Forum Laboratory; Hilda Bondi, soprano and Erich Weil, piano. Three of the songs performed and called on the program *Three Songs*: Daybreak, Springs Will Come [*sic*], The Bargain. Note: No.2 originally performed on Sept. 10, 1938 at Yaddo Festival by Ethel Luening.

Selected performances:

1974 (May 6): New York City, New York; Manhattan School of Music, Hubbard Recital Hall; Judith Bettina, soprano, pianist unknown.

1974 (May 10): New York City, New York; Kingsborough Community College, City University of New York, Judith Bettina, soprano, pianist unknown.

1976 (February 19): Saratoga Springs, New York; Skidmore College, Filene Recital Hall; Ruth Lakeway, soprano and Karen Bauman, piano.

1981 (December 19): New York City, New York; International House; Eric Li, piano, vocalist not identified.

1982 (May 9): Saratoga Springs, New York; Skidmore College, Filene Recital Hall; Nancy Jo Davidson, mezzo-soprano and Richard Hihn, piano.

1983 (June 1): Bennington, Vermont; Bennington College; Bette Goldberg, soprano, Jacob Glick, violin, Maxine Neuman, cello and Vivian Fine, piano.

1985 (April 7): Washington, DC; National Gallery of Art, West Building, East Garden Court, The F. Lammot Belin Concerts, 42nd American Music Festival, Nan Nall, soprano and Veda Zuponcic, piano, performed: Daybreak and The Bargain.

1986 (February 15): New York City, New York; Bruno Walter Auditorium, New York Public Library; Nan Nall, soprano, Lise Messier, soprano and Veda Zuponcic, piano.

1986 (February 18): New Brunswick, New Jersey; Faculty of Arts and Humanities, and New Jersey Guild of Composers, A-Wing Lecture Hall, Nan Nall, soprano and Veda Zuponcic, piano, performed: Daybreak.

1986 (February 19): Glassboro, New Jersey; Wilson Recital Hall, Department of Music, Glassboro State College; Nan Nall, soprano and Veda Zuponcic, piano, performed: Daybreak.

1987 (April 26): Buffalo, New York; Vivian Fine, A Retrospective; State University of New York at Buffalo,

Hallwalls, North American New Music Festival, Lois Stipp, soprano and Stephen Manes, piano.

OPUS 51   **JC24**

Dance titles: Opening Dance; March; Comedia; Solo; Duet; Spectacle
Ballet for Charles Weidman.
Piano and percussion
Catamount*; 22 min.
See: C. Ammer, 1980; E.R. Anderson, 1976; E. Armer, 1991; A. Block and C. Neuls-Bates, 1979; J. Carson, 1983; G. Claghorn, 1996; A. Cohen, 1987; V. Fine and L. Dlugoszewski, 1963; D. Ewen, 1982; S. Fuller, 1994; D. Humphrey, 1958; L. Jones, 1997; A. Kozinn, 2000; *Los Angeles Times*, 2000; Morton and Collins, 1992; N. Slonimsky, 1997; E. White, 1974.

Premiere:
1938 (August 6 & 10): Bennington, Vermont; Vermont State Armory, The Fifth Bennington Festival of the Modern Dance, The Bennington School of the Dance; Charles Weidman and members of the Concert and Apprentice Groups; Vivian Fine, piano and Franziska Boas, percussion.

Selected performances:
1938 (November 27): New York City, New York; Guild Theater, Charles Weidman and Doris Humphrey and members of the Concert Groups, accompanied by Lionel Nowak, percussion and Vivian Fine, piano.

1939 (January 13): Syracuse, New York; Syracuse Museum of Fine Arts, Lincoln Auditorium; Charles Weidman and Doris Humphrey and Group; accompanied by Lionel Nowak, piano.

1939 (January 19): Philadelphia, Pennsylvania; Temple University, Mitten Hall Auditorium; Charles Weidman and Group; accompanied by Lionel Nowak, piano.

1939 (February 22): Chapel Hill, North Carolina; Woman's College; Lecture-Entertainment Course; Charles Weidman and Group; accompanied by Lionel Nowak, piano.

1939 (March 2): Montevalto, Alabama; Alabama College, Palmer Auditorium; Charles Weidman and Group; accompanied by Lionel Nowak, piano.

1939 (March 11): Chicago, Illinois; Civic Theater, Chicago Concert Series; Charles Weidman and Group; accompanied by Lionel Nowak, piano.

1939 (April 11): Colorado Springs, Colorado; Fine Arts Center; Charles Weidman, Doris Humphrey and Company; accompanied by Lionel Nowak, piano.

1939 (November 21): Bryn Mawr, Pennsylvania; Bryn Mawr College, Goodhart Hall; Charles Weidman and Group; accompanied by Lionel Nowak, piano.

1939 (November 25): New York City, New York; Washington Irving High School, Municipal Auditorium; Charles Weidman, Doris Humphrey and Group; accompanied by Lionel Nowak, piano.

1939 (December 13): Lynchburg, Virginia; Doris Humphrey and Charles Weidman and Group; accompanied by Lionel Nowak, piano.

1939 (December 28): New York City, New York; Washington Irving High School Municipal Auditorium, Charles Weidman and members of the Concert Groups, accompanied by Lionel Nowak, percussion and Vivian Fine, piano.

1941 (February 8 and 9): New York City, New York; Studio Theater; Charles Weidman and Company.

1971 (Sundays, March-April): New York City, New York; The Expression of Two Arts Theatre; Charles Weidman and the Members of the Theatre Dance Company.

1972 (May 4): New York City, New York; YMCA; Charles Weidman and Theater Dance Company (Selby Beebe, Myra Hushansky, Margret O'Sullivan, Janet Towner and Janice Wodynski), Opening Dance accompanied by Vivian Fine.

1972 (April 6): Denton, Texas; Texas Women's College; Charles Weidman and Theater Dance Company (Selby Beebe,

Carol Geneve, Myra Hushansky, Janet Towner and Janice Wodynski), Opening Dance accompanied by Vivian Fine.

1974 (Sundays, April and May): New York City, New York; The Expression of Two Arts Theater; Charles Weidman with members of the Theater Dance Company and Workshop Group, accompanist not identified.

1986 (October 15): Bennington, Vermont; Greenwall Music Workshop, Bennington College, "Opening dance from the ballet," Vivian Fine and Allen Shawn, pianos.

MUSIC FOR STUDY   JC25
No.1. Children's Suite for Piano (1938)
          Shepherd Song, March, Waltz, The Small
          Sad Sparrow, Corn Song Irish Lament
          (Famine of 1845), The Brook; 5 min. 30 sec.
No.2. Two Preludes for Four Hands (1941); 2 min.
No.3. Five Little Canons (1941); 2 min.
No.4. Two Descriptive Pieces (1941); 3 min.
No.5. Study in Changing Meter (1935); 1 min. 30 sec.
Piano
E.H. Morris, "Contemporary American Piano Music," Two Pieces from Children's Suite; 5 min. 30 sec.; 2 min.; 2 min.; 3 min.; 1 min. 30 sec.
Also called: **Children's Suite for Piano** (see: Program for premiere)
See: E.R. Anderson, 1976; A. Cohen, 1987.

Premiere:
1940 (May 1): New York City, New York; Composer's Forum-Laboratory; Erich Weil, piano.

THE PASSIONATE SHEPHERD TO HIS LOVE
AND HER REPLY   JC26
Three part women's chorus: Soprano, alto, alto
Catamount*; 5 min.
Text: Poetry of Christopher Marlowe and Walter Raleigh.
See: A. Cohen, 1987; Morton and Collins, 1992; Veil of Isis, 1980.

Premiere:

1975 (April 23): Madison, Wisconsin; Anna Crusis Women's Choir, performers not identified.

Selected performances:
1977 (June): Philadelphia, Pennsylvania; Anna Crusis Women's Choir.

1980 (March 16): San Francisco, California; Community Music Center; The Veil of Isis, Joan Gallegos, conducting; Jan Aaland, Fran Burgess, Cheryl Keller, Lynne Morrow, Marlene Rozofsky, sopranos and Elizabeth Anker, Kathryn Brookes, Francie Conklin, Laura Gilliard, Claire Giovanetti, Linda Millerd Smeage, altos.

1981 (March 29): New York City, New York; New York University; First National Congress of Women In Music; Anna Crusis Women's Choir.

1981 (June 13): Philadelphia, Pennsylvania; Anna Crusis Women's Chorus, Catherine Roma, conducting.

DANCE SUITE   JC27
March, Waltz, Indian Dance, Mazurka (from **Opus 51** and **Race of Life**)
Orchestra: 2-2-3-2, 4-2-2-1, timpani, percussion, piano, 1 or 2 harps, strings
Catamount*; 10 min.
See: A. Cohen, 1987.

Premiere: Unknown

VARIATIONS ON AN AMERICAN THEME   JC28
Blues; Waltz; Jazz
Instrumentation unknown.
Publisher unknown (see App. 1); duration unknown.

Premiere:
1938 (April 4): New York City, New York; Concert League, Recital for Medical Aid to Spain under auspices of Artists Union, performers not identified.

ADIOS BILBADITO   **JC29**

Tenor, cello and bell
Catamount*; duration unknown
Text: Anonymous
Also: Part 1 of **Canzones Y Dances** (JC137) for guitar, flute,
and cello.
See: Albany Records, 1992; *Bennington Banner*, 1970; L.
Jones, 1997; D3.

Premiere:
1970 (May 24): Bennington, Vermont; Mt. Anthony Union
High School Auditorium; Frank Baker, tenor, George Finckel,
cello and Nina Karp, bell.

1939

TRAGIC EXODUS   **JC30**

Ballet for Hanya Holm.
Baritone and piano.
Catamount*; 9 min.
Note: Hanya Holm received the 1939 *Dance Magazine* Third
Annual Award for this ballet.
See: C. Ammer, 1980; A. Cohen, 1987; D. Ewen, 1982; S.
Fuller, 1994; L. Jones, 1997; A. Kozinn, 2000; *Los Angeles
Times*, 2000; N. Slonimsky, 1997; E. White, 1974.

Premiere:
1939 (February 19): New York City, New York; Guild
Theater; Hanya Holm and Dance Company; accompanied by
Peter Throne, baritone and Vivian Fine, piano.

Selected performances:
1939 (November 2): Durham, North Carolina; Duke
University, Women's College Auditorium; Hanya Holm and
Concert Group, accompanists not identified.

1940 (January 7): New York City, New York; Adelphi Theater; Hanya Holm and Company, accompanists not identified.

1940 (January 10, 11, 12, 13): Chicago, Illinois; Art Institute
of Chicago, Kenneth Sawyer Goodman Memorial Theater;
Hanya Holm and Company, accompanists not identified.

1940 (February 3): Colorado Springs, Colorado; Colorado College; Koshare; Hanya Holm and Company, accompanists not identified.

1940 (February 5): Denton, Texas; Texas State College for Women (now: Texas Women's University); Artist's Course; Hanya Holm and Company, accompanists not identified.

1940 (February 15): Muncie, Indiana; Ball State Teachers College (now: Ball State University), Assembly Hall; Hanya Holm and Company, accompanists not identified.

1940 (February 19): Harrisonburg, Virginia; Madison College; Hanya Holm and Company, accompanists not identified.

1940 (April 7): New York City, New York; Theresa L. Kaufmann Auditorium; The Dance Theater Series of the Young Men's Hebrew Association; Hanya Holm and Company, accompanists not identified.

1940 (April 13): New York City, New York; Washington Irving High School, Municipal Auditorium; Hanya Holm and Company, accompanists not identified.

THEY TOO ARE EXILES   JC31

Ballet for Hanya Holm.
Piano and percussion.
Catamount*; 15 min.
See: C. Ammer, 1980; *Associated Press*, 2000; A. Cohen, 1987; D. Ewen, 1982; S. Fuller, 1994; A. Kozinn, 2000; N. Slonimsky, 1997; E. White, 1974.

Premiere:
1940 (January 7): New York City, New York; Adelphi Theater; Hanya Holm and Dance Company; Vivian Fine, piano.

Selected performances:
1940 (January 10, 11, 12, 13): Chicago, Illinois; Art Institute of Chicago, Kenneth Sawyer Goodman Memorial Theater; Hanya Holm and Company, probably Vivian Fine, piano.

1940 (February 3): Colorado Springs, Colorado; Colorado College; Koshare; Hanya Holm and Company, probably Vivian Fine, piano.

1940 (February 5): Denton, Texas; Texas State College for Women (now: Texas Women's University); Artist's Course; Hanya Holm and Company, accompanist not identified.

1940 (February 15): Muncie, Indiana; Ball State Teachers College (now: Ball State University), Assembly Hall; Hanya Holm and Company, accompanist not identified.

1940 (February 19): Harrisonburg, Virginia; Madison College; Hanya Holm and Company, accompanist not identified.

1940 (April 7): New York City, New York; Theresa L. Kaufmann Auditorium; The Dance Theater Series of the Young Men's Hebrew Association; Hanya Holm and Company, accompanist not identified.

1940 (April 13): New York City, New York; Washington Irving High School, Municipal Auditorium; Hanya Holm and Company, accompanist not identified.

1941 (May 17): New York City, New York; Mansfield Theater; Hanya Holm and Company, accompanist not identified.

SONATINA FOR OBOE AND PIANO   JC32
Allegro moderato, Lute sostenuto, Allegretto
Also arranged for cello and piano; violin and piano.
Catamount*; 7 min. 30 sec.
Also called: **Suite for Oboe and Piano**
Note: This piece won the 1942 season award chosen by the Judges of the Music Guild, Ethical Society, Philadelphia, Pennsylvania.
See: E.R. Anderson, 1976; A. Cohen, 1987.

Premiere:
1942 (September 7): Buenos Aires, Argentina; Teatro del Pueblo; Grupo Renovacion, Undécimo Ciclo de Cultura Musical, Esther Castro, oboe and Rodrigo Storani, piano.

Selected performances:
1943 (April): Philadelphia, Pennsylvania; The Music Guild in the Ethical Society Auditorium; Marcel Tabuteau, oboe and Edith Braun, piano.

FIVE PRELUDES   JC33

Allegro; Adagio Calmato; Allegro un poco rubato; Allegro Moderato; Allegro Brillante
Piano
Catamount*; 5 min.
Note: Composed in the time period between the years 1939 and 1941
See: *Algemeen Handelsblad*, 1962; L. Chapin, 1963; F. Church, 1984; A. Cohen, 1987; C. Hall, 1996; J. Haskins, 1962; *Het Vrije Volk*, 1962; K. Mengelberg, 1962; *Montclair Times*, 1951; WNYC, 1986.

Premiere:
1951 (March 4): Montclair, New Jersey; Montclair Art Museum, Vivian Fine, piano.

Selected performances:
1962 (June 8): Mohonk Lake, New York; Lake Mohonk Mountain House; Robert Guralnik, piano.

1962 (June 12): Washington, DC; Phillips Gallery; Robert Guralnik, piano.

1962 (Fall): Amsterdam, Rotterdam, The Hague, Innsbruck, Linz, Berlin and other cities in Europe; Robert Guralnik, piano.

1962 (December 29): New York City, New York; Town Hall; Robert Guralnik, piano.

1963 (June 14): Mohonk Lake, New York; Lake Mohonk Mountain House; Robert Guralnik, piano.

1963 (November 7): Nuremberg, Germany; Robert Guralnik, piano.

1963 (November 13-15): Kiel, Regensburg and Munich, Germany; Staedisches Konservatorium, Am Katharinenkloster 6;

Amerika Hous Munchen Karolinenplay 3; Robert Guralnik, piano.

1964 (January 19): Cornwall-on-Hudson, New York; Museum of the Cornwall Countryside at the Boulevard; benefit by Robert Guralnik, piano.

1966 (March 30): Genova, Italy; Associaziano Italo-Americana-Palazzo Lerconi-Via Garbaldi 3; Robert Guralnik, piano.

1966 (March 31): Milano, Italy; United States Information Service; Robert Guralnik, piano.

1975 (August 7): Hanover, New Hampshire; Dartmouth College, Rollins Chapel; Vivian Fine, piano.

1975 (December 1): Lansing, Michigan; Michigan State University, Department of Music; Sylvia Kahan, piano.

1984 (September 26): Bennington, Vermont; Bennington College, Greenwall Music Workshop, Kit Young, piano.

1984 (November 26): Richmond, Virginia; University of Richmond, North Court Recital Hall, Kit Young, piano.

Broadcasts:
1986 (March 8, September 28): National Public Radio, first in a series by the International League of Women Composers called "Live from Merkin Concert Hall "; a tribute on Fine's 73rd birthday by Ev Grimes and Karen Pearlman.

LIKE A DRIVEN LEAF   JC34
Dance for Corinne Chochem
Piano
Publisher unknown (see App. 1); duration unknown.
Text: Bialick, In No Man's Land: "The refugee driven from place to place asks himself and the world, 'Why?'"

Premiere:
1939 (November 21): Bensonhurst, Brooklyn, New York; Jewish Community House of Bensonhurst, Corinne Chochem and dance company, accompanied by Vivian Fine, piano.

1940

SUITE IN E-FLAT   JC35
Prelude; Sarabande; Gavotte; Air; Gigue
Piano
Catamount*; 7 min.
See: C. Hall, 1996; L. Jones, 1997; *Philadelphia Evening Bulletin,* 1946.

Premiere:
1944 (March 4): Congers, New York; Congers High School; International Society for Contemporary Composers, The Forum Group of the American Section, Vivian Fine, piano.

Selected performances:
1946 (November 21): Philadelphia, Pennsylvania; Temple University; Vivian Fine, piano.

1955 (July 24): Plainfield, Vermont; The Haybarn Theater, Upper Winooski Development Association; Vivian Fine, piano.

1975 (April 25): Albany, New York; Free Music Store, Music of Vivian Fine program, Vivian Fine, piano.

1975 (August 7): Hanover, New Hampshire; Rollins Chapel, Dartmouth College; Vivian Fine, piano.

1975 (November 16): Manchester, New Hampshire; The Currier Gallery of Art; in observance of International Women's Year by the New Hampshire Commission on the Status of Women, presentation of "Women In Music," Vivian Fine, piano.

Broadcasts:
1942 (February 18): New York City, New York; WNYC, Third Festival of American Music, performed by Vivian Fine, piano.

THREE PIECES FOR VIOLIN AND PIANO   JC36
Moderato, Andante, Vivace
Catamount*; 9 min.
See: A. Cohen, 1987; R-M. Johnson, 1989; M. Schubert, 1946.

Premiere:
1946 (April 16): New York City, New York; New York Times
Hall; International Society for Contemporary Music Forum
Group, United States Section; Orrea Pernel, violin and
Beveridge Webster, piano.

1941

EPIGRAM AND EPITAPH   JC37
Mezzo-soprano, piano
Catamount*; 3 min.
Texts: Sir William Jones and Sir Henry Wolton
See: A. Cohen, 1987.

Premiere: Unknown

TIN-HORN REBELLION   JC38
Dance for George Bockman and the Adelphi Dance Theater
Piano
Publisher unknown (see App. 1); duration unknown.

Premiere:
1941 (December 7, 14 and 21): New York City, New York;
Studio Theater; George Bockman and the Adelphi Dance
Theater; accompanied by Genevieve Pitot, piano.

1942

"DOLLARS AND CENTS" — MUSIC FOR PLAY   JC39
Subtitle: A Tropical Review
Voices and piano
Note: Written jointly with Margret Bonds
Five parts: Fine wrote the following three songs: "I Don't
Believe Everything They Say," "You've Got to Get Wise," and
"I'm a Very Simple Fellow"
Publisher unknown (see App. 1); duration unknown (a "longer
work")
See: A. Cohen, 1987.

Premiere:

1942 (Spring): New York City, New York; Henry Street
Settlement, performers not identified.

1943

SONGS OF OUR TIME   JC40
I. Stabat Mater (text: Jozef Wittlin)
II. And what did she get, the soldier's wife (text: Bertolt
Brecht)
Mezzo-sopranos, piano, (percussion optional)
Catamount*; 4 min. 30 sec.; 3 min.
See: *Bennington Banner*, 1970; A. Cohen, 1987.

Premiere: Stabat Mater
1970 (May 24): Bennington, Vermont; Mt. Anthony High
School; Nina Karp, alto, Catherine Satterlee, mezzo-soprano,
Sarah Tenney, percussion, and Vivian Fine, piano.

RHAPSODY ON A RUSSIAN FOLK SONG   JC41
Piano
Catamount*; 6 min.
Also known as **Capriccio on a Russian Theme**
See: A. Cohen, 1987; C. Hall, 1996.

Premiere:
1944 (April 30): New York City, New York; Town Hall; a
concert in honor of Russia sponsored by Congregation Emanu-
El and the University Women's Chorus; Vivian Fine, piano
with the title: *Capriccio on a Russian Theme*.

Selected performances:
1948 (April 17): New York City, New York; City Center;
International Society for Contemporary Music, Forum Group,
Vivian Fine, piano.

1944

CONCERTANTE FOR PIANO AND ORCHESTRA   JC42
Andante con moto; allegro risoluto
Piano, 2-2-2-2, 2-2-0-0, timpani, strings
Catamount*; 17 min. 30 sec.

See: E.R. Anderson, 1976; E. Armer, 1991; J. Carson, 1983; A. Cohen, 1987; A. Cohn, 1960, 1981; D. Cummings, 1998; R. French, 1960; S. Fuller, 1994; D. Greene, 1985; C. Hall, 1996; *HiFi Stereo Review*, 1960; S. Husarik, 1992; R. Jones, 1960; E. Kahn, 1980's; Morton and Collins, 1992; *New Paltz Independent and Times*, 1962; *Playbill*, 1960; J. Raymond, 2000; W. Riegger, 1958; N. Slonimsky, 1997; S. Tyler, 1998; D4, D5.

Premiere:
1988 (December 2): Brunswick, Maine; Pickard Theater, Bowdoin College; Martin Perry, piano and Bowdoin College Community Orchestra, Zae Munn, conducting.

Broadcasts:
1972: The National Federation of Music Clubs produced a series of 13 programs to be aired on radio. Program 1 began with Fine's CRI 135-A recording of *Concertante for Piano and Orchestra*, movements I and II. On June 5, 1972, Minnesota Educational Radio, stations KSJR, KSJN and KCCM, carried this radio show.

1983: WAMC, Albany, New York, National Public Radio, Robert Lurtsema, host of Morning Pro Musica.

Recordings:
1960: CRI SD-135 by The Japan Philharmonic Symphony Orchestra, A. Watanabe conducting; Composers Recordings Inc., New York. See: D4
1995: CRI 692, American Masters, **Music of Vivian Fine**; remastered onto compact disc; Composers Recordings Inc., New York. See: D5

1946

CAPRICCIO FOR OBOE AND STRING TRIO   JC43
Oboe, violin, viola, cello
Catamount*; 10 min.
Also called: **Capriccio for Oboe Quartet**
See: E. Armer, 1991; A. Cohen, 1987; R-M. Johnson, 1989; E. Salzman, January 7 and 10, 1959; N. Slonimsky, 1997.

Premiere:

1948 (April 17): New York City, New York; ICSM Forum Group; Lois Wann, oboe, Sherman Goldscheid, violin, Sol Greitzer, viola, and Eula Schock, cello.

Selected performances:
1958 (December 21): New York City, New York; Nonagon Gallery; Composers' Showcase; Lois Wann, oboe, The New York String Trio, Sterling Hunkins, cello, Lilla Kalman, violin, Bernard Zaslov, viola.

1979 (May or June): Charleston, North Carolina; Simons Arts Center Recital Hall; performers unidentified.

1979 (August 21): Bennington, Vermont; Greenwall Auditorium; The Chamber Music Conference and Composer's Forum of the East, music by the composers-in-residence; Patricia Stenberg, oboe, Joseph Schor, violin, May Elliott James, viola, and Charlotta Klein Ross, cello.

1980 (May 30): Charleston, North Carolina; Piccolo Spoleto; Patricia Stenberg, oboe, Rinaldo Couto, violin, Melissa Trier, viola, and David Moore, cello.

Broadcasts:
1958 (December 22): Music of Vittorio Rieti and Vivian Fine from the December 21, 1958 performance heard over WQXR.

1947

CHACONNE   JC44
Piano
Catamount*; 15 min.
See: A. Cohen, 1987; L. Jones, 1997.

Premiere:
This work has never been performed.

THE GREAT WALL OF CHINA   JC45
Medium high or medium voice, flute, cello, piano
New Music Press, New York; 12 min.
See: E.R. Anderson, 1976; A. Berger, 1948; G. Claghorn, 1996; A. Cohen, 1987; W. Crutchfield, Jan. 24, 1985; M.

Jacobson, 1990; Library of Congress, 1982; Morton and Collins, 1992; N. Slonimsky, 1997.
Text: Franz Kafka

> I. I can still remember quite well us standing as small children, scarcely sure on our feet . . .
> II. But instead how vainly does he wear out his strength; . . .
> III. Long-dead emperors are set on the throne. . .
> IV. Try with all your might to comprehend the decrees of the high command. . .

Premiere:
1948 (May): New York City, New York; Macmillan Theater; Alice Ditson Fund Concert; Shirlee Emmons, soprano, Ralph Freundlich, flute, Claus Adam, cello, and Alvin Bauman, piano.

Selected performances:
1966 (June 17): Bennington, Vermont; Bennington College; Carey Daniels, soprano, Sharon Powers, flute and Michael Finckel, cello. Parts I and II only.

1975 (March 8): New York City, New York; International House; International Women's Arts Festival; Walden Trio, Gwendolyn Mansfield, flute, Joan Stein, piano, Maxine Neuman, cello and LouAnn Lee, soprano; celebrating International Women's Day.

1975 (March 9): New York City, New York; Community Church; Walden Trio, Gwendolyn Mansfield, flute, Joan Stein, piano, Maxine Neuman, cello and LouAnn Lee, soprano.

1975 (April 25): Albany, New York; Free Music Store, Music of Vivian Fine program, LouAnn Lee, mezzo-soprano, Irvin Gilman, flute, David Gibson, cello and Vivian Fine, piano.

1985 (January 22): New York City, New York; The Juilliard Theater, The Juilliard School, Lincoln Center; performers unidentified.

1990 (March 26): Washington, DC; Ward Recital Hall, Catholic University; The Contemporary Music Forum, Sara

Landgren, flute, Lori Barnet, cello, Mark Markham, piano and Pamela Jordan, soprano.

SECOND SOLO FOR OBOE   JC46
Catamount*; 5 min.
See: A. Cohen, 1987; E. Salzman, January 7 and 10, 1959

Premiere:
1958 (December 21): New York City, New York; Nonagon Gallery, Lois Wann, oboe.

Selected performances:
1964 (February 17): New York City, New York; Donnell Library; Lois Wann, oboe.

1976 (February 19): Saratoga Springs, New York; Skidmore College, Filene Recital Hall; Gene Marie Green, oboe.

1980 (October 30): Innsbruck, Austria; Hall at the Center for New Music; tour of James Ostryniec, oboe.

1985 (May 4): Philadelphia, Pennsylvania; Sigma Alpha Iota, Philadelphia Alumnae Chapter, Rheta Smith, oboe.

Broadcasts:
1958 (December 22): Music of Vittorio Rieti and Vivian Fine from the December 21, 1958 performance heard over WQXR.
1964 (Winter/spring): WNYC broadcast
1980 (November): Austrian radio re-broadcast of James Ostryniec's concert.

THERE IS A GARDEN IN HER FACE   JC47
Soprano, flute, violin, cello, piano.
Publisher unknown (see App. 1); 4 min.
Text: Thomas Campion
See: A. Cohen, 1987.

Premiere:
This piece has not been performed.

1951

DIVERTIMENTO   JC48

Cello and percussion (timpani, snare-drum, cymbal, tambourine, wood-block)

Catamount*; 5 min.

See: M. Berliner, 1964; A. Borg, 1958; A. Cohen, 1987; R. Ericson, 1972; R-M. Johnson, 1989; I. Lowens, 1964; C. Mersel, 1962; *New Paltz News*, 1958; K. Pennell, 1962

Notes: The following notes by Fine were published as part of the Program Notes for the 1978 performance by the San Francisco Conservatory. *"The Divertimento* was written in 1951 and has been widely performed. It was originally written for a percussionist and his cellist wife. They were taken aback by the idiom —— perhaps expecting something 'typical' for cello and drumming — and never performed the work. The dramatic dialogue between the players contrasts the linear quality of the cello with the more varied sounds of percussion."

Premiere:

1962 (August 19): Mountainville, New York; Storm King Art Center, Hudson Valley Philharmonic Chamber Music Concerts, Sterling Hunkins, cello and James Coover, percussion.

Selected performances:

1958 (November 18): New Paltz, New York; State University Teachers College, College Union Lounge; Sterling Hunkins, cello, and Warren Smith, percussion.

1962 (August 26): Millbrook, New York; Millbrook Pavilion, The Innisfree Chamber Music Concerts; Sterling Hunkins, cello and James Coover, percussion (see also next two dates)

1962 (October 31 and November 6): Poughkeepsie, New York; Vassar College, Skinner Recital Hall, see above.

1962 (November 2): New Paltz, New York; State University of New York at New Paltz; College Union Lounge, A Program of Baroque and Contemporary American Music, see above.

1963 (February 19): Union College, New York; Memorial Chapel, A Program of Baroque and Contemporary American Music, Sterling Hunkins, cello and James Coover, percussion.

1963 (March 31): Annandale-on-Hudson, New York; Bard College; all by Sterling Hunkins, cello and James Coover, percussion.

1964 (June 8): Washington, DC; Phillips Collection Gallery; Jesse Kergal, cello and Takayori Atsumi, piano.

1972 (May 12): Boston, Massachusetts; Isabella Stewart Gardner Museum; Barbara Mallow, cello and Louis Calabro, percussion.

1972 (May 15): New York City, New York; Carnegie Recital Hall, Barbara Mallow, cello and Takayori Atsumi, piano.

1978 (February 16): San Francisco, California; Hellman Hall, The San Francisco Conservatory of Music; New Music Ensemble, Jerry LeClerc and Kevin Walker, cello, Andy Lewis, Jim Reynolds, percussion, directed by Joan Gallegos and Hermann Le Roux.

1952

VARIATIONS   JC49
Piano
Publisher unknown (see App. 1); 20 min.
See: A. Cohen, 1987; C. Hall, 1996.

Premiere:
1952 (June 11): New Paltz, New York; State University of New York at New Paltz; Conference on the Fine Arts; Vivian Fine, piano.

SONATA FOR VIOLIN AND PIANO   JC50
Energico, con fuoco; Lento; Allegro con spirito.
Catamount*; 16 min.
Also called: **Violin Sonata**
See: Ariel, 1983; A. Cohen, 1987; D. Cummings, 1998; C. Hall, 1996; R-M. Johnson, 1989; D. Landis and L. Edelman, 1982; *New York Times*, 1958; R. Parmenter, 1959; E. Salzman, January 7 and 10, 1959; San Francisco Symphony, 1982; H. Tircuit, 1983

Premiere:
1958 (December 21): New York City, New York; Nonagon Gallery; Composer's Showcase Concert; Matthew Raimondi, violin and Yehudi Wyner, piano.

Selected performances:
1961 (May 23): New York City, New York; Bethasbee de Rothschild Foundation; Matthew Raimondi, violin and Yehudi Wyner, piano.

1983 (January 9): San Francisco, California; Old First Church; "Vivian Fine Week" (January 5-13) sponsored by San Francisco Symphony; Daniel Kobialka, violin and Machiko Kobialka, piano.

Broadcast:
1958 (December 22): Music of Vittorio Rieti and Vivian Fine from the December 21, 1958 performance heard over WQXR.

SINFONIA AND FUGATO   JC51
Piano
Lawson-Gould, New York, in: New Music for Piano; distributed by G. Schirmer; 5 min. 40 sec.
See: E.R. Anderson, 1976; A. Cohen, 1987; D. Greene, 1985; M. Hinderaker, 1968; H. Klein, 1966; M. Miller, 1989; C. Samford, 1968; L. Trimble, 1972; D16, D17, D18.

Premiere: unknown

Selected performances:
1966 (October 24): Annandale-on-Hudson, New York; Bard Hall, Bard College, a lecture-recital on 20th Century piano music including this work, Vivian Fine performing.

1968 (February 26): Oshkosh, Wisconsin; Panorama of Arts program, Wisconsin State University-Oshkosh; a lecture-recital Vivian Fine performed on 20th Century piano music. [Review article by Hinderaker (See: M. Hinderaker, 1968) indicated that she performed Sinfonia and Fugato, not Piano Pieces as indicated on the copy of the program]

1968 (May 12): Williamsburg, Virginia; Collegium Musicum series, William and Mary College, a lecture-recital Vivian Fine performed on 20th Century piano music.

1975 (August 7): Hanover, New Hampshire; Rollins Chapel, Dartmouth College; Vivian Fine, piano.

1976 (November 6): Baltimore, Maryland; American Musicological Society, Statler Hilton; Arthur Tollefson, piano.

1989 (April 20): Boston, Massachusetts; Northeastern University, Department of Music, Music at Noon, Ell Center Ballroom; Emily Corbato, piano. A performance as part of Vivian Fine Appreciation Week in Boston.

1989 (April 23): Watertown, Massachusetts; First Parish Church; American Women Composers Fourth Annual Marathon; Emily Corbato, piano.

1989 (October 22): New York City, New York; Weill Recital Hall; Emily Corbato, piano.

Recordings:
1966: CRI SD-288 by Robert Helps, piano; **New Music for Piano**; Composers Recordings Inc., New York. See: D16.
1966: LM 7042 2-disks and LSC 7042 Stereo; ibid.; RCA New Victor, New York. See: D17.
1995: CRI 692, American Masters, **Music of Vivian Fine**; remastered onto compact disc; Composers Recordings Inc., New York. See: D18.

1953

PSALM 13   **JC52**

Three-part women's chorus, baritone solo.
Two sopranos, alto, baritone, piano or organ.
Catamount*; 4 min. 30 sec.
See: A. Cohen, 1987; N. Slonimsky, 1997.

Premiere: Never performed.

VARIATIONS FOR HARP   **JC53**

Remembrance of things in the past of Erik Satie
Theme: Andante; Variation 1: Poco piu mosso; Variation 2:
Ancora piu mosso; Variation 3: Poco meno mosso; Variation
4: Invertus; Finale.
Lyra Music; 5 min.
Comment: Honorable Mention, Northern California Harpists
Association Contest, 1954.
See: A. Cohen, 1987; E.R. Anderson, 1976.

Premiere:
1955 (April 22): Woodstock, New York; Maverick Theater;
Joyce Rosenfield, harp.

Selected performances:
1963 (June 14): Mohonk Lake, New York; Lake Mohonk
Mountain House; Joyce Rosenfield, harp.

1967 (March 6): New Paltz, New York; Duzine Auditorium;
The League of Women Voters of New Paltz; Joyce Rosenfield,
harp.

1985 (October 16): Bennington, Vermont; Bennington College,
Greenwall Music Workshop, Vivian Fine, piano and Elizabeth
Wright, piano. Arrangement for two pianos by Fine and
Wright.

1954

COMPOSITION FOR STRING QUARTET   **JC54**

Two violins, viola, cello
ACA; 12 min.
See: A. Cohen, 1987; C. Hall, 1996; R-M. Johnson, 1989.

Premiere:
This work was written for the educational film "New Ways of
Seeing," by Roger Tilton, based on ideas of Benjamin Karp,
sculptor.

1956

A GUIDE TO THE LIFE EXPECTANCY OF A ROSE   JC55

Soprano, tenor, flute, violin, cello, clarinet, harp
Catamount*; 16 min.
Commission: Bethasbee de Rothschild Foundation
Text: Article in the *New York Times* garden section by S.R.
Tilley.
See: C. Ammer, 1980; E.R. Anderson, 1976; B., A.E., 1959;
G. Claghorn, 1996; A. Cohen, 1987; D. Cummings, 1997; D.
Ewen, 1982; S. Fuller, 1994; R-M. Johnson, 1989; B. Jones,
1999; L. Jones, 1997; N. Lebrecht, 1992; Morton and Collins,
1992; **Music in Print**, 1999; *New Paltz Independent*, 1959;
New York Times, 1959; R. Parmenter, 1956; Parsons, 1986;
Playbill, 1960; J. Raymond, 2000; W. Riegger, 1958; S. Sadie,
1988; E. White, 1974.

Premiere:
1956 (May 16): New York City, New York; Bethasbee de
Rothschild Foundation; Bethany Beardslee, soprano, Earl
Rogers, tenor, Jacques Monod, conducting.

Selected performances:
1959 (February 7): New York City, New York; Donnell
Library Center; Fifth Concert of the Composer's Forum;
Bethany Beardslee, soprano, William McGrath, tenor, Sam
Baron, flute, Herbert Baumel, violin, Jack Kreiselman, clarinet,
Otto Deri, cello, Sonya Kahn, harp and Carlos Surinach,
conducting.

1957

STRING QUARTET   JC56

Allegro appassionato, allegro di bravura, lento, allegretto a la
danza.
Two violins, viola, cello
Catamount*; 19 min.
See: T. Brookes, 1986; A. Cohen, 1987; D. Cummings, 1998;
C. Hall, 1996; R-M. Johnson, 1989; *New Paltz Independent*,
1959; S. Tyler, 1998; WNYC, 1986.

Premiere:
1957 (November 21): Poughkeepsie, New York; Skinner
Recital Hall, Vassar College; Claremont String Quartet, Marc

Gottlieb, violin, Vladimir Weisman, violin, William Schoen, viola, Irving Klein, cello.

Selected performances:
1959 (February 7): New York City, New York; Donnell Library Center; Fifth Concert of the Composer's Forum; Claremont String Quartet, Marc Gottlieb and Vladimir Weisman, violins, William Schoen, viola, and Irving Klein, cello. First New York performance.

1963 (June 23): Washington, DC; Phillips Gallery; Claremont String quartet, sponsored by the National Council of Women of the United States.

1976 (February 19): Saratoga Springs, New York; Skidmore College, Filene Recital Hall; George Green and Sander Strenger, violins, Jacob Glick, viola and Maxine Neuman, cello.

Broadcasts:
1986 (April 19): Boston, Massachusetts; WGBH 89.7 FM, Vivian Fine: A Celebration of Her Music.

1986 (March 8, September 28): National Public Radio, first in a series by the International League of Women Composers, WNYC program "Live from Merkin Concert Hall."; a tribute on Fine's 73rd birthday by Ev Grimes and Karen Pearlman.

1959

VALEDICTIONS   **JC57**
Soprano, tenor, mixed chorus, ten instruments
Catamount*; 16 min.
Text: Poetry of John Donne
See: E.R. Anderson, 1976; A. Cohen, 1987; C.J. Hall, 1989; N. Slonimsky, 1997.

Premiere:
1959 (May 1959): New York City, New York; Bethasbee de Rothschild Foundation; Shirlee Emmons, soprano, William McGrath, tenor and the Schola Cantorum of New York, Hugh Ross, conducting.

1960

ALCESTIS   **JC58**

Alcestis and Thanatos; The Revelling Hercules; Battle between
Hercules and Thanatos; Dance of Triumph: Rescue of Alcestis.
Ballet for Martha Graham
Catamount*; 27 min.
See: C. Ammer, 1980; E.R. Anderson, 1976; *Associated Press*,
2000; C. Barnes, 1968; A. Block and C. Neuls-Bates, 1979; T.
Brookes, 1986; A. Cohen, 1987; M. Connell, 1986; D.
Cummings, 1989; D. Ewen, 1982; V. Fine and L.
Dlugoszewski, 1963; W. Flanagan, 1962; R. Fruchter, 1989; S.
Fuller, 1994; D. Greene, 1985; C. Hall, 1996; S. Husarik,
1992; B. Jones, 1999; A. Kozinn, 2000; *Los Angeles Times*,
2000; Morton and Collins, 1992; *New Paltz Independent*, 1960;
New Paltz Independent and Times, 1962; *Playbill*, 1960; D.
Randel, 1996; R. Sabin, 1960; S. Sadie, 1988; N. Slonimsky,
1997; E. Stodelle, 1975; *Washington Post*, 2000; E. White,
1974; D1, D2.

ALCESTIS   **JC59**

Suite from ballet for orchestra
Catamount*; 10 min. 45 sec.
Commission: Martha Graham
See: C. Ammer, 1980; **American Record Guide**, 1962; J.
Carson, 1983; A. Cohn, 1962, 1981; Fanfare, 1962; W.
Flanagan, 1962; S. Galardi, 1985; C. Hall, 1996; R. Jones,
1961; E. Kahn, 1960's; A. Levine, 1983; D. Randel, 1996; E.
White, 1962; D1, D2.

Premiere:
1960 (April 29): Ballet; New York City, New York; 54th
Street Theater; Martha Graham in title role assisted by
members of her Dance Company; chamber orchestra conducted
by Robert Irving. Subsequent performances: April 30, May 5,
8, 1960.

1983 (November 5): Orchestral Suite from ballet; Bennington,
Vermont; Bennington College; Vermont Symphony Orchestra,
Efrain Guigui, conducting.

Selected performances:
1961 (April): New York City, New York; 54th Street Theater;
Martha Graham and company.

1962 (March 5, 9, 11, 13, 15): New York City, New York; Broadway Theater; Martha Graham and company.

1962 (August 18): New London, Connecticut; 15th American Dance Festival, Palmer Auditorium, Connecticut College; Martha Graham and her Dance Company; Robert Irving, conducting.

1962 (October): Israel; Martha Graham and company.

1968 (October 23 through November 3): Brooklyn, New York; Brooklyn College of Music; Martha Graham and company.

1989 (March 3): Wayne, New Jersey; Shea Auditorium, William Paterson College; Suite from the ballet, Wayne Chamber Orchestra, Murray Bernard Colosimo, conducting.

Broadcasts:
1986 (March 8, September 28): National Public Radio broadcast, first in a series by the International League of Women Composers.
1972: National Federation of Music Clubs produced a series of thirteen programs to be aired on radio during 1972. Program 3 featured *Alcestis* from CRI 145 a, band 2.

Recordings:
1961: CRI SRD 145 by The Imperial Philharmonic Symphony Orchestra of Tokyo, William Strickland, conducting; Composers Recordings Inc., New York City, New York. See: D1
1995: CRI 692 American Masters, **Music of Vivian Fine**, remastered onto compact disc, Composers Recordings Inc., New York. See: D2

1961

DUO FOR FLUTE AND VIOLA   **JC60**
War Against Images
Carl Fischer, Inc.; 5 min. 30 sec.
Also called: **Iconomachy**; **Duo for Violin and Viola**
See: A. Cohen, 1987; *New Paltz Independent and Times*, 1962.

Premiere:

1962 (February 22): New York City, New York; Carnegie
Recital Hall; Claude Monteux, flute and Walter Trampler,
viola.

Selected performances:
1962: London; Heidelberg, Bremen, Berlin, Stuttgart,
Germany; European tour of Claude Monteux and Walter
Trampler.

1964 (January 30): London, England; American Embassy
Theatre; Claude Monteux, flute and Walter Trampler, viola.

1970 (November 15): Staten Island, New York; The Unitarian
Church; Stanley Hoffman, viola and Mary Barto, flute.

1975 (February 12): Boston, Massachusetts; Boston University;
Samuel B. Bronski, flute and violist unidentified.

1976 (February 19): Saratoga Springs, New York; Skidmore
College, Filene Recital Hall; George Green, violin and Jacob
Glick, viola.

Broadcast:
1962: Hamburg Radio, European tour performance of Claude
Monteux and Walter Trampler.

THREE PIECES FOR FLUTE, BASSOON AND HARP   **JC61**
Catamount*; 6 min.
See: A. Cohen, 1987.

Premiere:
1961: Ellsworth, Maine; Claude Monteux, flute, Loren
Glickman, bassoon, Cynthia Otis, harp.

1962

MORNING   **JC62**
Mixed chorus
Mixed chorus, narrator, piano or organ.
Catamount*; 5 min.
Text: Henry David Thoreau (from **Walden**)
Commission: New York Society for Ethical Culture

See: G. Claghorn, 1996; A. Cohen, 1987.

Premiere:
1973 (June 6): Bennington, Vermont; Bennington Armory, Bennington College Motet Choir, Stanley Scott, narrator, Beth Eisenberg, organ, and Vivian Fine, conducting.

FANTASY FOR CELLO AND PIANO   JC63
Slow; Allegro; Adagio; Presto; Lento molto.
Catamount*; 7 min. 30 sec.
See: A. Cohen, 1987; M. Cooper, 1976; L. Jones, 1997; M. Richter, 1970; D. Spengler, 1975; D7.

Premiere:
1970 (February 13): New York City, New York; Carnegie Chamber Hall; John Thurman, cello and Robert Guralnik, piano. Concert of works by American women sponsored by National Federation of Music Clubs.

Selected performances:
1975 (November 1 or 2): Ridgewood, New Jersey; Anderson Auditorium; The Walden Trio, Maxine Neuman, cello and Joan Stein, piano.

1976 (March 11): Hackensack, New Jersey; Johnson Free Public Library; Walden Trio.

1976 (April 18): Bronx, New York; Bronx Museum of the Arts, Sunday Afternoon Concert Series; Maxine Neuman, cello and Joan Stein, piano.

1976 (October 8): New York City, New York; The New School for Social Research; Meet the Woman Composer; Maxine Neuman, cello and Joan Stein, piano.

1978 (July 8): Bennington, Vermont; Bennington College; Michael Finckel, cello and Vivian Fine, piano.

1979 (February 17): New York City, New York; Carnegie Recital Hall; Maxine Neuman, cello and Joan Stein, piano.

1979 (February or March): Ridgewood, New Jersey; Anderson Auditorium; Maxine Neuman, cello and Joan Stein, piano.

1981 (October 21): Bennington, Vermont; Bennington College, Greenwall Music Workshop; Maxine Neuman, cello and Vivian Fine, piano.

Recordings:
1990s: No number, by Maxine Neuman, cello and Joan Stein, piano; Opus One Records, Greenville, Maine and Napanoch, NY. See: D7

OCTOBER PIECES   JC64
Piano and percussion
Published unknown (see App. 1); duration unknown.
Dedication: Sterling Hunkins
See: C. Mersel, 1962.

Premiere:
1962 (Fall): Poughkeepsie, New York; Vassar College, performers unidentified.

1963

THE CONFESSION   JC65
Soprano, flute, violin, viola, cello, piano
Catamount*; 11 min. 20 sec.
Text: Racine
See: E.R. Anderson, 1976; A. Cohen, 1987; D. Ewen, 1982; D. Henahan, 1973.

Premiere:
1963 (March 21): New York City, New York; Carnegie Recital Hall; Karen Ranung, soprano, Claude Monteux, flute, Robert Rudie, violin, Lilla Kalman, viola, Sterling Hunkins, cello, and Robert Guralnik, piano.

Selected performances:
1973 (April 15): New York; Finch College Concert Hall; an All-Vivian Fine program; Jan DeGaetani, soprano, Jeanne Benjamin, violin, Sue Kahn, flute, Jacob Glick, viola, Barbara Mallow, cello, and Robert Guralnik, piano.

1975 (April 4): Berkeley, California; 1750 Arch Street, University of California at Berkeley, Department of Music,

Morrison Hall, lecture-recital; Miriam Abramowitsch, mezzo-soprano, Karla Warnke, flute, Mardell Kuntz, violin, Joan Carl, viola, Kevin Walker, cello, and Alan Martin, piano, San Francisco Conservatory Players, and Vivian Fine, conducting.

1975 (April 6): Hayward, California; California State University at Hayward; Music Building; Miriam Abramowitsch, mezzo-soprano, Karla Warnke, flute, Mardell Kuntz, violin, Joan Carl, viola, Kevin Walker, cello, and Alan Martin, piano, San Francisco Conservatory Players, and Vivian Fine, conducting.

1964

DREAMSCAPE   JC66
Percussion ensemble, three flutes, cello, piano, lawnmower
Catamount*; duration unknown
See: A. Cohen, 1987; D. Cummings, 1998; N. Slonimsky, 1997; S. Tyler, 1998.

Premiere:
1964 (November 25): Bennington, Vermont; Bennington College, Carriage Barn; Simone Juda, Deborah Pollack and Sharon Powers, flutes, George Finckel, cello, Reinhoud van der Linde, piano, Deborah Chaffee and George Gilman, Chinese temple blocks, Nan Newton, claves and maracas, Pril Smiley, woodblock, Louis Calabro, snare drum and gong, Elaine Buxbaum and Carolyn Heimburger, water whistles, Lisa Tate, bells, Barbara Glasser, triangle, Wendy Erdman, lawn mower and conducted by Henry Brant.

MELOS   JC67
Solo double bass
Catamount*; 6 min.
See: A. Cohen, 1987.

Premiere:
1964 (April 8): Bennington, Vermont; Bennington College; Bertram Turetzky, double bass.

Selected performances:
1964 (May 26): Hartford, Connecticut; Hartt College of Music,

University of Hartford, Auerbach Hall; Bertram Turetzky, double bass.

1973 (October 24): Bennington, Vermont; Bennington College, Roy Wiseman, double bass.

1979 (date unknown): La Jolla, California; University of California at San Diego, Bertram Turetzky, double bass.

1988 (April 3): Bennington, Vermont; Bennington College, Greenwall Music Workshop, Jeffery Levine, contrabass.

THE SONG OF PERSEPHONE   JC68
Adagio, with intense expressiveness; Allegro, with bombastic, flamboyant exaggeration and rhythmic elasticity; Molto moderato e tranquillo.
Solo viola
Catamount*; 9 min.
See: E.R. Anderson, 1976; A. Cohen, 1987; C.J. Hall, 1989; A. Hughes, 1968.

Premiere:
1968 (August 6): Lenox, Massachusetts; High Point Inn and Galleries; Berkshire Chamber Players concert, guest artist - Jacob Glick, viola.

Selected performances:
1968 (September 18): New York City, New York; Town Hall, Jacob Glick, viola. Part of a program presenting eight composers.

1969 (September 23): Bennington, Vermont; Bennington College; Jacob Glick, viola.

1974 (December 5): Albany, New York; The Music Store, State University of New York at Albany, Jacob Glick, viola.

1975 (January 19): New York City, New York; concert "Music from Bennington," Jacob Glick, viola.

1975 (February 4): Santa Cruz, California; Crown College, University of California at Santa Cruz, Sesnon Gallery, College V; Jacob Glick, viola.

1975 (April 25): Albany, New York; Free Music Store, Music
of Vivian Fine program, Jacob Glick, viola.

1978 (April 8): DeKalb, Illinois; Northern Illinois University;
Jacob Glick, viola.

1978 (October 4): Bennington, Vermont; Bennington College,
Greenwall Music Workshop; Jacob Glick, viola.

1980 (January 29): Eugene, Oregon; University of Oregon,
School of Music, Beall Concert Hall; Jacob Glick, viola.

1980 (January 30): Seattle, Washington; Cornish Institute,
Cornish Theater, New Performance Group; Jacob Glick, viola.

1980 (March 6): Grinnell, Iowa; Grinnell College, Department
of Music, Herrick Chapel; Jacob Glick, viola.

1965

CONCERTINO FOR PIANO AND PERCUSSION ENSEMBLE   JC69
Allegretto agitato, Cadenza, Lento appassionata, Tempo di
gige, Andante tranquillo, Moderato
Xylophone, vibraphone, marimba, three tom-toms, and timpani.
Catamount*; 11 min.
See: A. Cohen, 1987; D. Ewen, 1982; L. Jones, 1997.

Premiere:
1965 (March 18): New York City, New York; Manhattan
School of Music; Paul Price Ensemble, Richard Allen, Wayne
Brotherton, Edward Burnham, Fred Eckler, John Feddersen,
Alan Silverman, and Howard Zwickler, Paul Price conducting
and Vivian Fine, piano.

Selected performances:
1968 (February 11 to April 7): European-Asian Tour of The
Manhattan School of Music Percussion Ensemble, Paul Price,
conducting, Robert Abrahamson, piano.
>   (February 19): Keerbergen, Belgium.
>   (March 7): Belgrade, Yugoslavia; taping and radio
>   (March 8): Ljubljana, Yugoslavia.
>   (March 15): Athens, Greece; Hellenic-American
>   Union.

(March 18): Izmir, Turkey; Turkish-American Association.

(March 20): Ankara, Turkey; Turkish-American Association

(March 20): Ankara, Turkey; taping for Turkish radio

(March 23): Istanbul, Turkey; Academy of Fine Arts

(March 27): Beirut, Lebanon; American University of Beirut.

(April 2): Teheran, Iran; Iran-American Society.

1968 (November 5): Fredonia, New York; Mason Hall Auditorium, Department of Music, State University of New York at Fredonia; Fredonia Percussion Ensemble, Lawrence Balestra, Harold Coons, Robert Hammer, Kenneth Harbison, Stephen Henry, John Keon Jr., Paul Manton (string bass), Joseph Murphy, and Virginia Sadkin with Theodore Frazeur, conducting and Robert Marvel, piano.

1969 (February 4): Rutherford, New Jersey; Fairleigh-Dickinson University, Dreyfuss Hall; Fredonia Percussion Ensemble, Theodore Frazeur, conducting and Robert Marvel, piano.

1969 (February 5): Indiana, Pennsylvania; Indiana University of Pennsylvania, Cogswell Auditorium; Robert Marvel, piano and the Fredonia Percussion Ensemble, Lawrence Balestra, Harol Coons, Robert Hammer, Kenneth Harbison, Stephen Henry, John Keon Jr., Paul Manton (string bass), Joseph Murphy, Virginia Sadkin with Theodore Frazeur, conducting.

1973 (May 9): Newark, New Jersey; Newark State College, Union Theater for the Performing Arts; Newark State College Percussion Ensemble, Paul Price conducting and William Feldman, piano.

1977 (March 11): Poznan, Poland; Poznan Percussion Ensemble, Jerzy Zgodzinski conducting.

1986 (November 22): Buffalo, New York; Department of Music, State University of New York at Buffalo, Slee Concert Hall, UB Percussion Ensemble, Charles Gray, pianist, Timothy Moon, David Hershey, Robert Schulz, Kevin Soltis, Eric Zak, and Jan Williams, conducting.

MY SON, MY ENEMY   JC70

Ballet for Jose Limon
Visions, Fantasies, Judgment and Vengeance
String quartet, piano, percussion.
Publisher unknown (see App. 1); 30 min.
Commission: Connecticut College through assistance of funds
from The Rockefeller Foundation
Text: "If you obey me, I assure you and I promise, in the
name of God, that I will not punish you, and if you return I
will love you more than ever. But if you do not, I give you as
your father my eternal curse; and as your sovereign, I assure
you that I shall find the means of punishing you." Letter from
Peter, Czar of Russia, to his son Alexis.
See: C. Ammer, 1980; *Associated Press*, 2000; A. Cohen,
1987; D. Ewen, 1982; C. Hall, 1996; A. Hughes, 1965; E.
Kahn, 1980's; A. Kozinn, 2000; *Los Angeles Times*, 2000; N.
Slonimsky, 1997; W. Terry, 1965; *Washington Post*, 2000; E.
White, 1974.

Premiere:
1965 (August 13, 14, 15): New London, Connecticut; Frank
Loomis Palmer Auditorium, Connecticut College; 18th
American Dance Festival, Jose Limon and Company, Limon
as father, Louis Falco as son, and Jennifer Muller as Venus.
Musicians conducted by Vivian Fine.

1966

CHAMBER CONCERTO FOR CELLO AND SIX INSTRUMENTS
JC71

Solo cello, oboe, violin, viola, cello, double bass, piano
Catamount*; 10 min.
See: A. Cohen, 1987; D. Cummings, 1998; L. Jones, 1997; N.
Slonimsky, 1997; S. Tyler, 1998.
Text: I. Recitative: A Sequence for St. Michael. (Alcuin)
II. Declamation: Prayer. (W.H. Auden)
III. Recitative: Lament. (David's Lament for Jonathan -
Abelard)

Premiere:
1979 (December 5): Putney, Vermont; Newman Hall,
Windham College; George Finckel, cello, Gunnar Schonbeck,
clarinet, Eric Rosenblith, violin, Alice Webber, viola, Pamela

Bostelmann, cello, Marianne Finckel, double bass, Lauren Levey, piano and Vivian Fine, conducting.

Selected performances:
1966 (December 15): Bennington, Vermont; Carriage Barn, Bennington College; George Finckel, cello, Gunnar Schonbeck, clarinet, Eric Rosenblith, violin, Alice Webber, viola, Pamela Bostelmann, cello, Marianne Finckel, double bass, Lauren Levey, piano and Vivian Fine, conducting.

FOUR PIANO PIECES   JC72

Catamount*; 7 min. 15 sec.
See: A. Cohen, 1987; C. Hall, 1996; F. Schmidt, 1966.

Premiere:
1966 (April 28): South Bend, Indiana; University of Notre Dame; Vivian Fine, piano.

Selected performances:
1966 (October 24): Annandale-on-Hudson, New York; Bard College, Bard Hall; Vivian Fine, piano as part of lecture-recital on 20th century piano music.

1966 (November 7): Bennington, Vermont; Carriage Barn, Bennington College; Vivian Fine, piano as part of lecture-recital on 20th century piano music.

1972 (April 3): Ithaca, New York; Cornell University, Barnes Hall, Festival of Women in the Arts; Vivian Fine, piano.

1967

QUINTET FOR STRING TRIO, TRUMPET AND HARP   JC73

Lento-Teneramente; Passacaglia; Duo 1. Violin and Viola; Duo 2. Viola and Harp; Pavane, for those who are dying in this war; Cadenza and Ritornello Caleidoscopico.
Violin, viola, cello, trumpet, harp
Catamount*; 16 min.
Commission: Wykeham Rise School for the Commencement of the Class of 1967.
See: E.R. Anderson, 1976; A. Cohen, 1987; D. Cummings,

1998; C. Hall, 1996; R-M. Johnson, 1989; N. Slonimsky, 1997;
S. Tyler, 1998.

Premiere:
1967 (June 3): Washington, Connecticut; The Church on the
Green, Wykeham Rise School; Renato Bonacini, violin,
Leonello Forzante, viola, David Wells, cello, Ronald Kutik,
trumpet, and Barbara Pniewska, harp.

EPITAPH: MY SLEDGE AND MY HAMMER LY RECLINED JC74
Catamount*; 5 min. 30 sec.
See: A. Cohen, 1987; C. Hall, 1996; N. Slonimsky, 1997.

Premiere:
1967 (May 26): Bennington, Vermont; Mount Anthony Union
High School Theater; High school, college and community
singers and musicians, Louis Calabro, conducting.

1969

PAEAN   **JC75**
Brass ensemble (six trumpets, six trombones), female chorus
and narrator (tenor).
Catamount*; 11 min. 35 sec.
Text: John Keats "Ode to Apollo"
See: C. Ammer, 1980; E.R. Anderson, 1976; J. Carson, 1983;
A. Cohen, 1987; A. Cohn, 1981; D. Cummings, 1997; A. F.,
1971; A. Frankenstein, 1971; S. Fuller, 1994; D. Greene, 1985;
B. Jones, 1999; J.C. Press, 1983; D. Randel, 1996; *Richmond
Times-Dispatch*, 1973; S. Sadie, 1988; E. Schupp, 1971; D13.

Premiere:
1970 (April 1): Bennington, Vermont; Bennington College,
Carriage Barn; Frank Baker, narrator and leader of the chorus,
The Bennington Choral Ensemble, The Eastman Brass
Ensemble, Vivian Fine, conducting.

1975 (August 7): Hanover, New Hampshire; Dartmouth
College, Rollins Chapel; performers unidentified.

1975 (October 21): DeKalb, Illinois; Northern Illinois
University, College of Visual and Performing Arts, Department

of Music; Women's Choir, Brass Ensemble, Lawrence Rast, narrator and singer, Barbara Steg, conducting.

Broadcasts:
1973: French National Radio Network.

Recordings:
1971: CRI SD-260 by F. Baker, soloist and narrator; Bennington Choral Ensemble conducted by Vivian Fine; Composers Recordings Inc., New York. See: D13.

THE DELTA   JC76

Brass ensemble, narrator, chorus
Publisher unknown (see App. 1); duration unknown.
Text: Michael Dennis Browne
See: *Bennington Banner*, 1970.

Premiere:
1970 (May 24): Bennington, Vermont; Mt. Anthony Union High School Auditorium; Eastman Brass Ensemble, Community Chorus Ensemble, Michael Dennis Browne, reader, and tape.

1971

TWO NERUDA POEMS (La Tortuga and Oda al Piano)   JC77

Mezzo-soprano and piano
Catamount*; 14 min.
Text: Poetry of Pablo Neruda
See: C. Ammer, 1980; E.R. Anderson, 1976; A. Cohen, 1987; D. Henahan, 1973; P. Hertelendy, 1983; L. Jones, 1997; R. Pontzious, 1983; J.C. Press, 1983; C. Shere, 1981; H. Tircuit, 1983.

Premiere:
1971 (December 1): Bennington, Vermont; Bennington College; Carriage Barn; Jan DeGaetani, soprano and Vivian Fine, piano.

Selected performances:
1973 (April 15): New York City, New York; Finch College

Concert Hall; All Vivian Fine program; Jan DeGaetani, soprano and Vivian Fine, piano.

1974 (March 7): Oakland, California; Center for Contemporary Music, Women's Festival, Mills College; Stephanie Friedman, mezzo-soprano.

1976 (October 8): New York City, New York; The New School for Social Research; Meet the Woman Composer; Mary Lee Farris, mezzo-soprano and Vivian Fine, piano.

1976 (December 8): Bennington, Vermont; Bennington College, Carriage Barn; Mary Lee Farris, soprano and Vivian Fine, piano.

1978 (February 27): New York City, New York; City University of New York Graduate Center, First Festival of Women's Music; Morey Ritt, piano and Sheila Schonbrun, soprano.

1983 (January 9): San Francisco, California; Old First Church; "Vivian Fine Week" (January 5-13) sponsored by San Francisco Symphony; Stephanie Friedman, mezzo-soprano and Vivian Fine, piano.

SOUNDS OF THE NIGHTINGALE   JC78
Soprano, female chorus ensemble, chamber orchestra (two flutes, oboe/English horn, clarinet, bass clarinet, violin, viola, cello, percussion).
Catamount*; 12 min.
Text: "From various sources" (V. Fine)
See: A. Cohen, 1987; C. Hall, 1996; N. Slonimsky, 1997.

Premiere:
1971 (May 19): Bennington, Vermont; Bennington College; Valerie Lamoree, soprano, Bennington Choral and Instrumental Ensembles, Vivian Fine, conducting.

1972

MISSA BREVIS   JC79

Sacred, electronic

I. Praeludium (cellos); II. Kyrie - Lord (voice); III. Omnium - Lord (voice); IV. Omnien visibilium et invisibilium - All Things Visible and Invisible (cellos); V. Lacrymosa - Weeping (cellos); VI. Teste David Cum Sibylla - So Spoke David and the Sibyl (cellos, voice); VII. Dies Irae - Day of Wrath (cellos, voice); VIII. Eli, Eli, Lomo asov toni - My God, Why Hast Thou Forsaken Me (from the 22nd Psalm, voice); IX. Sanctus - Holy (cellos); X. Omein -Amen (voice, cellos).

Four to eight cellos, taped voice

Catamount*; 20 min.

See: C. Ammer, 1980; E.R. Anderson, 1976; E. Armer, 1991; T. Brookes, 1986; J. Carson, 1983; A. Cohen, 1987; R. Commanday, Oct. 24, 1982, 1990; J. Ditsky, 1982; J. Donner, 1982; S. Fuller, 1994; D. Greene, 1985; C. Hall, 1996; N. Hasden, 1982; D. Henahan, 1973; P. Hertelendy, Mar. 10, Mar. 17, 1974, 1983, 1988; S. Husarik, 1992; L. Jones, 1997; C. Kino, 1983; B. Sable, 1982; S. Sadie, 1988; D. Shepfer, 1982; C. Shere, 1983; WNYC, 1986; D9, D10.

Premiere:

1973 (April 15): New York City, New York; Finch College Concert Hall; all Vivian Fine program; Gail Alcock, Lori Barnet, Michael Finckel and Barbara Mallow, cellos, and taped voice, Jan DeGaetani, soprano.

Selected performances:

1973 (May 9): Bennington, Vermont; Bennington College; Gael Alcock, Michael Finckel, Christopher Finckel and Barbara Mallow, cellos and taped voice of Jan DeGaetani, soprano.

1974 (March 7): Oakland, California; Mills College, Center for Contemporary Music, Women's Festival; Jan De Gaetani, taped voice, Jenny Goss, Phyllis Luckman, Susan Napper, and Irene Sharp, cellos.

1974 (May 26): Berkeley, California; California Cello Club, Northbrae Community Church; Jan De Gaetani, taped voice, Jenny Goss, Phyllis Luckman, Susan Napper, and Irene Sharp, cellos; arranged by Phyllis Luckman.

1975 (April 4): Berkeley, California; 1750 Arch Street, University of California at Berkeley, Department of Music, Morrison Hall, lecture-recital; Kevin Walker, Joanne Ludbrook, Steve Pereira and Jerry LeClerc, cellos, San Francisco Conservatory Players, and Miriam Abramowitsch, mezzo-soprano.

1975 (April 6): Hayward, California; California State University at Hayward, Music Building; Kevin Walker, Joanne Ludbrook, Steve Pereira and Jerry LeClerc, cellos, San Francisco Conservatory Players, and taped voice of Jan DeGaetani.

1975 (April 25): Albany, New York; Free Music Store, Music of Vivian Fine program, David Gibson, cello, Ingrid Porter, cello, Ann Sheldon, cello, Jacob Glick, viola and taped voice of Jan DeGaetani.

1976 (October 8): New York City, New York; The New School for Social Research; Meet the Woman Composer; David Finckel, Michael Finckel, Maxine Neuman and Richard Locker, cellos and voice on tape, Jan De Gaetani.

1981 (January 31): San Francisco, California; San Francisco State University, Hellman Hall; featured concert of Bay Area Congress on Women in Music; San Francisco Conservatory Cello Ensemble, Jennifer Culp, Jennifer Epler, Dawn Foster, Joan Garvin, Bonnie Hampton, Elisabeth Le Guin, Mara Parker, Irene Sharp and Jan De Gaetani, voice on tape, conducted by Vivian Fine.

1986 (December 7): Oneonta, New York; Catskill Conservatory and State University of New York at Oneonta, Goodrich Theater, Composers Chamber Music Series, Catskill Chamber Players, Janet Nepkie, Stephen Stalker, Lucy Bardo, Susan Ruzow, cellos and taped voice of Jan DeGaetani, Vivian Fine, conducting.

1987 (August 28): Oneonta, New York; Windfall Dutch Barn, Catskill Chamber Players, Janet Nepkie, Stephen Stalker, Lucy Bardo and Susan Ruzow, cellists, Scott Miller, tape operator, Jan DeGaetani, taped voice.

1990 (October 2): San Francisco, California; Composer's Inc., Green Room, Veteran's War Memorial Building.

Broadcasts:
1983: WAMC, Albany, New York, National Public Radio, Robert Lurtsema, host of Morning Pro Musica.

1986 (April 19): Boston, Massachusetts; WGBH 89.7 FM, Vivian Fine: A Celebration of Her Music.

1986 (March 8, September 28): National Public Radio, first in a series by the International League of Women Composers; WNYC program "Live from Merkin Concert Hall"; a tribute on Fine's 73rd birthday by Ev Grimes and Karen Pearlman.

Recordings:
1982: CRI SD-434 by Jan DeGaetani, mezzo-soprano and Bartlett, Finckel and Neuman, cellos; Composers Recordings Inc., New York. See: D9.
1995: CRI 692, American Masters, **Music of Vivian Fine**; remastered onto compact disc; Composers Recordings Inc., New York. See: D10

CONCERTO FOR PIANO STRINGS AND
PERCUSSION FOR ONE PERFORMER   **JC80**
Variations, Fanfare, Eclogue, Variations
Solo piano and percussion
Catamount*; 9 min.
Commission: Woolley Fund
See: C. Ammer, 1980; E.R. Anderson, 1976; A. Cohen, 1987; Composers Forum, 1974; D. Ewen, 1982; E. French, 1974; D. Henahan, 1973; P. Hertelendy, 1974; H. Tircuit, 1974; E. White, 1974.

Premiere:
1973 (April 15): New York City, New York; Finch College Concert Hall; all Vivian Fine program; Vivian Fine, piano and percussion.

Selected performances:
1974 (February 5): Santa Cruz, California; Crown College, University of California at Santa Cruz, Vivian Fine, piano and percussion.

1974 (March 7): Oakland, California; Center for Contemporary Music, Women's Festival, Mills College; Vivian Fine, piano and percussion.

1974 (November 20): Albany, New York; The Arts Center, Composer's Forum, Contemporary Music for Viola and Piano; Vivian Fine, piano and percussion.

1974 (December 4): Bennington, Vermont; Bennington College, Vivian Fine, piano and percussion.

1975 (April 4): Berkeley, California; University of California at Berkeley, Department of Music, Morrison Hall, lecture-recital; Vivian Fine, piano.

1975 (April 25): Albany, New York; Music of Vivian Fine program, Vivian Fine, piano.

1975 (April 30): New Haven, Connecticut; Southern Connecticut State College, Music Department; Vivian Fine, piano and percussion.

1975 (August 7): Hanover, New Hampshire; Rollins Chapel, Dartmouth College; Vivian Fine, piano and percussion.

1976 (February 19): Saratoga Springs, New York; Skidmore College, Filene Recital Hall; Vivian Fine, piano and percussion.

1976 (October 8): New York City, New York; The New School for Social Research; Meet the Woman Composer; Vivian Fine, piano and percussion.

Broadcasts:
1975 (August 29): Schenectady, New York; WMHT Radio Program "The Composers Forum," Vivian Fine, piano and percussion.

THREE VALEDICTORY SONGS   JC81
Soprano, viola, three cellos
Publisher unknown (see App. 1); duration unknown

Premiere:

1972 (October 25): Bennington, Vermont; Bennington College; Stephanie Turash, soprano, Jacob Glick, viola, Michael Finckel, cello, Gael Alcock, cello and Lori Barnet, cello.

1973

THE FLICKER JC82
Solo flute
Gunmar Music, Inc.; 8 min. 30 sec.
Also called: **MOVEMENT**
Text: Roger Tory Peterson. "The flight is deeply undulating, produced by several quick beats and a pause." Bird-song is also heard, and flight and song intermingle.
See: A. Cohen, 1987; D. Landis and L. Edelman, 1982; B. Lynerd, 1997; R. Pontzious, 1983; San Francisco Symphony, 1982; H. Tircuit, 1983; D8.

Premiere:
1974 (March 7): Oakland, California; Center for Contemporary Music, Women's Festival, Mills College; Maquette Kuper, flute.

Selected performances:
1981 (October 6): Bennington, Vermont; Bennington College, Greenwall Music Workshop; Lionel Nowak, piano.

1982 (October 20): Bennington, Vermont; Bennington College; flutist unknown.

1983 (January 9): San Francisco, California; Old First Church; as part of "Vivian Fine Week" (January 5-13) sponsored by the San Francisco Symphony; Leone Buyse, flute.

1983 (May 13): Bennington, Vermont; Bennington College; Bennington College Chorus.

1983 (August 2): Philadelphia, Pennsylvania; Bellevue Stratford Hotel; National Flute Association; Leone Buyse, flute.

1986 (April 22): New York City, New York; Carnegie Recital Hall, Jayn Rosenfeld, flute, New York Premiere.

1988 (February 5): Poultney, Vermont; Green Mountain College, Ackley Auditorium, Capitol Chamber Artists.

1988 (February 7): Albany, New York; State University of New York at Albany, Page Hall, Capitol Chamber Artists.

Recording:
1990s: CD317, by Leone Buyse, flute, Martin Amlin, piano, and Fenwick Smith, alto flute and flute; **Music for Flute**; Crystal Records, Camas, Washington. See: D8

1975

TEISHO   JC83
Eight solo singers and small chorus, string quartet
Version for mezzo-soprano, violin and piano written for the Aviva Players, The Mannes College of Music, New York.
Version for violin and piano called **Three Buddhist Evocations for Violin and Piano** (JC88).
Part One: I. The Stringless Harp; II. With the Passing of Winter; III. Let the Difference be Even a Tenth of an Inch.
Part Two: IV. If people ask me what Zen is like I will say that it is like learning the art of burglary; V. The King of Good Memory; VI. The 10-Thousand Things.
Catamount*; 20 min.
Commission: National Endowment for the Arts grant of $8000, 1974, written for the Aviva Players.
See: Ariel, 1983; A. Cohen, 1987; C. Fulkerson, 1988; D. Greene, 1985; P. Hertelendy, 1988; R-M. Johnson, 1989; L. Jones, 1997; D. Landis and L. Edelman, 1982; *The Music*, 1979; R. Pontzious, 1983; San Francisco Symphony, 1982; H. Tircuit, 1983.

Premieres:
1976 (May 22): Bennington, Vermont; Bennington College; Sine Nomine Singers, Contemporary Quartet, Jean Ingraham, violin, Thomas Kornacker, violin, Jacob Glick, viola, and Chris Finckel, cello, Vivian Fine, conducting.

1979 (March 26): New York City, New York; The Mannes College of Music, Mannes Recital Hall; Mira Spektor, mezzo-soprano, Erika Schenker, piano, and Asiya Meshberg, violin, other singers not identified.

1977 (October 4): Bennington, Vermont; Bennington College; Daniel Kobialka, violin and Machiko Kobialka, piano. See citations under **Three Buddhist Evocations for Violin and Piano** (JC88).

Selected performances:
1979 (June 12): New York City, New York; Christ and Stephen's Church; a version written for mezzo-soprano, violin and piano for the Aviva Players, The Mannes College of Music, New York City; Mira Spektor, mezzo-soprano, Asiya Meshberg, violin, Dorothy Indenbaum, piano. New York premiere of this version.

See 1983 (January 9): San Francisco, California, performance of violin and piano version of **Teisho** called **Three Buddhist Evocations for Violin and Piano** (JC88).

1988 (May 20): San Francisco, California; San Francisco Community Center; Ariel (Cheryl Keller, Ruth Peabody, Claire Kelm, sopranos; Marcia Gronewold, mezzo-soprano; Douglas Wright, Jon Ellis tenors; John Conry, Doug Wyatt, baritones), Christopher Fulkerson, Music Director.

1976

MEETING FOR EQUAL RIGHTS 1866   JC84
Cantata for narrator, soprano, bass-baritone, chorus, orchestra. Re-scored for organ, percussion, winds, bass-baritone, mezzo-soprano and narrator (see May 20, 1976 performance) Catamount*; 20 min.
Commission: The Cooper Union for its Great Hall, the actual locale of the Women's Rights Association meetings, and funded by the National Endowment for the Arts.
See: C. Ammer, 1980; *Associated Press*, 2000; B. Belt, 1976; J. Carson, 1983; A. Cohen, 1987; A. Der, 1976; D. Ewen, 1982; S. Fuller, 1994; D. Henahan, 1976; L. Jones, 1997; A. Kozinn, 2000; J.C. Press, 1983; J. Raymond, 2000; N. Slominsky, 1994, 1997; *Stuart News*, 2000.

Premieres:
1976 (April 23): New York City, New York; Great Hall of the Cooper Union; Cooper Union Forum; Chorus and Symphony Orchestra of the Oratorio Society of New York, Lyndon

Woodside, conducting the chorus and Roberta Kosse and Joseph Rescigno, conducting the orchestra with Mary Lee Farris, mezzo-soprano, Richard Frisch, bass-baritone, Nancy Deering, narrator.

1976 (May 20): New York City, New York; Alice Tully Hall, Lincoln Center for the Performing Arts; Chorus and Orchestra of the Oratorio Society of New York, Mary Lee Farris, mezzo-soprano, Richard Frisch, bass-baritone, Patricia Robbins, narrator, David Ralph, organ, and Lyndon Woodside, conducting assisted by Roberta Kosse and Joseph Rescigno, using the re-scored version.

Selected performances:
1976 (December 8): Bennington, Vermont; Bennington College, Carriage Barn; Mary Lee Farris, mezzo-soprano, Henry Brant, organ, Marta Ptaszynska, timpani, String Orchestra conducted by Vivian Fine and Wind Ensemble conducted by Louis Calabro.

THE NIGHTINGALE   JC85

Solo singer (mezzo-soprano) accompanying herself with triangle, woodblock and cymbal.
Catamount*; 6 min.
Commission: Composers Forum, Albany Arts Center, Albany, New York
Texts: Keats, T.S. Eliot, John Lyly, Richard Barnefield, and the **Encyclopaedia Britannica**.
See: R. Capparela, 1977; A. Cohen, 1987; R. Pontzious, 1983; San Francisco Symphony, 1982; H. Tircuit, 1983.

Premiere:
1977 (March 4): Albany, New York; Albany Arts Center; Julie Kabat, mezzo-soprano.

Selected performances:
1983 (January 9): San Francisco, California; Old First Church; part of "Vivian Fine Week" (January 5-13) sponsored by the San Francisco Symphony; Stephanie Friedman, mezzo-soprano.

ROMANTIC ODE   JC86

Solo violin, solo viola, solo cello and string orchestra.

GunMar Music, Inc.; 11 min.
Commission: The Chamber Music Conference of the East
See: A. Cohen, 1987; D. Cummings, 1998; **Music in Print**,
1999; J.C. Press, 1983; N. Slonimsky, 1997; S. Tyler, 1998; R.
Woolmington, 1976.

Premiere:
1976 (August 28): Bennington, Vermont; Bennington College,
Performing Arts Center; Chamber Music Conference of the
East, George Grossman, conducting with Joel Berman, solo
violin, Jacob Glick, solo viola, Ralph Oxman, solo cello.

Selected performances:
1976 (October 30): Bennington, Vermont; Ernestine Schor,
violin, Maureen Gallagher, viola and Dana Rusinak, cello and
The Vermont Symphony, Efrain Guigui, conducting.

1977 (April 26): Pittsburgh, Pennsylvania; Tuesday Musical
String Ensemble, George Grossman, conducting.

1978 (December 3): Cambridge, Massachusetts; Harvard
University, Sanders Theater; Jean Lamon, violin, Danna
Young, viola, Janet Cochran, cello with Vivian Fine,
conducting.

1981 (January 15): San Francisco, California; San Francisco
Jewish Community Center; Concordia Chamber Orchestra,
Jeffery Levine, conducting with Anne Crowden, solo violin,
Ruth Freeman, solo viola and Richard Eade, solo cello.

SONNETS FOR BARITONE AND ORCHESTRA   **JC87**
Catamount*; 10 min.
Text: John Keats
Commission: The Sage City Symphony
An earlier composition which became part of this composition
was called **Sonnet, To A Cat** for SATB.
See: N. Slonimsky, 1997.

Premiere:
1976 (December 5): North Bennington, Vermont; Sage City
Symphony, Louis Calabro, conducting with Wayne Dalton,
baritone.

1977

THREE BUDDHIST EVOCATIONS FOR VIOLIN AND PIANO JC88

Catamount*; 11 min.

Note: A version of parts of **Teisho**, for violin and piano (see JC67, 1975); **Teisho** are the talks or sermons given by the Zen masters to the disciples.

See: A. Cohen, 1987; R-M. Johnson, 1989.

Premiere:

1977 (October 4): Bennington, Vermont; Bennington College; Daniel Kobialka, violin and Machiko Kobialka, piano.

Selected performances:

1977 (October 5): Albany, New York; State University of New York at Albany; Daniel Kobialka, violin and Machiko Kobialka, piano.

1983 (January 9): San Francisco, California; Old First Church; Daniel Kobialka, violin and Machiko Kobialka, piano. (Called **Teisho** on the program).

THE WOMEN IN THE GARDEN   JC89

Chamber opera for five singers: Isadora Duncan - dramatic soprano; Virginia Woolf - lyric soprano; Emily Dickinson - mezzo-soprano; Gertrude Stein - contralto or dark mezzo; and tenor - tenor, and nine instruments ((flute, B flat clarinet interchangeable with bass clarinet, bassoon, piano, viola, cello, double bass, percussion (2 players: snare drum, triangle, suspended cymbal, wood block, field drum, gong, castanets, temple blocks, sleigh bells, wind chimes, vibraphone, marimba, chimes, glockenspiel, medium and low timpani, and tuned tom-toms), and handbells (played by cast)).

Catamount*; 55 minutes.

Commission: National Endowment for the Arts grant of $8000, 1974

See: S. Albahari, 1983; C. Ammer, 1980; *Associated Press*, 2000; *Burlington Free Press*, 1985; M. Burrell, J. Carson, 1983; A. Cohen, 1987; R. Commanday, March 31, 1982, April 3, 1982, January 7, 1983; J. Coon, 1987; ; D. Cummings, 1997, 1998; D. Ewen, 1982; S. Fuller, 1994; E. George, 1984; M. Goldstein, 1981; D. Gorin, 1979; D. Greene, 1985; C.J. Hall, 1989; C. Hall, 1996; P. Hertelendy, 1978, 1983, 1988; J.

Jamieson and V. Fine, 1984; R-M. Johnson, 1989; B. Jones, 1999; L. Jones, 1997; A. Kaplan, 1981; A. Kozinn, 2000; D. Landis and L. Edelman, 1982; N. Lebrecht, 1992; A. Levine, 1983; *Los Angeles Times*, 2000; P. Moor, 1983; K. Moore, 1984; B. Paris, 1979; R. Pontzious, 1983; J.C. Press, 1983; T. Putnam, 1986; C.S., 1978; D. Randel, 1996; J. Raymond, 2000; San Francisco Symphony, 1982, 1983; C. Shere, 1982, 1983; N. Slominsky, 1994, 1997; P. Swift, 1984; H. Tircuit, 1978; M. Tucker, 1982; S. Tyler, 1998; A. Ulrich, 1982; S. Von Bachau, 1982; W. West, 1984.

Premiere:
1978 (February 12): San Francisco, California; San Francisco Conservatory, Hellman Hall; Port Costa Players, Anna Carol Dudley, Vicky Van Derwark, Susan Rode Morris, sopranos, Barbara Baker, mezzo-soprano and John Duykers, tenor with chamber ensemble, Alan Balter, conducting. Co-sponsored by the L.J. and Mary C. Skaggs Foundation and Laney College Community Services.

Selected performances:
1978 (February 17 and 19): Oakland, California; Laney College, Laney College Theater; Port Costa Players, see above.

1979 (February 22-25): Pittsburgh, Pennsylvania; Carnegie-Mellon University; College of Fine Arts, Alumni Concert Hall, Opera Theater Program, David Gorin, guest director and Istvan Jaray, conducting; Lynne Engstrom, Joette Salandro, Myrna Paris, sopranos, Kathleen Kelleher, mezzo-soprano and Patrick Gibson, tenor.

1981 (August 29 and 30): Cambridge, New York; L'Ensemble Chamber Music Center; members of L'Ensemble, Marsha Andrews, soprano, Judith Bettina, soprano, Ida Faiella, soprano, Julia Heyer, mezzo-soprano, Peter Shea, tenor, and Joshua Rifkin, conducting the L'Ensemble Chamber Orchestra, and Cynthia Wands, stage director.

1981 (October 2): Cambridge, Massachusetts; Sanders Theater, Harvard University; members of the Boston Musica Viva, Jeanette Hall-Wood, soprano, Sue Ellen Kuzma, soprano, Valerie Walters, mezzo-soprano, Eunice Alberts, contralto, Jeffrey Gall, tenor, Richard Pittman, conducting and Nicholas Deutsch, stage director.

1981 (October 4): New Haven, Connecticut; Sprague Hall, Yale University; members of the Boston Musica Viva, Jeanette Hall-Wood, soprano, Sue Ellen Kuzma, soprano, Valerie Walters, mezzo-soprano, Eunice Alberts, contralto, Jeffrey Gall, tenor, Richard Pittman, conducting and Nicholas Deutsch, stage director.

1982 (April 1): San Francisco, California; Herbst Theater; Kathryn Gamberoni, Kaaren Erickson, Wendy Hillhouse, sopranos, Laura Brooke Rice, mezzo-soprano, and Jeffrey Thomas, tenor, Richard Bradshaw, conducting and Martha Schlamme, stage director.

1984 (March 26): Syracuse, New York; Carrier Theatre, Civic Center, Society for New Music; Karen Holohan, Neva Pilgrim, sopranos, JoElyn Wakefield-Wright, mezzo-soprano and Jean Loftus, contralto, and Maurice Black, tenor with Rhonda Kess, conducting.

1984 (July 12): Buffalo, New York; State University of Buffalo, Amherst Campus, Slee Concert Hall, Society for New Music, Karen Holohan, Neva Pilgrim, sopranos, JoElyn Wakefield-Wright, mezzo-soprano and Jean Loftus, contralto, and Maurice Black, tenor with Rhonda Kess, conducting.

1978

MOMENTI   JC90
Poco allegretto, delicato; Andante lusingando; Allegro; Con tenerezza; Moderato; Lento
Piano solo.
GunMar Music, Inc.; 8 min. 50 sec.
Comment: Written for the 150th Anniversary of Schubert's death in 1828 and having as their point of departure the *Moment Musicaux* of Franz Schubert.
Dedication: Roger Sessions
See: T. Brookes, 1986; J. Carson, 1983; A. Cohen, 1987; R. Commanday, Oct. 24, 1982; J. Ditsky, 1982; J. Donner, 1982; D. Greene, 1985; N. Hasden, 1982; A. Kozinn, May 26, 1988; **Perspectives of New Music**, 1985; D. Randel, 1996; D. Shepfer, 1982; D11, D12.

Premiere:

1979 (March 26): New York City, New York; Mannes College Auditorium; Lionel Nowak, piano.

Selected performances:
1979 (April 29): Washington, DC: National Gallery of Art; Claudia Stevens, piano.

1980 (March 28): Bennington, Vermont; Greenwall Music Workshop; Lionel Nowak, piano.

1980 (April 14): Williamsburg, Virginia; The College of William and Mary, Phi Beta Kappa Hall; Claudia Stevens, piano.

1981 (December 2): Bennington, Vermont; Bennington College, Greenwall Music Workshop; Vivian Fine, piano.

1988 (May 22): New York City, New York; Weill Recital Hall, Christine Diwyk, piano.

Broadcasts:
1986 (April): Boston, Massachusetts; WGBH 89.7 FM, Vivian Fine: A Celebration of Her Music.

1986 (March 8, September 28): National Public Radio, first in a series by the International League of Women Composers; WNYC program "Live from Merkin Concert Hall"; a tribute on Fine's 73rd birthday by Ev Grimes and Karen Pearlman.

Recordings:
1982: CRI SD-434 by Lionel Nowak, piano; Composers Recordings Inc., New York. See: D11.
1995: CRI 692, American Masters, **Music of Vivian Fine**; remastered onto compact disc; Composers Recordings Inc., New York. See: D12.

QUARTET FOR BRASS   JC91
Variations, Fanfare, Eclogue, and Variations.
Trumpets, trombone and french horn
GunMar Music Inc.; 12 minutes
Commission: Metropolitan Brass Quartet
See: J. Carson, 1983; A. Cohen, 1987; R. Commanday, Oct. 24, 1982; Composers, Inc., 1986; D. Cummings, 1998; J.

Ditsky, 1982; J. Donner, 1982; D. Greene, 1985; N. Hasden, 1982; S. Husarik, 1992; *Schenectady Gazette*, 1979; W. Severinghaus, 1987; D. Shepfer, 1982; N. Slonimsky, 1997; D15, D16.

Premiere:
1979 (April 20): Schenectady, New York; Union College Memorial Chapel; Metropolitan Brass Quartet, Douglas Hedwig, trumpet, William Parker, French horn, Bruce Bonvissuto, trombone and Kristian Solem, trumpet.

Selected performances:
1979 (May 20): New York City, New York; Solomon R. Guggenheim Museum; Metropolitan Brass Quartet, Douglas Hedwig, trumpet, William Parker, French horn, Bruce Bonvissuto, trombone and Kristian Solem, trumpet.

1979 (May 22): New York City, New York; Hunter College, Hunter College Playhouse; Metropolitan Brass Quartet, Douglas Hedwig, trumpet, William Parker, French horn, Bruce Bonvissuto, trombone and Kristian Solem, trumpet.

1982 (August 2): Lenox, Massachusetts; Tanglewood; Lawrence DiBello, French horn, Thomas Smith, trumpet, Justin Cohen, trumpet and Paul Eachus, bass trombone.

1986 (March 11): San Francisco, California; Green Room, San Francisco Veteran's Building; Composers, Inc. series; San Francisco Brass quartet: William Essert, trumpet, John Pearson, trumpet, Douglas Hall, french horn, and Craig McAmis, bass trombone.

1986 (April 26): Oneonta, New York; Anderson Center Theatre, Hartwick College, Catskill Brass Quintet, Carleton Clay, trumpet, Ben Aldridge, trumpet, Donald Robertson, trombone, and Julia Hasbrouck Clay, french horn.

1986 (April 26): Oneonta, New York; Hunt Union Ballroom, Catskill Conservatory;, Catskill Brass Quintet, Carleton Clay, trumpet, Ben Aldridge, trumpet, Donald Robertson, trombone, and Julia Hasbrouck Clay, french horn.

1986 (September 7): Rensselaerville, New York; Rensselaerville Institute, Catskill Brass Quintet, Carleton Clay, trumpet, Ben Aldridge, trumpet, Donald Robertson, trombone, and Julia Hasbrouck Clay, french horn.

1986 (December 7): Oneonta, New York; Catskill Conservatory and State University of New York at Oneonta, Goodrich Theater, Composers Chamber Music Series, Catskill Chamber Players, Ben Aldridge, trumpet, Carleton Clay, trumpet, Donald Robertson, trombone, Julia Hasbrouck Clay, french horn.

1986 (April 4): Oneonta, New York; Henry Cowell Festival; Catskill Brass Quintet, Ben Aldridge, trumpet, Carleton Clay, trumpet, Donald Robertson, trombone, Julia Hasbrouck Clay, french horn.

1987 (April 15): Bennington, Vermont; Bennington College; The Purchase Brass, Ron Carson, trumpet, Ron Stinson, trumpet, Jean Martin, French horn, Richard Clark, tenor trombone and David Titcomb, bass trombone.

Broadcasts:
1986 (March 8, September 28): National Public Radio, first in a series by the International League of Women Composers.

Recordings:
1982: CRI SD-434 ; by Ronald K. Anderson and Allan Dean, trumpets, David Jolley, french horn, and Lawrence Benz, trombone; Composers Recordings Inc., New York. See: D14.
1995: CRI 692, American Masters, **Music of Vivian Fine**; remastered onto compact disc; Composers Recordings Inc., New York. See: D15.

1979

A BUST FOR ERIC SATIE   **JC92**
Soprano, mezzo-soprano, narrator, flute, bassoon, trumpet, trombone, cello, double bass.
Catamount*; 20 min.
Text: Georges Guy
See: A. Cohen, 1987; *Music Educators Journal,* 1980.

Premiere:
1979 (May 11): Bennington, Vermont; Greenwall Auditorium;

Judith Bettina, soprano; Johanna Albrecht, mezzo-soprano; Georges Guy, Leroy Logan and Harry Matthes, narrators; Sue Ann Kahn, flute; Maurice Pachman, bassoon; Douglas Hedwig, trumpet; Bruce Bonvissuto, trombone; Michael Finckel, cello; Dean Crandall, double bass; and Vivian Fine, conducting.

NIGHTINGALES, MOTET FOR SIX INSTRUMENTS   JC93
Flute, oboe, violin, 2 violas, double bass
CFE; 5 min.
Text: John Lyly, "What bird so sings yet so does wail? O 'tis the ravish'd nightingale."
Commission: Chamber Music Conference and Composer's Forum of the East

Premiere:
1979 (August 21): Bennington, Vermont; Greenwall Auditorium; The Chamber Music Conference and Composer's Forum of the East, Music by the composers-in-residence; Robert Ackerberg, flute, Sylvia Ackerberg, oboe, Nancy Dunetz, violin, Marc Bastuscheck, viola, Bernard Schlanger, viola, and Marji Danilow, bass.

Selected performances:
1981 (November 14): Bennington, Vermont; Bennington College, Greenwall Music Workshop; Lilo Kantorowicz-Glick, violin, Jacob Glick, viola, Gunnar Schonbeck, clarinet, Su Lian Tan, flute, Edith Bicknell-Finckel, oboe and Jeffrey Levine, bass, with Vivian Fine, conducting.

LIEDER FOR VIOLA AND PIANO   JC94
Allegretto (The Balcony); Molto tranquillo (Moon-Stream); Allegretto rustico (The Song of the Trout); Lento (Jewels); Sustained, with fervor (In the Garden of the Crucifixion); and, Flowing (Transfiguring Night).
Arsis Press; 14 min.
See: A. Cohen, 1987; **Music in Print**, 1999.

Premiere:
1980 (May 2): New York City, New York; Composers' Forum, A Program of 20th Century Music for Viola and Piano, Bruno Walter Auditorium, Lincoln Center Library; Jacob Glick, viola and Vivian Fine, piano.

Selected performances:
1979 (January 27): Chicago, Illinois; Jacob Glick, viola and Vivian Fine, piano.

1980 (May 2): New York City, New York; Women in the Arts: Composers, The Center for the Study of Women and Sex Roles, Graduate School and University Center, City University of New York; Jacob Glick, viola and Vivian Fine, piano.

1980 (May 7): Bennington, Vermont; Bennington College, Greenwall Music Workshop, A Concert of 20th Century Music for Viola and Piano; Jacob Glick, viola and Vivian Fine, piano.

1981 (February 15): San Francisco, California; Guild Hall Congregation Emanu-El; Jacob Glick, viola and Vivian Fine, piano.

1982 (May 15): Bennington, Vermont; Bennington College; Jacob Glick, viola and Vivian Fine, piano.

1983 (April 29): New York City, New York; Manhattan School of Music, Hubbard Recital Hall; Elizabeth Rodgers, piano and unknown, viola.

1985 (March 27): Bennington, Vermont; Bennington College, Greenwall Music Workshop, Jacob Glick, viola and Elizabeth Wright, piano.

1990 (April 22): Queens, New York; Garden City Chamber Music Society; Toby Appel, viola and Doris Stevenson, piano.

DUO FOR KETTLEDRUMS AND PIANO   JC95
Publisher unknown (see App. 1); duration unknown.
Also called: **Duo for Piano and Timpani** (1969)

Premiere:
1978 (September 7): Bennington, Vermont; Bennington College, Greenwall Music Workshop; Rick Sacks, percussion and Vivian Fine, piano.

Selected performances:
1979 (September 6): Bennington, Vermont; Greenwall Music Workshop; Louis Calabro, percussion and Vivian Fine, piano.

TWO SONGS   **JC96**
Soprano
Publisher unknown (see App. 1); duration unknown.

Premiere:
1979 (October 8): Bethlehem, Pennsylvania; Lehigh University,
Lamberton Hall; Sheila Schonbrun, soprano.

1980

TRIO FOR VIOLIN, CELLO AND PIANO   **JC97**
I. Fluente - L'istesso tempo, ma pesante e marcato -
Passacaglia (Lento, in memory of Gregor Piatigorsky); II.
Allegretto - Allegro - Elegy on a theme by Ravel.
GunMar Music; 18 minutes
Commission: Mirecourt Trio
See: Ariel, 1983; Castleton State College, 1987; A. Cohen,
1987; D. Cummings, 1998; N. Slonimsky, 1997; S. Tyler,
1998.

Premiere:
1981 (April 4): Oak Park, Illinois; Frank Lloyd Wright Unity
Temple; The Mirecourt Trio, Kenneth Goldsmith, violin, Terry
King, cello, and John Jensen, piano.

Selected Performances:
1983 (January 9): San Francisco, California; Old First Church;
a part of "Vivian Fine Week" (January 5-13) sponsored by the
San Francisco Symphony; Daniel Kobialka, violin, Peter
Shelton, cello and Machiko Kobialka, piano.

1987 (March 7): Albany, New York; Page Hall, State
University of New York at Albany; Mary Lou Saetta, violin,
David Decker, cello and Annette Covatta, piano.

1987 (March 8): Castleton, Vermont; Castleton State College,
Fine Arts Center; Women In Music Program, Mary Lou Saetta,
violin, David Decker, cello and Annette Covatta, piano.

ODA A LAS RANAS   **JC98**
Women's chorus, flute, oboe, cello and percussion
Catamount*; 6 minutes.

Also: Part 2 of **CANZONES Y DANCES** (JC137) for guitar, flute and cello.
Text: Pablo Neruda
Commission: Anna Crusis Women's Choir
<u>See</u>: L. Jones, 1997; D3.

Premiere:
1981 (June 13): Philadelphia, Pennsylvania; Anna Crusis Women's Ensemble, Jean Leavitt, narrator, Lore Silverberg, flute, Mary Ellen Corwin, oboe, Lori Barnett, cello, Flossie Ierardi, percussion, Catherine Roma, conducting.

Selected performances:
1983 (July 29): Berkeley, California; First Congregational Church; Jane Lenoir, flute, William Banovetz, oboe, Carol Negro, bassoon and Sandra Mabee, percussion and Veil of Isis, vocal ensemble, Joan Gallegos, conducting.

MUSIC FOR FLUTE, OBOE AND CELLO   JC99

Molto moderato, Allegretto, Lento espressivo, Leggiero.
Flute (alto flute), oboe (English horn), cello
Catamount*; 10 minutes
Commission: Huntingdon Trio
<u>See</u>: M. Brandt, 1983; A. Cohen, 1987; J. Reinthaler, 1981.

Premiere:
1980 (July 20): Philadelphia, Pennsylvania; Huntingdon Trio, Diane Gould, flute, Rheta Smith, oboe and Lloyd Smith, cello.

Selected performances:
1980 (July 27): Lancaster, Pennsylvania; Atrium, Steinman College Center, Franklin and Marshall College; Huntingdon Trio, Diane Gould, flute, Rheta Smith, oboe and Lloyd Smith, cello.

1980 (November 22): Philadelphia, Pennsylvania; Huntingdon Trio, Diane Gould, flute, Rheta Smith, oboe and Lloyd Smith, cello.

1981 (February 8): Haverford, Pennsylvania; Haverford College; Huntingdon Trio.

1981 (April 12): State College, Pennsylvania; Pennsylvania State University, Music Academy; Huntingdon Trio.

1981 (May 3): Washington, District of Columbia; National Gallery of Art, 38th American Music Festival; Huntingdon Trio.

1981 (July 13): Cazenovia, New York; A Summer Classic at "Old Trees," home of Bob and Faith Knapp, Society for New Music, John Oberbrunner, flute, Patricia Sharpe, oboe, and Gregory Wood, cello.

1981 (September 13): Brunswick, Maine; Bowdoin College, Daggett Lounge; Huntingdon Trio, Rheta Smith, oboe, Lloyd Smith, cello and Diane Gould, flute.

1981 (September 14): Waterville, Maine; Colby College, Lorimer Chapel; Huntingdon Trio (see above).

1981 (October 11): Lewisburg, Pennsylvania; Bucknell University, Vaughn Literature Auditorium; Huntingdon Trio.

1983 (May 29): Oglebay Institute, Mansion Museum, Oglebay Park; Huntingdon Trio.

1983 (September 4): Arnhem, The Netherlands; Huntingdon Trio.

1983 (September 11): Kiddington, England; Kiddington Parish Church; Huntingdon Trio.

1986 (November 11): Geneva, New York; Hobart and William Smith Colleges, Department of Music, Warren Hunting Smith Library, Geneva Room, Concert of New American Music; Linda Greene, flute, Patricia Sharpe, oboe, Barbara Rabin, clarinet and Gregory Wood, cello.

1986 (July 13): Cazenovia, New York; "Old Trees," Society of New Music, home of Bob and Faith Knapp; John Oberbrunner, flute, Patricia Sharpe, oboe and Gregory Wood, cello.

Broadcasts:
1981 (May 3): National Public Radio, music of the 38th American Music Festival at the National Gallery of Art.

1981

GERTRUDE AND VIRGINIA   JC100

Soprano, mezzo-soprano, small ensemble
Catamount*; 9 minutes
See: B. Holland, 1981.

Premiere:
1981 (June 8): New York City, New York; Carnegie Recital
Hall; Kimball Wheeler, mezzo-soprano, Rosalind Rees,
soprano, Sarah Tenney, percussion, Daniel Levitan, percussion,
Virgil Blackwell, clarinet, Lewis Paer, double bass and Vivian
Fine, conducting.

1982

DRAMA FOR ORCHESTRA (after paintings of Edvard Munch) JC101

Large orchestra: 4 flutes (3rd and 4th doubling on piccolo), 4
oboes (4th doubling on English horn), 4 clarinets (4th doubling
on bass clarinet), 4 bassoons (4th doubling on contrabassoon),
6 horns, 4 trumpets, 3 trombones, tuba, timpani, percussion
(vibraphone, xylophone, chimes, gong, whip, triangle, temple
blocks, wood block, suspended cymbal), harp, piano, celesta,
and strings.
Catamount*; 16 minutes
Commission: Dr. and Mrs. Ralph I. Dorfman for the San
Francisco Symphony
Comment: Runner-up for 1983 Pulitzer Prize
See: S. Albahari, 1983; Ariel, 1983; E. Armer, 1991;
Burlington Free Press, 1985; J. Carson, 1983; G. Claghorn,
1996; A. Cohen, 1987; R. Commanday, Jan. 7, 1983; M.
Connell, 1986; C. Crawford, 1983; D. Cummings, 1997, 1998;
T. Flandreau, 1983; S. Fuller, 1994; E. George, 1984; W.
Glackin, 1983; C.J. Hall, 1989; C. Hall, 1996; P. Hertelendy,
Jan. 4, Jan. 7, 1987; B. Jones, 1999; L. Jones, 1997; C. Kino,
1983; D. Landis and L. Edelman, 1982; A. Levine, 1983; N.
Malitz, 1983; P. Moor, 1983; Morton and Collins, 1992; R.
Pontzious, Jan. 6, Jan. 10, 1983; J.C. Press, 1983; D. Randel,
1996; J. Raymond, 2000; San Francisco Symphony, 1982; C.
Shere, Jan. 7, Jan 9, 1983; N. Slonimsky, 1997; P. Swift, 1984;
M. Tucker, 1982; S. Tyler, 1998; WNYC, 1986.

Premiere:

1983 (January 5-8): San Francisco; Davies Symphony Hall; Cupertino, California; Flint Center; San Francisco Symphony, Edo de Waart, conducting. Part of "Vivian Fine Week" (January 5-13) sponsored by San Francisco Symphony.

Selected performances:
1983 (January 7 or 8): Cupertino, California; Flint Center; San Francisco Symphony, Edo de Waart, conducting. Part of "Vivian Fine Week" (January 5-13) sponsored by San Francisco Symphony.

Broadcasts:
1986 (April 19): Boston, Massachusetts; WGBH 89.7 FM, Vivian Fine: A Celebration of Her Music.

1986 (September 28): New York City, New York; WNYC 94 FM, "The Music of Vivian Fine"; a tribute on Fine's 73rd birthday by Ev Grimes and Karen Pearlman for the International League of Women Composers.

DOUBLE VARIATIONS FOR PIANO SOLO   JC102
Catamount*; 10 minutes
Commission: Claudia Stevens in honor of Elliott Carter's 75th birthday
See: S. Albahari, 1983; J. Carson, 1983; C. Hall, 1996; B. Luse, 1983; Morton and Collins, 1992.

Premiere:
1983 (December 5): New York City, New York; Composers Forum, Carnegie Recital Hall; Claudia Stevens, piano.

Selected performances:
1983 (October 30): Williamsburg, Virginia; The College of William and Mary; Claudia Stevens, piano.

1983 (November 6): Richmond, Virginia; University of Richmond; Claudia Stevens, piano.

1983 (November 13): Norfolk, Virginia; Old Dominion University; Claudia Stevens, piano.

TOCCATINA   JC103

Piano
Publisher unknown (see App. 1); duration unknown.
Commission: Mary Ellen and Timothy Fine, 1981

Premiere:
1982 (March 12): Berkeley, California; recital of the Music
Teacher's Association of California, Alameda County Branch;
Town and Gown Club; Rachel Fine, piano.

Selected performances:
1982 (May 2): Berkeley, California; Berkeley Piano Club;
Rachel Fine, piano.

1982 (June 25): Orange, California; Chapman College; The
Music Teacher's Association of California; Rachel Fine, piano.

1982 (June): Oakland, California; Pacific Musical Society,
Lutheran Trinity Church; Rachel Fine, piano.

1983

CANTICLES FOR JERUSALEM   JC104

Song-cycle for mezzo-soprano (or soprano) and piano
Catamount*; 15 minutes
Commission: Stephanie Friedman and Lois Brandynne
Text: In Hebrew and English from the Bible (IV. By the rivers
of Babylon, Psalm 137), Judah Halevi (I. My heart's in the
East; V. Ode to Zion), Yehuda Amichai (II. this year I traveled
far; III. Light against the Tower of David)
See: S. Albahari, 1983; J. Carson, 1983; E. George, 1984.

Premiere:
1989 (April 16): Cambridge, Massachusetts; Harvard
University, Paine Hall; part of "Vivian Fine Appreciation
Week in Boston" and presented by the magazine **Mosaic**,
Maria Tegzes, soprano and Geoffrey Burleson, piano.

1984

ODE TO HENRY PURCELL   JC105

Soprano and string quartet

Catamount*; 16 minutes.
Commission: Elizabeth Sprague Coolidge Foundation.
Text: Rainer Maria Rilke and Gerald Manley Hopkins.
See: Library of Congress, Oct. 28 & 30, 1985; J. McLellan, 1985; N. Slonimsky, 1997.

Premiere:
1985 (October 30): Washington, District of Columbia; The Coolidge Auditorium, Library of Congress; Founder's Day Concert; Phyllis Bryn-Julson, soprano and the Atlantic String Quartet, Linda Quan and Timothy Baker, violins, Lois Martin, viola, and Christopher Finckel, cello.

Broadcasts:
1985 (December 12): Washington, District of Columbia; WETA-FM (90.9). Also, the program was made available to American Public Radio under the auspices of the Katie and Walter Louchheim Fund of the Library of Congress.

QUINTET FOR VIOLIN, OBOE, CLARINET, CELLO AND PIANO
JC106

I. Adagio, calmo ("Summer Evening"); II. Allegro ma non troppo ("Jealousy"); III. with a warm lyrical impulse ("The Kiss")
C.F. Peters, Inc.; 11 minutes
Commission: Sigma Alpha Iota
Comments: Inspired by the works of Norwegian artist, Edvard Munch.
See: D. Cummings, 1998; R-M. Johnson, 1989; N. Slonimsky, 1997; S. Tyler, 1998.

Premiere:
1984 (July 29): Chicago, Illinois; The Palmer House, Grand Ballroom, Sigma Alpha Iota 1984 National Convention; Shirley Thomson, violin, Jo Anne Fosselman, oboe, Ona Pinsonneault, clarinet, Patricia Germain, cello and Vivian Fine, piano.

Selected performances:
1984 (November 19): Minneapolis-St. Paul, Minnesota; Westminster Church, Sigma Alpha Iota Incorporation Day, Patricia Nortwen, piano, Laura Nortwen, oboe, Ona Pinsonneault, clarinet, Shirley Thomson, violin and Patricia Germain, cello.

1986 (February 13): Minneapolis, Minnesota; The Thursday Musical, Shirley Thompson, violin, Laura Nortwen, oboe, Ona Pinsonneault, clarinet, Lucia Magney, cello, and Patricia Nortwen, piano.

1986 (April 27): Minneapolis, Minnesota; Church of the Annunciation, Sigma Alpha Iota and Annunciation Music Series, Contemporary American Music, Shirley Thompson, violin, Laura Nortwen, oboe, Ona Pinsonneault, clarinet, Lucia Magney, cello, and Patricia Nortwen, piano.

Broadcasts:
1986 (February 20): Minneapolis-St. Paul, Minnesota; Saint Olaf College, WCAL-FM Public Radio.

POETIC FIRES   JC107
Orchestra: 2 flutes (2 double piccolos), 2 oboes (2 double English horns), 2 clarinets (2 double bass clarinets), 2 bassoons (2 double contrabassoons), 4 horns, 2 trumpets, 2 tenor trombones, bass trombone, tuba, timpani, percussion (Glockenspiel, Xylophone, Vibraphone, Temple blocks, wood blocks, ratchet, suspended cymbals, triangle), harp, strings; and solo piano
Catamount*; 14 min.
Commission: Koussevitsky Foundation
See: A. Cohen, 1987; D. Cummings, 1997, 1998; S. Fuller, 1994; S. Galardi, 1985; C. Hall, 1996; R-M. Johnson, 1989; B. Jones, 1999; T. Page, 1985; N. Slonimsky, 1997; P. Swift, 1984; S. Tyler, 1998.

Premiere:
1985 (February 21): New York City, New York; Alice Tully Hall, Lincoln Center; American Composers Orchestra, Gunther Schuller, conducting and Vivian Fine, piano.

1985

A SONG FOR ST. CECILIA'S DAY   JC108
Mixed chorus, soprano and baritone soloists, string orchestra and two trumpets.
Catamount*; 17 min.
Commission: Trinity College, Burlington, Vermont in

conjunction with the 60th anniversary of the founding of Trinity by the Sisters of Mercy; and supported in part by a grant from the Vermont Council for the Arts.

Text: Poetry of John Dryden

See: *Burlington Free Press*, 1985; J. Donoghue, 1985.

Premiere:

1985 (October 25): Burlington, Vermont; Mann Hall Auditorium, Trinity College; Trinity College Chorus, Bennington College Chorus, University of Vermont Concert Choir and Trinity Choir, Vermont Symphony Orchestra string and trumpet ensemble, Vivian Fine, conducting.

AEGEAN SUITE   JC109

Piano solo

1. Melos (Song), 2. The Blue Aegean, 3. Meltemi (The strong, constant, northerly winds of summer experienced in the eastern Mediterranean)

Catamount*; 6 min.

Commission: Timothy and Mary Ellen Fine for their daughter, Rachel

Premiere:

1986 (March 9): Berkeley, California; Memorial Scholarship Foundation of the Music Teachers' Association of California, Alameda County Branch, Scholarship and Award Winning Students, Berkeley Piano Club, Rachel Fine, piano (she won a $500 first place scholarship).

Selected performances:

1986 (March 16): Berkeley, California; Piano Recital by the students of Jennie Lois Windle, Berkeley Piano Club, Rachel Fine, piano.

1986 (May 11): Berkeley, California; Piedmont-East Bay Music Festival, Solo Competition Final Concert, Rachel Fine, piano.

1986

SHEILA'S SONG JC110[2]

Voice, piano and double bass
Catamount*; 3 minutes

Premiere: Not yet performed.

INSCRIPTIONS JC111

1. One's Self I Sing; 2. Look Down Fair Moon; 3. A child
said, What is the grass?; 4. When Lilacs Last in the Dooryard
Bloom'd; 5. Inscriptions.
Two voices, piano
Catamount*; 13 min.
Grant: Living Composers grant from the New England
Foundation for the Arts.
Text: Poetry of Walt Whitman (1. One's Self I Sing; 2. Look
Down Fair Moon; 3. A child said, What is the grass?; 4. When
Lilacs Last in the Dooryard Bloom'd; 5. Inscription.)
Note: Dedicated to Nan Nall and Lise Messier.
See: W. Severinghaus, 1987.

Premiere:
1987 (January 8): Boston, Massachusetts; Isabella Stewart
Gardner Museum; Nan Nall, Lise Messier, sopranos, Glenn
Parker, piano.

Selected performances:
1987 (January 11): Rutland, Vermont; Nourse Hall, Trinity
Church, Nan Nall and Lise Messier, sopranos and Glenn
Parker, piano.

1987 (January 12): Middlebury, Vermont; Mead Chapel, The
Middlebury College, Nan Nall and Lise Messier, sopranos and
Glenn Parker, piano.

1987 (January 17): West Brattleboro, Vermont; The Brattleboro
Music Center, West Village Meeting House, Nan Nall and Lise
Messier, sopranos, and Glenn Parker, piano.

---

[2] *Song* is included only for the reader's convenience, since it is listed in
many places. But Fine expressly noted that it was not part of her compendium.

1987 (September 13): North Bennington, Vermont; Park-McCullough House Associations, Inc., Nan Nall and Lise Messier, sopranos and Glenn Parker, piano.

1989 (August 30): Chicago, Illinois; Talman Dame Myra Hess Memorial Concerts; Chicago Public Library Cultural Center; Nan Nall and Lise Messier, sopranos; Glenn Parker, piano.

TOCCATAS AND ARIAS (FOR HARPSICHORD)   JC112
Toccata I; Aria I; Toccata II; Aria II; Toccata III.
Solo harpsichord
Commission: Barbara Harbach
Catamount*; 9 minutes
See: R. Chon, 1987; J. Coon, 1987; A. Kozinn, 1989; T. Putnam, 1987; D19.

Premiere:
1987 (February 9): Buffalo, New York; Department of Music, State University of New York at Buffalo, Baird Recital Hall; Barbara Harbach, harpsichord.

Selected performances:
1987 (April 26): Buffalo, New York; Vivian Fine, A Retrospective; State University of New York at Buffalo, Hallwalls, North American New Music Festival, Barbara Harbach, harpsichord.

1989 (January 30): New York City, New York; Weill Recital Hall, Glassboro (N.J.) State College; Veda Zuponcic, piano.

Recording:
1990s: GSCD-266, by Barbara Harbach, **20th Century Harpsichord Music**, Volume II; Gasparo Records, Jaffrey, New Hampshire. See: D19.

SONATA FOR VIOLONCELLO AND PIANO   JC113
I. Poco Lento, rubato - Tempo guisto; II. Elegia; III. Allegro; IV. Con piena voce.
Hommage a Claude Debussy
Catamount*; 11 min.
See: D. Cummings, 1998; N. Slonimsky, 1997; S. Tyler, 1998.

Premiere:
1988 (March 13): New York City; Christ and St. Stephen's
Church; Cordier Ensemble, Maxine Neuman, cello and Joan
Stein, piano.

Selected performances:
1988 (March 23): Bennington, Vermont; Bennington College,
Greenwall Music Workshop, Maxine Neuman, cello and Joan
Stein, piano.

1990 (January 9): Warburg, Germany; the Aula; Maxine
Neuman, cello and Rainer Hoffman, piano.

1990 (January 9): Frankfort, Germany; Stadthalle; Maxine
Neuman, cello and Rainer Hoffman, piano.

1990 (July 27): Vail, Colorado; Bravo Colorado Music
Festival; Warren Lash, cello and William Tritt, piano.

1990: Manchester, Vermont; Manchester Music Festival;
Michael Rudiakov, cello and David James, piano.

PIZZICATO FANFARE   JC114

Cello solo
Catamount*; 2 minutes
Note: Written especially for the occasion "A Concert for
Lionel Nowak."

Premiere:
1986 (October 15): Bennington, Vermont; Greenwall Music
Workshop, Bennington College, Maxine Neuman, cello.

DANCE WITH THE FROG PRINCE   JC115

Dance for Pierre Dalaine
Piano
Quadrivium Press; 3 minutes.
Also called: **Tango with the Frog Prince**
See: M. Connell, 1986.

Premiere:
1986 (February 28): New York City, New York; Dance
Theater Workshop's Bessie Schonberg Theater, Composers

Forum, Tango Marathon; Yvonne Marceau, artistic director, Yvar Mikhashoff, piano.

1987

MA'S IN ORBIT   JC116
The 30's revisited from the ballet **The Race of Life** (JC17): the race — the cuckoo — spring dance — the race resumes — faster! — night time — shifting images — Indians! — shifting images — finish line.
Violin, double bass, percussion and piano
Catamount*; 8 min.
See: R. Chon, 1987.

Premiere:
1987 (April 26): Buffalo, New York; Vivian Fine, A Retrospective; State University of New York at Buffalo, Hallwalls, North American New Music Festival, Thomas Halpin, violin, William Staebell, contrabass, Yvar Mikhashoff, piano and Jan Williams, percussion.

EMILY'S IMAGES   JC117
Flute and piano.
Anthology of American Flute Music by the National Flute Association with the Oxford University Press, Catamount; 8 minutes
Text: First lines of poems by Emily Dickinson: A Spider sewed at Night; A Clock stopped — Not the Mantel's; Exultation is the going; The Robin is a Gabriel; After great pain, a formal feeling comes; The Leaves like Women interchange; A Day! Help! Help! another Day.
Dedication: Jayn Rosenfeld
See: W. Crutchfield, 1988; P. Hertelendy, 1988; B. Lynerd, 1997; D6.

Premiere:
1987 (September 15): Recinto de Rio Piedras, Puerto Rico; Teatro Universidad de Puerto Rico, Fundacion Latinoamericano para la Musica Contemporanea, Jayn Rosenfeld, flute and Evelyne Crochet, piano.

American premiere:

1988 (February 28): Berkshire, Massachusetts; Concert Series at the Berkshire Museum, Jayn Rosenfeld, flute and Evelyn Crochet, piano.

Selected performances:
1988 (April 13): Cambridge, Massachusetts; Edward Pickman Concert Hall, Longy School of Music, Jayn Rosenfeld, flute and Evelyne Crochet, piano.

1988 (April 17): New York City, New York; Merkin Concert Hall; Jayn Rosenfeld, flute and Evelyne Crochet, piano.

1988 (November 2): New York City, New York; Music by American Composers; Third Street Music School settlement; John Ranck, flute and Mitchell Vines, piano.

1989 (October 11): Bennington, Vermont; Greenwall Music Workshop; Sue Ann Kahn, flute and Marianne Finckel, piano.

1990 (April 26): New York City, New York; Renee Weiler Music Center, Greenwich House Music School; Bernard Rose, piano, and Jayn Rosenfeld, flute.

Recording:
1990s: CD317, by Leone Buyse, flute, Martin Amlin, piano, and Fenwick Smith, alto flute and flute; **Music for Flute**; Crystal Records, Camas, Washington. See: D6.

THE HUMAN MIND   JC118

Mezzo-soprano and piano.
Catamount*; 5 min.

Premiere: Not yet performed.

DANCING WINDS   JC119

Woodwind quintet (flute, oboe, clarinet, horn, bassoon)
Catamount*; 12 minutes
Commission: Catskill Conservatory on behalf of the Catskill Woodwind Quintet with assistance of the New York Council on the Arts.
See: D. Cummings, 1998; A. Kozinn, June 9, 1988; N. Slonimsky, 1997; S. Tyler, 1998.

Premiere:
1987 (August 28): Salt Springville, New York; Windfall Dutch Barn; Catskill Woodwind Quintet, Floyd Herbert, flute, Rene Prins, oboe, Julia Robin Seletsky, clarinet, Hasbrouck Clay, horn, and Spencer F. Phillips, bassoon.

1988 (June 9): New York City, New York; Weill Recital Hall; Catskill Woodwind Quintet, Carleton Clay, trumpet and director, Floyd Herbert, flute, Rene Prins, oboe, Timothy Perry, clarinet, Hasbrouck Clay, horn, and Stephen Walt, bassoon.

TOCCATAS AND ARIAS FOR PIANO   JC120
Passionato; style of instrumental cantillation
Catamount*; 11 minutes
Commission: Veda Zuponcic
See: A. Kozinn, 1989

Premiere:
1989 (January 30): New York City, New York; Weill Recital Hall, Carnegie Hall; Veda Zuponcic, piano.

IN MEMORIAM: GEORGE FINCKEL   JC121
Four cellos and multiples thereof
Catamount*; duration unknown
See: L. Jones, 1997.

Premiere:
1987 (September 13): Bennington, Vermont; Bennington College, Greenwall Auditorium; an ensemble of 16 cellos conducted by Vivian Fine, Elizabeth Brunton, Thomas Calabro, Joan Esch, Chris Finckel, David Finckel, Michael Finckel, Connie Gordon, Maxine Neuman, Robert Nowak, William Peck, Ingrid Porter, Michael Severens, Jared Shapiro, Martha Siegel and Jennifer Weiss.

LIGHT IN SPRING POPLARS   JC122
Mixed chorus, soprano solo, viola solo, piano.
Catamount*; 5 minutes
Text: Stephen Sandy

Premiere:

1987 (October 11): Bennington, Vermont; Bennington College; Janet Gillespie, soprano and Jacob Glick, viola with performers of Bennington College conducted by Randall Neale on the occasion of the inauguration of Elizabeth Coleman as President of the College.

AFTER THE TRADITION   JC123

Kaddish; My heart's in the East and I at the end of the West; Hark! Jaweh causes the wilderness to dance.

Orchestra: 2 flutes (double piccolo), 2 oboes (double English horn), 2 clarinets, 2 bassoons (double contrabassoons), 2 horns, trumpet, trombone, timpani, percussion (xylophone, triangle, tambourine), and strings.

Catamount*; 11 minutes

Commission: Bay Area Women's Philharmonic

See: E. Armer, 1991; R. Bramhall, 1988; D. Cummings, 1997, 1998; S. Fuller, 1994; P. Hertelendy, April 29 & May 2, 1988: B. Jones, 1999; J. Kosman, 1988; N. Slonimsky, 1997; S. Tyler, 1998.

Premiere:
1988 (April 29): Berkeley, California; First Congregational Church; Bay Area Women's Philharmonic, JoAnn Falletta, conducting.

Selected Performances:
1989 (April 14): Minneapolis, Minnesota; Macalester College; Civic Orchestra of Minneapolis, Robert Bobzin, conducting.

1989 (April 16): Minneapolis, Minnesota; St. John's Lutheran Church; Civic Orchestra of Minneapolis, Robert Bobzin, conducting.

1988

THE GARDEN OF LIVE FLOWERS   JC124

Soprano, tenor, baritone, piano.
Catamount*; 8 minutes
Text: Lewis Carroll

Premiere:
1988 (March 27): Bayside, New York; Queensboro Community

College Theater; Meet The Composer program, After Dinner Opera Company, MaryEllen Landon, Richard Holmes, and Bert Lindsey, piano and conductor, Conrad Strasser.

Selected performances:
1988 (March 28): New York City, New York; Bruno Walter Auditorium, Lincoln Center, After Dinner Opera Company, MaryEllen Landon, Richard Holmes, and Bert Lindsey, piano and conductor, Conrad Strasser.

L'ECOLE DES HAUTES ETUDES   JC125
Piano, clarinet, bass, percussion.
Catamount*; 8 minutes
Note: based on etudes of Czerny, Cramer and Chopin. Parts: 1. Intrada; 2. Twirling; 3. Tango; 4. Feu Follet (Will o' the Wisp); 5. Glockenspiel und Contra Bass; 6. Sturm und Drang (Storm and Stress); 7. A Difference of Opinion; 8. Chinese Medley (dedicated to Phebe Chao).

Premiere:
1988 (April 3): Bennington, Vermont; Bennington College; Lionel Nowak, piano, Gunnar Schonbeck, clarinet, Jeffrey Levine, bass, Louis Calabro, percussion with Jonathan Green, conducting.

VICTORIAN SONGS   JC126
Voice, flute, clarinet, violin-viola, cello
Catamount*: 14 minutes
I. Aloof; II. Cadmus and Harmonia; III. Spring and Fall: to a young child; IV. Invictus; V. Sonnet from the Portuguese
Commission: The Capitol Chamber Artists, through a grant from the New York State Council on the Arts
Text: Christina Rossetti, Matthew Arnold, Gerald Manley Hopkins, William Ernest Henley and Elizabeth B. Browning.

Premiere:
1988 (March 4): Poultney, Vermont; Green Mountain College; Capitol Chamber Artists, Mary Lou Saetta, violin, viola; Irvin Gilman, flute; Charles Stancampiano, clarinet; Ann Alton, cello; Janet Stasio, soprano.

Selected performances:

1989 (March 23): New York City, New York; Weill Recital Hall; Capitol Chamber Artists (performers same as above).

1989 (October 30): Richmond, Virginia; University of Richmond, North Court Recital Hall, Lisa Edwards Burr, soprano, Patricia Werrell, alto flute, Charles West, clarinet, Robert Murray, violin, Judy H. Cohen, viola, Anne Bakker-Stokes, cello and Fred Cohen, conducting. Guest composer: Vivian Fine.

ASPHODEL   **JC127**

Coloratura soprano, flute, clarinet, violin, viola, cello, percussion, piano
Catamount*; 13 minutes.
Commission: Boston Musica Viva
Text: William Carlos Williams
See: R. Dyer, 1989.

Premiere:
1989 (April 10): New York City, New York; Kathryn Bache Miller Theater; Maria Tegzes, soprano, Leone Buyse, flute, William Wrzesien, clarinet, Nancy Cirillo, violin, Katherine Murdock, viola, Kim Scholes, cello, Dean Anderson, percussion, Sally Pinkas, piano, and Richard Pittman, conducting. Performed as part of the 20th Anniversary Season of Boston Musica Viva.

Selected performances:
1989 (April 21): Plymouth, New Hampshire; Plymouth State College; Maria Tegzes, soprano, Leone Buyse, flute, William Wrzesien, clarinet, Nancy Cirillo, violin, Katherine Murdock, viola, Kim Scholes, cello, Dean Anderson, percussion, Sally Pinkas, piano and Richard Pittman, conducting.

1989 (April 21): Cambridge, Massachusetts; Longy School; Maria Tegzes, soprano, Leone Buyse, flute, William Wrzesien, clarinet, Nancy Cirillo, violin, Katherine Murdock, viola, Kim Scholes, cello, Dean Anderson, percussion, Sally Pinkas, piano and Richard Pittman, conducting. In conjunction with a "Meet the Composer" session at Boston Conservatory of Music.

THE TRIPLE-GODDESS   **JC128**
> Wind ensemble
> Catamount*; 8 1/2 minutes.
> Commission: Harvard Wind Ensemble
> <u>See</u>: M. Caldwell (1989); M. Miller, 1989.

> Premiere:
> 1989 (April 22): Cambridge, Massachusetts; Sanders Theater,
> Harvard University, Harvard Wind Ensemble, Thomas Everett,
> conducting.

1989

DISCOURSE OF GOATHERDS   **JC129**
> Amorous, Boisterous
> Solo bass (or tenor) trombone
> Catamount*; 5 minutes.
> Commission: Tom Everett
> <u>See</u>: M. Caldwell (1989); **ITA Journal**, 1990.

> Premiere:
> 1989 (April 20): Boston, Massachusetts; Northeastern
> University, Department of Music, Music at Noon, Ell Center
> Ballroom; Matthew Guilford, bass trombone. A performance
> and interview as part of Vivian Fine Appreciation Week.

> Selected Performances:
> 1990 (October 3): Bennington, Vermont; Bennington College;
> Gerlad Zaffuts, trombone.

MADRIGALI SPIRITUALI   **JC130**
> Trumpet and string quartet.
> Catamount*; 16 minutes.
> Commission: Music from Angel Fire Festival
> <u>See</u>: E. Armer, 1991, **Chamber Music**, 1989; **Symphony**, 1990.

> Premiere:
> 1989 (August 27): Angel Fire, New Mexico; Ida Kavafian,
> Pamela Frank, violins, Toby Appel, viola, Warren Lash, cello,
> Stephen Burns, trumpet.

> Selected performances:

1990 (October 14): Saratoga, New York; Filene Recital Hall, Skidmore College; Saratoga Chamber Players, Janet Rowe, Lucy Joseph, violins, Susan St. Amour, viola, Susan Ruzow, cello and James Morris, trumpet.

1990 (November 3): San Francisco, California; First Congregational Church; Bay Area Women's Philharmonic, JoAnn Falletta, conducting.

THE HEART DISCLOSED   **JC131**
Voice and piano (monodrama)
Commission: Claudia Stevens
Catamount*; 18 minutes.

Premiere:
1990 (October 6): Providence, Rhode Island; Athenaeum; Claudia Stevens, piano and voice.

Selected performances:
1990 (October 31): Charlottesville, Virginia; University of Virginia; Claudia Stevens, piano and voice.

1990 (October 31): Virginia Beach, Virginia; Virginia Beach Center for the Arts; Claudia Stevens, piano and voice.

1990

PORTAL   **JC132**
Violin and piano
Commission: Pamela Frank
Catamount*; 7 minutes.
See: E. Armer, 1991; A. Kozinn, 1990; P. Schiavo, 1990.

Premiere:
1990 (March 19): Philadelphia, Pennsylvania; Philadelphia Free Library; Pamela Frank, violin and Wu Han, piano.

Selected Performances:
1990 (April 19): New York City, New York; Alice Tully Hall, Lincoln Center; Pamela Frank, violin and Wu Han, piano.

SONGS AND ARIAS   JC133
French horn, violin, cello.
Catamount*; 13 minutes.
See: E. Armer, 1991.

Premiere:
1990 (July 12): Portland, Oregon; Chamber Music Northwest;
David Jolley, horn, Eriko Sato, violin, and Fred Sherry, cello.

Selected Performances:
1990: Bravo! Colorado Festival.

1991

HYMNS   JC134
Two pianos, French horn, and cello.
Catamount*; duration unknown

Premiere:
Never performed.

SONGS OF LOVE AND WAR   JC135
Soprano, violin, oboe, bassoon, percussion and piano.
Catamount*; duration unknown
Texts: Walt Whitman, Emily Dickinson, Jozef Wittlin
(translated by Loy Davidson), and "The Song of Songs" from
the Old Testament.

Premiere:
1991 (August 14): Williamstown, Massachusetts; Clark Art
Institute; Marlene Walt, soprano; Jeannie Shames, violin;
Ralph Gomberg, oboe; Stephen Walt, bassoon; Thomas
Gayger, percussion; and Gilbert Kalish, piano.

CANZONES Y DANCES   JC136
Classical guitar, flute and cello.
1. Adios, Bilbadito; 2. Oda a las Ranas; 3. The Frog Prince
and the Señorita; 4. Sililoquio; and 5. Jiga de la Muerta.
Catamount*; 3:28, 3:17; 1:45; 3:01; 2:38.
Also called: **Canciones y Danzas**
Commission: Joel Brown

See: E. Armer, 1991; MacAuslan and Aspen, 1997; D3.

Recording:
1992: TROY 086, compact disc; by Joel Brown, guitar; Jan
Vinci, flute; and Ann Alton, cello; **Five Premieres: Chamber
Works for Guitar**; Albany Records; Albany, New York. See:
D3

1993

CANTICLE FROM THE OTHER SIDE OF THE RIVER   JC137
Violin, cello, flute, clarinet, percussion, and piano.
Catamount*; duration unknown

Premiere: never performed or performance is not known.

MEMOIRS OF ULIANA ROONEY   JC138
A multimedia chamber opera. Soprano, two baritones, and two
female voices as chorus. Chamber orchestra: flute, clarinet,
violin, cello, double bass, piano and percussion.
Libretto and film/slide sequences: Sonya Friedman
Catamount*; duration unknown.
Commission: Meet the Composer/Reader's Digest Commis-
sioning Program, in partnership with the National Endowment
for the Arts, and the Lila Wallace-Reader's Digest Fund.
Grants: Film and slide projections supported in part by New
York State Council on the Arts, and research support provided
New York Council for the Humanities.
See: R. Baxter, 1997; S. Fuller, 1994; L. Jones, 1997; A.
Kozinn, 2000; *Los Angeles Times*, 2000; J. Raymond, 2000; D.
Webster, 1997.

Premiere:
1994 (September 9 and 10): Richmond, Virginia; University of
Richmond, Camp Theater, Currents Resident Ensemble, Fred
Cohen, artistic director and conductor, Christine Schadeberg,
soprano, David Pelton, narrator and baritone, Stephen Kalm,
baritone, Jennifer Cable, soprano and chorus, and Tamara
Wright, soprano.

Selected Performances:
1994 (February): Preview, New York City, New York;

American Opera Projects Inc., Grethe Barret Holby, producer and artistic director, Miriam Charney, pianist and music director (not a full production).

1996 (August 1): New York City, New York; same as above (see Leslie Jones, 1996).

1997 (February 28): Philadelphia, Pennsylvania; Annenberg Center; Relache Ensemble and American Opera Projects; National Women's Month celebration; Melanie Helton, soprano, James Busterud, tenor, David Stoneman, narrator, staged by Grethe B. Holby with Fred Cohen, conducting.

1996

"UNTITLED"   **JC139**
Voice and piano
Text: Nina Karp
Unpublished; 20-25 minutes.
Note: Schoenbergian in concept. This is Fine's last known composition, it may be unfinished.
See: Jones, Leslie 1997.

Premiere:
Unknown.

Group Composition:

1983

AUGURIES   **JC140**
Processional to honor the inauguration of Michael Hooker as president of Bennington College
Soprano, piano, trumpet, clarinet and percussion
Note: Written with Jeffrey Levine and Lionel Nowak
See: Teeter, Paul, 1983.

Premiere:
1983: Bennington, Vermont; Bennington College, performers not identified.

Chapter 4

FINE AT THE PIANO

Vivian Fine was justifiably proud of her prowess as a pianist in concert. Not only had she been a child prodigy, later she became acclaimed for her remarkable ability to instantly sight read and play any given music, this while her pianistic ability was also extolled (see B266, B304 and B266). Music reached Fine not only in an intellectual sense; she possessed an innate musician's mastery allowing her to respond to, and comprehend this auditory sphere directly "through the fingers" on the keys.[1] It was with the piano as her instrument that she earned her livelihood for many years.

Fine was quick to explain that she had worked hard as an accompanist to the pacesetter dancers, and also as a performer to earn a wage. She was only too aware of the actual physical effort involved when a pianist must accompany the demands of the dance, through countless rehearsals, until something like perfection is satisfied in the eye of the scrutinizing choreographer, and later, the audience. She knew how "playing for the dancers" exhausted the keenest mind, fatigued the back, the hands, after longs days bent over the piano. This, no matter how satisfying the final event in ballet performance.[2]

Her parents could contribute little financial help, only their support and love. She was not a pampered young talent at all, but a struggling musician who also had to earn a living with her piano. Vivian Fine was a young talent with grit as well as gift. She not only managed to support herself during the overwhelming poverty of the American Great Depression years, but she managed to support and nurture her own talent as a composer in what time remained after working hours. For while there might be a bit of money in arranging or composing a work for a particular ballet, there was little, if any cash for a composer of an original work. Fortunately, music was always performed live in Fine's era, the living musician always needed.[3] Therefore, as Fine might have concluded, in her reserved, somewhat down-to-earth tone . . . So, it was the piano!

There is something of a mystery in these many decades that Fine accompanied and concertized at her piano. On the countless occasions through the many decades of her life, she had performed her own piano compositions, plus the piano compositions of other composers, both classical and modern. Tragically, for though her playing was well praised and rewarded, there seems to be but a single professional recording of her performing at the piano (D20 and ex. P63). Yet strangely, for her solitary recording, she does not choose to play one of her own piano compositions (see Appendix 8); rather, she performs the neglected composition of her long-dead friend and teacher, Ruth Crawford.

Fine was dedicated to Ruth's music legacy. She was the last living link to an important composition that Crawford had composed fifty-seven years before Fine's Week. Even at the height of her own fame, Fine appeared willing to share that success with another long-gone composer, in some sense of her own devising. She would perform her own music during her busy and exciting San Francisco Vivian Fine Week (see Chapter 1, 1982). Then she would manage to find the time and energy necessary to perform Ruth's *Sonata for Violin and Piano* that same week in January 1983 (see P64). Slightly more than a month later she traveled to New York City to perform the *Sonata* again (see P65). Fine then traveled to Washington, D.C., that fall to perform her childhood mentor's *Sonata* at the Kennedy Center (see P66).

Ruth's piece was in four parts: Agitated-vibrant-andante lusingando; Buoyant; Mystic-intense; and Fast with bold energy.[4] Although Vivian was now seventy-years-old, she was still able to bring "bold" excitement, vigor, and controlled interpretation to the keys in her concert performances of Crawford's piece. The long dormant music was awakened, received with keen admiration by critics who were probably not even born when it was conceived (B256, B167).

Speaking from the modesty of an earlier era, Fine often referred to herself as a "musician" rather than a "composer." She would smile with a certain pride when she would call herself a "professional pianist"; but after all, she had worked so hard to earn that claim.[5] Besides performing her own music, and others, "from 1933 until 1938 [she] was active as pianist for dance, serving as accompanist for the Humphrey-Weidman Company, Tina Flada, Pauline Koner, Nini Theilade, Eleanor King, Jose Limon, and others."[6] Fine would continue performing on piano until well into her seventh decade. In one of her last public concerts, Fine was on-stage at Lincoln Center in New York City performing with her orchestral *Poetic Fires,* in 1985 (see P67). Since it sadly seems that the only extant recording of Fine's long career as a pianist will be simply a written one, the following selections, where she was the performer, are given as somewhat characteristic of her years on the keyboard.[7]

In this catalog, individual concert or music events are given a P number (e.g., P1); P numbers are listed chronologically; next, the title of the event (e.g., Formal Musicale), is underlined. Where records could be found, each event is cross-referenced to the Bibliography, Chapter 2; in some cases these are the actual reviews for the particular event. In other cases, an example (ex.) of the type of review a specific category of event probably elicited is given (ex. B66).

CATALOG OF SELECTED PIANO PERFORMANCES

1930
P1 "Formal Musicale, by the Gamma Chapter of Sigma Alpha Iota:" *Home Thoughts* and *Joy*, by Ruth Crawford; with Arvesta Parrish, voice. Cordon Club, Chicago, Illinois, April 15.

1931-1932
P2 The Dance Center, Second Subscription Bill of Ballet Repertoire: *Salome*, from the opera score of Richard Strauss, an original ballet version devised by Gluck-Sandor. Intimate Theatre Studio, New York City, New York (NY).

P3 The Dance Center, Third Subscription Bill of Ballet Repertoire: *El Amor Brujo*, by De Falla and *Flor de Noche*, Spanish folk songs arranged by J. Nin. Intimate Theatre Studio, New York City, NY.

P4 The Dance Center, Fourth Subscription Bill of Ballet Repertoire: *The Prodigal Son*, by Prokofieff, ballet. Intimate Theatre Studio, New York City, NY. (see B217).

1932
P5 The Young Composers' Group: *Sonatina*, by Israel Citkowitz; *"Phobias"* by Lehman Engel, and *Music for Five and Ten Cent Store* by Henry Brant on percussion and Bertram Brant, violin on the latter two pieces. The New School Auditorium, New York City, NY, January 15 (see B118; B202; B231).

P6 Seminar and Symposium on American Polyphonic Music, conducted by Henry Cowell: first performance of *Study in Mixed Accents* by Ruth Crawford. Participants included Crawford, Adolph Weiss, Carl Ruggles and Wallingford Riegger. New School of Social Research, New York City, NY, January 27 (see B17).

P7 Roerich Society Series of Dance Evenings of Felicia Sorel and Gluck-Sandor and the Dance Center Company: *El Amor Brujo*, by De Falla and *Salome*, by Richard Strauss. Roerich Hall, New York City, NY, February 10.

P8 Concert, conducted by Nicholas Slonimsky: "what may have been the first performance" of Charles Ives' *Set for Theatre Orchestra*. The New School, New York City, NY, February 16.

P9 "Symposium for Moderns:"*Salutations to the Depths; Tenderness; The Earth-Pull; Crucifixion, No.1* by Dane Rudhyar; and *Four Polyphonic Pieces*

(JC7) by Fine. The Dance Center, New York City, NY, April 21 (see B213 and B27).

P10   First Festival of Contemporary American Music: *Four Polyphonic Piano Pieces* (JC7) by Fine. Yaddo, Saratoga Springs, NY, April 30 (see B212 and B91).

P11   The Dance Center: *Petrouchka* by Igor Stravinsky. Intimate Theatre Studio, New York City, NY, May 4 (see ex. B212).

1933
P12   The League of Composers: six songs from *Das Marienleben* by Paul Hindemith; with Ada MacLeish, soprano. French Institute, New York City, NY, January 8.

P13   Concert: *Sonatina for Piano* by Israel Citkowitz and *Music for a Five and Ten Cent Store* by Henry Brant on percussion with Bertram Brant, violin. The New School, New York City, NY, January 15.

P14   The Neighborhood Playhouse Studios: *Spanish Folk Songs* by Serafin and Joaquin Alvares Quintero and "Peace and Quiet" performed by the students. New York City, NY, (n.d.).

P15   The Pan American Association of Composers: *Sonata for Piano* by Carlos Chavez, and *Piano Study* by Gerald Strang. Carnegie Chapter Hall, New York City, NY, March 6 (see ex. B18).

P16   The Pan American Association of Composers Series: *String Quartet; Songs—To a Lovely Myrtle Bound; Joy Song; Music in the Earth and Air; and Sonatina (for piano)* by Israel Citkowitz; with the Arion String Quartet, and Helen Marshall, soprano. Radio Station WVED, University of the Air, New York City, NY, April 30.

P17   Charles Weidman Ballet Group: *Candide*, arranged and composed by Genevieve Pitot and John Coleman; instrumentation by Vivian Fine. The Booth Theatre, New York City, NY, May 13.

P18   Dance Recital of the "The Little Group" of Ernestine Henoch, Letitia Ide, Eleanor King and Jose Limon, members of the Doris Humphrey-Charles Weidman Concert Group: *Tango Rhythms* and *Notturno*, percussion by Fine. Provincetown Playhouse Festival, NY, May 25.

P19   The Pan American Association of Composers Series: *Mists; The New River; The Indians; Walt Whitman; Evening, Walking* by Charles Ives; *Where*

She Lives and *Manaunaun's Birthing* by Henry Cowell; *My Little Pool* by Nicolas Slonimsky; *Ave Maria* by Umberto Allende; and *Bito Manue* by Alejandro Caturla; with Mary Bell, soprano and Adolph Weiss, piano. Radio Station WVED, University of the Air, New York City, NY, June 4.

P20   Dance Recital by Charles Weidman and Doris Humphrey: *Alcina Suite,* by Handel; *Danza (La Puerta del Vino)* and *Danse Profane* by Debussy; *Sarabande* by Roussel; *Poeme,* and *Etude* by Scriabin; *Two Ecstatic Themes, A- Circular Descent* by Medtner and *B- Pointed Ascent* by Malipiero; *Scherzo* by Borodin; *Rude Poema* by Villa-Lobos; *Air on a Ground Bass* by Purcell; and, *Burlesca* by Bossi. Bennington Theater Guild, Bennington College, Vermont (VT), November 13.

P21   The "Y" Pop Series, Dance Recital by Nini Theilade, premiere danseuse of Max Reinhardt Theatre: *Danish Porcelain (La Plus Que Lente)*; *Diana (The Huntress); Lotus Flower* and *Dance* by Debussy; *Miniature Suite* by Felix Felton; *Pizzicato Arabesque* by Fanchetti; *The Flute Player (Mazurka Op.7, No.2); Mazurka (Op.33, No.2); Three Preludes (B flat major, F minor, F major)* and *Polonaise in B Flat* by Chopin; *Impression from Tahiti* by Sherwood; *Serenade (Tango)* by Albeniz; *Sonata in F major* by Haydn; and, *Viennese Dance* by Johann Strauss. Fuld Hall, Newark, New Jersey (NJ), December 28; (see ex. B1).

1934
P22   Student's Dance Recitals of Doris Humphrey and Charles Weidman and their Concert Group: *Three Dances* by Tansman; *Credo* by Chavez; *Dance Profane* by Debussy; *Two Ecstatic Themes*; *Circular Descent* by Medtner and *Pointed Ascent* by Malipiero; *Kinetic Pantomime* by McFee; *Variations of a Theme by Handel* by Brahms; *Memorial to the Trivial* by Moross; *Rude Poema* by Villa-Lobos; *Affirmations* by V. Fine; *Counterpoint No.2* by Pollins; and *Alcina Suite* by Handel. Municipal Auditorium, Washington Irving High School, New York City, NY, November 17 (see B7; B32; B143; and ex. B145).

P23   Recital by Vivian Fine and Pauline Koner: *Organ Prelude* by Bach-Liszt; *Three Preludes* by Chopin; *Rhapsody in G Minor* by Brahms; *Waldesrauschen* by Liszt; and *La Maja Maldita (The Wicked Enchantress)* by Gaillard. Green Mansions, probably New York City, NY, (n.d.).

1935
P24   Dance Recitals of Nini Theilade, premiere danseuse of Max Reinhardt Theatre on a North American Tour: *Danish Porcelain (La Plus Que Lente)*; *Diana (The Huntress)*; *Lotus Flower (En Bateau)*; and *"Ballett"* by Debussy; *Miniature Suite* by Felix Felton; *Pizzicato Arabesque* by Fanchetti; *The Flute Player (Mazurka Op.7, No.2)* and *Three Preludes (B flat major, F minor, F*

major) by Chopin; *Waldesrauschen* by Liszt; *Impression from Tahiti (Hawaiian Sunset)* by Sherwood; *The Sylph* by Rubenstein; *Serenade (Tango)* by Albeniz; and *Presto (Andante and Rondo Capriccioso)* by Mendelssohn (see exs. B1; B14; B83; B239; B309 and B311).

> The Women's Musical Club, Concert Hall, Winnipeg Auditorium, New York City, NY, January 8.
> Library Auditorium, New York City, NY, January 14.
> Presser Hall, Western College, Oxford, Ohio, January 22.
> Guild Theater, New York City, NY, January 28.
> Orchestra Hall, Detroit Town Hall Series, Detroit, Michigan, January 31.
> Glebe Collegiate Auditorium, Ottawa, Canada, February 19.
> Imperial Theatre, Montreal, Canada, March 11.
> McFarlin Auditorium, The Dallas Civic-Community Music Association, Dallas, Texas (TX), May 6 [Possibly 1934].
> North Texas State Teachers College, Wichita Falls, TX, May 8.

P25   Dance performance of Doris Humphrey and Charles Weidman and their Concert Group: *Prelude from Suite in F* by Roussel; *Two Ecstatic Themes; Circular Descent* by Medtner, and *Pointed Ascent* by Malipiero; *Studies in Conflict* by Rudhyar; *Poeme, No.1 - Sentimentale and Etude, No. 12 - Patetico* by Scriabin; *Dance of Work*, and *Dance of Sport* by Cowell; *Kinetic Pantomime* by McFee; *Dionysiaques* by Schmitt; and *Alcina Suite* by Handel (see ex. B145).

> Eastman School of Music, University of Rochester, Kilbourn Hall, Rochester, NY, January 15.
> Eaton Auditorium, Toronto, Canada, January 16.
> Repertory Theatre, Boston, Massachusetts, March 14 and 15.

P26   Solo Recital of dancers Rose Crystal, Ernestine Henoch and Eleanor King with other dancers: *Attis Sophistication* by Satie; *Gossip* by Hindemith; *Valse* by Larmanjat; *The Mothers* by Reutter; *Despair* by Bartok; and *Invictus* by Milhaud. Civic Repertory Theatre, probably New York City, NY, April 7 (see B81).

P27   Dance Recital of Rose Crystal: *Prelude, Danza (La Puerto del Vino)*, and *Valse, La Plus Que Lente* by Debussy; *Attis Sophistication*, and *Integrity* by Eric Satie; *Rhapsody* by Brahms; *Conviction (JC14)*, and *Invictus (JC15)* by Fine; *Despair; Adolescence and Maturity; Dynamic* by Bartok; *Exuberance* by Milhaud; *Etude in E Major* by Liszt; and *Gossip* by Hindemith. Henry W. Saxe Junior High School, New Canaan, Connecticut (CT), September 13.

P28   Dance Program of Charles Weidman and Doris Humphrey, The "Y" Concert Series: *Prelude* by Roy Harris; *Affirmations (JC11)* by Vivian Fine; *Variations on a Theme of Handel* by Brahms; *Rudepoema* by Villa-Lobos; *Alcina*

Suite by Handel; *Two Ecstatic Themes: Circular Descent* by Medtner, and *Pointed Ascent* by Malipiero; *Kinetic Pantomime* by Colin McFee; *Etude* by Scriabin; *Exhibition Pieces* by Nicolas Slonimsky. Fuld Hall, Young Men's and Young Women's Hebrew Association, Newark, NJ, October 30.

P29   A Roger Sessions Program: *Symphony for Orchestra* (1927) by Roger Sessions (transcription for two pianos). Sessions conducting and also with Lehman Engel, piano. The New School, New York City, NY, November 22.

1938
P30   The Fifth Bennington Festival of the Modern Dance, Dance Performances of Charles Weidman and Group: *Opus 51* (JC24) by Fine at the piano with Franziska Boas, percussion. The Bennington School of the Dance, Bennington College, State Armory, Bennington, VT, August 6 and 10.

1940
P31   Composer's Forum-Laboratory Concert: *Three Ostinati with Chorales*, for flute and piano, with Robert McBride. Lennox Gallery, New York Public Library, New York City, NY, February 11.

1941
P32   Concert: Works of Bach, Scarlatti, Schumann, Schoenberg, Chopin and Fine. Steinway Hall, Studio 621, New York City, NY, June 2.

1942
P33   Concert of The League of Composers: *Rye Sextet with Voice* by Lazare Saminsky, with Maria Maximovitch, soprano and an ensemble from the New York Philharmonic. Museum of Modern Art, New York City, NY, December 27.

1943
P34   Concert, under the auspices of The National Conference of Christians and Jews, under the direction of Lazare Saminsky: Excerpt from *Seven Last Words* by Norman Lockwood (first performance), and *Incaic Air*, arranged by Andres Sas, with Maria Maximovitch, soprano and Gottfried Federlein, organ. Town Hall, New York City, NY, February 23.

1944
P35   Third Faculty Concert of the Metropolitan Music School: *Sonata for Flute and Piano* by Miriam Gideon, with Harry Moskovitz, flute. Steinway Hall, Studio 621, New York City, NY, January 30.

P36   A Salute to the New Russian Concert: premiere of Fine's *Rhapsody on a Russian Folk Song* (JC41); and piano part in *Turn, O Libertad* for chorus and piano by Roger Sessions. Town Hall, New York City, NY, April 30 (see B211).

1946
P37   Concert: works of Bach, Scarlatti, Schumann, Liszt, and Fine. Temple University, Pennsylvania, November 21 (see B234).

1947
P38   Concert of Sonatas of K.P.E. Bach, Scarlatti: *Sonatina for Oboe and Piano* (JC4), and *Suite in E Flat* (JC35) for piano solo by Fine, with Lois Wann, oboe. New York University, Music Education Department, New York City, NY, April 17.

1951
P39   Concert presented by United World Federalists: works of Bach, Scarlatti, Beethoven, Debussy, Chopin, Liszt, and Fine. Montclair State Teachers College, Montclair, NJ, February 26 and Montclair Art Museum, Montclair, NJ, March 4 (see B195).

1953
P40   Concert presented by the International Society for Contemporary Music and Mu Sigma Epsilon: works by Bach, Hindemith, Szymanoski, Beethoven, and Fine's *Three Pieces for Violin and Piano* (JC36), with Alice Smiley, violin. New Paltz State Teachers College, New Paltz, NY, April 16 (see B209).

1954
P41   Concert presented by the Artist Series: Works of Vivaldi-Respighi, Tansman, Brahms, Mozart, Guarnieri, Suk, McBride, and Fine's *Sonatina for Violin and Piano* (JC4), with Alice Smiley, violin. New Paltz State Teachers College, New Paltz, New York, March 9.

1955
P42   Program of Contemporary Music: Fine performed her own work *Suite in E flat* (JC35), and *Three Dialogisms* (composer unknown). Maverick Hall, Woodstock, NY, August 22.

1957
P43   Concert featuring, *Quintet for Piano and String Quartet, Opus 47* by Wallingford Riegger, with the Claremont Quartet, Marc Gottlieb, violin, Vladimir Weisman, violin, William Schoen, viola, and Irving Klein, cello. Vassar College, Poughkeepsie, NY, November 21.

1958
P44   Concert: *Serenade for Piano and Strings, Op. 39* by Ben Weber; *Quartet in G Minor for Piano and Strings, K. 478* by W.A. Mozart; and *Two From a Set of Five for Violin, Piano and Percussion* by Henry Cowell, with Lilla Kalman, violin, Sterling Hunkins, cello, Bernard Zaslav, viola and Warren Smith,

percussion. State University Teachers College, New Paltz, College Union
Lounge, New Paltz, NY, November 18 (see B34 and B210).

1960

P45   Concert in Honor of Riegger's 75th Birthday, by the Contemporary
Music Society, where Leopold Stokowski is president: *Quintet for Piano and
Strings* by Wallingford Riegger, with the quartet consisting of Fine, Matthew
Raimondi, Joseph Robuzhka, John Garvey and Sterling Hunkins. Caspary
Auditorium of Rockefeller Institute, New York City, NY, April 27 (see B207).

1963

P46   Program of Baroque and Contemporary American Music, sponsored by
the American Composers Alliance: *Invention for Piano* by Colin McPhee, and
Music for an Imaginary Ballet by Henry Brant. Union College, NY, February 19.

P47   Concert of Old and Contemporary music: *Sonata in B minor* by
Scarlatti, *Invention for Piano* by Colin McPhee, and *Music for an Imaginary
Ballet* by Henry Brant, with Claude Monteux, flute and James Coover,
percussion. Bard College, Annandale-on-Hudson, NY, March 31.

1965-1967

P48   Lecture-Recital of 20th Century Piano Music: works of Schoenberg, von
Webern, Messiaen, Cowell, Satie and Ives.
> University of Notre Dame, South Bend, Indiana, April 22, 1966.
> Bard College, Annandale-on-Hudson, NY, October 24, 1966.
> Bennington College, Bennington, VT, November 7, 1966 (see exs. B266
> and B275).

P49   "Satiana" danced by Lucas Hoving, Fine performed *Satiana* by Erik
Satie at:
> YMHA, New York City, NY, May 21, 1966.
> American Dance Festival, New London, CT, August 9, 1965.
> Village Theater, New York City, NY, May 1, 1967.
> New York Shakespeare Festival, Delacorte Theatre, Central Park, New
> York City, NY, August 30, 1967 (see ex. B56).

1968

P50   Lecture-Recital of 20th Century Piano Music: works of Schoenberg, von
Webern, Messiaen, Cowell, Satie, Ives., and Scriabin. Part of a week-long
residency, University of Wisconsin at Oshkosh, Wisconsin, February 26 - March
2; and College of William and Mary, Williamsburg, Virginia, May 12 (see
B265).

P51   Carl Ruggles Festival: *Toys* by Carl Ruggles, with Bethany Beardslee, soprano. North Bennington, VT, September 29.

1973

P52   Women In The Arts: accompanist to mezzo-soprano Betty Allen, Fine also acted as panel moderator; Schubert, Wolf, Ravel and Mendelssohn. Bennington College, Bennington, VT, Nov 15 (see B26).

1974

P53   Lecture-Recital of 20th Century Piano Music: works of von Webern, Messiaen, Cowell, Satie, Ives., and Scriabin. Giannini Auditorium, San Francisco, CA, March 5 (see B302).

P54   Composers Forum: *Hymn and Fuguing Tune No.7* by Henry Cowell; *Music for Viola and Piano* by Jean E. Ivey; and Fine's *Concerto for Piano Strings and Percussion for One Performer* (JC80), with Jacob Glick, viola. Albany, NY, November 24 (see ex. B103; also B66).

1975

P55   Recital: *Fuguing Tune No.7* by Henry Cowell, *Sonata for Viola and Piano* by Honneger and a group of pieces by Eric Satie, with Jacob Glick, viola. University of California at Santa Cruz, California (CA), February 4 (see ex. B103 and B275).

P56   All-Vivian Fine Concerts by the San Francisco Conservatory Players: Fine performed her *Concerto for Piano Strings and Percussion for One Performer* (JC80).
        University of California at Berkeley, CA, April 4.
        1750 Arch Street, Berkeley, CA, April 4.
        California State University at Hayward, CA, April 6.

P57   All-Vivian Fine Program: Fine performed her *Concerto for Piano Strings and Percussion for One Performer* (JC80), and *Suite in E-flat* (JC35). Free Music Store, Albany, NY, April 25.

P58   Concert: *Music for Viola and Piano* by Jean E. Ivey; and Fine's *Concerto for Piano Strings and Percussion for One Performer* (JC80), with Jacob Glick, viola. Southern Connecticut State College, New Haven, CT, April 30. (see B103)

P59   Concert: Fine performed her *Five Preludes* (JC33); *Concerto for Piano Strings and Percussion for One Performer* (JC80), and *Suite in E-flat* (JC35). Dartmouth College, NH, August 7.

1976
P60   All-Vivian Fine Program: she performed her *Concerto for Piano Strings and Percussion for One Performer* (JC80). Skidmore College, Saratoga Springs, NY, February 18.

P61   All-Vivian Fine Program: she performed her *Concerto for Piano Strings and Percussion for One Performer* (JC80), and accompanied her *Two Neruda Poems* (JC77). The New School, New York City, NY, October 8 (see B72).

1980
P62   A Concert of Twentieth Century Music for Viola and Piano: *Hymn and Fuguing Tune No.7* by Henry Cowell; *Four Preludes* by Ruth Crawford; *Filament* by Peter Golub; *Lieder for Viola and Piano* by Fine; and *Sonata for Viola and Piano - Opus 11, No.4* by Paul Hindemith. Bennington College, Bennington, VT.

1982
P63   Library of Congress Program of New Music Composers, organized by Vivian Fine: *Sonata for Violin and Piano* by Ruth Porter Crawford; *Sonatina for Violin and Piano* by Carlos Chavez; and, *"The Corpse"* by Leon Ornstein, with Ida Kavafian, violin and Judith Bettina, soprano. The Library of Congress, The Coolidge Auditorium, The McKim Fund, Washington, DC, November 12, (see exs. B109; B140 and B188).

1983
P64   Vivian Fine Week in San Francisco: As part of the S. F. "Vivian Week," Fine performed her *Two Neruda Poems* (JC77), with Stephanie Friedman, soprano. Old First Church, San Francisco, CA, January 9. In another performance during "Fine Week," she played, Crawford's *Sonata for Violin and Piano*, with Daniel Kobialka, violin. Vorpal Gallery, San Francisco, January 13 (see B64; B129; B256; B269; B286; B304).

P65   Concert: *Sonata for Violin and Piano* by Ruth Porter Crawford, with Ida Kavafian, violin.
          YHMA Concert Hall, New York City, NY, February 27.
          Tashi, 92nd Street Y Center, New York City, NY, March 1. with Ida Kavafian, violin.

P66   The 1983 Kennedy Center Friedheim Awards, Special Recognition and Performance: *Sonata for Violin and Piano* by Ruth Porter Crawford, with Rolf Schulte, violin. The Kennedy Center, Washington, DC, October 8.

1985
P67   American Composers Orchestra, Gunther Schuller conducting: *Poetic*

Fires (JC107). Alice Tully Hall, New York City, NY, February 21 (see B109 and B220).

P68   Concert: *Variations for Harp* (JC53), arranged for two pianos by Elizabeth Wright and Vivian Fine, also performed by them. Bennington College, Bennington, VT, October 16.

1986
P69   Concert: *Opening Dance* from the ballet *Opus 51*, written for Charles Weidman, arranged for two pianos by Fine, also with Alan Shawn, piano. Bennington College, Bennington, VT, October 15.

NOTES

1. "through the fingers:" Taped, by author, interview with Fine, Berkeley, California, afternoon of 4-29-1988.

2. quick . . . [to] . . . performance: Data, interview with Fine, by author, at the Karp's San Francisco apartment, November, 1990.

3. parents could . . . [to] . . . needed: Data, interview with Fine, by author, at her home, 9-20-1988. At one point in the interview, when asked, How many hours a day did you spend with the dancers? Fine answered emphatically, "A lot! A lot!"

4. Ruth's . . . [to] . . . energy: Data, from **Ruth Crawford Seeger, A Composer's Search for American Music,** by Judith Tick (see B301) p 362.

5. Speaking . . . [to] . . . "pianist:" Taped, by author, interview with Fine at her home, 9-19-1988.

6. "1933 until 1938 . . . [to] . . . others:" Letter from Fine, to author, 5-15-1990.

7. Many of the Fine piano performance selections were based on three lists from Fine sent to the author: May, 1990; June, 1990, and one in 1995. These were noted by her as, "activities as a pianist." Other selections were based on data taken, by the author, from the original event programs or news clippings in Fine's home; also, many copies sent to the author by Fine. CAC

⤞ *Chapter 5* ⤝

DISCOGRAPHY

Alcestis   (<u>See</u>: JC59)
D1   <u>CRI SRD 145</u>, Composers Recordings Inc., 1961
1/2 side, 12 in. 33.3 rpm. stereophonic; 10 min. 45 sec.
Title: **Alcestis**
Program Notes by Don Jennings on slipcase.
With: Louise Talma, *Toccato* (orchestra); Julia Perry, A short piece [*sic*]
(orchestra); M.W. Daniels, *Deep Forest*; Mary Howe (Carlisle), *Spring Pastoral*.

D2   <u>CRI 692 American Masters</u>, Composers Recordings CD, 1995
One sound disc (76 min.): digital; 4 3/4 in.; 10 min. 45 sec.
Title: **Music of Vivian Fine**
Notes: Biographical and program notes by Heidi Von Gunden inserted
in container; Composer Award Record from American Academy and
Institute of Arts and Letters.
The Imperial Philharmonic Symphony Orchestra of Tokyo
William Strickland, conductor.
Recorded in Tokyo

D3   *Canzones y Danzas*   (<u>See</u>: JC136)
<u>TROY 086</u>, Albany Records, Albany, New York, 1992
One sound disc (60 min., 20 sec.): digital; 4 3/4 in.; 14 min. 27 sec.
Title: **Five Premieres, Chamber Works with Guitar** (1992)
Joel Brown, classical guitar; Jan Vinci, flute; and Ann Alton, cello.
Recorded at Rutgers Church, New York City, January 20-23, 1992.
Program notes by the composers and notes on the performers in
container.
With: Loris O. Chobanian, *Images*; Anthony Holland, *Three Poems
Without Words*; Carver Blanchard, *Lament*; and *Frolic*; Andrew York,
Transilience.

Concertante for Piano and Orchestra   (See: JC42)

D4   CRI SD-135, Composers Recordings Inc., 1960
One side, 12 in. 33.3 rpm, microgroove; 17 min. 29 sec.
Title: **Concertante for Piano and Orchestra**
Program notes by William Flanagan on slipcase.
With: J.H.G. Franco, *Symphony No.5.*

D5   CRI 692 American Masters, Composers Recordings CD, 1995
One sound disc (76 min.): digital; 4 3/4 in.
Title: **Music of Vivian Fine**
Notes: see D2
Reiko Honsho, piano
Japan Philharmonic Symphony Orchestra
Akeo Watanabe, conductor.
Organization: Nihon Firuhamoni Kokyo Gakudan

D6   *Emily's Images* (See: JC117)
CD317, Crystal Records, Camas, Washington
One sound disc: digital; 4 3/4 in.
Title: **Music for Flute**
Leone Buyse, flute; Martin Amlin, piano; Fenwick Smith, alto flute and
flute.
With: Samuel Barber, *Canzone for Flute and Piano*; Ingolf Dahl,
Variations on a Swedish Folk Tune; John Cage, *Three Pieces for Flute
Duet*; Martin Amlin, *Sonata for Flute and Piano*; Theodore Antoniou,
Lament for Michelle; Juli Nunlist, *Twelve Bagatelles for Solo Flute*;
Gregory Tucker, *Idle Conversations for Two Flutes.*

D7   *Fantasy for Cello and Piano*   (See: JC63)
Stereo Number 123, Opus One Records
One disc; 12 in. 33.3 rpm.
Maxine Neuman, cello; Joan Stein, piano.
Note: Fluorescent colors on jacket and disc for black light use.
With: Jeffrey Levine, *Variations Romanesca*; Frank Martin, *Ballade for
Cello and Piano.*

D8   *Flicker* (See: JC82)
CD317, Crystal Records
See D6 above.

Missa Brevis   (See: JC79)
D9   CRI SD-434, Composers Recordings Inc., 1982
One disc, 12 in. 33.3 rpm; 20 min. 15 sec.
Title: **Vivian Fine/Quartet for Brass, Momenti, Missa Brevis**
D10   CRI 692 American Masters, Composers Recordings CD, 1995

One sound disc (76 min.): digital; 4 3/4 in.
Title: **Music of Vivian Fine**
Notes: see D2
Jan De Gaetani, mezzo-soprano; with an ensemble of four cellos, Eric Bartlett, David Finckel, Michael Finckel and Maxine Neuman (cellos).

D11

Momenti   (See: JC90)
CRI SD-434, Composers Recordings Inc., 1982
One disc; 12 in. 33.3 rpm; 8 min. 50 sec.
Title: **Vivian Fine/Quartet for Brass, Momenti, Missa Brevis**

D12
CRI 692 American Masters, Composers Recordings CD, 1995
One sound disc (76 min.): digital; 4 3/4 in.; 8 min. 50 sec.
Title: **Music of Vivian Fine**
Notes: see D2
Lionel Nowak, piano.

D13   *Paean*   (See: JC75)
CRI SD-260, Composers Recordings Inc., 1971
One sound disc: analog, 12 in. 33.3 rpm, stereo; 11 min. 35 sec.
Title: **Bennington Composers: Henry Brant, Vivian Fine, Lionel Nowak, Louis Calabro** (also called: **Music from Bennington**)
Frank S. Baker, tenor, narrator
Bennington Choral Ensemble and Eastman Brass Ensemble
Vivian Fine, conductor.
With: Henry Brant, *Hieroglyphics*; Lionel Nowak, *Concert Piece*; Louis Calabro, *Environments*.

Quartet for Brass   (See: JC91)
D14   CRI SD-434, Composers Recordings Inc., 1982
One disc; 12 in. 33.3 rpm; 11 min. 20 sec.
Title: **Vivian Fine/Quartet for Brass, Momenti, Missa Brevis**
Jacket notes by Henry Brant.

D15
CRI 692 American Masters, Composers Recordings CD, 1995
One sound disc (76 min.): digital; 4 3/4 in.; 11 min. 20 sec.
Title: **Music of Vivian Fine**
Notes: see D2
Ronald K. Anderson and Allan Dean, trumpets; David Jolley, french horn; Lawrence Benz, trombone.

Sinfonia and Fugato for Piano   (See: JC51)
D16   CRI SD-288, Composers Recordings Inc., 1966
D17   RCA Victor LM 7042; RCA Victor; 1966
Two sound discs: analog, 33.3 rpm, mono., 12 in.; 5 min. 40 sec.
Title: **New Music for Piano**

Biographies of the composers by Joseph Prostakoff, 12 pages, inserted. With: Samuel Adler, *Capriccio*; Josef Alexander, *Incantation*; Milton Babbitt, *Partitions*; Ernst Bacon, *The Pig Town Fling*; Arthur Berger, *Two Episodes*; Sal Berkowitz, *Syncopations*; Mark Brunswick, *Six Bagatelles*; Norman Cazden, *Sonata, op.53, no.3*; Ingolf Dahl, *Fanfares*; Miriam Gideon, *Piano Suite, no.3*; Morton Gould, *Rag-Blues-Rag*; Robert Helps, *Image*; Peggy Granville-Hicks, *Prelude for a Pensive Pupil*; Overton Hall, *Polarities, no.1*; Alan Hovhaness, *Allegro on a Pakistan Lute Tune, op.104, no.6*; Kent Wheeler Kennan, *Two Preludes*; Earl Kim, *Two Bagatelles*; Leo Kraft, *Allegro Giocoso*; George Perle, *Six Preludes, op. 20B*; Paul Amadeus Pisk, *Nocturnal Interlude*; Mel Powell, *Etudes*; Joseph Prostakoff, *Two Bagatelles*; Ben Weber, *Humoreske*.

D18   CRI 692 American Masters, Composers Recordings CD, 1995
        One sound disc (76 min.): digital; 4 3/4 in.; 5 min. 40 sec.
        Title: **Music of Vivian Fine**
        Notes: see D2
        Robert Helps, piano.

D19   ***Toccato and Arias***   (See: JC112)
        GSCD-266, Gasparo Records, Jaffrey, New Hampshire
        Barbara Harbach, harpsichord.
        Title: **20th Century Harpsichord Music, Volume II**
        Jacket notes by John Profitt.

Recording where Vivian Fine is the performer on piano (See p.262):

        Sonata for Violin and Piano by Ruth Crawford Seeger
        Ida Kavafian, violin and Vivian Fine, piano.
D20   CRI SD 508, Composers Recordings Inc., 1982
        Sound disc: analog, 33.3 rpm, 12 in.; 15 min. 30 sec.
D21   CRI American Masters, Composers Recordings CD
        One sound disc: digital; 4 3/4 in.; 15 min. 30 sec.
        Title: **Music of Ruth Crawford Seeger**
        Program notes by Judith Tick inserted in container.
        With (D20): **Piano Study with Mixed Accents** (Joseph Bloch, piano); **Nine Preludes for Piano** (Joseph Bloch, piano); **Diaphonic Suite for Solo Flute or Oboe** (Joseph Ostryniec, oboe); **Three Songs to Poems by Carl Sandburg** (Patricia Berlin, mezzo-soprano, Paul Hoffman, piano, and Dan Armstrong, percussion); and **Suite for Wind Quintet** (The Lark Quintet: Arthur Bloom, clarinet; John Wion, flute; Humbert Lucarelli, oboe; Howard T. Howard, horn; and, Alan Brown, bassoon).

→ *Chapter 6* ←

CHRONOLOGY OF LIFE EVENTS

NOTE: The italized years, in the left margin, correspond to the same years in the Biography, chapter 1, where each year is described in more detail.

1913   Vivian Fine was born on September 28, at Michael Reese Hospital, Chicago, Illinois, where her father worked.

1916   Fine demands piano lessons with "famous tantrum."

1918   Five-year-old Fine auditions and wins scholarship to Chicago Musical College (youngest child ever to win), until 1922; had first piano lessons from her mother, later Miss Rosen (see Appendix 5).

1920   Young Fine performs at her first concert at the college.

1921   **Composed:** *The Starving Children of Belgium* (Jci) on piano.
Events: plays first movement of Mozart's *C-major Sonata* at concerts.

1923   **Events:** ten-year-old Vivian is escorted to piano lessons by her mother; at age eleven she went to her lessons alone.

1924   **Events:** that fall she begins lessons with Djane Lavoie-Herz; starts going to concerts of Chicago Symphony Orchestra; Ruth Crawford takes Fine to concert of Ruth's *Violin and Piano Sonata*.

1925   **Composed:** "incidental piano pieces" (never written on paper) in a "Scriabin Style."

Events: that fall, Fine starts theory/composition lessons with Crawford, is influenced by and impressed with Ruth as a composer (see Chapter 1, 1924).

1927   Composed: *Lullaby* (JCii); first composition written on paper; many "early compositions" (see Chapter 3); first *creative explosion* begins (see Appendices 3 & 4).

1928   Composed: *Piece for Two Flutes* (JCiii); *Poem for Voice and Piano* (JCiv); *Song for Voice and Piano* (JCv); begins setting poetry to music.
Events: leaves Nicholas Senn High School; studies avant-garde music on her own; Henry Cowell becomes her mentor; performs a Christmas concert, of classical piano music, at a Chicago socialite's home.

1929   Composed: *Two Movements for Wind Instruments* (JCvi); *Piece for Soprano, Clarinet and Cello* (JCvii) *Prologue and Allegro* (JCviii); *Two pieces for Solo Clarinet* (JCix); *Solo for Oboe* (JC1).
Events: meets, is stylistically influenced by Dane Rudhyar; meets, is stylistically influenced by Imre Weisshaus.

1930   Composed: *Three Stanzas from the Japanese* (JCx); *Lizard* (JCxi); *Suite for Piano* (JCxii); *Four Pieces for Two Flutes* (JC2); *Trio for Strings* (JC3); *Sonatina for Violin and Piano* (JC4); *Canon and Fugue for Piano* (JC5); *Little Suite for Voice and Piano* (JC6).
Events: *Solo for Oboe* world premiered at the Pan American Association of Composers; scholarship studies with music traditionalist, Adolf Weidig; realizes that she must go elsewhere to study her music, there was no one suitable in Chicago; plays piano at "Formal Musicale," Cordon Club, Chicago, Illinois (P1).

1931   Composed: *Sonatina for Violin and Piano* (JC4); *A Drinking Song* (JCxiii); *Four Polyphonic Piano Pieces* (JC7).
Events: moves to New York City; meets Mrs. Blanche Walton; on December 13, 1931 has her New York composer debut concert at Walton's home; introduced to the New Music Circle; continues composing in a dissonant, avant-garde style; *Four Pieces for Two Flutes*, premiered at the Bauhaus, Dessau, Germany.

1932   Events: father loses job so parents join her in New York; Fine performs *Four Polyphonic Piano Pieces* at Yaddo "First Festival of Contemporary Music;" performs at first "Symposium for Moderns;" picked to be part of Aaron Copland's "Young Composers Group;" works as piano accompanist for numerous ballets, *Salome* (P2), also *El Amor Brujo* and *Flor de Noche* (P3), also *Prodigal Son* (P4), and *Petrouchka*, all at The Dance Center; premieres Charles Ives' *Set for Theatre Orchestra* at The New School (P8); plays piano for several performances of other "Young Composers'" work at The New School (see Chapter 1, 1932 & 1934); receives critical notice and acclaim.

1933   Composed: *Four Songs* (JC8); *Divertimento* (JC9); *Four Lyric Songs* (JC10).
Events: performs for League of Composers (P12); performs for The Pan American Association of Composers at Carnegie Chapter Hall (P15), and also their radio series (P16 & P19); accompanies Nini Theilade at "Y" Pop Series (P21); accompanies "Dance Recitals by Charles Weidman and Doris Humphrey" (P20) at Bennington College, Vermont.

1934   Composed: *Affirmations* (JC11); *This Believing World* (JC12); *Quest (Convergence and Affirmations)* (JC13).
Commissions: Charles Weidman for JC13; and Elizabeth Waters for JC12.
Events: regularly works accompanying, arranging, composing for modern dance choreographers (P22); quits after two lessons with Charles Seeger; starts harmony and counterpoint studies with Roger Sessions; begins tonal music; takes classes in improvisation and eurhythmics; Fine meets Benjamin Karp.

1935   Composed: *Conviction* (JC14); *Invictus* (JC15).
Commissions: Rose Crystal for JC14 and JC15.
Events: Vivian and Benjamin are married; Fine accompanies dancer, Nini Theilade on tour, "delights" audiences and critics (P24); continues accompanying the dance (P25, P26, P27, P28); performs on piano with Roger Sessions' *Symphony for Orchestra* (P29).

1937   Composed: *The Race of Life* (JC16, piano and percussion and JC17, orchestral); *Prelude for String Quartet* (JC18); *Piece for Muted Strings* (JC19); *Piece for Flute and Muted Strings* (JC20); *Lyric Piece for Violoncello and Piano* (JC21); *Lyric Piece for Violoncello and String Quartet* (JC22).
Commission: Doris Humphrey for JC16, JC17.
Events: begins piano studies with Abby Whiteside.

1938   Composed: *Four Elizabethan Songs* (JC23); *Opus 51* (JC24); *Music For Study* (JC25); *The Passionate Shepherd to His Love and Her Reply* (JC26); *Dance Suite* (JC27); *Variations on an American Theme* (JC28); *Adios, Bilbadito* (JC29).
Events: accompanies Charles Weidman and Group, with her *Opus 51* at Bennington College.

1939   Composed: *Tragic Exodus* (JC30); *They Too Were Exiles* (JC31); *Sonatina for Oboe and Piano* (JC32); *Five Preludes* (JC33); *Like a Driven Leaf* (JC34).
Commissions: Hanya Holm for JC30.
Events: *Sonatina for Oboe and Piano* won season award from the judges of the Music guild, Ethical Society, Philadelphia.

1940   **Composed:** *Suite in E-flat* (JC35); *Three Pieces for Violin and Piano* (JC36).

1941   **Composed:** *Epigram and Epitaph* (JC37); *Tin-Horn Rebellion* (JC38). **Events:** performs for Composer's Forum at the Lennox Gallery, New York City (P31); concert performance at Steinway Hall (P32).

1942   **Composed:** *"Dollars and Cents" — Music for Play* (JC39). **Events:** Peggy, first child is born; performs for The League of Composers, Museum of Modern Art, New York City (P33); stops studies with R. Sessions.

1943   **Composed:** *Songs of Our Times* (JC40); *Rhapsody on a Russian Folk Song* (JC41). **Events:** performs concert for The National Conference of Christians and Jews, Town Hall, New York City (P34); begins work on her "first big work for orchestra,"(JC42); Fine's music is now frankly tonal, without former dissonance.

1944   **Composed:** *Concertante for Piano and Orchestra* (JC42); *Capriccio for Oboe and String Trio* (JC43). **Events:** discovers herself as orchestral composer; studies with conductor George Szell; Fine's dad baby sits so that she can compose; performs at Steinway Hall, New York City (P35); premieres and performs her *Rhapsody on a Russian Folk Song* (P36), and music by Roger Sessions at Town Hall, New York City.

1945   **Events:** adjunct piano teacher until 1948 at New York University.

1947   **Composed:** *The Great Wall of China* (JC45); *Second Solo for Oboe* (JC46); *There is a Garden in Her Face* (JC47). **Events:** begins the *mid-life interlude* (see Appendices 3 and 4), decline in compositions; returns to more atonal idiom, drops traditional harmony; music becomes more diverse, dramatic and complex; continues concert performances of classic composers, Bach, Scarlatti, Liszt, etc., adding a solo or two of one of her own works to the concert (P38).

1948   **Events:** Nina, second child is born; writes paper and delivers talk to teachers, "Rhythm as the Basic Tool in the Learning of Musical Skills (B54);" family moves to Montclair, New Jersey, Benjamin heads Art Department at State Teacher's College; Fine is adjunct teacher at Juilliard School of Music.

1950   **Events:** Mr. and Mrs. Karp team up in an art and music project at Newtown, New York town hall, it was well reviewed in the local press.

1951   **Composed:** *Divertimento* (JC48). **Events:** family moves to New Paltz, New York; involved in family life, but keeps in touch with composing and music; teaches children theory, piano, composing; occasional performances; adjunct teacher State University Teacher's College at Potsdam, New York; performs classic composer concerts with a few "Fine" compositions at State Teachers College and Montclair Art Museum (P39).

1952   **Composed:** *Variations* (JC49); *Sonata for Violin and Piano* (JC50); *Sinfonia and Fugato* (JC51).
Events: Fine performs, premieres *Variations*, Conference on the Arts, New Paltz.

1953   **Composed:** *Psalm 13* (JC52); *Variations for Harp* (JC53).
Events: becomes music director of Rothschild Music Foundation until 1960; performs for International Society for Contemporary Music at New Paltz State Teachers College (P40); Hermann Trio premieres *Trio for Strings*, written 1930.

1954   **Composed:** *Composition for String Quartet* (JC54).
Events: concert performance at New Paltz State Teachers College (P41); *Variations for Harp* received Honorable Mention from Northern California Harp Association Contest.

1956   **Composed:** *A Guide to the Life Expectancy of the Rose* (JC55).
Commission: Bethasbee de Rothschild Foundation for JC55.
Events: gives concerts of her works; feels "cut off" from music mainstream.

1957   **Composed:** *String Quartet* (JC56).
Events: performs at concert of a Riegger composition at Vassar College (P43).

1958   **Events:** Fine's music is analyzed and acclaimed by expert Wallingford Riegger in his article; performs modern composers at College Union Lounge, New Paltz, NY (P44).

1959   **Composed:** *Valedictions* (JC57).

1960   **Composed:** *Alcestis* (JC58, ballet; JC59, orchestral).
Commission: Martha Graham for JC58 and JC59.
Events: critical success for *Alcestis;* performs concert to honor Wallingford Riegger's 75th birthday (P45); *Concertante for Piano and Orchestra* recorded during its first performance, 16 years after composition (D4).

1961   **Composed:** *Duo for Flute and Viola* (JC60); *Three Pieces for Flute, Bassoon and Harp* (JC61).
Commissions: New York Society for Ethical Culture for JC62 (1962).
Events: founder, vice president American Composer's Alliance until 1965; begins performing, on piano with a chamber group, in a concert series in Dutchess, Putnam, Westchester, and Ulster counties of New York State

performing contemporary composers works with commentary by Fine; Composers Recordings Inc., releases record with *Alcestis* (D1).

1962   **Composed:** *Morning* (JC62); *Fantasy for Cello and Piano* (JC63); *October Pieces* (JC64).
Events: Richard Guralnik, concert pianist, undertakes a concert tour of Europe, *Fine's Five Preludes* are included in his program; European reviewers are mostly very negative on the *Preludes* (see Chapter 3, JC33); a review of her *Alcestis* (JC59, also JC58) recording strongly praises the work (see B6).

1963   **Composed:** *The Confession* (JC65).
Events: Fine was teaching school when Kennedy was assassinated; performs concerts of modern music at several New York colleges (exs. P46 and P47); published article on music and dance in the May *Dance Perspectives*; elected to second term as vice president of the American Composers Alliance; Fine's work was part of exhibit of "Contemporary Women Composers in the United States," for the New York Public Library.

1964   **Composed:** *Dreamscapes* (JC66); *Melos* (JC67); *The Song of Persephone* (JC68).
Events: accepts $5000 a year part-time faculty position at Bennington College; likes "very lively scene" at the music department.

1965   **Composed:** *Concertino for Piano and Percussion Ensemble* (JC69); *My Son, My Enemy* (JC70).
Commission: Connecticut College and The Rockefeller Foundation for JC69.
Events: performs Satie's *Satiana* at the American Dance Festival; commissioned by Jose Limon to write *My Son, My Enemy;* develops and performs a lecture-recital series of 20th century piano music that is widely performed (ex. P48).

1966   **Composed:** *Chamber Concerto for Cello and Six Instruments* (JC71); *Four Piano Pieces* (JC72).
Events: *Dreamscape* performed at Bennington; gives her series of lectures and recitals of 20th century piano music; recipient of the Dollard Prize; Fine's compositions are "automatically" performed at Bennington, giving her new "impetus" to create; *Four Songs* revived since last performance in 1933; Composers Recordings Inc., releases record with Fine's *Sinfonia and Fugato for Piano* (D16); RCA Victor LM releases record of her *Sinfonia and Fugato for Piano*, among other composers for new music on piano (D17).

1967   **Composed:** *Quintet for String Trio, Trumpet and Harp* (JC73); *Epitaph: My Sledge and My Hammer Ly Reclined* (JC74).
Commission: Wykeham Rise School, Connecticut.
Events: Fine continues performing in many concerts at Bennington College, such

as accompanying the Bennington String Quartet, among other events; Benjamin
retires from teaching; Fine performs *Satiana* for dancer Lucas Hoving at many
events (P49).

1968   **Events:** Martha Graham's dance company performs Fine's ballet,
Alcestis, in New York City, and it is severely criticized (see B21).

1969   **Composed:** *Paean* (JC75); *The Delta* (JC76).
Events: family moves to Hoosick Falls, New York; Fine assumes full-time
faculty job at Bennington, her music is almost "automatically" performed there.

1970   **Events:** Fine organizes performances of her works on war themes, *The
Delta*, "Stabat Mater" from *Songs of Our Time*, and *Adios, Bilbadito*; mid-life
interlude ends.

1971   **Composed:** *Two Neruda Poems* (JC77); *Sounds of the Nightingale*
(JC78).
Events: second *creative explosion* begins; records and conducts *Paean*; receives
a Ford Foundation grant through Bennington College; her biography is in Virgil
Thomson's new book, **Music Since 1910**; Composers Recordings Inc., releases
record of "Bennington Composers" with Fine's *Paean*, she is also the conductor
on this record (D13); music is now thematically/instrumentally extremely
complex and will remain so for the rest of Fine's life.

1972   **Composed:** *Missa Brevis* (JC79); *Concerto for Piano, Strings and
Percussion for One Performer* (JC80); *Three Valedictory Songs* (JC81).
Commission: Woolley Fund for JC80.
Events: program of Fine's music broadcast on WNYC sponsored by National
Federation of Music Clubs; recorded works, *Paean, Alcestis*, and *Concertante* are
distributed to 70 radio stations in 34 states as part of a project by NFMC.

1973   **Composed:** *The Flicker* (JC82).
Events: accompanies mezzo-soprano and is panel moderator at "Women in the
Arts" program at Bennington College (P52); performs her lecture-recital program
at California Institute of the Arts, and at University of California, San Diego.

1974   **Events:** Gets $8000 grant from the National Endowment for the Arts
to write opera; continues her lecture-recital series (P53).

1975   **Composed:** *Teisho* (JC83).
Commission: National Endowment for the Arts for JC83.
Events: develops and performs her "All-Vivian Fine Concerts" at several venues
in California and New York, featuring her *Concerto for Piano Strings and
Percussion for One Performer* (exs. P56, P57, P58, P59); *Four Pieces for Two*

Flutes performed for first time in 43 years and *Four Polyphonic Piano Pieces* performed for first time since 1933.

1976   Composed: *Meeting for Equal Rights 1866* (JC84); *The Nightingale* (JC85); *Romantic Ode* (JC86); *Sonnets for Baritone and Orchestra* (JC87). **Commissions:** Cooper Union and the National Endowment for the Arts for JC84; Composers Forum, Albany Arts Center for JC85; The Chamber Music Conference of the East for JC86; and, Sage City Symphony for JC87. **Events:** *Meeting* was funded by National Endowment for the Arts; performs her "All-Vivian Fine Concerts" at Skidmore College, also at The New School (P60, P61); *Meeting* premieres at Great Hall of the Cooper Union, also Lincoln Center for the Performing Arts; Fine conducts *Meeting* at Bennington; mixed reviews.

1977   Composed: *Three Buddhist Evocations for Violin and Piano* (JC88); *Women in the Garden* (JC89). **Commission:** National Endowment for the Arts for JC89. **Events:** Fine's *Teisho*, 1975 (JC83) is reviewed, acclaimed and positively compared to Mozart (see B7).

1978   **Composed:** *Momenti* (JC90); *Quartet for Brass* (JC91). **Commission:** Metropolitan Brass Quartet for JC90. **Events:** *Women in the Garden* premiere by the Port Costa Players.

1979   Composed: *Bust for Eric Satie* (JC92); *Nightingales, Motet for Six Instruments* (JC93); *Lieder for Viola and Piano* (JC94); *Duo for Kettledrums and Piano* (JC95). **Commissions:** Chamber Music Conference and Composers Forum of the East for JC93. **Events:** Fine elected member of American Academy and Institute of Arts and Letters; *Women in the Garden* is performed at Carnegie-Mellon University; *Quartet for Brass* (JC91) premiered in Schenectady, New York, later at the Guggenheim Museum, then Hunter College.

1980   **Composed:** *Two Songs* (JC96); *Trio for Violin, Cello and Piano* (JC97); *Oda A Las Ranas* (JC98); *Music for Flute, Oboe and Cello* (JC99). **Commissions:** Mirecourt Trio for JC97; Anna Crusis Women's Chorus for JC98; and, Huntingdon Trio for JC99. **Events:** wins Guggenheim Fellowship for composition; *Solo for Oboe* performed for the first time since 1930.

1981   Composed: *Gertrude and Virginia* (JC100) **Events:** Fine conducts *Missa Brevis* at Bay Area Congress on Women in Music, in San Francisco, California; *Women in the Garden* performed at the L'Ensemble Chamber Music Center, then Harvard University, and at Yale University.

1982   **Composed:** *Drama for Orchestra* (JC101); *Double Variations for Piano Solo* (JC102); *Toccatina* (JC103). **Commissions:** Dr. and Mrs. Ralph Dorfman for San Francisco Symphony for JC101; Claudia Stevens in honor of Elliott Carter's 75th birthday for JC102.

Events: *Women in the Garden* performed by San Francisco Opera Center; *Drama for Orchestra* is first major commission to a woman by the S. F. Symphony; Fine organizes concert of new music composers for the Library of Congress, where she performs Ruth Crawford's *Sonata for Violin and Piano* to rave reviews (P63); Composers Recordings Inc. releases CD with *Missa Brevis, Quartet for Brass*, and *Momenti* (D9); Fine performs Ruth Crawford's, *Sonata for Violin and Piano* on a record release from Composers Recordings Inc.(D20).

1983   **Composed:** *Canticles for Jerusalem* (JC104).
Commission: Stephanie Friedman and Lois Brandynne.
Events: San Francisco Symphony creates "Vivian Fine Week," full week devoted to her music with *Drama for Orchestra* premiered, also performed at Flint Center, Cupertino, California during same week; *Drama* is broadcast on WGBH, also WNYC as part of programs devoted to Fine's music; *Drama* is critical success; *Four Songs* is revived after forty-three years for "Fine Week;" *Drama* voted runner-up for Pulitzer Prize; performs Crawford's *Sonata* as part of "Fine Week," also her *Two Neruda Poems* (JC77) (P64); performs Crawford's *Sonata* at the Kennedy Center (P66).

1984   **Composed:** *Ode to Henry Purcell* (JC105); *Quintet for Violin, Oboe, Clarinet, Cello and Piano* (JC106); *Poetic Fires* (JC107).
Commissions: Elizabeth Sprague Coolidge Foundation for JC105; Sigma Alpha Iota for JC106; and, Koussevitsky Foundation for JC107.
Events: *Women in the Garden* is performed at the Civic Center, Syracuse, New York, and at the State University of Buffalo, Buffalo, New York.

1985   **Composed:** *A Song for St. Cecilia's Day* (JC108); *Aegean Suite* (JC109).
Commissions: Trinity College and Vermont Council for the Arts for JC108, and Timothy and Mary Ellen Fine for JC109 for Rachel Fine.
Events: performs with orchestra for her *Poetic Fires* at Alice Tully Hall (P67).

1986   **Composed:** *Inscriptions* (JC111); *Toccatas and Arias* (JC112); *Sonata for Violoncello and Piano* (JC113); *Pizzicato Fanfare* (JC114); *Dance with the Frog Prince* (JC115).
Commissions: New England Foundation for the Arts, Living Composers grant for JC111.
Events: there is a one hour radio program devoted to Fine and her music sponsored by the International League of Women Composers; performs *Opus 51* ballet at Bennington College (P69); the Bay Area Women's Philharmonic, in

Berkeley, California, and Fine begin commission and artistic negotiations for
After the Tradition (Appendix 10).

1987   **Composed:** *Ma's In Orbit* (JC116); *Emily's Images* (JC117); *The
Human Mind* (JC118); *Dancing Winds* (JC119); *Toccatas and Arias for Piano
Solo* (JC120); *In Memoriam: George Finckel* (JC121); *Light in Spring Poplars*
(JC122); *After the Tradition* (JC123).
Commissions: Catskill Conservatory and New York Council on the Arts for
JC119; Bay Area Women's Philharmonic for JC123, and Veda Zuponcic for
JC120.
Events: Fine retires from Bennington College; SUNY-Buffalo has performance
retrospective of Fine's music.

1988   **Composed:** *The Garden of Live Flowers* (JC124); *L'Ecole des Hautes
Etudes* (JC125); *Victorian Songs* (JC126); *Asphodel* (JC127); *The Triple Goddess*
(JC128).
Commissions: The Capitol Chamber Artists for JC126, Boston Musica Viva for
JC127, and Harvard Wind Ensemble for JC128.
Events: *After the Tradition* premieres to wide critical acclaim; Fine invites
author to stay at her home to do research for Fine's bio-bibliography; *Tradition*
has two performances by Civic Orchestra of Minneapolis in Minnesota; premiere
of *Concertante for Piano and Orchestra*, composed in 1944.

1989   **Composed:** *Discourse of Goatherds* (JC129); *Madrigali Spirituali*
(JC130); *The Heart Disclosed* (JC131); *Portal* (JC132); *Songs and Arias*
(JC133).
Commissions: Claudia Stevens for JC131, Tom Everett for JC129, Music From
Angel Fire for JC130, and Pamela Frank for JC132.
Events: Boston declares "Vivian Fine Appreciation Week." *Canticles for
Jerusalem* (JC104), *Discourse of Goatherds* (JC129), and *The Triple-Goddess*
(JC128) all premiered as part of the Fine Week; *Madrigali Spirituali* (JC130)
premieres in Angel Fire, New Mexico; begins work on her last opera.

1990   **Events:** Fine contracts first major illness, pneumonia, and recovers with
concerns that she may have to "hold back" on her work; Ben and Vivian take an
apartment in San Francisco for several months; Fine composes a piece for her
granddaughter; premieres: *Portal* (JC132), *Songs and Arias* (JC133), and *The
Heart Disclosed* (JC131); *Madrigali Spirituali* (JC130) performed by Bay Area
Women's Philharmonic, and also at Skidmore College in Saratoga, New York.

1991   **Composed:** *Hymns* (JC134); *Songs of Love and War* (JC135); *Canzones
Y Dances* (JC136).
Commission: Joel Brown for JC136.
Events: completes first work for classical guitar, with flute and cello, *Canzones*

y Dances (JC136); premiere of *Songs of Love and War* (JC135).

1992   **Events:** Albany Records releases CD with Fine's *Canzones y Danzas* for chamber group with classical guitar, her first classical guitar work (D3).

1993   **Composed:** *Canticles for the Other Side of the River* (JC137); *Memoirs of Uliana Rooney* (JC138).
Commission: Meet the Composer/Reader's Digest Commissioning Program, National Endowment for the Arts, and also the Lila Wallace-Reader's Digest Fund for JC138.
Events: *Uliana*, an opera, was Fine's last major composition and her first openly autobiographical (though fictionalized) music exploration.

1994   **Events:** *Uliana* world-premieres at the University of Richmond; second creative explosion ends (see Summary, Chapter 1).

1995   **Events:** Composers Recordings Inc. releases CD recording devoted to Fine's music (D2).

1996   **Composed:** *"untitled"* (JC139).
Events: composes last known composition; discusses last work in long interview for *Contemporary Music Review; Uliana*, performed by American Opera Projects.

1997   **Events:** *Uliana* is performed at Pennsylvania's Annenberg Center.

2000   **Events:** Vivian Fine is killed in an automobile accident in Bennington, Vermont on March 20; some weeks later Fine's sister, Adelaide dies from the same accident; in December 2000, Fine's husband, Benjamin dies after an illness. (see obituaries: B10; B15; B173; B180; B246; B278; B294; B317)

APPENDICES

APPENDIX 1

LOCATING FINE'S MUSIC/SCORES

Many of Fine's scores were published and available through Catamount Facsimile Editions during Fine's lifetime. However, Catamount had been operated by Fine's sister, Adelaide, and with Adelaide's death Catamount ceased to function.

Some of Vivian Fine's music may be found with publishers and recording companies; a number of these are shown in Appendix 2. Fine had willed her entire music collection and her papers to the Library of Congress. It is there that her scores, including those scores that were formerly published by Catamount, are now available, at the Performing Arts Reading Room, Music Division. The reader is encouraged to learn about the Library of Congress' services to researchers and others via the Internet. The Library of Congress has a fee-for-service photoduplication service. A few resources of the Library are listed here for the researcher's convenience.

Library of Congress, Performing Arts Reading Room, Music Division.
Internet home page: http://lcweb.loc.gov/rr/perform/
Location: Room LM 113, James Madison Memorial Building
                   101 Independence Avenue, S. E.
                   Washington, D. C. 20540-4710
Photoduplication Service (Library of Congress) home page:
                   http://lcweb.loc.gov/preserv/pds/
Telephone: (202)707-5640; fax: (202)707-1771
Recorded general information for researchers: (202)707-6500

The reader should contact their nearest university music library for information on Fine's recordings or scores. The following list has some examples of archives and libraries where the researcher will find works by Fine:

American Music Center
30 West 26th Street, Suite 1001
New York City, NY 10010-2011
(212) 366-5260; fax: -5265
e-mail: center@amc.net   http://www.amc.net/amc/

New York Public Library
Performing Arts Library
Lincoln Center
New York City, NY

New York Public Library Publications
New York Women Composers Inc.
114 Kelbourne Avenue
Tarrytown, NY 10591
(914) 631-4361; fax: -6444

Music Library
Music Department
University of Richmond,
Richmond, VA 23173   (804) 289-8277

Music Library
Bennington College
Bennington, VT

National Women Composer Resource Center
Bay Area Women's Philharmonic
330 Townsend Street, Suite 218
San Francisco, CA 94107
(415) 543-2297; fax: -3244

Braun Music Center
Music Library and Archive of Recorded Sound
Stanford University
Stanford, CA 94305-3076   (650) 723-3811

University of California
Music Library
Berkeley, CA 94720 and MUSIC@GARNET.BERKELEY.EDU

APPENDIX 2

PUBLISHERS AND RECORDING COMPANIES

MUSIC PUBLISHERS:
American Composers Alliance
American Composers Edition Inc.
170 West 74th Street
New York City, NY 10023
(212)362-8900
fax: (212)362-8905
e-mail: 75534.2232@compuserve.com

Arsis Press
Plymouth Music Co., Inc.
170 North East 33rd Street
Fort Lauderdale, FL 33334
(305)563-1844
fax: (305)563-9006

Carl Fischer Inc.
62 Cooper Square
New York City, NY 10003
(212)777-0900
fax: (212)477-4129

Catamount Facsimile Editions
(no longer in business)

C.F. Peters Corp./Music Publishing
70-30 80th Street
Glendale, NY 11385
(718)416-7800
fax: (718)416-7805
sales@cfpeters-ny.com

Edwin H. Morris and Co.
39 West 54th Street
New York City, NY 10019

G. Schirmer Inc.
257 Park Ave. South, 20th Floor
New York City, NY 10010

(212)254-2100
fax: (212)254-2013
71360.3514@compuserve.com

Instituto Interamericano Musicologia
Montevideo, Uruguay

Lawson-Gould Music Publishers, Inc.
250 West 57th Street, Suite 1005
New York City, NY 10107
(212)247-3920
fax:(212)247-3991

Lyra Music Co.
43 West 61st Street
New York City, NY 10023

MarGun Music Inc./GunMar Music Inc.
167 Dudley Road
Newton Centre, MA 02159
(617)332-6398
fax: (617)969-1079

New Music Editions
Theodore Pressor Co.
Pressor Place
Bryn Mawr, PA 19010
(610)525-3636
fax: (610)527-7841

Oxford University Press Inc.
Music Department
198 Madison Avenue
New York City, NY 10016-4314
(212)726-7044 to 7051
fax: (212)726-6444

RECORDING COMPANIES:

Albany Records, Classical Music
Box 5011
Albany, NY 12205

Composers Recordings Inc.
773 Spring Street, Room 506
New York City, NY 10012

Crystal Records Inc.
28818 North East Hancock Road
Camas, WA 989607

Gasparo Records
P.O. Box 600   Jaffrey, NH 03452

Opus One Recordings Inc.
Box 604   (Nov-April) Box 795
Greenville, ME 04441   Napanoch, NY 12458

RCA Victor/BMG Classics
1540 Broadway, 41st Floor
New York City, NY 10036-6758

APPENDIX 3

VIVIAN FINE'S LIFETIME CREATIVE PERIODS

<u>Year</u>	<u>Fine's Age</u>	<u>Period & Number of Works Fine Created</u>
1913	(birth)	
1918	age 5	Fine began piano studies on a scholarship to the Chicago Musical College
1920	age 7	Fine's first known work played on piano; many incidental works
from 1927	age 13	Fine's first written score: *Lullaby*

First Creative Explosion:

Fine composed 54 compositions

to 1946	age 33	

Mid-Life Interlude:

Fine composed 33 compositions

to 1970	age 57	

Second Creative Explosion:

Fine composed 62 compositions

to 1993	age 80	

one untitled composition

2000	(death) age 86	

<u>Note to Appendices 3 & 4:</u> In #3 we see the three major periods of music composition in Vivian Fine's lifetime outlined here by the name of each creative period shown in boldface type.

(*continued on page 296*)

APPENDIX 4

ANALYSIS OF FINE'S CREATIVE PRODUCTIVITY

	1926-1946	1947-1970	1971-1994
			JC140
			JC139
			JC138
			JC137
			JC136
			JC135
			JC134
			JC133
	JC43		JC132
	JC42		JC131
	JC41		JC130
	JC40		JC129
	JC39		JC128
	JC38		JC127
	JC37		JC125
	JC36		JC124
	JC35		JC123
	JC34		JC122
	JC33		JC121
	JC32		JC120
	JC31		JC119
	JC30		JC118
	JC29		JC117
	JC28		JC116
	JC27		JC115
	JC26		JC114
	JC25		JC113
	JC24		JC112
	JC23		JC111
	JC22		JC110
	JC21	JC76	JC109
	JC20	JC75	JC108
	JC19	JC74	JC107
	JC18	JC73	JC106
	JC17	JC72	JC105
	JC16	JC71	JC104
W	JC15	JC70	JC103
O	JC14	JC69	JC102
R	JC13	JC68	JC101
K	JC12	JC67	JC100
S	JC11	JC66	JC99
	JC10	JC65	JC98
N	JC9	JC64	JC97
U	JC8	JC63	JC96
M	JC7	JC62	JC95
B	JC6	JC61	JC94
E	JC5	JC60	JC93
R	JC4	JC59	JC92
S	JC3	JC58	JC91
	JC2	JC57	JC90
	JC1	JC56	JC89
	JCxiii	JC55	JC88
	JCxii	JC54	JC87
	JCxi	JC53	JC86
	JCx	JC52	JC85
	JCix	JC51	JC84
	JCviii	JC50	JC83
	JCvii	JC49	JC82
	JCvi	JC48	JC81
	JCv	JC47	JC80
	JCiv	JC46	JC79
	JCiii	JC45	JC78
	JCii	JC44	JC77

Each of Fine's composing life was charted according to the amount of finished music she composed in a given year. Only the number of finished works were quantified and not the size of work, type of work, awards or any other factor. This would have been difficult anyway. Her sheer amount of creativity was noted.

Appendix #4 is a graphic illustration of Fine's creative periods as contrasted to Appendix #3. Something like a bar graph, the stack of JC numbers corresponds to the title of each work (see Chapter 3) that Fine produced in each of the "creative periods" of her life. The years at the top of each JC number stack or "bar" correspond to the three creative periods shown in boldface type in Appendix #3.

Statistical study of all of Fine's music compositions throughout her lifetime yielded these figures when plotted onto a curve. Two high peaks of her work emerged, 1926 to 1946 and 1971 to 1994, this being a bimodal or "two modes" shape (see Chapter 1, Summary). Most expectations, mine included, and those of other writers on this issue, were that the amount of her music would follow what the conventional bias on aging predicts: a central peak (the bell-shaped curve) or two until "middle age," then afterwards, a slight but relentless decline in creative production until "old age." At that point, cultural bias says that productivity all but ceases due to inevitable loss of "mental" ability.

When the actual numbers of Fine's works were put to the test of arithmetical study and modeled, the outcome was dramatically different than most might expect. Indeed, quite the opposite, as the greater amount of her work was accomplished in what some might call "old age, declining years, etc.," In fact if I had analyzed her entire life's work somewhat differently, by actual time lengths of each of her compositions, as opposed to just the amount of works, for example, then the curve would have probably doubled in height in her second creative explosion. This would have been true, since her music in her second creative explosion was quite a bit longer in performance time than in the first creative explosion of her youth.

APPENDIX 5

FINE'S MUSIC AND COMPOSITION EDUCATION[1]

Teacher	Subject	Fine's age	Time period	City
Rose Finder Fine (Fine's mother)	piano	5 years	2-3 months	Chicago
Miss Rosen (neighborhood teacher)	piano	5 years	2-3 months	"
Chicago Musical College Helen Ross, teacher	piano scholarship	5 years	3 years	"
Mr. Weinstein & Mr. Lempkoff (neighborhood teachers)	piano	9-10 years	1 year	"
American Conservatory of Music, Silvio Scionti violin teacher	violin scholarship	10 years	1 lesson	"
Djane Lavoie-Herz piano teacher, Chicago	piano	11-18 years	7 years	"
Ruth Crawford composer, teacher	theory & composition	13-17 years	1926-1930	"
Adolf Weidig composer, teacher	harmony & composition	17-18 years	1930-1931	"
Roger Sessions composer, teacher	harmony & composition	22-30 years	1935-1943	NYC
Abby Whiteside piano teacher	piano	25-30 years	1938-1943	"
George Szell conductor	orchestration	31 years	one term, 1944	"

---

[1]data from Fine's letter to author, 5-14-1990. Her dates are always the deciding factor in this book.

APPENDIX 6

WORKS LISTED ALPHABETICALLY

Adios, Bilbadito (1938) JC29
Aegean Suite (1985) JC109
Affirmations (1934) JC11
After the Tradition (1987), JC123
Alcestis (1960) JC58 (ballet), JC59
  (orchestral)
Asphodel (1988) JC127

A Bust for Eric Satie (1979) JC92

Canon and Fugue for Piano (1930)
  JC5
Canticles for Jerusalem (1983)
  JC104
*Canticles for the Other Side of the
  River* (1993) JC137
*Capriccio for Oboe and String Trio
  (1947)* JC43
Canzones Y Dances (1991) JC136
Chaconne (1947) JC44
*Chamber Concerto for Cello and
  Six Instruments* (1966)
  JC71
Composition for String Quartet
  (1954) JC54
*Concertante for Piano and
  Orchestra* (1944) JC42
*Concertino for Piano and
  Percussion Ensemble*
  (1965) JC69
*Concerto for Piano Strings and
  Percussion for One
  Performer* (1972) JC80
The Confession (1963) JC65
Conviction (1935) JC14

Dance Suite (1938) JC27
Dancing Winds (1987) JC119
Delta, The (1969) JC76

Discourse of Goatherds (1989)
  JC129
Divertimento (1933) JC9
Divertimento (1951) JC48
*"Dollars and Cents" – Music For
  Play* (1941) JC39
Double Variations for Piano Solo
  (1982) JC102
Drama for Orchestra (1982) JC101
Dreamscape (1964) JC66
Duo for Flute and Viola (1961)
  JC60 (also: *Iconomachy*)
Duo for Kettledrums and Piano
  (1979) JC95

Emily's Images (1987) JC117
Epigram and Epitaph (1941) JC37
*Epitaph: My Sledge and My
  Hammer Ly Reclined*
  (1967) JC74

Fantasy for Cello and Piano (1962)
  JC63
Five Preludes (1939) JC33
The Flicker (1973) JC82
Four Elizabethan Songs (1938)
  JC23
Four Piano Pieces (1966) JC72
Four Pieces for Two Flutes (1930)
  JC2
Four Polyphonic Piano Pieces
  (1931) JC7
Four Songs (1933) JC8
Four Lyric Songs (1933) JC10

The Garden of Live Flowers (1988)
  JC124
Gertrude and Virginia (1981) JC100

The Great Wall of China (1947)
    JC45
*A Guide to the Life Expectancy of
    the Rose* (1956) JC55

The Heart Disclosed (1989) JC131
The Human Mind (1987) JC118
Hymns (1991) JC134

In Memoriam: George Finckel
    (1987) JC121
Inscriptions (1986) JC111
Invictus (1935) JC15

L'Ecole des Hautes Etudes (1988)
    JC125
Lieder for Viola and Piano (1979)
    JC94
Light in Spring Poplars (1987)
    JC122
Like a Driven Leaf (1939) JC34
Little Suite for Voice and Piano
    (1930) JC6
*Lyric Piece for Violoncello and
    Piano* (1937) JC21
*Lyric Piece for Violoncello and
    String Quartet* (1937) JC22

Madrigali Spirituali (1989) JC130
Ma's In Orbit (1987) JC116
Meeting for Equal Rights 1866
    (1976) JC84
Melos (1964) JC67
Memoirs of Uliana Rooney (1993)
    JC138
Missa Brevis (1972) JC79
Momenti (1978) JC90
Morning (1962) JC62
Music for Flute, Oboe and Cello
    (1980) JC99
Music For Study (1938) JC25
My Son, My Enemy (1965) JC70

The Nightingale (1976) JC85

*Nightingales, Motet for Six
    Instruments* (1979) JC93

October Pieces (1962) JC64
Oda A Las Ranas (1980) JC98
Ode to Henry Purcell (1984) JC105
Opus 51 (1938) JC24
    Also: *Commedia*

Paean (1969) JC75
*The Passionate Shepherd to His
    Love and Her Reply* (1938)
    JC26
Piece for Muted Strings (1937)
    JC19
Piece for Flute and Muted Strings
    (1937) JC20
Pizzicato Fanfare (1986) JC114
Poetic Fires (1984) JC107
Portal (1989) JC132
Prelude for String Quartet (1937)
    JC18
Psalm 13 (1953) JC52

Quartet for Brass (1978) JC91
*Quest (Convergence and
    Affirmations)* (1934) JC13
*Quintet for String Trio, Trumpet and
    Harp* (1967) JC73
*Quintet for Violin, Oboe, Clarinet,
    Cello and Piano* (1984)
    JC106

The Race of Life, The (piano and
    percussion) (1937) JC16
    (orchestra) JC17
Rhapsody on a Russian Folk Song
    (1943) JC41
Romantic Ode (1976) JC86

Second Solo for Oboe (1947) JC46
Sheila's Song (1986) JC110
Sinfonia and Fugato (1952) JC51
Solo for Oboe (1929) JC1

Sonata for Violin and Piano (1952)
JC50
Sonata for Violoncello and Piano
(1986) JC113
Sonatina for Oboe and Piano (1939)
JC32
Sonatina for Violin and Piano
(1930) JC4
A Song for St. Cecilia's Day (1985)
JC108
The Song of Persephone (1964)
JC68
Songs and Arias (1989) JC133
Songs of Love and War (1991)
JC135
Songs of Our Time (1943) JC40
Sonnets for Baritone and Orchestra
(1976) JC87
Sounds of the Nightingale (1971)
JC78
String Quartet (1957) JC56
Suite in E-flat (1940) JC35

Tango with the Frog Prince (1986)
JC115
Teisho (1975) JC83
There Is A Garden In Her Face
(1947) JC47
They Too Are Exiles (1939) JC31
This Believing World (1934) JC12
Three Buddhist Evocations for
Violin and Piano (1977)
JC88
Three Pieces for Flute, Bassoon and
Harp (1961) JC61
Three Pieces for Violin and Piano
(1940) JC36
Three Valedictory Songs (1972)
JC81
Tin-Horn Rebellion (1941) JC38
Toccatas and Arias (1986) JC112
Toccatas and Arias for Piano Solo
(1987) JC120
Toccatina (1982) JC103

Tragic Exodus (1939) JC30
Trio for Violin, Cello and Piano
(1980) JC97
Trio for Strings (1930) JC3
The Triple Goddess (1988) JC128
Two Neruda Poems (1971) JC77
Two Songs (1979) JC96

Valedictions (1959) JC57
Variations (1952) JC49
Variations for Harp (1953) JC53
Variations on an American Theme
(1938) JC28
Victorian Songs (1988) JC126

Women in the Garden (1977) JC89

APPENDIX 7

**WORKS LISTED BY JC
NUMBER**

JCi   *The Starving Children of
Belgium* (about 1921)

JCii   *Lullaby* (1927)

JCiii   *Piece for Two Flutes*
(1928)

JCiv   *Poem for Voice and Piano*
(1928)

JCv   *Song for Voice and Piano*
(1928)

JCvi   *Two Movements for Wind
Instruments* (1929)

JCvii   *Piece for Soprano, Clarinet
and Cello* (1929)

JCviii   *Prologue and Allegro*
(1929)

JCix   *Two Pieces for Solo
Clarinet* (1929)

JCx   *Three Stanzas from the
Japanese* (1930)

JCxi   *Lizard* (1930)

JCxii   *Suite for Piano* (1930)

JCxiii   *A Drinking Song* (undated,
probably 1930-1931)

JC1   *Solo for Oboe* (1929)

JC2   *Four Pieces for Two Flutes*
(1930)

JC3   *Trio for Strings* (1930)

JC4   *Sonatina for Violin and
Piano* (1930)

JC5   *Canon and Fugue for
Piano* (1930)

JC6   *Little Suite for Voice and
Piano* (1930)

JC7   *Four Polyphonic Piano
Pieces* (1931)

JC8   *Four Songs* (1933)

JC9   *Divertimento* (1933)

JC10   *Four Lyric Songs* (1933)

JC11   *Affirmations* (1934)

JC12   *This Believing World*
(1934)

JC13   *Quest (Convergence and
Affirmations)* (1934)

JC14   *Conviction* (1935)

JC15   *Invictus* (1935)

JC16   *Race of Life, The* (piano
and percussion) (1937)

JC17   *Race of Life, The*
(orchestra) (1937)

JC18   *Prelude for String Quartet*
(1937)

JC19   *Piece for Muted Strings*
(1937)

JC20   *Piece for Flute and Muted
Strings* (1937)

JC21   *Lyric Piece for Violoncello
and Piano* (1937)

JC22   *Lyric Piece for Violoncello
and String Quartet* (1937)

JC23   *Four Elizabethan Songs*
(1938)

JC24   *Opus 51* (1938)   Also:
Commedia

JC25   *Music For Study* (1938)

JC26   *Passionate Shepherd to His
Love and Her Reply, The*
(1938)

JC27   *Dance Suite* (1938)

JC28   *Variations on an American
Theme* (1938)

JC29   *Adios, Bilbadito* (1938)

JC30   *Tragic Exodus* (1939)

JC31   *They Too Are Exiles* (1939)

JC32   *Sonatina for Oboe and
Piano* (1939)

JC33   *Five Preludes* (1939)
JC34   *Like a Driven Leaf* (1939)
JC35   *Suite in E-flat* (1940)
JC36   *Three Pieces for Violin and Piano* (1940)
JC37   *Epigram and Epitaph* (1941)
JC38   *Tin-Horn Rebellion* (1941)
JC39   *"Dollars and Cents"— Music for Play* (1942)
JC40   *Songs of Our Time* (1943)
JC41   *Rhapsody on a Russian Folk Song* (1943)
JC42   *Concertante for Piano and Orchestra* (1944)
JC43   *Capriccio for Oboe and String Trio* (1947)
JC44   *Chaconne* (1947)
JC45   *Great Wall of China, The* (1947)
JC46   *Second Solo for Oboe* (1947)
JC47   *There Is A Garden In Her Face* (1947)
JC48   *Divertimento* (1951)
JC49   *Variations* (1952)
JC50   *Sonata for Violin and Piano* (1952)
JC51   *Sinfonia and Fugato* (1952)
JC52   *Psalm 13* (1953)
JC53   *Variations for Harp* (1953)
JC54   *Composition for String Quartet* (1954)
JC55   *Guide to the Life Expectancy of the Rose, A* (1956)
JC56   *String Quartet* (1957)
JC57   *Valedictions* (1959)
JC58   *Alcestis* (1960) (ballet)
JC59   *Alcestis* (1960) (orchestral)
JC60   *Duo for Flute and Viola* (1961)
JC61   *Three Pieces for Flute, Bassoon and Harp* (1961)

JC62   *Morning* (1962)
JC63   *Fantasy for Cello and Piano* (1962)
JC64   *October Pieces* (1962)
JC65   *Confession, The* (1963)
JC66   *Dreamscape* (1964)
JC67   *Melos* (1964)
JC68   *Song of Persephone, The* (1964)
JC69   *Concertino for Piano and Percussion Ensemble* (1965)
JC70   *My Son, My Enemy* (1965)
JC71   *Chamber Concerto for Cello and Six Instruments* (1966)
JC72   *Four Piano Pieces* (1966)
JC73   *Quintet for String Trio, Trumpet and Harp* (1967)
JC74   *Epitaph: My Sledge and My Hammer Ly Reclined* (1967)
JC75   *Paean* (1969)
JC76   *Delta, The* (1969)
JC77   *Two Neruda Poems* (1971)
JC78   *Sounds of the Nightingale* (1971)
JC79   *Missa Brevis* (1972)
JC80   *Concerto for Piano, Strings and Percussion for One Performer* (1972)
JC81   *Three Valedictory Songs* (1972)
JC82   *Flicker, The* (1973)
JC83   *Teisho* (1975)
JC84   *Meeting for Equal Rights 1866* (1976)
JC85   *Nightingale, The* (1976)
JC86   *Romantic Ode* (1976)
JC87   *Sonnets for Baritone and Orchestra* (1976)
JC88   *Three Buddhist Evocations for Violin and Piano* (1977)
JC89   *Women in the Garden*

(1977)

JC90   *Momenti* (1978)

JC91   *Quartet for Brass* (1978)

JC92   *Bust for Eric Satie, A* (1979)

JC93   *Nightingales, Motet for Six Instruments* (1979)

JC94   *Lieder for Viola and Piano* (1979)

JC95   *Duo for Kettledrums and Piano* (1979)

JC96   *Two Songs* (1979)

JC97   *Trio for Violin, Cello and Piano* (1980)

JC98   *Oda A Las Ranas* (1980)

JC99   *Music for Flute, Oboe and Cello* (1980)

JC100 *Gertrude and Virginia* (1981)

JC101 *Drama for Orchestra* (1982)

JC102 *Double Variations for Piano Solo* (1982)

JC103 *Toccatina* (1982)

JC104 *Canticles for Jerusalem* (1983)

JC105 *Ode to Henry Purcell* (1984)

JC106 *Quintet for Violin, Oboe, Clarinet, Cello and Piano* (1984)

JC107 *Poetic Fires* (1984)

JC108 *Song for St. Cecilia's Day, A* (1985)

JC109 *Aegean Suite* (1985)

JC110 *Sheila's Song* (1986)

JC111 *Inscriptions* (1986)

JC112 *Toccatas and Arias* (1986)

JC113 *Sonata for Violoncello and Piano* (1986)

JC114 *Pizzicato Fanfare* (1986)

JC115 *Dance with the Frog Prince* (1986) (also: *Tango with . . .*)

JC116 *Ma's In Orbit* (1987)

JC117 *Emily's Images* (1987)

JC118 *Human Mind, The* (1987)

JC119 *Dancing Winds* (1987)

JC120 *Toccatas and Arias for Piano Solo* (1987)

JC121 *In Memoriam: George Finckel* (1987)

JC122 *Light in Spring Poplars* (1987)

JC123 *After the Tradition* (1987)

JC124 *Garden of Live Flowers, The* (1988)

JC125 *L'Ecole des Hautes Etudes* (1988)

JC126 *Victorian Songs* (1988)

JC127 *Asphodel* (1988)

JC128 *Triple Goddess, The* (1988)

JC129 *Discourse of Goatherds* (1989)

JC130 *Madrigali Spirituali* (1989)

JC131 *Heart Disclosed, The* (1989)

JC132 *Portal* (1989)

JC133 *Songs and Arias* (1989)

JC134 *Hymns* (1991)

JC135 *Songs of Love and War* (1991)

JC136 *Canzones Y Dances* (1991)

JC137 *Canticles for the Other Side of the River* (1993)

JC138 *Memoirs of Uliana Rooney* (1993)

JC139 *"Untitled"* (1996)

JC140 *Auguries* (1983)

APPENDIX 8

WORKS LISTED BY GENRE

Piano Compositions:
Piano Solos:

> *The Starving Children of Belgium* (JCi); *Lullaby* (JCii); *Suite for Piano* (JCxii); *Canon and Fugue for Piano* (JC5); *Four Polyphonic Piano Pieces* (JC7); *Music for Study* (JC25); *Five Preludes* (JC33); *Suite in E-Flat* (JC35); *Tin-Horn Rebellion* (JC38); *Rhapsody on a Russian Folk Song* (JC41); *Chaconne* (JC44); *Variations* (JC49); *Sinfonia and Fugato* (JC51); *Four Piano Pieces* (JC72); *Momenti* (JC90); *Double Variations for Piano Solo* (JC102); *Toccatina* (JC103); *Aegean Suite* (JC109); *Dance with the Frog Prince* (JC115); *Toccatas and Arias for Piano* (JC119).

Piano Duets:

> *Poem for Voice and Piano* (JCiv); *Song for Voice and Piano* (JCv); *A Drinking Song* (JCxiii); *Sonatina for Violin and Piano* (JC4); *Little Suite for Voice and Piano* (JC5); *Four Lyric Songs* (JC10); *Lyric Piece for Violoncello and Piano* (JC21); *Four Elizabethan Songs* (JC23); *Sonatina for Oboe and Piano* (JC32); *Three Pieces for Violin and Piano* (JC36); *Epigram and Epitaph* (JC37); *"Dollars and Cents" —Music for Play* (JC39); *Songs of Our Time* (JC40); *Sonata for Violin and Piano* (JC50); *Fantasy for Cello and Piano* (JC63); *Two Neruda Poems* (JC77); *Three Buddhist Evocations for Violin and Piano* (JC88); *Lieder for Viola and Piano* (JC94); *Canticles for Jerusalem* (JC104); *Sonata for Violoncello and Piano* (JC113); *Emily's Images* (JC117); *The Human Mind* (JC118); *The Heart Disclosed* (JC131); Portal (JC132); "Untitled" (JC140).

Piano and Chamber Group:

> *Three Stanzas from the Japanese* (JCx); *Lyric Piece for Violoncello and String Quartet* (JC22); *The Great Wall of China* (JC45); *There is a Garden in Her Face* (JC47); *Morning* (JC62); *The Confession* (JC65); *My Son My Enemy* (JC70); *Trio for Violin, Cello and Piano* (JC97); *Quintet for Violin, Oboe, Clarinet, Cello and Piano* (JC106); *Inscriptions* (JC111); *Ma's in Orbit* (JC116); *Light in Spring Poplars* (JC122); *The Garden of Live Flowers* (JC124); *L'Ecole des Haute Etudes* (JC125); *Asphodel* (JC127); *Hymns* (JC134); *Canticle from the Other Side of the River* (JC137).

Piano and Modern Dance:

> *Affirmations* (JC11); *This Believing World* (JC12); *Quest (Convergence*

and *Affirmations*)(JC13); *Conviction* (JC14); *Invictus* (JC15); *The Race of Life* (JC16); *Opus 51* (JC24); *Tragic Exodus* (JC30); *They Too Are Exiles* (JC31); *Like a Driven Leaf* (JC34); *Alcestis* (JC58); *My Son My Enemy* (JC70).

Piano and Percussion:

The Race of Life (JC16); *Opus 51* (JC24); *They Too Are Exiles* (JC31); *October Pieces* (JC64); *Concertino for Piano and Percussion Ensemble* (JC69); *Chamber Concertino for Cello and Six Instruments* (JC71); *Concerto for Piano Strings and Percussion for One Performer* (JC80); *Duo for Kettledrums and Piano* (JC95).

Piano and Orchestra:

Concertante for Piano and Orchestra (JC42); *Poetic Fires* (JC107).

Chamber music:

Piece for Soprano, Clarinet and Cello (JCvii); *Prologue and Allegro* (JCviii); *Lizard* (Jcxi); *Four Pieces for Two Flutes* (JC2), also called: *Four Pieces for Violin and Oboe* (JC2); *Trio for Strings* (JC3); *Four Songs* (JC8); *Divertimento* (JC9); *Four Lyric Songs* (JC10); *Prelude for String Quartet* (JC18); *Piece for Flute and Muted Strings* (JC20); *Lyric Piece for Violoncello and String Quartet* (JC22); *Variations of an American Theme* (JC28); *Capriccio for Oboe and String Trio* (JC43); *The Great Wall of China* (JC45); *There is a Garden in Her Face* (JC47); *Divertimento* (JC48); *Variations for Harp* (JC53); *Composition for String Quartet* (JC54); *A Guide to the Life Expectancy of a Rose* (JC55); *String Quartet* (JC56); *Valedictions* (JC57); *Duo for Flute and Piano* (JC60); *Three Pieces for Flute, Bassoon and Harp* (JC61); *The Confession* (JC65); *Dreamscape* (JC66); *Melos* (JC67); *The Song of Persephone* (JC67); *Chamber Concerto for Cello and Six Instruments* (JC71); *Quintet for String Trio, Trumpet and Harp* (JC73); *Epitaph: My Sledge and My Hammer Ly Reclined* (JC74); *Missa Brevis* (JC79); *Three Valedictory Songs* (JC81); *The Flicker* (JC82); *Teisho* (JC83); *A Bust for Eric Satie* (JC92); *Nightingales, Motet for Six Instruments* (JC93); *Trio for Violin, Cello and Piano* (JC97); *Oda a las Ranas* (JC98); *Music for Flute, Oboe and Cello* (JC99); *Gertrude and Virginia* (JC100); *Ode to Henry Purcell* (JC105); *Quintet for Violin, Oboe, Clarinet, Cello and Piano* (JC106); *Toccatas and Arias (for Harpsichord)*(JC112); *Pizzicato Fanfare* (JC114); *In Memoriam: George Finckel* (JC120); *Victorian Songs* (JC126); *Asphodel* (JC127); *Discourse of Goatherds* (JC129); *Madrigali Spirituali* (JC130); *Portal* (JC132); *Songs and Arias* (JC133); *Hymns* (JC134); *Songs of Love and War* (JC135); *Canzones Y Dances* (JC136); *Canticle from the Other Side of the River* (JC137); *Auguries* (JC139).

Modern Dance:

Affirmations (JC11); *This Believing World* (JC12); *Quest (Convergence and Affirmations)*(JC13); *Conviction* (JC14); *Invictus* (JC15); *The Race of Life* (JC16, JC17); *Dance Suite* (JC27); *Tragic Exodus* (JC30); *Like a Driven Leaf* (JC34); *Tin-Horn Rebellion* (JC38); *Alcestis* (JC58, JC59); *My Son My Enemy* (JC70).

Opera:

A Guide to the Life Expectancy of a Rose (JC55); *The Women in the Garden* (JC89); *The Memoirs of Uliana Rooney* (JC138).

Orchestra/Symphony:

The Race of Life (JC17); *Piece for Muted Strings* (JC19); *Dance Suite* (JC27); *Concertante for Piano and Orchestra* (JC42); *Alcestis* (JC59); *Sounds of the Nightingale* (JC78); *Meeting for Equal Rights 1866* (JC84); *Romantic Ode* (JC86); *Sonnets for Baritone and Orchestra* (JC87); *Drama for Orchestra (after the paintings of Edvard Munch)*(JC101); *Poetic Fires* (JC107); *A Song for St. Cecilia's Day* (JC108); *After the Tradition* (JC123).

Vocal, Choral music:

Poem for Voice and Piano (JCiv); *Song for Voice and Piano* (JCv); *Piece for Soprano, Clarinet and Cello* (JCvii); *Prologue and Allegro* (JCviii); *Three Stanzas from the Japanese* (JCx); *Lizard* (JCxi); *A Drinking Song* (JCxiii); *Little Suite for Voice and Piano* (JC5); *Four Songs* (JC8); *Four Lyric Songs* (JC10); *Four Elizabethan Songs* (JC23); *The Passionate Shepherd to His Love and Her Reply* (JC26); *Adios, Bilbadito* (JC29); *Tragic Exodus* (JC30); *Epigram and Epitaph* (JC37); *Songs of Our Time* (JC40); *The Great Wall of China* (JC45); *There is a Garden in Her Face* (JC47); *Psalm 13* (JC52); *A Guide to the Life Expectancy of a Rose* (JC55); *Valedictions* (JC57); *Morning* (JC62); *The Confession* (JC65); *Epitaph: My Sledge and My Hammer Ly Reclined* (JC74); *Paean* (JC75); *The Delta* (JC76); *Two Neruda Poems* (JC77); *Sounds of the Nightingale* (JC78); *Missa Brevis* (JC79); *Three Valedictory Songs* (JC81); *Teisho* (JC83); *Meeting for Equal Rights 1866* (JC84); *The Nightingale* (JC85); *Sonnets for Baritone and Orchestra* (JC87); *A Bust for Eric Satie* (JC92); *Two Songs* (JC96); *Oda a las Ranas* (JC98); *Gertrude and Virginia* (JC100); *Canticles for Jerusalem* (JC104); *Ode to Henry Purcell* (JC105); *A Song for St. Cecilia's Day* (JC108); *Inscriptions* (JC111); *The Human Mind* (JC118); *Light in Spring Poplars* (JC122); *The Garden of Live Flowers* (JC124); *The Heart Disclosed* (JC131).

Wind Instruments:

Piece for Two Flutes (JCiii); *Two Movements for Wind Instruments* (JCvi); *Two Pieces for Solo Clarinet* (JCix); *Lizard* (JCxi); *Solo for Oboe* (JC1); *Four Pieces for Two Flutes* (JC2); *Divertimento* (JC9); *Second Solo for Oboe* (JC46); *Three Pieces for Flute, Bassoon and Harp* (JC61); *Music for Flute, Oboe and Cello* (JC99); *Dancing Winds* (JC119); *The Triple-Goddess* (JC128).

Brass Ensembles:

Paean (JC75); *The Delta* (JC76); *Quartet for Brass* (JC91); *Discourse of Goatherds* (JC129).

APPENDIX 9

FINE'S USE OF POETRY IN MUSIC

Aeschylus. *Poetic Fires (from the Greeks)*, JC107.

Alcuin. "A Sequence for St. Michael," *Chamber Concerto for Cello and Six Instruments*, JC71.

Amichai, Yehuda. "This year I traveled far" and "Light against the Tower of David," *Canticles for Jerusalem*, JC104.

Anonymous. Stanzas from the Japanese, 10th century, *Three Stanzas from the Japanese*, JCx.

Anonymous. 16th century, "The lover in winter plaineth for the Spring," *Four Songs*, JC8.

Anonymous. "Adios, Bilbadito," *Four Lyric Songs*, JC10; *Adios Bilbadito*, JC29; and *Canzones Y Dances*, JC137.

Anonymous. *Sounds of the Nightingale*, JC78.

Arnold, Matthew. "Cadmus and Harmonia," *Victorian Songs*, JC126.

Auden, W.H. Prayer. "O God, put away justice and truth . . . ," *Chamber Concerto for Cello and Six Instruments*, JC71.

Barnefield, Richard. *The Nightingale*, JC85.

The Holy Bible. Psalm 13, *Psalm 13*, JC52; Psalm 22, *Missa Brevis*, JC79; Psalm 137, *Canticles for Jerusalem*, JC104; "The Song of Songs" from the Old Testament, *Songs of Love and War*, JC135.

Brecht, Bertolt. "And what did she get, the soldier's wife," *Songs of Our Time*, JC40.

Browne, Michael Dennis. *The Delta*, JC76.

Browning, Elizabeth Barrett. "Sonnets from the Portuguese," *Victorian Songs*, JC126.

Campion, Thomas. *There is a Garden in Her Face*, JC47.

Dehmel, Richard. *Song for Voice and Piano*, Jcv.

Dickinson, Emily. "The Riddle," *Four Lyric Songs*, JC10; *The Women in the Garden*, JC89; "A Spider sewed at Night," "A Clock stopped — Not the Mantel's," "Exultation is the going," "The Robin is a Gabriel," "After great pain, a formal feeling comes," "The Leaves like Women interchange," "A Day! Help! Help! another Day," *Emily's Images*, JC117; poetry, *Songs of Love and War*, JC135.

Donne, John. "Daybreak," *Four Elizabethan Songs*, JC23; *Valedictions*, JC57.

Dryden, John. *A Song for St. Cecilia's Day*, JC108.

Eliot, T.S. *The Nightingale*, JC85.

Galsworthy, John. *Poem for Voice and Piano*, Jciv.

Guy, Georges. *A Bust for Eric Satie*, JC92.

Halevi, Judah. 12th century Hebrew poet, "My heart's in the East" and "Ode to Zion," *Canticles for Jerusalem*, JC104; also used in *After The Tradition*, JC123.

Henley, William Ernest. "Invictus," *Victorian Songs*, JC126.

Herrick, Robert. "Comfort to a youth that had lost his love," *Four Songs*, JC8.

Homer. *Poetic Fires (from the Greeks)*, JC107.

Hopkins, Gerald Manley. *Ode to Henry Purcell*, JC105; "Spring and Fall: to a young child,"*Victorian Songs*, JC126.

Jones, Sir William. *Epigram and Epitaph*, JC37.

Joyce, James. "She weeps over Rahoon," and "Tilly," *Four Songs*, JC8; "A Flower Given to My Daughter," *Four Lyric Songs*, JC10.

Keats, John. "Sonnet, To one who has been long in city pent," *Four Lyric Songs*, JC10; poetry, "Ode to Apollo," *Paean*, JC75; *The Nightingale*, JC85; "Sonnet, To A Cat," Sonnets for Baritone and Orchestra, JC87.

Lawrence, D.H. *Lizard*, Jcxi.

Lyly, John. "Spring's Welcome," *Four Elizabethan Songs*, JC23; *The*

Nightingale, JC85; "What bird so sings yet so does wail? O 'tis the ravish'd nightingale," *Nightingales, Motet for Six Instruments*, JC93.

Marlowe, Christopher. *The Passionate Shepherd to His Love and Her Reply*, JC26.

Neruda, Pablo. "La Tortuga" and "Oda al Piano," *Two Neruda Poems*, JC77; poetry, "Oda a las Ranas," *Oda A Las Ranas*, JC98; and *Canzones Y Dances*, JC137.

Ono No Yoshiki. *Three Stanzas from the Japanese*, JCx.

Racine. *The Confession*, JC65.

Raleigh, Walter. *The Passionate Shepherd to His Love and Her Reply*, JC26.

Rilke, Rainer Maria. *Ode to Henry Purcell*, JC105.

Rossetti, Christina. "Aloof," *Victorian Songs*, JC126.

Sandburg, Carl. "Sea Chest;" "Sleep Impression;" "Two Stranger's Breakfast," *Little Suite for Voice and Piano*, JC6.

Sandy, Stephen. *Light in Spring Poplars*, JC122.

Shakespeare, William. "Dirge," *Four Elizabethan Songs*, JC23.

Sidney, Sir Philip. "The Bargain," *Four Elizabethan Songs*, JC23.

Whitman, Walt. 1941, *Four Lyric Songs*, JC10; "One's Self I Sing, "Look Down Fair Moon, "A child said, What is the grass?," "When Lilacs Last in the Dooryard Bloom'd," "Inscription," *Inscriptions*, JC111; *Songs of Love and War*, JC135.

Williams, William Carlos. *Asphodel*, JC127.

Wittlin, Jozef. "Stabat Mater," *Songs of Our Time*, JC40; *Songs of Love and War*, JC135.

Wolton, Sir Henry. *Epigram and Epitaph*, JC37.

APPENDIX 10

ICONOGRAPHY FOR FINE'S *AFTER THE TRADITION*

The following exchange of letters, between Fine and administrators of the Bay Area Women's Philharmonic, outlines many of the details leading to the commission and world premiere of *After the Tradition* (JC123). Contract negotiations, fees, copying fees, available orchestration, instrumental considerations, possible grants to finance costs were some of the numerous details written about in this long discourse on the production matters for a major orchestral composition in the San Francisco Bay Area (Berkeley, California).

The work was performed in April 29, 1988 (see Chapter 1, 1988). Fine was most gratified with the final result on premiere night in Berkeley. The excellent response had led to rumors that *Tradition* might be submitted for Pulitzer Prize consideration.

- Nan H. Washburn, Artistic Director, Bay Area Women's Philharmonic, San Francisco, CA to Fine. November 5, 1986: Vivian Fine's personal collection, Library of Congress, Washington, D. C., See: Appendix 1.
- Fine to Washburn. November 19, 1986: ibid.
- Washburn to Fine. January 8, 1987: ibid.
- Fine to Washburn. January 28, 1987: ibid.
- Washburn to Fine. April 7, 1987: ibid.
- Washburn to Fine. April 15, 1987: ibid.
- Washburn to Fine. April 15, 1987: ibid.
- Washburn to Fine. May 15, 1987: ibid.
- Fine to Washburn. June 17, 1987: ibid.
- Washburn to Fine. August 25, 1987: ibid.
- Fine to Washburn. October 29, 1987: ibid.
- Fine to Washburn. October 29, 1987: ibid.
- Miriam Abrams, Executive Director, Bay Area Women's Philharmonic, San Francisco, Ca to Fine. December 14, 1987: ibid.
- Fine to [copyist]. February 9, 1988: ibid.
- Fine to Miriam Abrams. June 6, 1988: ibid

APPENDIX 11

GUIDE TO AUTHORS

INDEX

Memories, Music B112, 32n28, 33n40, 33n42
Rutland Daily Herald B295, B298
Ruzow, Susan JC79, JC130

Sabin, Robert B260
Sable, Barbara Kinsey B261
Sacks, Rick JC95
Sacramento Bee B2, B115
Sadie, Stanley B262
Sadkin, Virginia JC69
Saetta, Mary Lou JC97, JC127
Sage City Symphony 284, JC87
Salandro, Joette JC89
Salzedo, Carlos B127
Salzman, Eric B214, B263, B264
Samford, C. Clement B265
Saminsky, Lazare B19, B73, B251, B266, B267, P33, P34
Sandburg, Carl 10, 308, B256, JC6
Sandy, Stephen JC122
San Francisco (SF, CA) 22-23, 25, 26, 36n76, 262, 286, 311, B2, B11, B43, B46, B52, B60, B61, B62, B63, B64, B67, B96, B101, B107, B108, B129, B164, B166, B167, B174, B176, B184, B196, B221, B236, B237, B238, B245, B259, B269, B270, B286, B302, B303, B306, B312, B315, JC8, JC26, JC48, JC50, JC77, JC79, JC82, JC83, JC85, JC86, JC88, JC89, JC91, JC94, JC97, JC101, JC130, P64
San Francisco Chamber Music Society B282
San Francisco Chronicle B2, B60, B61, B62, B63, B64, B65, B166, B167, B268, B302, B303, B304
San Francisco Community Center JC83
San Francisco Conservatory B128, B237, B269, JC48, JC65, JC79, JC89
San Francisco Conservatory of Players (and Music Players) JC2, JC65, JC79, P56
San Francisco Conservatory Cello Ensemble JC79
San Francisco Examiner B236, B237, B238
San Francisco Jewish Community Center JC86
San Francisco Opera B174, B196, B269, B270
Showcase B238, B283
San Francisco Opera Center 23, 285, B60,

B156, B306, B308, B315
San Francisco State University B52, JC79
San Francisco Symphony 23, 285, B2, B11, B36, B38, B46, B62, B70, B101, B115, B129, B130, B164, B167, B174, B176, B196, 221, B236, B237, B238, B269, B270, B284, B285, B286, B304, B306
San Jose Mercury B129, B130, B131, B132
Sandved, Kjell Bloch B271
Saratoga Chamber Players JC130
Saratoga Springs (NY) 10, 286, JC7, JC9, JC23, JC46, JC56, JC60, JC80, JC130, P10, P60
Sartori, Claudio B272
Satie, Erik 21, 282, B29, B56, B199, B259, B265, B275, B283, B292, B302, JC53, JC92, P26, P27, P48, P49, P50, P53, P55
Sato, Eriko JC133
Satterlee, Catherine JC40
Scarecrow Press B51, B112, B136, B316
Scarlatti, Alessandro 6, 280, B156, B169, P32, P37, P38, P39, P47
Schadeberg, Christine JC8, JC138
Schnectady Gazette B273
Schenker, Erika JC83
Schiavo, Paul B274
Schirmer Books 291, B59, B110, B121, B287, B288, JC51
Schlamme, Martha JC89
Schlanger, Bernard JC93
Schmidt, Frank G. B275
Schmitt, Florent P25
Schock, Eula JC43
Schoen, William JC56, P43
Schoenberg, Arnold 1, 9, 30n3, B73, B149, B265, B275, B284, B310, P32, P48, P50
Schola Cantorum (NY) JC57
Scholes, Kim JC127
Schonbeck, Gunnar JC71, JC93, JC125
Schonbrun, Sheila B255, JC77, JC96
Schor, Ernestine JC86
Schor, Joseph JC43
Schubart, Mark A. B276
Schubert, Franz 30n1, B26, B233, JC90, P52
Schuller, Gunther B38, B109, B220, JC107, P67
Schulte, Rolf P66
Schulz, Robert JC69
Schuman, William 3, B266
Schumann, Clara B127, B132, B218, B255

About the Author

JUDITH CODY is a writer, independent researcher, poet, and composer, who has won national awards in both writing and composing. Also a pianist and classical guitarist, she has composed numerous chamber works, published a collection of her poetry, and written on the "creative explosions" of composers. The Smithsonian Institution has placed her *Women's Year Poem* in its permanent collection of American history.